&
UNTOLD STORIES
COLLECTED
BY HOA TRUONG

THE
GLOBAL FEATURES
&
UNTOLD STORIES
COLLECTED
BY HOA TRUONG

Clover Leaves
Publishing LLC

Library of Congress Control Number 2021940571

ISBN 978-1-0879-7114-8

Published in the United States by
Clover Leaves Publishing LLC.

Manufactured in the United States of America

10 9 8 7 6 5 4 3 2 1

Books are available in quantity for promotional or premium use.

CONTENTS

FOREWORD
BY HOA TRUONG

I was born in the Indochina War, despite the Second World War was over, but my country faced the unfortunate situation when the rapacious colony of France colluded with Vietnam Communist Party to create the Indochina War. Vietnamese communist leader Hồ Chí Minh exploited the French troops returned to Vietnam after Hồ Chí Minh shook the hand with French colonial official Marius Moutet to agree on Fountainebleau Agreement in 1946 to accept France coming back, therefore when French troops landed Vietnamese shore, Hồ Chí Minh called to fight for independence and cheated the people. If the British occupied Vietnam, the Vietnam War didn't happen, Vietnamese people and the US, allies avoided the war. The deep cause of the Vietnam War came from France and Vietnam Communist Party.

I grew up in the Vietnam War and volunteered to join the

Army of the Republic of Vietnam. I knew the cruelty of Vietcong, the early terror organization to terrorize its people. I survived in the fierce battlefields and survived after imprisoned for six years in the re-education, the hell of prison as Hitler's concentration camp. After Vietcong attempted the last invasion on April 30, 1975, the ruthless regime congregated 800,000 members of South Vietnam soldiers and public servants, the worst treatment in the re-education camps killed 165,000 political prisoners.

I must escape Vietnam after releasing from the hell of prison when the Vietcong regime applied hostile policies to the South Vietnam soldiers. I was alive after the desperate journey for freedom with a small boat in August 1982 and I spent a month in a refugee camp in Malaysia (Pulau Bidong island), eventually, I resettled a new life in Australia. During working for livelihood and saved the money to help my mother in Vietnam, I learned English myself at the working places, neighbors, shopping, and the lesson of my daughter from year one to university.

My life's journey was not easy as a normal person in Western, I had the risky plan to learn English in the re-education camps of Vietcong, the camps strictly banned the foreign language's learning, actually, the English called Empire American is the counter-revolutionary language. My mother torn off a pocket dictionary and created a newspaper sheet with rice glue, she wrapped the foods sending to prison, if Vietcong knew, my life would be ended by killing or torture, so I secretly learned English in a dangerous situation. I promised to write the untold stories in the re-education of Vietcong if I survived, so I accomplished my promise with the first book" The Dark Journey" published in 2010, this book is chosen by the Library of America Congress. The second book published in 2011" Good Evening Vietnam", the third book" from laborer to author" published in 2012, Sci-Fi" Nick Morrow" published in 2015, and the fifth book" a humble Vietnamese woman" to keep the promise for my wife's story.

I started to write the sixth book, but in 2016, my mother passed away in Vietnam, I couldn't return to attend her funeral, which causes me to stop writing the book. On March 5, 2017, I founded the daily online news" thedawnmedia.com". My features interested readers around the world, including author THU PHONG NGUYEN who collected my works and refer to the people. Obviously, I would like to thank everyone for reading my articles, particularly, I deeply thank author Thu Phong Nguyen who brings my voice to the public.

Hoa Minh Truong

BIOGRAPHY

Hoa Minh Truong was born after 4 years of the Indochina War occurred between the French colonial and Viet Minh Front. Mostly communist-controlled its organization and Ho Chi Minh drove the fighting for the independence of Vietnam to serve the global communist Bloc, Hoa's situation was incredible, the family escaped in the countryside under the crossfire of both sides.

After the Geneva Convention signed on July 20, 1954, between the French colonial with the French Prime Minister Mendes and the Global Communist Bloc represented by Mr. Pham Van Dong (Vietnam communist party), Mr. Zhou Enlai (China), and Molotov (Soviet Union), his family moved to Ca-Mau city and rebuilt the new life. The Geneva conference is the consequence of the conspiracy between the French colonial and the International Communist Bloc, therefore this period the communist was lost the Korean war, so they had to confess and South Vietnam remained in freedom, if not the communist is strong, they would take over South Vietnam. However, the communist has never given up the ambition, their essential strategy takes one step back then preparing the three steps toward. Vietnam War occurred that came from the communist.

He grew up in the Vietnam War and volunteered to join the South Vietnam Army when he was a young man. Graduated from the Political Warfare Academy as the first lieutenant, regular army. He was launched into the fierce battle after the Paris treaty signed on January 27, 1972. He served in the Black Panther battalion, held the psychological warfare officer and company leader. In 1974 he transferred to the province and served in the political warfare company then held the espionage team leader of the province. In February 1975 he transferred to Vinh Long province and held the vice commander of a sub-district.

The historic event on April 30, 1975, that pushed his life into the disaster, he was arrested on May 2, 1975, the Vietcong sent him to 9 re-education camps, he was among 800, 000 members of the South Vietnam armed force personnel to be congregated into the hell of the prison camp. The Vietcong killed 165,000 people by barbarous behaviors: the worse accommodation, execution, illness without medical and treatment, frequently spiritual terror, starvation, hard labor. He survived after 6 years and escaped successfully by a small boat then resettled a new life in Australia.

During living in the re-education camp, he vowed and promised himself to write the deadly stories in the camp if surviving. Obviously, he told his mother to separate an

English dictionary and stuck by the rice glue, she made it looked like newspaper used to wrap the foods, she provided for her son in the prison camp. Hoa learned English quietly, because the Vietcong strictly banned the foreign language, actually English to be condemned as the American empire language. If the Vietcong discovered a prisoner who learned English, then his life would be cut short or the heavy punishment (torture, putting in the cell). Hoa couldn't afford the pronunciation, he used a finger-written word by word, so his prisoner mates called him a mad man; he learned almost all of the dictionary in 5 years; after resettled a new life in Australia, he started to fulfill his promise. Finally, he spent about 30 years on the first book:

- The Dark Journey: inside the reeducation camps of Vietcong" published in 2010 in New York by SBPRA. After then he wrote the following books:

- Good Evening Vietnam: the aftermath of an unknown journey (Fiction)

- From laborer to the author. The flowers in heaven are rooted in hell (his life in Australia)

- Nick Morrow: After a half-century, a missing man returns (Scientific fiction)

- A Humble Vietnamese woman: Multiple colorful lives to be dyed by society).

Hoa Minh Truong is also the senior journalist of the Vietnamese language from 1984, he held the editor of Chinh Luan's monthly magazine in Western Australia (1996-2003). Now he continues to write and contribute the experiences and knowledge to the late generations and who want to study the dark side of history or the untold stories./.

XV

BRIEF WORDS TO READERS

I have an opportunity to access thedawnmedia.com of author Hoa Minh Truong, founder and editor, I feel like sharing the notorious views of a Vietnamese man about the global impact and the untold stories written throughout thousands of articles published since 2017. I believe the readers can find the interesting in this book. The articles of Hoa Minh Truong are variable into multiple themes, those are like the shinning stars emerge in the dark sky, his features based on the truth and the resolution to raise the ideas for whom wants to carry out some problems, the concerned people and community can use his proposals as the helpful options. I collected some articles below, thank very much for reading. I hope you enjoy the interest article.

Writer Phong Thu.

THE ARTICLES

1. THE COMMUNISM STARTS TO APPLY IN AMERICA

Americans are endangered after the mongrel communist Joe Biden robbed the White House with the certification of the major traitor Mike Pence and John Roberts. The American communist Joe Biden applies the same methods as Mao Tse Tung in 1949, Vietcong in 1975, Pol Pot in 1975, Lenin in 1917, and other communists. The US people face the impoverishment's policy and the obscurantism of Joe Biden, now, the people start to live in the nightmare of communism as Chinese people, Vietnamese people, Russian, and others spent the bloody experiences.

The mongrel communist Joe Biden will target the wealthy persons, the enemies of communists, they label the capitalists or counter-revolutionary elements. The innocent people voted and supported Joe Biden plus the wealthy persons poured many into Joe Biden's campaign, all will be faced the peril of communism. It is too late after President Donald Trump didn't trigger the EO-13848 to crack-down the communist movement in the United States of America, the disaster comes. When seeing the coffin, it is too late for crying.

The communist parties, the left parties in democratic countries are the siblings as tiger snake and Cobra. The

1

different kinds of poisonous snakes expose the different colors in the territories, certainly, the poisonous snakes are not python. The innocent people in Western and democratic countries can not distinguish between the tiger snake and python, so the country risks with the left parties are the hidden communist parties. Commonly, the communist and the left parties' formula is **3 D= Deception + Demagogy + Destruction**. The communist parties in China, Vietnam, North Korea, Cuba, and others have applied the same formula:

1-The Deception has applied since the communist party didn't rob the government and after taking over the country. The propaganda brainwashes people plus the terror contributed to the succession of the communist parties in Russia, Eastern European states, China, Vietnam. The nice languages as revolution, class struggle, socialism, the communist paradise, all are the pies on the sky as Boris Yeltsin warned. Chinese people have enjoyed the roast Peking duck in the painting of Mao Tse Tung since 1949 and now Xi Jinping continues to give the picture of the roast Peking duck to 1.4 billion people. In the US, Democratic Party has deceived the people with the benefit, democracy, freedom, and other languages, so many innocent people joined and support the hidden communist party in the United States of America. Nowadays, hateful communist faces appeared like Bill Clinton, Barrack Obama, Joe Biden, Kamala Harris, Adam Schiff, Chuck Schumer, Nancy Pelosi who combined the Mafia and communist, Bernie Sanders, and others.

2-The Demagogy to cover the communism as the tiger snake disguises python, the demagogic policies lie about the hoax climate change, the hypocritical humanity is the human rights turn human wrong with the support of the illegal migrants. The same-sex-marriage legislation challenges human history, religious faith, and social valuation. Those demagogic policies woo the ballots in the election. *Do not listen to what the communist talks, let's watch what the communist did.* The professional lie is the essential character of the communist *when a communist is born, initially, a midwife sees the mouth.*

3-The Destruction is the last stage on the 3D's formula, after the communist party or the left parties controlled the government, initially, destruction is the essential tactic to destroy the hostile government, they call the capitalist or counter-revolutionary regime. The communist parties and the left parties have applied the same method. Before driving the country to communism, Karl Marx's pupils destroy the fundamental society and economy.

After Mao Tse Tung robbed the authentic government of Chinese people in 1949, China's Communist Party destroyed the society by the bloodshed campaigns that were Great Leap Forward, Hundred of Flowers, the Culture Revolution, particularly, the Landlord Reform campaign to beat the wealthy component including the intellectuals including the innocent wealthy persons and intellectuals contributed the victory of China's Communist Party. Socialism is the dawn of communism but in the Western, the mongrel communist Bill Clinton deceived the world by the word" GLOBALIZATION". The impoverishment applies to destroy the economy from the grassroots.

In Vietnam, after the last invasion succeeded on April 30,

3

1975, Vietcong launched the beaten capitalist campaign, the ruthless regime confiscated the assets of the wealthy persons and launched three times to change the currency, so the South Vietnam people to be impoverished, it caused a million Vietnamese people fled the country to find the freedom. Everywhere is the same situation after the communist party or the left party controlled the government. Mostly, **the Australian Labor Party** advocates the debt, after the Coalition government lost in the election in 2007, Labor Prime Minister Kevin Rudd *(a mongrel communist of Beijing)* and Finance Minister Penny Wong *(the hidden communist)* spent $A 42 billion surpluses of Prime Minister John Howard and Treasurer Peter Costello, then Labor government of Prime Minister Kevin Rudd, Julia Gillard created the debt to help China taking control Australia's economy. Nowadays the Australian people wake up after China terrorizes Australia's imports and China humiliates the people.

The Democratic Party succeeded in the deception and demagogic policies, eventually, Democrats colluded with China, Deep State to rob the US government by using the rotten Constitution of 1871. The rigged election was legalized by Chief Justice John Roberts, House Speaker Nancy Pelosi, and Vice-President, Senate Speaker Mike Pence to inaugurate the presidential robber Joe Biden who illegally occupied the White House on January 20, 2021, **while the rigged election has not solved yet as a legal case is processing, no one claims the winner.** Unfortunately, three heads of the US certified the robber Joe Biden. **However, Joe Biden is not the 46th president until the rigged election cleared, so Joe Biden is an illegal president to storm the White House as a**

4

communist leader robs the government. It tells the people about the illegal presidency of Joe Biden. Once again, after January 20, 2021, Vice President Kamala Harris and her husband have not moved to the Naval Observatory, instead, they stay at the Blair House, it is the president's official guest residence located right across from the White House, why?

Initially, **the mongrel communist leader Joe Biden enters the White House is like Pol Pot entered Pnom Penh, Mao Ste Tung controlled Beijing**. The mongrel communist Joe Biden has started to destroy the economy and impoverish the United States of America from the first day in the White House, he signed 17destructive executive orders to lose 70,000 jobs. Within two weeks, Joe Biden signed 40 destructive executive orders, he becomes the champion of executive orders in US history. Communism or socialism starts to apply in the United States of America starts, so innocent people like the employees and union of Keystone Pipeline Xl regret to support the mongrel communist is Joe Biden. Now, they lost the job, but they do nothing to save after the decree of Joe Biden issue.

The next step will carry out the tactic of throwing the lemon's skin after the juice emptied. The bloody lesson Vietnam's Communist Party after Vietcong occupied Saigon. The tool of Hanoi was the members of the National Liberation Front were purge, many henchmen kicked out from the government, and the prominent henchmen like lawyer Trịnh Đình Thảo and his wife detained at their house, their comrades cut the food and water, eventually, they died in silence. Medical Doctor Dương Quỳnh Hoa, activist student Huỳnh Tấn Mẫm and others received bad treatment from Vietnam's Communist Party. The Chinese people who lived at

5

Cholon faced the impoverishment policy, despite in the Vietnam War, the rich Chinese people in Cholon contributed money for Vietcong.

The mongrel communist Joe Biden and his Democratic Party will purge the henchmen like Mitch McConnell, Mitt Romney, Mike Pence, the Rino, and others. It is the essential methods of communists, therefore, the regret is too late, the innocent people and the turncoat Republicans must pay the dire consequences. It is a better way to save the country when the Republican states unite to fight and nullify the destructive executive orders of Joe Biden, now there are more 200 companies file the lawsuit against Joe Biden and seeking the compensation. **The mongrel communist Joe Biden applies the bush law and he has never respected the people, the states, why do the states comply with the illegal executive orders of Joe Biden? Let's reject all unlawful executive orders of the illegal president Joe Biden.**

The hidden communist party robs the US government while the bullshit Constitution ties the patriotism, so the US Army, Police, Intelligence become a robot and Joe Biden who holds the remote control, which conducts the United States of America is on the brink of collapse. The presidential robber regime of Joe Biden has the comrade is Norwegian MP Petter Edi who nominated Black Lives Matter for the Nobel Peace Prize in 2021, it conflicts the signification, everyone knows Antifa and Black Lives Matters are the terror organizations. If the global thug and global war-maker Barrack Obama awarded the Nobel Peace Prize in 2009, so Black Lives Matter should be awarded.

The US presidential election in 2020 has not

concluded yet while the rigged election has not been solved, so Joe Biden has no authority to inaugurate on January 20, 2021. The basic law confirms a legal case doesn't decide yet, so no one can not claim the winner. Therefore, Joe Biden illegally inaugurated the 46th president at Capitol Hill on January 20, 2021. Certainly, Joe Biden is not the lawful president, instead, he is the presidential robber.

-President Donald Trump was the winner from the night of November 3, 2020, therefore, Joe Biden robbed the election by stealing the ballots, everyone and the world know the truth, **President Donald Trump is the victim of the bullshit Constitution and Chief Justice John Roberts, traitor Mike Pence**. The bullshit Constitution causes the presidency to expire on January 20, 2021, and Chief Justice John Roberts illegally presided over the illegal inauguration of Joe Biden. Moreover, President Donald Trump didn't hand over the government and the White House to the presidential robber Joe Biden, so Donald Trump still authorizes the US president. The tenant of the White House is President Donald Trump expired the contract on January 20, 2021, the owner (*US people agreed Donald Trump with four years more of the contract*). Instead, a new tenant Joe Biden who cheated the contract, so he is not a new tenant until the rigged election cleared, the official tenant of the White House is President Donald Trump moved to the new office in Florida, he is still working without a salary. On the other hand, Donald Trump is still the US president, not Joe Biden.

-The presidential robber Joe Biden is not the US president: Without Mike Pence certified the 306 fraudulent electoral colleges of Joe Biden, he couldn't inaugurate, so Mike Pence is the treason at the high level and Chief Justice

John Roberts presided the inauguration is the major traitor.

What happens after the rigged election proved by the courts, recently, the judge in Virginia decided the Election Board violated the law with mail-in-voting. Its case can apply to the swing states or 50 states. Moreover, the Federal Election Commission confirmed the US presidential election in 2020 is illegitimate. The circumstance of Joe Biden is like a doping athlete loses the medal after the cheat was discovered. When the rigged election of the swing states, even 50 states are concluded by the courts, certainly, Joe Biden must oust from the White House despite he inaugurated and he will be arrested with Justice John Roberts, Mike Pence, and the accomplices commit the treason in the high level.

-The Republican states, including the waken the Democratic States damaged by the destructive executive orders of mongrel communist Joe Biden, let's unite and reject the illegal president Joe Biden plus the unlawful executive orders. The states can deny the executive orders issued by the illegal president Joe Biden and also dismiss any orders of Joe Biden.

–The wealthy persons in America must know the mongrel communist Joe Biden will confiscate their assets after Democrats controlled the government, Congress, Senate, and the Supreme Court. The bloody experiences alert about the beaten capitalists as China, Vietnam, and other communist regimes did.

Certainly, the presidential robber Joe Biden was legalized by the Supreme Court, Senate, and Congress that humiliates the United States of America when the robber becomes the US president and the Vice President's nickname is" *let's go to bed*" should replace an old imbecile president anytime. Nevertheless, Joe Biden and Kamala Harris are the mongrel communists.

The government's robbery proved Joe Biden is the professional robber, he is the super and great master of Al Capone because Joe Biden robs the US government, the White House and Congress, Senate plus Supreme Court certified. On the other hand, Joe Biden is the world's super robber, his robbery becomes the black spot of US history./.

2. AMERICA SOFT COMMUNIST REVOLUTION IN 2020

The first communist revolution occurred in October 1917 in Russia, the world has been complicated, the bloodshed appeared in Europe, Asia, Africa, South America. The genocide strayed and distorted to revolutionary morality. The massive massacrers have never repented, instead, they were happy to enjoy the killing, robbing, and enslave its people. The Cold War following the Second World War, the communist movement is dangerous than Hitler. From Karl Marx released the evil bible, the communists killed more than 100 million people and enslaved more than a billion people.

After many years activated throughout the countryside, the demagogic propaganda of Vladimir Lenin succeeded to deceive the major peasant component plus the low and illiterate component in the countryside. The communist revolution of 1917 was carried out by poor people with revolutionary violence. Certainly, the first communist revolution created bloodshed and the huge prison camp covered the countries were occupied by the communist parties. Commonly, the communist always applies terror plus propaganda to rob the government, so Lenin took the Russian government and imposed the inhumane regime in 70 years.

Therefore, after the Communist Party of the Russian Federation robbed the government and eliminated the monarchical Tsar. Vladimir Lenin transformed the so-called proletarian regime into the red capitalist, the communist dictatorial regime robbed all the assets and enslaved the people. Instead, the members of the communist party lived on the people's sweat, they become the red noble class in Russia. The communist revolution in 1917 spread worldwide and Soviet-Union became the cradle of global communism. In Asia appeared China's Communist Party was led by genocide Mao Tse Tung, Vietnam founded Vietnam's Communist Party with traitor leader Ho Chi Minh, Cuba with Fidel Castro, North Korea with Kim Il Sung...

Global Communist Bloc collapsed in the early 1990s, Europe's communist countries changed, therefore, China's Communist Party has applied the lizard changes color's skin tactic and succeeded to cheat the Western. Indeed, **Communism is not over yet, it changes from the Cold War to Cool War**, and China leads the communist vestige states to remain the global hegemonic ambition, China has invaded the world, particularly, the United States of America is the main target.

The first communist revolution in 1917 was created by Vladimir Lenin with the poor people and peasants plus the illiterate component. Therefore, the communist revolution on November 3, 2020, is commanded by China's Communist

Party, the cradle of the post-communism movement after the Soviet Union collapsed. The communist revolution in 2020 occurs in the most democratic country as a stratagem of Sun Tzu:" *defeat the enemy by capturing their chief"*, China couldn't send the People's Liberation to invade the US, instead, the domestic thugs are the Democratic Party and the Deep State carry out the communist revolution in 2020 in the United State of America as Sun Tzu:" *kill with a borrowed knife"*. Democrats, execute and henchman Joe Biden, and Kamala Harris are the zombies, the soft communist revolution in 2020 in the US to make the coups with the rigged election and technological Dominion voting system. If China succeeded in America, Beijing will control the world, in human history, China is the most dangerous enemy on the planet.

The communist revolution in November 2020 was pregnant a long time, it prepared China to join the free market after the historic visit of US President Richar Nixon that opened the pathway by Henry Kissinger carried out in 1972. China has exploited the trade ties, a free trade agreement, diplomacy, the innocent leaders, the dishonest investors, and businesses placing the profit above the national interest and the country. China sent the soft army to infiltrate the Western and also sowing the members of the Deep State, the domestic thugs deployed in government, courts including the Supreme Court, FBI, CIA, and other agencies. The most active henchman is the Supreme Court with nine Justices using the attorney power to impose the bush law. The US presidential election in 2020 proved the Supreme Court is not different from the People Court in China and Vietnam., so chief Justice John Roberts becomes the leader of legal terror. Nevertheless,

China's Communist Party also deployed 1,950,0000 espionage agents inserted into 70,000 cells in Western countries. The soft communist revolution in 2020 is the long-term plan.

Mostly, the Deep State gathered the wealthy persons, treasonous and corrupt politicians, the dishonest academics. The small numerous traitors control the national economy, financial system, the media, and influence the government. **The revolutionary locomotive** leads the United State of America and the democratic countries into the orbit of communism. After the first communist revolution in 1917 in Russia, the second communist revolution occurs in 2020 in the United States of America.

China's Communist Party, Democrats, and the Deep State couldn't use the poor people, the low and illiterate components to rob the US government as Lenin did in Russia. Instead, China uses the social top class in the United States of America with the billionaires, CEOs of the giant media companies, and the giant tech communication companies like Facebook, Twitter, and Google, and the treasonous politicians, the judges including the Justices in Supreme Court. Nevertheless, China used biological warfare launched before the election to support the communist revolution in 2020, the mail-in voting was easily applied to the rigged election. Dogtor Anthony Fauci and W.H.O director, Dogtor Tedros Adhanom Ghebreysus activated the soft communist revolution in 2020.

The communist revolution in November 2020 is carried by the top social class and the wealthy component using money and technology to rob the US government. The US presidential election on November 3, 2020 purposes to rob the government is like Vladimir Lenin robbed the Tsar's monarchy in 1917 with the peasant, low and illiterate component. However, the communist revolution in November 2020 in the United States of America is carried out by the rich people and the high education component. The revolution in 2020 is the coup to rob the US government by the rigged election.

In society, money is the most important for everyone, the poor and rich, politicians and the people including the religions do need the money. On the other hand, money becomes the blood of human society. The Western people quote:" *Money is a passport to everything"*. China has applied the money to buy the politicians, particularly the national leaders become the main target to carry out the global hegemonic ambition. China's Communist Party has applied a very old tactic, is bribery and Beijing succeeded to buy dishonest, treasonous presidents like Bill Clinton, Barrack Obama, Vice-President Joe Biden, and others. China just spent a small monetary amount but got huge profits fetched from the policies of the corrupt leaders and the politicians. Mostly, President Bill Clinton is the prominent global thug, he helped China to grow faster with the Most Favored Nation's policy and Bill Clinton curbed the Western industry with the hoax climate change while China freely releases the dioxide.

China uses money and malicious methods to establish the global Deep State, the largest Deep State located in the US. After many decades of preparation for the soft communist revolution in the strongest democratic country on the planet, China commands the members of the Deep State in

13

America to make the communist revolution on November 3, 2020, with the henchman Joe Biden, Kamala Harris, Chief Justice John Roberts, and many traitors. However, the communist revolution of November 2020 has met the strong reaction of the US people and the patriotic President Donald Trump vows to fight and draining out the White House's swamp.

The important members of the Deep State appeared after the deceitful and imaginary victory of imposter President Joe Biden. Unfortunately, Joe Biden is underway to lose the dream and the intrigue of China ruined. The Deep State's members were eradicated, they appeared the treasonous faces like Attorney-General William Barr, Senate leader Mitch McConnell, Senator Mitt Romney, and the turncoat Republicans congratulated the illegal president Joe Biden. Whoever supports Joe Biden, they are the Deep State's members, the wealthy persons like George Soros, Bill Gates, traitors are Bill and Hillary Clinton, Barrack Obama, Nancy Pelosi, and others commit treason.

The soft communist revolution in November 2020 in the US that is the last standing up of communism on the planet. The US people have never given up the fight, so Joe Biden, Democrats are waiting for the disaster. Certainly, China's perpetrator failed the coup in America and China will receive the dire consequences after January 20, 2021, and an actual henchman Joe Biden is going to inaugurate at Guantanamo Bay.

Nowadays, the communist revolution is obsolete when the Marxism-Leninist was no longer to operate as after the Second World War. The soft communist revolution in 2020 in the United States of America failed, the coup leader Joe Biden is going to jail with the accomplices, the Executive order in 2018 is waiting for them. On the other hand, the communist revolution in 2020 in the US that is the last wave of communism on the planet. The master of the global Deep State is China will face the disaster as Soviet-Union when the world community wakes up.

The soft communist revolution in 2020 in the United States of America is the crucial battle of China's Communist Party. If Joe Biden robs the US with the rigged election, China will colonize the US and control the world. The Deep State intrigues the communism imposing in the US, the US people will be enslaved and the top social class, wealthy persons control global finance forever. The Western's wealthy component becomes the actual henchmen and servants of China to conspire and execute the global communism, initially, the United States of America is the first place to test the communist paradise. Globalization has the same signification as communism, the demagogic title debunked in the soft communist revolution in 2020 in the United States of America./.

3. ALL EXECUTIVE ORDERS OF BIDEN ARE UNLAWFUL

America is dead by BIDEN, the presidential robber created by Chief Justice John Roberts, Nancy Pelosi, and Mike Pence, China commands the government's robbery with the Deep State supports. The rigged election conducts the illegal President Joe Biden, an actual henchman of China, the professional traitor, and corruption. The Vice-

Presidential robber is thuggish Kamala Harris who can sell the United States of America for China, even her body sold to Willie Brown for her political promotion. **When the traitor and whore politician illegally storm the White House and control the government, including the Nuclear Codes, the United States of America is endangered.** The presidential robber Joe Biden destroyed just one day all great achievements did by President Donald Trump in four years. **Joe Biden is not the US 46th president while the legal argument about the rigged election is fighting,** instead, Joe Biden is the illegal president, so the Constitution and the US people have not mandated Joe Biden to sign an executive order and authority to run the government. **All executive orders of Joe Biden are illegal when the White House is occupied by the terrorist's Joe Biden and Kamala Harris. The US people, National Guard, the Republican states, and the militias can come to Washington D.C to expel and arrest Joe Biden and Kamala Harris as soon as possible. Do not comply with the illegal executive orders and waiting for the rigged election solved. If not, the United States of America is on the brink of collapse, and American will live in the communist paradise as China, North Korea, Vietnam, Cuba.**

Vice President Mike Pence stabbed in the back of the United States of America and President Donald Trump after certified the 306 fraud electoral colleges of the professional traitor Joe Biden, which conducts the presidential robber Joe Biden to inaugurate on January 20, 2021. The inauguration carried out as a fictional film of Hollywood like Harry Potter, therefore the disgraced sitcom debunked when the people wonder about the inauguration was life at noontime, but why the shadows were not at noon? The illegal inauguration without traditional music, nor 21 gunshots, moreover, the US presidential inauguration of Joe Biden broadcast on Spanish television before 10 hours? The illegal president inaugurated as fake news, the left stream media can not conceal the ugliest inauguration of Joe Biden.

Unfortunately, the US Constitution becomes the legal garbage's tip, so the lawful and virtual Constitution mixed the bush-Constitution like the pure gold placed with excrement, despite the pure gold and excrement are yellow, but the people can recognize what is it? However, the dishonest judges and Justices, the thuggish Senator, Representatives recognize the pure gold and excrement are the same kind. It means they can eat the shit as a hamburger. Whoever doesn't recognize right and wrong, good and bad, they are the animal-covered human body.

The fate of the United States of America must be decided by the people, not House Speaker Nancy Pelosi, Chief Justice of Supreme Court John Roberts, and Senate Speaker Mike Pence or the animals control the highest firms in America. Three persons sold the country to China after certified China's henchman Joe Biden to win the rigged election with the illegal ballots, stolen ballots, fraudulent counting, and the Dominion voting system plus the interference of China and 65 nations. The independence and national security of America are threatened by foreign enemies and the domestic thugs to rob the government.

From January 20, 2021, the US people strongly condemn Vice President Mike Pence who distorted the function of Senate Speaker to certify the 306 fraudulent electoral colleges of traitor Joe Biden while the legal battle has not concluded yet. Moreover, President Donald Trump and the legal team hold the massive evidence plus the witnesses. Nevertheless, the Director of the National Intelligence John Lee Ratcliffe reported China and other nations interfered with the US presidential election in 2020. Therefore, President Donald Trump didn't trigger EO 13848 and the presidential robber Joe Biden stormed the White House on January 20, 2021.

The Supreme Court turns the thuggish highest court with Chief Justice John Roberts places the justice for sale, they waive the lawsuit of Texas and 20 states with 126 lawmakers to raise the unconditional election in the swing states. The Supreme Court legalized the illegal ballots of Joe Biden and on January 6, 2021, the last unlawful practice at Congress with the Senate to conclude Joe Biden becomes the 46th President. Indeed, Joe Biden lost the election, and President Donald Trump won the landslide victory on the night of November 3, 2020. The bullshit, rotten and ugly Constitution mandates too much power of three head persons of the Supreme Court, Senate, and Congress. China just buys three persons and Beijing can take the US easily, and China just paid $US 1.5 billion for traitor Joe Biden who peacefully transits the United States of America to China's colony. Certainly, Joe Biden ready to repay China the invention, top secrets including the nuclear program.

When the legal argument has not concluded yet, a judge can not decide who is a winner or loser. Unfortunately, the three domestic thugs exploited the presidency expired on January 20, 2021, and they admitted Joe Biden to take the White House on January 20, 2021. The people's outrage, the

Constitution distorted to serve for the traitors. Despite, the presidential robber Joe Biden inaugurated on January 20, 2021, the pedophile and corrupt Chief Justice John Roberts presided the ugly and illegal inauguration, but the people reject the presidency of Joe Biden. They confirm" JOE BIDEN IS NOT OUR PRESIDENT", certainly, Joe Biden is not the 46th President of the United States of America, the people didn't vote for Biden, instead of the left stream media terror companies, the left tech communication companies the Deep State and China's Communist Party selected Joe Biden and Mike Pence made the last decision on January 20, 2021.

The presidential robber Joe Biden is not the US president, the rotten Constitution plus John Roberts, Nancy Pelosi, and Mike Pence decided Joe Biden taking the White House, so the unlawful inauguration without the people, because Joe Biden storms the White House with the head of Supreme Court, House Speaker, and Senate Senate Speaker. The illegal president Joe Biden can not access any government's services and facilities including the Intelligence and Defense and cabinet. His cabinet recycled Barrack Obama's staff, the mongrel communist or mongrel Ape Joe Biden occupies the US government with the cabinet is like ANIMAL FARM of George Orwell.

Certainly, the traitor Joe Biden is not the president, he can not issue an executive order and scraps a heap of President Donald Trump's executive orders. The presidency must certify after the Supreme Court concluded and decided. The legal battle of the rigged election is not over yet, despite the Supreme Court rejected all legal files of President Donald Trump, but the rigged election has not been solved yet (*). Why didn't Chief Justice John Roberts preside the inauguration of Joe Biden while the legal battle is processing?. The thuggish Chief Justice with the traitor Mike Pence and others inaugurated the illegal president Joe Biden. The US people must act and Republican Congress, Senate plus the concerned Justices in the Supreme Court can review the unlawful authorities of the presidential robber Joe Biden. All his executive orders are illegal is like a robber can not sell the occupied property. Certainly, Joe Biden has no authority to sign anything, his presidency must wait until the rigged election is solved. The people are the highest justice, so the voices of 74,000,000 people disqualify the illegal presidency of Joe Biden and the unlawful Vice Presidency of Kamala Harris. The inauguration is illegal, it breaches the Constitution and the common law including the election law./.

NOTES: (*) THE LEGAL BATTLE IS NOT OVER YET, WHY DID JOE BIDEN INAUGURATE?

Sidney Powell Launches Super PAC to 'Fight Vigorously for Our Constitutional Rights'

Attorney Sidney Powell, who filed third-party election lawsuits on behalf of former President Donald Trump, has launched a Super PAC dedicated to a range of aims, including freedom of speech, Constitutional rights, and "the sacred right of free and fair elections."

In a statement on Saturday, Powell announced the launch of the Restore the Republic Super PAC, which is an independent expenditure-only political action committee that may receive unlimited contributions and may engage in unlimited political spending on initiatives, provided it does not coordinate directly with campaigns or candidates.

A Jan. 22 filing with the Federal Elections Commission shows Powell as the entity's Custodian of Records, while former Trump campaign attorney Jesse Binnall serves as the Super PAC's Treasurer.

Powell said what prompted the move is that Americans are "starved for truth, restoration of the Rule of Law, and even-handed accountability," and are fed up with government corruption and an "elitist political class that views them with condescension and contempt."

"The American people deserve a voice that exposes and rejects the self-interest of political parties, the control of tech giants, and the lies of the fake news," she said.

Vowing to be a "voice for honesty, integrity, and a return to government by We the People," Powell said the Restore the Republic Super PAC "will be dedicated to supporting candidates who will fight vigorously for our Constitutional rights, freedom of speech, and the sacred right of free and fair elections."

"The PAC will promote candidates who fight for truth and the Rule of Law, and we will strenuously oppose any candidate who discards the Constitution for his own short-term or political gain—regardless of her party," she said.

Powell, who successfully defended retired Army Lt., Gen. Michael Flynn, was introduced by the Trump legal team in November, although the team later distanced themselves from her and said she wasn't working on their behalf.

She is known for filing a number of contest-of-election lawsuits in the wake of the November election, which claimed fraud and other irregularities.

On the eve of President Joe Biden's inauguration, Powell withdrew her lawsuit in the U.S. Supreme Court challenging Georgia's election results. She and other attorneys on the case filed an appeal with the high court after the case was struck down in district court for lack of standing and being brought too late

Of the dozens of post-election lawsuits filed by the Trump legal team and supporters, just one ended up getting a win, striking down a deadline extension to correct mail-in ballots in Pennsylvania that were missing proof of identification.

From The Epoch Times *(*January 23, 2021)

4. JOE BIDEN BRINGS MAOIST PANDEMIC TO AMERICA

The medical doctor bases on pathology and radical illness for treatment, the radically medical research is the best method to cure the sickness including cancer. Fighting against the communist is the same, the anti-communism experts focus on the vulnerabilities of the malicious enemy on the planet, and communism is the most dangerous pandemic to kill a hundred million people, and infected many million people in China, Vietnam, Laos, Cuba, North Korea, Venezuela. Moreover, the communism pandemic eliminated in Russia, Eastern Europe by the" *democratic vaccine*" in the early 1990s, therefore, the communism virus-transformed Maoist virus has developed the new form a pandemic, so China's mainland becomes the central pandemics with SARS, H1NI and now China virus threatens the world. Unfortunately, the Western countries neglect the Maoist virus, the left parties, the left stream media, and the left tech communication companies help Maoist pandemic spread in their states to infect the mind of its people. On the other hand, the communism or Maoist virus is the most dangerous pandemic, because the Maoist virus is the master of all kinds of pandemics, so the concerned people must fight against Maoist pandemic to strike on the right target, so the wrong method to fight against Maoist pandemic that is useless and wastes the time, the common treatment based in the rule:

Do not fear what the communist does.

Let's do what the communist fears.

The backbone of communism is based on Karl Marx's theories coming from his books, unfortunately, most strategists and academics just follow the tactics of communism exposing the languages as class struggle, socialism, revolution, and the communist paradise. Indeed, those are the shade of Karl Marx, the wrong targets lose time and useless, so the high profiles in Western couldn't solve the evil theory that causes more than a hundred million people massacred and a billion people enslaved by the super gang labeled revolution. On the other hand, the wrong target has conducted the Western and democratic countries falling into the traps of communists, the deadlock unsolved from the 19th century to the 21st century.

The personality of Karl Marx is the main target, no one trusts a traitor, and dishonest person who lived on the income support of Frederick Engel, but Karl Mark wrote the books teaching the dishonest component that called the working class to kill the wealthy people. Karl Marx betrayed Fredric Engel since he and his family lived from a wealthy person. Do not trust and respect dishonest Karl Marx, plus the books. If the innocent component in Western condemns dishonest Karl Marx and his books, the evil theory couldn't influence. Nevertheless, Western academics, strategists have made the mistake to remove the evil theory from society, education. They have fought against communism on the shades, the demagogic languages of Karl Marx, Lenin, Mao Ste Tung, Hồ Chí Minh, and other communist leaders are just the mist to cover the deception. The political languages are a class struggle, the revolution, socialism, communist paradise, proletariat, capitalists are the decoys to cheat the democratic countries and Western. Indeed, fighting on the languages couldn't nullify communism, instead, the communists are very happy when the enemy attacking the wrong target. The funny and useless fighting against communism on the language battle couldn't eliminate the ruthless regimes like China, Vietnam, except the people standing up like Soviet-Union, Eastern Europe Communist Bloc. Certainly, fighting against the communist on languages that follows the traps with the common and basic tactics are the buying time, talking during the fighting, and taking one step back to prepare three steps forward.

The US President Bill Clinton enriched the positive conditions for China, instead, the sanction could force China to stop the global hegemonic ambition and Bill Clinton also led the US, the world to respond to the strategy of China. The hoax climate change has curbed the industry and China has made a profit by selling solar power, moreover, the hoax climate change has created mayhem in Western with the protests to support and oppose.

The communists have never respected the people's lives, the Korean War, Vietnam War proved the communists barbecued many million troops. However, the death vulnerability of communists is the economy. The Western and the US can prevent China to create the war by attacking the economy, it matches a saying of Napoleon Bonaparte: " *an army marches on its stomach*". When the communist proposes the negotiation that means they fall into the low tide of revolution. The talk means helps the communist to buy the time, it is the trap to cheat the innocent politicians, the national leaders, and the naïve people in the Western.

President Donald Trump curbed the deceitful tactics of China from 2017 to 2021, China failed to apply the tactics like buying time, taking one step back to prepare three steps forward, and talking while fighting. Unfortunately, the rigged election was conspired by the Deep State, Democrats, and China to create the bloody old, imbecile and mongrel Ape Joe Biden to storm the White House. Chief Justice John Roberts exploited the 45th presidency expired on January 20, 20-2012 to illegally preside the unlawful inauguration of Joe Biden who is the presidential robber. Certainly, Joe Biden is an actual henchman of China after Hunter Biden received $US 1.5 billion. The national disaster comes from presidential robber Joe Biden that panics the US people with 52 destructive executive orders signed within 20 days in the White House. The thuggish Chief Justice John Roberts and former Vice-President Mike Pence are the prominent traitors of the White House's tragedy, the US people have not tolerated the traitors, particularly, and a million jobless condemn Joe Biden, John Roberts, and Mike Pence.

Moreover, the traitor Joe Biden eases the death vulnerability of China while President Donald Trump made China being crippled. So Joe Biden, Democrats, and the turncoat Republicans help China survives and also bringing the Maoist virus to America. President Donald Trump has the vaccine of China virus and the US people have infected by Maoist pandemic, the disaster is coming with the bloody old, mad, imbecile mongrel Ape Joe Biden and his animal cabinet as the animal farm of George Orwell. President Donald Trump nullified the traps of China in four years, therefore, the illegal president Joe Biden brings China's traps to deploy in the US and the world, Joe Biden is the loyal servant of China's Communist Party as Carrie Lam in Hong Kong, the domestic thugs are dangerous than the foreign enemy./.

5. THE WORLD NEEDS TO TREAT THE VIRAL MAOIST

The viral Maoist or viral Communism is the master of all kinds of viruses, it has spread in the mainland labeled the viral Maoist, it is the most deadly virus on the planet. Unfortunately, since the US President Richard Nixon attended the first visit to the land of viral Maoists in 1972 and the deadly virus has started to spread silently by transmitting from China's mainland to the US then develop everywhere on the planet. Nowadays, viral Maoists infected worldwide including the United Nations, the World Health Organization, even the Vatican has a socialist Pope Francis who has the syndromes of viral Maoists *(on September 22, 2018, Pontiff signed an agreement with the den of red evil, the Vatican accepts China appoints bishop and Pope Francis supposes the COVID-19 comes from the climate change)*. Any country could infect the viral Maoists after contacting China by trade ties and diplomatic relations. The viral Maoists created SARS and now the Coronavirus *(or Chinese Virus)*, initially, the world needs to find an effective treatment for viral Maoists that causes global pandemics. On the other hand, viral Maoists are the master of all kinds of viruses.

After the Second World War, the viral Maoists spread in Vietnam and rebellious organizations occurs in India, the Philippines, South America, and other countries. Therefore, the viral Maoists infected the US and spread widely under the rule of President Bill Clinton, George. H.W Bush, George W. Bush, and Barrack Obama. If Hillary Clinton elected in 2016, the viral Maoists would infect the whole 51 states of the United States of America. However, the US people elected the patriotic President Donald Trump who can find an effective treatment to treat the viral Maoist.

The original Maoist virus derives from viral Karl Marx and following Lenin, it called viral Communism or Socialism. When the deadly virus spread to China, it renamed viral Maoists that infected Vietnam, Cambodia, Laos, and somewhere else. The Maoist virus killed a hundred million Chinese people and has infected 1.4 billion people in the mainland and brainwashing the world's largest population. The Maoist virus killed 2 million Cambodian people from 1975 to 1979, it killed about 10 million people in Vietnam from 1949 after the viral Maoist spread to this country. The Maoists covered under the viral Ho-Chi-Minh and continues to infect 90 million Vietnamese people in Vietnam and the overseas Vietnamese community. The major media companies of the Vietnamese language in the US and overseas are leftists despite they fled from Vietnam after Vietcong claimed the unpredictable victory on April 30, 1975.

The viral Maoist has infected the illiterate, low educated, and innocent people in China, Vietnam, Laos, Cambodia. Therefore, in the Western, the innocent components, the profit lover's businesses, dishonest academics, and the left media easily infected by the viral Maoist. In pandemic history, the viral Maoist or viral Marxism-Leninist is the longest pandemic, it has perpetuated from the 19th century to the 21st century with the massive death and infected population, the most dangerous pandemic on the planet is the viral Maoist.

Commonly, the pandemics must have the vaccine, but the viral Maoists can cure by isolation of the economy and stop providing the money to the den of the pandemic in the mainland. The viral Maoist can not spread when the world stops the trade, and the viral Maoist disabled, all the viruses killed as Sun Tzu quoted:" *defeat the enemy by capturing their chief"*.

President Donald Trump has effective medicine to cure the viral Maoist, the tariff medicine plus the isolation pushing the viral Maoist into the dead road. On the other hand, viral Maoists, a master of all kinds of viruses can treat with the economic sanction, so when viral Maoist treated and all pandemics stop. Moreover, the Western countries need to stop Chinese students, almost, Chinese students have been infected by the Maoist virus, they bring the deadly virus to intoxicate the young generations.

After more than 70 years, Chinese people have lived in

the fear, the viral Maoists infected Chinese people in the mainland, while Taiwanese and Hong Kong people are Maoist free. So Chinese people do need to cure themselves by standing up, it is the only way to help Chinese people escape the deadly virus and joining the world community./.

6. THE DEADLOCK OF LEFT PARTIES IN WESTERN

Communism is the most dangerous theory on the planet, the death toll of Communism was up to 100 million people and a billion people enslaved (*it means a billion people infected by viral communism*). On the other hand, Communism is like the deadly pandemic by viral Karl Marx has struck the people's minds and spread worldwide. Obviously, the viral Communism spread to Russia (*that is like the Novel Coronavirus starts from Wuhan*) and its outbreak occurred in October 1917, it called the October Revolution by Lenin. The viral Communism came to China, it has activated by the label Maoist and the outbreak occurred in 1949 that cause 65 million people killed (*the viral Maoist is very dangerous than any kind of virus, Maoist continues to kill its people in the mainland, there were about 100 million people killed. Moreover, the viral Maoists have spread the terror of rebels in India, the Philippines, South America, and somewhere else.*). When the viral Marxism-Leninist came to Vietnam by a viral form called Hồ Chí Minh's thoughts, it killed tens of millions of Vietnamese people and infected nearly 100 million Vietnamese people from Viral Hồ Chí Minh activated the outbreak on February 3, 1930 (*The Vietnam Communist Party founded on February 3, 1930*).

29

Cambodia struck by a viral Khmer Rouge that killed 2 million people. There are many countries infected by viral communism as the Eastern Europe Communist Bloc *(the virus treated from the early 1990s),* Cuba, Laos, North Korea, and Venezuela still infected. Viral communism is the longest pandemic that has infected human life on the planet, it has attacked people's minds since the 19th century. The viral Communism transforms Socialism and it has infected into the democratic countries, actually, the Western.

The viral Socialism has appeared in the Western under multiple forms as the left parties, the left media. The viral Socialism causes the current mayhem in Western, actually, the virus silently has struck the democracy, the free speech by the fake news, misleading the public. The left parties are the dangerous form of viral Communism because the dangerous virus hides under the political parties.

The left parties in Western are the hidden communist parties, the essential policies based on the demagogy, lie, cheat to cover the fallen policies on the economy, border protection, while the national interest abandons:

-The hoax climate change has deceived the people, actually, the young generations have not enough knowledge about climate change, they are infected by viral Socialism. The left parties, the left media, and perpetrators of the hoax climate change have exploited the ebullient character of the primary-high school students as Mao Tse Tung used the young people into the Cultural Revolution from 1966 to 1976. The Green Guard of hoax climate change is a form of Mao Tse Tung's Red Guard.

-The same-sex-marriage legislation: the left parties are

keen to woo the ballot by any tactic, so the left parties advocate homosexuality despite the homosexual couple is a minority in society, but their ballot can change the election's outcome.

-The hypocritical humanity exposes the protection of asylum seekers: the left parties woo the ballot of ethnic by supporting the illegal migrants.

The communist parties have applied the demagogic policies, so psychological warfare becomes a vital weapon to intoxicate the people by the propaganda. The people who live in communist regimes couldn't access the impartial information, instead of the government's propaganda, so their ears filled full by the regime's policies, and the eyes forced to see slogans. In Vietnam, people quote" *eating is like a prisoner, sleeping is like a monk and talking is like a national leader"*. The people face poverty but the countries are rich in the red flag, slogans, and the communist leader's statue plus the portrait. The cheat language has applied in the communist countries, commonly, the nice words are the class struggle, socialism, beaten the capitalist, landlord reform, the hell of prison labeled re-education, actually, the communist paradise is the last rest of communism, but Boris Yeltsin quoted: " *Communism was just an idea, just pie in the sky*". On the other hand, the communist paradise has never come, therefore, the communist paradise just deserves for the Red noble class, the communist members work nothing but they afford anything from the people's sweat, actually, the high ranking cadres of communist parties are the millionaire and billionaires. The viral Communism is like a beautiful cloth that covers the garbage bin, so Communism has no solution to reach the highest level is the communist paradise.

The left parties in Western and democratic countries are the same circumstance as the communist countries. The so-called Socialism became the deadlock, therefore, the demagogic policies cover the carcass of Socialism, the socialists are paranoids like Democratic Senator Bernie Sanders, French President Emmanuel Macron who attacks nationalism, Secretary-General Antonio Guterres, and others. Socialism applies in Western and democratic countries that couldn't cheat the people after the demagogic policies debunked. The circumstance of the Democratic Party in the US proved the fallen Socialism. Nowadays, the world wakes up after the viral Communism and Socialism infected the human's minds by the crazy theory of Karl Marx who was the dishonest jobless to avenge the society by the books teaching the dishonest elements and the social dregs how to rob, kill and enslave the people.

The communist countries in Europe collapsed from the early 1990s, actually, the cradle of viral Communism in Russia quarantined and expelled viral Communism. Therefore, in Asia, the viral Maoists still infects 1.4 billion people on the mainland, actually, the communist paradise in China becomes the wonderful paradise of corruption and deadly viruses like SARS, Novel Coronavirus, Bird flu, Swine Flu. So Chinese people need to expel the viral Maoists as soon as possible, it is the cause of the deadly pandemics.

The left parties in the Western face the deadlock, the demagogic policies, and the propaganda couldn't cheat the people, the high technological communication kills the fake news and misleading the public. There is the only way to escape if the left parties give up Socialism and joining the political competition in the elections, actually, the demagogic policies on immigration, climate change can not attract the people. Nevertheless, the patriotic policy can save the left parties, the patriotism and the nationalism are effective medicine to treat viral socialism./.

7. KEN BURNS AND LYNN NOVICK DIDN'T UNDERSTAND THE VIETNAM WAR BUT THEY MADE THE DOCUMENTARY FILM

FOREWORD: The writer has no favor to discuss the derailed and biased facts in The Vietnam War's film made by Ken Burns and Lynn Novick. The debate argues on the wrong issues that are useless and wasted the time. Therefore, the article analyses the misleading to the public of the filmmakers and also corrects the Vietnam War's information after more than a half-century has been sullied by the leftists in the Western countries, the domestic thuggeries in the Cold War stood alongside with Vietcong and the Global Communist Bloc. The writer would like to send a strong message to Ken Burns and Lynn Novick about the wrongly basic facts in their documentary film, the people and Vietnam veteran couldn't find any new in this film, instead, the old propaganda's fashion that devalues the film and the prestige of the filmmakers despite both spent more than a decade to achieve.

(Hoa Minh Truong, Vietnam veteran)

In Western countries respect knowledge, experience, and professionalism. Except someone cheats the people with the fake qualification. Mostly the job and career are trained from the colleges or university. The electrician, plumber, even a chef cook have to graduate from school. Every job and career must have a license, certainly, it is like a mechanic couldn't do the medical doctor's practice or an untrained electrician couldn't allow working in the electrical field.

Ken Burns and Lynn Novick achieved the documentary film is the Vietnam War and released the multiple parts on PBS. Unfortunately, the filmmakers didn't know much about the Vietnam War although they made the film about the Vietnam War, the filmmakers are likely the doctors couldn't realize the cause of the disease and the virus, so how could Ken Burns and Lynn Novick convince the people to trust their film? The documents displayed the facts about the Vietcong, US and allies, mostly met the Vietcong propaganda those appeared since 1954 and the documents are not impartial, it repeats as the boring sounds of an old disgraced song. The information has been used in the film The Vietnam War to be recycled from the rotten materials of the anti-war, pro-communist movement in the Vietnam War as Jane Fonda, John Kerry, Joe Biden, Bill, and Hillary Clinton plus the left media as CNN (Communist News Networks) and the others in the US, Europe, Australia (Channel 7, ABC, SBS), all have poisoned the people and have misled the public, now the toxic still remains in the Western society, actually in the film The Vietnam War performs the obsolete psychological warfare in the 21st century. The biased document has been dropped the mask. Nevertheless, once again, the documents repeated and sullied the American soldiers and the South Vietnam Army (ARVN). They are the respectable soldiers who fought for freedom and democracy and against the early terror Vietcong for more than a half-century in the Vietnam battlefield. The Vietnam War's filmmakers have done the last effort of the pro-communist movement's vestige, but they couldn't cover up the truth because all the facts of the Vietnam War unveiled by the victims (Vietnamese refugee and others), the allies Vietnam veteran, actually the high technology of internet couldn't allow the deception as the Vietnam War's period again.

Obviously, the Vietnam War film posed in the wrong clause, it is like a building has no basement, so the document drove in the wrong direction. The original causes of the Vietnam War came from:

1-Vietcong was early terrorism, they were cruel than ISIS, Al Qaeda, therefore, Ken Burns and Lynn Novick spent more than 10 years making The Vietnam War film, they have enough time to collect the impartial document. Therefore, both just used the documents provided by Vietcong. As the hard evidence showed off the Military Museum at Mỏ Cày district, Bến Tre province where displays the Sledgehammer and below appraised Mr. Nguyễn Văn Thắng, vice district Mỏ Cày who used it to break the skull of 10 people. The Museum officially opens, the foreign tourist could come and on the internet, the sledgehammer broke the skulls of 10 people was available, why didn't Ken Burns and Lynn Novick ignore? The Vietnam War film dodged Vietcong was the barbaric terror's organization, indeed the most Vietnamese people and allied knew as well. Ken Burns and Lynn Novick also ignored the death of 165,000 members of ARVN and public servants killed in the hell of re-education camp after Vietcong claimed the unpredictable victory on April 30, 1975, and the tyranny regime in Vietnam is the hub of human rights violation.

2-The cruel policy of the colonial French that causes the outrage of the Vietnamese people: after the Second World War, France wanted to return the Indochina despite the French had not recovered yet while the Vietcong (Vietnam Communist party) was just a small group, but Hồ Chí Minh conspired to gather all the people into the communist movement and he exploited the interim government for inviting the French coming back by the Franco-Vietnam Agreement on March 6, 1946. Hồ Chí Minh and French had the same purpose although they stood the different sides, so the communist collaborated with the colonial French that created the Vietnam War. After Vietnam communist party invited France to come back when the first French military unit landed at the Vietnam shore, Hồ Chí Minh appealed the total resistant fight against the colonial French for independence, it was a farce but happened in Vietnam. If the British came to Vietnam, they returned the independence for the Vietnamese people like India, Malaysia...certainly, the Vietnam War didn't occur. In history, almost all the old French colonies fell into the communists after France withdrew.

3-Vietcong created the war under the order of the Global Communist Bloc: Since 1959, South Vietnam had not any the US and the ally military unit. However, in May 1959, Hồ Chí Minh ordered Major General Bùi Xuân Đăng who established the Special Task Force code 559, they gathered more than 100,000 laborers to repair the abandoned road linking three-nation of Vietnam-Laos-Cambodia, it was the Hồ Chí Minh trails where became the main road for the North Vietnam communist troop invaded and military equipment for the war, indeed the US just came to Vietnam from 1965. The Vietnam War film didn't explain the original cause of the Vietnam War or both Ken Burns and Lynn Novick didn't know much about the Vietnam War. Nevertheless, they tried to ignore an announcement of Mr. Lê Duẩn, the General Secretary of the Vietnam Communist party (or the Vietnam Workers Party) who was in charge of the Vietnam War. After winning the unpredictable war on April 30, 1975, Mr, Lê Duẩn said:" we fought against the American empire for Russia and China". Therefore the slogan" fighting against the American empire" is the cheat.

The Vietnam War film doesn't reflect the genocide of the Vietnam Communist Party since the super terror gang founded on February 3, 1930. The documentary filmmakers lacked the Land Reform Campaign that occurred at North after the Geneva Convention signed on July 20, 1954. Obviously, Hồ Chí Minh ordered his closest comrades Mr. Trường Chinh and Hồ Quyết Thắng executed the bloody campaign that the Vietcong officially confirmed about 200,000 Vietnamese people massacred, but the numerous victim could estimate about a million. Moreover, Hồ Chí Minh killed 1,700,000 people, he raped a 15-year-old girl named Tuyết LAN in 1929 at Thailand and Hồ Chí Minh was the famous pedophile in Vietnam. Besides the massive massacres, the Tet offensive in 1968, there was only at Huế city, Vietcong killed more than 7,200 people, including the foreigners, worked in Huế's university. The crime was at Tiananmen Square in 1989 in Beijing but most left media ignored it..

The serious crimes of Vietcong couldn't hide, the picture of Major General Nguyễn Ngọc Loan executed a uniform captain of Vietcong Bảy Lốp that has used as the peak propaganda of Vietcong, but the leftists have no explained

Mr. Bảy Lốp who killed all family members of Lieutenant Colonel Nguyễn Tuấn in the Tet's offensive. (* References). Once again, The Vietnam War film continues to carry out the tricky mission of the communist and protects the wrongdoing of the leftists in the US and the allies. The filmmaker's Ken Burns and Lynn Novick have not given up the misleading public and continuing to poison the people, actually the late generations in Western. In Vietnam, the ideologist and also the iconic herbalist Lê Hữu Trác, alias Hải Thượng Lãn Ông (1720-1791) who advised:" It is good to discover the positive of a book, but the best is finding out the negative". There is not only the writer recognizes The Vietnam War film is untrue, biased, and met the disgraced propaganda of Vietcong, but this film has been facing a strong reaction from the viewers, actually the Vietnam veteran and the concerned intellectuals. Finally, the writer congratulates Ken Burns and Lynn Novick who spent more than 10 years and money to create the documentary film. They are courageous to make The Vietnam War film despite both have no much knowledge about the Vietnam War so this film doesn't bring the perception instead it conflicts against the truth and the Vietnam War's history. The Vietnam War film based on the wrong facts and repeated the rotten psychological warfare of the Vietcong, so it has not convinced the people, instead the strong reaction has to have. The anti-war, pro-communist movement in the Vietnam War buried in the historic cemetery nearly a half-century ago, therefore the filmmaker's Ken Burns and Lynn Novick try to revive the carcass and transforming into a zombie in the Vietnam War film.

(*) References: the website UNCENSORED HISTORY (in the title" Was South Vietnam Police chief Ngoc Loan a bad guy?") Written below:

" In the morning of the second day of Tet, January 31st, 1968, when general Nguyen Ngoc Loan was leading a fierce fight near An Quang Pagoda in Saigon's Chinese quarter, two of his officers brought to him a communist cadre who had murdered many innocents in cold-blood in the past couple days. He was Captain Nguyen Van Lem, alias Bay Lop. Minutes before he was captured, Bay Lop had killed the ARVN policeman's wife and all of his family members including his children. Around 4:30 A.M., Nguyen Van Lem led a sabotage unit along with Viet Cong tanks to attack the Armor Camp in Go Vap. After communist troops took control of the base, Bay Lop arrested Lieutenant Colonel Nguyen Tuan with his family and forced him to show them how to drive tanks. When Lieutenant Colonel Tuan refused to cooperate, Bay Lop killed all members of his family including his 80-year-old mother. There was only one survivor, a seriously injured 10-year-old boy.

Nguyen Van Lem was captured near a mass grave with 34 innocent civilian bodies. Lem admitted that he was proud to carry out his unit leader's order to kill these people. Lem was in his shorts and shirt. His arms were tied from the back. The pistol was still in his possession. General Loan executed.

Nguyen Van Lem on the spot.Suggested Reading

1. The Dark Journey: Inside the Reeducation Camps of Viet Cong By Hoa Minh Truong (Page 131)

2. Encyclopedia of the Vietnam War: A Political, Social, and Military History Edited by Spencer C. Tucker (Page 829)"

-Book of the author: Hoa Minh Truong's books being sold around the world, mostly the populated bookstores as Amazon, Barnes & Noble, Booktopia....

The dark journey: inside the reeducation camps of Viet Cong/.

Hoa Minh Truong.

LC Control Number: 2013376006

Brief Description: Truong-Minh-Hoa.

The dark journey: inside the reeducation camps of Viet Cong/

Hoa-Minh-Truong.

238 pages : illustrations ; 23 cm

ISBN: 9781609111618 (pbk)

LC Call Number: HV9800.5 .T78 2010

Dewey Number: 959.704/37 23

The Library of Congress is open to researchers and the public for in-house research only. Researchers must register in person at the Reader Registration Station; the Library cannot accept registrations via mail, telephone, or electronically.

-Book fifth" A humble Vietnamese woman" refers by US Federal Government (Memos for the general public of White House) also ULOOP (university of Washington DC) introduces as the Textbook to 1,500 universities and colleges in the US:

http://washington.uloop.com/textbooks/view.php/1631 359045/A-Humble-Vietnamese-Woman. And being sold at Walmart, the largest super market in the US./

8. THE WESTERN UNIVERSITY LOST THE PRESTIGE BY THE UNDER LEVEL FOREIGN STUDENT

In common sense, money could purchase a house, car and some facilities in society but money couldn't buy knowledge, personality, and health. In the Western and the developed countries, education is the source of national development, the poor resource countries as Japan, Singapore invested the education and the national economy grew. Instead, the communist countries have invested the Red seed than talent as the saying quotes" the family record wins over the education level" and in the government agency, government company recruiting and employment based on criteria is" the Red is a priority than capacity". Most communist countries are such as China, Vietnam, and others apply the same rule. As the situation in Vietnam, education deserves the priority for the Vietcong family and the so-called counter-revolution family have been treated as the second class in society including the education, mostly the children of the non-communist relation family to be kicked out from the university and college despite they have enough the level, even talented student. After many decades, the high education in Vietnam filled full the Vietcong's background student. In Vietnam and the other communist countries, the universities granted the qualification that based on the family's record, even the students come from the Vietcong's noble could force the university issue the degree without examination or assist the fallen student passed over. The domestic high education always supports the communist family, actually, the overseas students are the high class in the communist countries. In the communist states, while the major population struggling the

41

food, mostly low income, the non-communist family has not enough finance for study, so overseas studying is a luxury, but the communist student could afford and enjoy the gamble and vacation in the Western. Moreover, some powerful communist family's students purchased by cash expensive houses in a good location. On the other hand, the overseas students to be chosen by the regime, therefore, the communist also accords the espionage agents following, infiltrating into the Western universities.

The Western government often granted the scholarship to some communist states like Vietnam. Certainly, the students are chosen by the government and the Western universities endorse the scholarship students as the diplomat ties and deserve the facilities. Mostly the communist overseas student has not enough level to attend the Western universities because the university degree or high school graduated based on the family record, so most students come from the communist countries should use the bogus degree, even the fake qualification for overseas study. Nevertheless, the overseas students who come from non-English speaking have not enough language level, but they attended the university. The language skill is difficult for the overseas students, it worsens for the communist students as Vietnam, China.

The Western universities funded by the government, actually the private universities commercialize education as a business, there are many universities that advertise and deserved easiness for overseas students, so Western universities have been overwhelmed by overseas students including the students who come from communist states. Some universities aim to make money, it is the loophole in the education field. Nowadays, after few decades, Western universities have been losing prestige with the low-level academics. Moreover, the skill migrant policy in the Western countries as Australia, the US, and Europe created the opportunity for the under level overseas students to stay after graduated from the native universities. The garbage academics who come from the communist family background migrated easily and they sponsored the family. In Australia, Mr. Hieu Van Le, now he is the 35th and current Governor of South Australia (he stepped in the office on September 1, 2014) Mr. South Australia Governor Hieu Van Le activated the Vietcong overseas student since he served in the Labor government in South Australia. Nevertheless, the private office of legal services for migrants helped the communist overseas students study and staying after graduated.

The overseas students come from the communist regime who attended and graduated which raises grave concern the national security as the China overseas student propagate the communist theory and the obsolete Confucian (gender discrimination) influence the native students. The Australian Intelligence alerted the China overseas students in the universities.

The Western universities get lost the education's signification instead the education business so in the Western society appeared the Doctor, Ph. D with low level, lacking knowledge, but they have used the qualify for working. A Vietcong overseas student named Trương Huy San, pen name Huy Đức, came to the US studied at the University of Maryland from 2005 to 2006 under a Hubert H. Humphrey Fellowship and in 2012 he received a fellowship from the

Nieman Foundation for Journalist to study at Harward University in Cambridge (Massachusetts). A Vietcong propaganda activist Huy Đức represented as a communist overseas student, despite the English skill doubts, unfortunately, he attended a well-known university in the US. He couldn't write a book in English but he wrote the propaganda book" Bên Thắng Cuộc" by the Vietnamese language. Moreover, Ken Burns with Lynn Novick interviewed Huy Đức in the Vietnam War's documentary film, although Mr. Huy Đức has never joined the Vietnam War. There is another untrue of the phony film. The Western universities lost the prestige of the under level foreign student, actually, the students come from communist countries. Education is not a business, money could buy the degree but couldn't buy the knowledge. The Western universities need to review the foreign students, actually the strict English level test and checking the qualification granted by their university./.

9. THE PARADISE OF ROBBERS WITH WOODEN HAMMER

The communist paradise is the dead land of humanity, without human rights, neither democracy nor free speech. The communist party uses terror plus propaganda to oppress the people. Certainly, the communist paradise is just a pie on the sky as Boris Yeltsin's quote in Russia or the roast Peking duck painting in China. The communist paradise has the bush-law with the People's Court, the law is led by socialism, and the justice is decided by the communist party that is the super gang labeled revolution symbolizes the hammer for breaking the people skull and sickle for cutting the people throat.

In the US, the fake democracy has occurred at least 150 years ago, the second Constitution 1871 grants to license to rob, so the robbery exposes on multiple forms from society to the courts including the Supreme Court, the Congress, and Senate, those places are the bases of the white collar's robbers.

The Constitution in 1871 is like a hamburger drawing on the beautiful painting, **the free speech becomes speech free** (*the left stream media and the tech communication companies are Facebook, Google, and Twitter gag the free speech, propaganda, and censor*). The legal system reflects the bush-law, so America is the hidden communist government, moreover, when the Democratic Party rules the White House and controls the Senate, Congress, the Supreme Court, the Donkey super gang deployed the bush law system as the safety net to protect the corruption and treason of the high profiles. Particularly, the recent President Barrack Obama inserted many Democratic judges into the courtrooms from the district, state, and Supreme Court plus the FBI, CIA, Intelligence and the Police become the tools of Democrats. Its reason explains FBI Director James Comey didn't indict 32,000 emails of comrade Hillary Clinton in the presidential election in 2016 and many mysterious deaths linking Bill Clinton and Hillary Clinton's friends, workers including four deaths of Benghazi sunk in the forgotten cases. Moreover, the legal system and investigating bodies waived the corruption, treason of Joe Biden, Hunter Biden. Instead, the presidential robber Joe Biden inaugurated on January 20, 2021, despite the Constitution's consent the sitting president can be removed from the office if commits treason, corruption.

The white collar's robbers rule the US with the bush law, the unconstitutional practice based on the Constitution of 1871. In the US, the number of lawyers in 2020 is 1,330,000. Among the legal servants, the dishonest lawyers are plenty, they are the ROBBERS WITH PAPER-KNIFE and the dishonest judges are the ROBBERS WITH WOODEN HAMMER. Moreover, almost, the Democratic lawmakers in Congress and Senate are the ROBBERS IN THE HIGHEST LEVEL. Certainly, Americans have lived in the paradise of bush law. So-called America is the land of an opportunity that is a farce.

The robbers with wooden hammers control the legal system and decide the justice that based on individual favor, the political purposes, so Americans have no justice, nor equal opportunity and the fair election. The Vietnamese people must obey the order of the cruel communist regime in Vietnam as a saying" *eating is like a prisoner, sleeping is like a monk and speaking is like the national leader"*. The people in the communist regime have no right to expose the opinion, and in Americans, the people have been suffered the bush-law with the judge's order is like the decree of the emperor in medieval. Moreover, the legal system deserves the absolute attorney power for the judges with the high legal fees that gag the justice when a victim wants to appeal, initially, the legal fees increase for every stage to hamper the people.

The white-collar robbers oppress the people with the bush-law and wild rules of the kings without a throne in the courtrooms. The robbers with wooden hammers legalized the rigged election of Democrats, Joe Biden. The victims are

President Donald Trump and 75,000,000 people do nothing to show the truth when the local courts at the swing states dismissed the rigged election that proved with the mountain of evidence while President Donald Trump won 2/3 lawsuits. Eventually, Texas and 20 states plus 126 Republican lawmakers filed the lawsuits against the swing states, but six Justices and Chief Justice John Roberts rejected despite they knew the rigged election is the crime. The victims of the robbers with the wooden hammer do nothing to prove the truth as former Lieutenant General Michael Flynn harmed by the bush-law, even the US President Donald Trump couldn't protect the presidency expired on January 20, 2021, and the thuggish Chief Justice John Roberts exploited the Constitution to preside the illegal inauguration of the presidential robber, Joe Biden, while 75,000,000 people elected President Donald Trump in the second term. The thuggish Chief Justice John Roberts is the presidential maker, he reflects the highest robbery level in America.

Despite President Donald Trump moved out of the White House after the first term expired, indeed, President Donald Trump won the second term. Therefore, the robbers with the white-collar of Democratic Congress and Senate applied the bush lawmaker to impeach President Donald Trump. Therefore, the bullshit impeachment failed because the Senate didn't have enough 67 votes, if not, President Donald Trump will be a victim of the bush-lawmakers. Once again, the Representative of Democrats in Mississippi is Bennie Thompson who applies the bush law to sue President Donald Trump and lawyer Rudy Giuliani over the so-called riot at Capitol Hill on January 6, 2021, although the Congress and Senate failed. Certainly, the bullshit lawsuit of the thuggish white-collar Bennie Thompson files at a Democratic court of the robber with the wooden hammer.

The fake democratic country called the United States of America exposes the Corporation of the United States of America. The US people have been suffered the bush law plus the bush lawmakers, so America has collapsed the democracy since 1871. The people need to get back the Constitution of 1776 or Americaxit to reform the virtual United States of America. Certainly, the legal system (*the judges and Supremes Justices*), Congress, Senate, and the White House have not reflected the democracy, although the land decorated the Statue of Freedom to cover the rotten government's system./.

10. CHINESE MIGRANTS HAVE INVADED THE WESTERN

Commonly, the communist party always applies the discrimination policy to its people but deserves priority for communist members and family. After the communist party robbed the government, initially, the main enemies of communists are the wealthy and intellectual components to be eliminated, the victims were killed, jailed, the family members suffered the worst treatment applying to three generations (*). The counter-revolutionary components have been treated as the second citizen's class, their descendants to be discriminated in education, working places. Instead, the communist families have anything, the Red noble class controls the national economy, assets, they become the Red capitalist. The communist regime empowered its members and families the right to rob, confiscate the people's land, properties, all labeled" *public interest and social benefit"*. The brainwash, obscurantism, and terror policy plus the impoverishment create the communist paradise, but the people live in hell. The people work as a slave, but the communist members become the millionaires and billionaires.

"In China, the asset of Premier Wen Jiabao is worth at least $USD 2.7 billion after 10 years sitting above his people. Before Mr. Xi Jinping controlled the communist party, he had owned the asset estimated up to a hundred million pounds, now he is richer than any previous leaders, despite his monthly wage is 11, 385 Yuan ($USD 1,830).

In Vietnam, the salary of a prime minister is roughly 17,000, 000 đồng Vietnam a month ($USD 805) it's equivalent to the dole benefit in Australia, but most of the Prime Minister, Secretary-General, Government Chairperson are the billionaires: Phan Văn Khải has $USD 2 billion, Võ Văn Kiệt has $1.15 billion, Trần Đức Lương has $USD 2.1 billion, General Lê Đức Anh has $USD 1.15 billion, Lê Khả Phiêu has $USD 1.43 billion, Nông Đức Mạnh has $USD 1.43 billion...as former Prime Minister Nguyễn Tấn Dũng, his asset is worth $USD 1.78 billion.

During power, Prime Minister Nguyen Tan Dung transferred a lot of money to their daughter and son-in-law who bought a soccer club Chivas in Los Angeles worth $USD 100 million, not including the properties purchased in the US. The incumbent Prime Minister Nguyễn Xuân Phúc is not an exception, the Vietnamese people expect that man is the most corrupt. **In Vietnam, he has many properties and in the US, he is the owner of the mansions located in Anaheim,**

California CA 92804: 636 South Halliday Street and 7556 East Calle Durango Street. Prime Minister Nguyễn Xuân Phúc's son is Nguyễn Xuân Hiếu, now lives in the US, his drive license registered address of a mansion 636 South Halliday Street." Cited from the article" VIETCONG PRIME MINISTER NGUYỄN XUÂN PHÚC, THE MOST CORRUPTED OFFICIAL IN VIETNAM" of Hoa Truong posted on June 1ˢᵗ, 2017.

The bloodshed campaigns occurred in China after 1949, North Vietnam after 1954, North Korea after the war, Russia after 1917, and other communist regimes in Eastern Europe states. The victims of communism were up to a hundred million people, therefore, the genocides like Mao Tse Tung, Hồ Chí Minh, Kim Il Sung, Fidel Castro, Pol Pot have never appeared at the International Court.

The discrimination policy strictly applies to communist countries. In Vietnam, the Red Noble class lives on the people's sweat, the social priority always deserves the communist family, the education rules" *the family record wins over the ta*lent" and working place (*government job*) applies the rule" *Red is rather than professionals*". Particularly, the Police force and the Public Security Guard force recruit the officers based on three generations.

The people in communist countries must struggle so hard to pay the cost of living, overseas trips, and migrants, students deserve the priority for the communist family. The Western countries made a terrible mistake by negligent immigration policy, so the communists, espionage agents, communist students (*Red seeds*) inundated.

China and Vietnam have exploited the immigration

policy of Western-like skilled migrants, business migrants (*the Red wealthy persons legally migrated with the corrupted money or communist regime's businesses*), the family reunion (*mostly the fake marriage*) has become the good business of private immigration firms with the ethnic lawyers. The Western immigration policy failed badly, **the multiple cultures turn multiple troubles** after the communists legally invaded. Vietcong has sent the espionage agents and the criminals to Western, mostly, the Vietnamese migrants come from the Northern background who have developed the Marijuana's plantations in Europe, the US, Canada, Australia. The Vietnamese refugees oppose the dregs of socialism, unfortunately, the Western countries accepted Vietcong migrants. A circumstance of Vietcong migrant named Pete Hoang that is an iceberg floating on the surface. Mr. Pete Hoang is a nephew of Vietcong's acting Prime Minister Hoàng Trung Hải, he migrated to Australia and he has never worked, certainly, Pete Hoang was the current recipient of Centrelink. Therefore, the Australian Police arrested them when he brought $US 1.5 million to Crown Casino. Pete Hoang told $US 90 million's winning from the gambling, he told to lose about $US 8 million. Possibly, Mr. Pete Hoang involved in the money-laundering ring of Vietcong in Australia. During Australian Police was investigating, he was killed by someone, Vietcong should send the secret agents to kill Pete Hoang to destroy the witness and protect the spy network. Crown Casino employed Mr. Ming Chai holds a high role (VIP), but he is the cousin of Xi Jinping.

From many decades ago, China and Vietcong sent the communist members to Western, certainly, the communist regimes easily granted the visa for their members, students including the communists covered under the Buddhist monks (*Vietnamese temples overseas are the den of a communist*), the communist's Catholic priests easily travel overseas including the so-called political prisoners, Vietcong has exploited the human rights to send the fake opponents like Điếu Cày (*Nguyễn Văn Hải*), Cù Huy Hà Vũ, Trần Khải Thanh Thủy and recently, Mẹ Nấm (*Nguyễn Ngọc Như Quỳnh*) to the US, instead, South Vietnam Captain Nguyễn Cầu who was imprisoned 37 years is still under the house detention in Vietnam (*Nelson Mandela spent 27 years in prison*).

Chinese travelers, migrants, workers, students, and others are communists, the rogue regime always deserves the facilities for communist members and family to travel overseas and migrated. **Every Chinese migrant who comes from the mainland is a communist, espionage agent, financial agent, and propaganda activist**. The trade war and the Chinese virus arouse the Western and the world, Chinese communists infiltrated and activating into the Western soil after joining the world community. The damages are inevitable, the domestic thugs present everywhere from society, school, university, multiple levels of government's system, and the free market including the stock market.

President Donald Trump does not rule out banning the visa for millions of Chinese people who come from the mainland. They are the communists, not migrants, travelers, and students who have exploited the opening's education policy, the profit lover Vice-chancellors who transformed the education to business. China's Communist Party has sent many students to study at the Western. The high level of technological thieves stole the technologies and propagated communism in Western universities, so the native students have been intoxicated and brainwashed in their own country.

Chinese migrants, Chinese students, and Chinese travelers who come from the mainland are dangerous. Nevertheless, Chinese travelers helped China's Communist Party spread the Coronavirus pandemic with the support of the World Health Organization. The visa ban of the US can affect millions of Chinese migrants, espionage agents, and technological thieves. The negligent immigration policy created an opportunity for China's communist regime to invade and carry out global hegemonic ambition. The Western countries alert Chinese migrants, students, they are dangerous and become domestic thugs after granted a residential status.

China always conspires to global hegemonic ambition with the soft army (*businesses, investors*), and the military intimidation are supported by China's communist government and embassy plus the consulate-general around the world. Nevertheless, Chinese migrants have invaded the Western, **some media social predict China's Communist Party aims to migrate about 92 million communist members to the US. In Australia, a rumor spread in the federal election on May 18, 2019, about Labor Opposition leader Bill Shorten and Labor Senate leader Penny Wong planned to accept 10 million** Chinese migrants come from the mainland. Moreover, Senator Penny Wong promised to admit Huawei operates 5G if the Australian Labor Party wins the election./.

NOTES: (*) the writer (*Hoa Minh Truong*) imprisoned for 6 years in the hell of a re-education camp after the Vietnam

War ended on April 30, 1975. The repression policy of Vietcong caused the writer to escape by a small boat to find freedom from August 1982 and have never returned to Vietnam. Despite my mother passed away on February 14, 2016, but I couldn't return for my mother's funeral.

11. THE COMMUNISM STARTS TO APPLY IN AMERICA

Americans are endangered after the mongrel communist Joe Biden robbed the White House with the certification of the major traitor Mike Pence and John Roberts. The American communist Joe Biden applies the same methods as Mao Tse Tung in 1949, Vietcong in 1975, Pol Pot in 1975, Lenin in 1917, and other communists. The US people face the impoverishment's policy and the obscurantism of Joe Biden, now, the people start to live in the nightmare of communism as Chinese people, Vietnamese people, Russian, and others spent the bloody experiences.

The mongrel communist Joe Biden will target the wealthy persons, the enemies of communists, they label the capitalists or counter-revolutionary elements. The innocent people voted and supported Joe Biden plus the wealthy persons poured many into Joe Biden's campaign, all will be faced the peril of communism. It is too late after President Donald Trump didn't trigger the EO-13848 to crack-down the communist movement in the United States of America, the disaster comes. When seeing the coffin, it is too late for crying.

The communist parties, the left parties in democratic countries are the siblings as tiger snake and Cobra. The different kinds of poisonous snakes expose the different colors in the territories, certainly, the poisonous snakes are not python. The innocent people in Western and democratic countries can not distinguish between the tiger snake and python, so the country risks with the left parties are the hidden communist parties. Commonly, the communist and the left parties' formula is **3 D= Deception + Demagogy + Destruction**. The communist parties in China, Vietnam, North Korea, Cuba, and others have applied the same formula:

1-The Deception has applied since the communist party didn't rob the government and after taking over the country. The propaganda brainwashes people plus the terror contributed to the succession of the communist parties in Russia, Eastern European states, China, Vietnam. The nice languages as revolution, class struggle, socialism, the communist paradise, all are the pies on the sky as Boris Yeltsin warned. Chinese people have enjoyed the roast Peking duck in the painting of Mao Tse Tung since 1949 and now Xi Jinping continues to give the picture of the roast Peking duck to 1.4 billion people. In the US, Democratic Party has deceived the people with the benefit, democracy, freedom, and other languages, so many innocent people joined and support the hidden communist party in the United States of America. Nowadays, hateful communist faces appeared like Bill Clinton, Barrack Obama, Joe Biden, Kamala Harris, Adam Schiff, Chuck Schumer, Nancy Pelosi who combined the Mafia and communist, Bernie Sanders, and others.

2-The Demagogy to cover the communism as the tiger snake disguises python, the demagogic policies lie about the hoax climate change, the hypocritical humanity is the human rights turn human wrong with the support of the illegal migrants. The same-sex-marriage legislation challenges human history, religious faith, and social valuation. Those demagogic policies to woo the ballots in the election. *Do not listen to what the communist talks, let's watch what the communist did.* The professional lie is the essential character of the communist *when a communist is born, initially, a midwife sees the mouth.*

3-The Destruction is the last stage on the 3D's formula, after the communist party or the left parties controlled the government, initially, destruction is the essential tactic to destroy the hostile government, they call the capitalist or counter-revolutionary regime. The communist parties and the left parties have applied the same method. Before driving the country to communism, Karl Marx's pupils destroy the fundamental society and economy.

After Mao Tse Tung robbed the authentic government of Chinese people in 1949, China's Communist Party destroyed the society by the bloodshed campaigns that were Great Leap Forward, Hundred of Flowers, the Culture Revolution, particularly, the Landlord Reform campaign to beat the wealthy component including the intellectuals including the innocent wealthy persons and intellectuals contributed the victory of China's Communist Party. Socialism is the dawn of communism but in the Western, the mongrel communist Bill Clinton deceived the world by the word"

GLOBALIZATION". The impoverishment applies to

destroy the economy from the grassroots.

In Vietnam, after the last invasion succeeded on April 30, 1975, Vietcong launched the beaten capitalist campaign, the ruthless regime confiscated the assets of the wealthy persons and launched three times to change the currency, so the South Vietnam people to be impoverished, it caused a million Vietnamese people fled the country to find the freedom. Everywhere is the same situation after the communist party or the left party controlled the government. Mostly, **the Australian Labor Party** advocates the debt, after the Coalition government lost in the election in 2007, Labor Prime Minister Kevin Rudd *(a mongrel communist of Beijing)* and Finance Minister Penny Wong (*the hidden communist*) spent $A 42 billion surpluses of Prime Minister John Howard and Treasurer Peter Costello, then Labor government of Prime Minister Kevin Rudd, Julia Gillard created the debt to help China taking control Australia's economy. Nowadays the Australian people wake up after China terrorizes Australia's imports and China humiliates the people.

The Democratic Party succeeded in the deception and demagogic policies, eventually, Democrats colluded with China, Deep State to rob the US government by using the rotten Constitution of 1871. The rigged election was legalized by Chief Justice John Roberts, House Speaker Nancy Pelosi, and Vice-President, Senate Speaker Mike Pence to inaugurate the presidential robber Joe Biden who illegally occupied the White House on January 20, 2021, **while the rigged election has not solved yet as a legal case is processing, no one claims the winner**. Unfortunately, three heads of the US certified the robber Joe Biden. **However, Joe Biden is not the**

46ᵗʰ president until the rigged election cleared, so Joe Biden is an illegal president to storm the White House as a communist leader robs the government. It tells the people about the illegal presidency of Joe Biden. Once again, after January 20, 2021, Vice President Kamala Harris and her husband have not moved to the Naval Observatory, instead, they stay at the Blair House, it is the president's official guest residence located right across from the White House, why?

Initially, **the mongrel communist leader Joe Biden enters the White House is like Pol Pot entered Pnom Penh, Mao Ste Tung controlled Beijing**. The mongrel communist Joe Biden has started to destroy the economy and impoverish the United States of America from the first day in the White House, he signed 17destructive executive orders to lose 70,000 jobs. Within two weeks, Joe Biden signed 40 destructive executive orders, he becomes the champion of executive orders in US history. Communism or socialism starts to apply in the United States of America starts, so innocent people like the employees and union of Keystone Pipeline Xl regret to support the mongrel communist is Joe Biden. Now, they lost the job, but they do nothing to save after the decree of Joe Biden issue.

The next step will carry out the tactic of throwing the lemon's skin after the juice emptied. The bloody lesson Vietnam's Communist Party after Vietcong occupied Saigon. The tool of Hanoi was the members of the National Liberation Front were purge, many henchmen kicked out from the government, and the prominent henchmen like lawyer Trịnh Đình Thảo and his wife detained at their house, their comrades cut the food and water, eventually, they died in silence. Medical Doctor Dương Quỳnh Hoa, activist student

Huỳnh Tấn Mẫm and others received bad treatment from Vietnam's Communist Party. The Chinese people lived at Cholon faced the impoverishment policy, despite in the Vietnam War, the rich Chinese people in Cholon contributed money for Vietcong.

The mongrel communist Joe Biden and his Democratic Party will purge the henchmen like Mitch McConnell, Mitt Romney, Mike Pence, the Rino, and others. It is the essential methods of communist, therefore, the regret is too late, the innocent people and the turncoat Republicans must pay the dire consequences. It is a better way to save the country when the Republican states unite to fight and nullify the destructive executive orders of Joe Biden, now there are more 200 companies file the lawsuit against Joe Biden and seeking the compensation. **The mongrel communist Joe Biden applies the bush law and he has never respected the people, the states, why do the states comply with the illegal executive orders of Joe Biden? Let's reject all unlawful executive orders of the illegal president Joe Biden.**

The hidden communist party robs the US government while the bullshit Constitution ties the patriotism, so the US Army, Police, Intelligence become a robot and Joe Biden who holds the remote control, which conducts the United States of America is on the brink of collapse. The presidential robber regime of Joe Biden has the comrade is Norwegian MP Petter Edi who nominated Black Lives Matter for the Nobel Peace Prize in 2021, it conflicts the signification, everyone knows Antifa and Black Lives Matters are the terror organizations. If the global thug and global war-maker Barrack Obama awarded the Nobel Peace Prize in 2009, so Black Lives Matter should be awarded.

The US presidential election in 2020 has not concluded yet while the rigged election has not been solved, so Joe Biden has no authority to inaugurate on January 20, 2021. The basic law confirms a legal case doesn't decide yet, so no one can not claim the winner. Therefore, Joe Biden illegally inaugurated the 46th president at Capitol Hill on January 20, 2021. Certainly, Joe Biden is not the lawful president, instead, he is the presidential robber.

-President Donald Trump was the winner from the night of November 3, 2020, therefore, Joe Biden robbed the election by stealing the ballots, everyone and the world know the truth, **President Donald Trump is the victim of the bullshit Constitution and Chief Justice John Roberts, traitor Mike Pence**. The bullshit Constitution causes the presidency to expire on January 20, 2021, and Chief Justice John Roberts illegally presided over the illegal inauguration of Joe Biden. Moreover, President Donald Trump didn't hand over the government and the White House to the presidential robber Joe Biden, so Donald Trump still authorizes the US president. The tenant of the White House is President Donald Trump expired the contract on January 20, 2021, the owner (*US people agreed Donald Trump with four years more of the contract*). Instead, a new tenant Joe Biden who cheated the contract, so he is not a new tenant until the rigged election cleared, the official tenant of the White House is President Donald Trump moved to the new office in Florida, he is still working without a salary. On the other hand, Donald Trump is still the US president, not Joe Biden.

-The presidential robber Joe Biden is not the US president: Without Mike Pence certified the 306 fraudulent electoral colleges of Joe Biden, he couldn't inaugurate, so

Mike Pence is the treason at the high level and Chief Justice John Roberts presided the inauguration is the major traitor.

What happens after the rigged election proved by the courts, recently, the judge in Virginia decided the Election Board violated the law with mail-in-voting. Its case can apply to the swing states or 50 states. Moreover, the Federal Election Commission confirmed the US presidential election in 2020 is illegitimate. The circumstance of Joe Biden is like a doping athlete loses the medal after the cheat was discovered. When the rigged election of the swing states, even 50 states are concluded by the courts, certainly, Joe Biden must oust from the White House despite he inaugurated and he will be arrested with Justice John Roberts, Mike Pence, and the accomplices commit the treason in the high level.

-The Republican states, including the waken the Democratic States damaged by the destructive executive orders of mongrel communist Joe Biden, let's unite and reject the illegal president Joe Biden plus the unlawful executive orders. The states can deny the executive orders issued by the illegal president Joe Biden and also dismiss any orders of Joe Biden.

–**The wealthy persons in America must know the mongrel communist Joe Biden will confiscate their assets after Democrats controlled the government, Congress, Senate, and the Supreme Court.** The bloody experiences alert about the beaten capitalists as China, Vietnam, and other communist regimes did.

Certainly, the presidential robber Joe Biden was legalized by the Supreme Court, Senate, and Congress that humiliates the United States of America when the robber becomes the US president and the Vice President's nickname is" *let's go to bed*" should replace an old imbecile president anytime. Nevertheless, Joe Biden and Kamala Harris are the mongrel communists.

The government's robbery proved Joe Biden is the professional robber, he is the super and great master of Al Capone because Joe Biden robs the US government, the White House and Congress, Senate plus Supreme Court certified. On the other hand, Joe Biden is the world's super robber, his robbery becomes the black spot of US history./.

12. THE TECH COMPANIES ARE MONGREL COMMUNISTS

The left parties in Western are the hidden communist parties, the political activities carry out with the demagogic policies as the hoax climates change, the fake human rights (*protect the illegal migrants*). Therefore, communism's backbone has never changed.

After Soviet-Union collapsed in the early 1990s, Communism has weakened, and the Marxism-Leninist eradicated in Europe, the cradle of Communism and Revolution 1917. Therefore, Communism has remained in Asia, China's Communist Party gathered the vestiges are Vietnam, Cambodia (*Khmer Rouge*), North Korea, Laos, and Cuba battle the new Communism movement. China's Communist Party stole the label of Marxism-Leninist made in China, it calls Maoist and applying the deceitful tactic as the lizard changes skin's color. The Cold War transforms into the Cool War with the soft army using the trade, free trade agreement, diplomat to invade the democratic countries, the essential targets are Western and the United States of America. The cheating economic pattern" *the free market is led by socialism*" bluffed in innocent leaders, the naïve academics, and the profit love's businesses. The global economic terror of China succeeded, but the democratic states didn't know, so the Western countries fell into the trap. China couldn't develop Maoist or Communism into Western countries and the world community, therefore, GLOBALIZATION disguises COMMUNISM or MAOIST. Democratic President Bill Clinton advocated and activated globalization, it is MONGREL COMMUNISM or MONGREL MAOIST silently developed and rooted in the Western. The Democratic Party has brought the Maoists invading the US for a long time. The tiger snake and Cobra are poisonous reptiles, Maoist, Communism, Marxism-Leninist, and Globalization are the same. China has at least a quarter of a century to influence Maoist in the US with two terms of President Bill Clinton, George. W.Bush and Barrack Obama, now Joe Biden continues to apply Maoist if taking the White House.

The essential tactics of communists are terror and propaganda, those tactics have applied in the US, the presidential election in 2020 exposes the terror and propaganda of Democrats, coup leader Joe Biden, and the left tech communication companies are Facebook, Google, Twitter. Commonly, the left parties, the left stream media terror companies, and the left tech communication terror companies have the formulas:

1-The left media: 3 F = False poll +Fake news

+Fabricated story

2-Democrats: 3 D = Deception +Demagogy + Destruction

3-The tech communication: 3C =Cancel + Conceal + Censor

The US presidential election wakes Americans and the world, the rigged election destroyed the country and the tools of Democrats are Facebook, Twitter, Google appeared the mongrel communists. The propaganda to help traitor Joe Biden made the coups and they also use the technology to terrorize President Donald Trump and the supporters.

The victims of communists have never forgotten the most barbarous regime on the planet. The essential tactics are propaganda plus terror force the people to shut the mouth, if not, the hell of re-education camps, killing have applied from the local government to the highest level government.

The communists can not hide the inhumane policies when the experts and the victims of Marxism-Leninist-Maoist-Ho Chi Minh's thoughts accuse the super gang rules the country under the demagogic propaganda called" *Communist Paradise*". On the other hand, the communist party is a super gang, well-organized, the genocide is sophisticated by the evil bible of Karl Marx.

In a communist country, people become slave, the communist party reflects the cruel speech of Mr. Nguyễn Hộ, a high ranking cadre of Vietnam's Communist Party. The so-called Liberation's day on April 30, 1975, Mr. Nguyễn Hộ and his gang invaded South Vietnam, at Saigon's Town Hall, he told to his comrades*:" their house, we occupy-their wife, we take-their children, we enslave"*. Vietnam, China, and other communist states are the same policies. The communist members are the Red noble class to earn anything from the people's sweat and the proletariat class. The priority always deserves for the communist family as the medieval. The lying propaganda can not conceal the discrimination policies applying throughout the country. The discrimination policy is the backbone of the communist to keep the regime remaining, it strictly applies in multiple fields:

1-The education focuses to deserve priority for the communist family and relatives:

The education system applies the rule:" *the family history wins over talent*", the high education prioritizes communist family, instead, the counter-revolutionary families can not afford the higher education, their children are curbed the future by the family's background. The university eliminates the non-communist family, so the major overseas students come from China, Vietnam, and others are the communists. The red seeds become the technological thieves and also the propaganda activists in a Western university.

2-The employment prioritizes the communist families as a saying:" *Red is better than the professionals*", the government job, government-owned companies just employ the communist family. Particularly, the Public Security Guard Force recruit the member that based on three generations, so the Public Security Guard Force is like SS of Hitler.

3-The social rules apply communist policies:

-The social relation must comply with communism, the people must obey the order of government, whoever exposes the different view with the government, the treason labeled and the heavy punishment applies.

-The activities of the communist regime are based on THREE GENERATIONS, the counter-revolutionary components like wealthy families, opponents, and others become the second class. The discrimination applies to eliminate the non-communist components, in the communist country, the communist gang members dominate the nation and society. Corruption is the hidden policy to feed the communist members, so the major high profiles of communist parties in China, Vietnam are the millionaires, billionaires. Therefore, the Red wealthy persons didn't keep the money in their banks, instead, they sent the corrupted money to the counter-revolutionary bank in the US, Europe.

The left parties in Western are the hidden communist parties, the Democratic Party in the US, the Australian Labor Party, the UK Labor Party, the Socialist Party in France, the Greens Party...have applied the communist methods. Therefore the MONGREL COMMUNISTS covered under the label of GLOBALIZATION can not succeed in democratic countries, moreover, the communist paradise couldn't apply in Western including the United States of America. The scam President Joe Biden has never won the election, therefore three traitors are Chief Justice John Roberts of Supreme Court, House Speaker Nancy Pelosi, and the Senate Speaker Mike Pence certified the traitor Joe Biden to win the presidency with the rigged election while the US people strongly oppose and President Donald Trump continues to fight for the country. Despite Joe Biden doesn't rule the White House, but Democrats intimidate to send 74,000,000 to the re-education camps as Mao Tse Tung did in China, Ho Chi Minh applied in Vietnam and Pol Pot carried out in Cambodia *(1975-1979)*.

The mongrel communists expose the hostile attitude of Facebook, Google, Twitter, the domestic thugs of the left tech communication terror companies banned President Donald Trump, former Lieutenant General Micheal Flynn, lawyer Lin Wood, lawyer Sidney Powell and the supporters of President Donald Trump. Twitter suspended 88 million followers after the incident at Capitol Hill on January 6, 2021 (*Democrats and Antifa are the culprits*). The left tech communication terror companies commit suicide, the users abandoned and the advertising plunged. The shares of Twitter Inc plunged 6% just a day after the ban of President Donald Trump, Facebook lost 3%, Google dropped 1.5%.

The mongrel communists apply discrimination in communication's services, Twitter banned Donald Trump and also banned his son is Barron Trump, 14-year-old. The CEO of Twitter Jack Dorsey plays a kid game like Jane Fonda's younger brother Peter Fonda attacked Barron Trump when he was 11-year-old (*he returned to communist paradise in 2019*).

The real communists succeeded in the terror and propaganda in China, Vietnam, Cuba, and others. Therefore, the leftists in the Western are the mongrel communists, the ban applies on Facebook, Twitter, Google can not gag free speech. President Donald Trump authorized to appeal to the 230 Act and President has the other media companies like Newsmax, OAN, gab.com, Duckduckgo." *When Trump is ready, he will announce it over the Emergency Broadcasting System. Twitter, FB, and other socialist social media groups that think they've stopped Trump will look like deer caught in the headlights.*" (Arch Bonnema). The internet is the common public place, Google, Facebook, Twitter, Youtube, and others just the businesses. The competitive era dethrones the exclusive position of the left stream terror and the left tech communication terror companies. When a business loses customers, bankruptcy is waiting for them. The tech giants make a terrible mistake, they declare war with the US government and terrorize the US president. Unfortunately, the communist methods of tech giants are useless, instead, the people boycott and joining other media services including the new media companies./.

13. THE SCLEROSIS CHARACTER OF ECONOMIC SOCIALISM

In the Cold War, the Global Communist Bloc applied the propaganda forwarding the technology, and the weapon advanced by the US to bluff the world. Indeed, Soviet-Union failed the arms race with the US, actually, the Star War Program (*The Strategic Defense Initiative*) promoted by President Ronald Reagan on March 23, 1983, ruined the developed missile of the cradle of the Global Communist Bloc. Nevertheless, after Soviet-Union collapsed, the world knew well the propaganda of the communist reflects a saying" **do not listen to what the communist talks, let's watch what the communist did."** Actually, the demagogic propaganda praised the communist paradise to deceive the innocent people and the lazy thinking of the lacking knowledge of inexpert communism's academics in the Western.

The books of Karl Marx are like the beautiful cloth cover a garbage bin, the naive Western people have attracted by the utopian theory, they have become craziness to believe communism and socialism can create the best society. Indeed, communism causes the death of more than 100 million people and a billion people enslaved.

The Marxism-Leninist's paranoid get lost the mind despite they knew the communism born the totalitarian regimes in Soviet-Union, China, Vietnam, Cambodia *(Khmer Rouge),* Cuba, and the others. On the other hand, the socialists in Western are the hypocritical component, they often raise the mouthful condemnation of the dictatorial regimes, actually, the human rights violation currently occurs in communist countries. Therefore, they adore and follow socialism that derived from communism, actually, Karl Marx is the mastermind of communism. The fake moral person opposes the crimes, gang but adores Mafia, it is a farce of the socialists in the Western countries.

Communism is the most disastrous humanity on the planet, Marxism-Leninist has intoxicated the people since Lenin succeeded in the Ape Revolution in October 1917. The communists lost the human mind, instead of the animal instinct, so the communists pride the genocide, robbery, they have enjoyed the serious crimes that titled the revolution. The communist regimes have eradicated human history from the grassroots and destroyed society. The mind purge covered under the languages of class struggle, social reform, communist paradise, and many nice titles brainwashed its people, even the hell of prison that called the re-education. The anti-communist expert's quote:" *when a communist is born, obviously, a midwife sees the mouth "*.

Communism is the enemy of human development. In China, Vietnam, the Soviet Union, and the other communist regimes eliminated the wealthy component, abolished the intellectuals. Vietnam Communists carried out the bloody campaign called LandLord Reform, Hồ Chí Minh and propaganda machine launched the slogan:" *uproot the intellectual, wealthy, landlord components"*. China did the same policy so after communist-controlled the country, the illiterate peasants and the low-educated members replaced the intellectuals. Moreover, the education of the communist regime applies the rule is" ***family history wins over the talent"***. The Communist regime eliminated the talent, but the regime prioritizes for their children in the education, actually, the overseas study always deserves for the communist members. The intellectuals and academics are the red seeds of the communist regime, they lack the talent and invention.

Socialism is a prime stage of communism, unfortunately, Marxism-Leninist rotted from the fundamental base, so socialism commits suicide the communist regimes and the lagging technology comes from lost democracy. Free speech comes to the freedom that conducts the mind's development and encouraging the invention. The sclerosis character of socialism hit back the communist regime on the economy:

-The financial system tied by the government, so the people including the communist members distrust the banks, they deposit the money to the" *counter-revolution banks"* in Western, even Hong Kong.

-The product that affected socialism with the untold rule is" *negligent work but the best report"*. The products made from the communist countries, including the Soviet-Union, Eastern Europe communist Bloc, all products couldn't compare with the US, European countries *(democratic states)*.

-The people who live in communist regimes lose freedom and the patriotic concern is led by socialism, the scam spirit deeply destroyed the people's invention. The mind contributes to the invention of and national spirit. Unfortunately, socialism framed patriotism and brainwashed the people's minds. The vital motive of national development to be murdered by socialism and communism.

Despite Soviet-Union changed the communist regime from the early 1990s, therefore, toxic communism still remains in Russia. Nowadays, Russia's car can not compare with German cars, the US, even Japan with Toyota and South Korea has Hyundai.

China has faced the lacking invention, Beijing solved the problem by stolen technology, so China becomes the den of thieves, the hub of counterfeit, and the center of a cheat. After more than 70 years, China's communist party built the regime from the bloodshed, demagogic policy, propaganda, and terror policy. China's products worsen the quality, poison, contamination, and short life. However, the poor quality products of China inundated the global market that promoted by the innocent leaders and the profit lover's business. **The naïve traitors helped China's growth** and nowadays, China uses the money to carry out the hegemonic ambition. Unfortunately, sclerosis's character hampered the invention, actually, the stolen technology on the space race, the arms race that conducts China into failure. In the Cold War, Soviet-Union failed the arms race with the US. Nowadays, China can not fight with the copied military technology. The aircraft carriers made in China but copied from Ukraine (*the old model of the Cold War*), so China has sunk into the quagmire of the Chinese dream. The nightmare is coming while the US fights against the global economic terror, China loses the major battles on the economy, finance, the potential damages to be recognized by China's currency devalued over the alert-level.

China should hire "*the comrade*" left media to propagate the fake news and fabricated stories about the unbelievable developments of China's economy like Chinese scientists made a pig that weighed more than 500 kilograms. China made the laser weapon, actually, the military strength. Therefore, the high technological communication era, the multiple information sources, and social media defeat fake news, so China also loses the psychological warfare in Western. Every time, the left media and the inexpert academics praise China's strength, actually, the concealment of loss in the economic battle with the US, the disgraced propaganda debunked promptly after the fake news was released. The sclerosis character of socialism has pulled Chinese people in the mainland lagging behind Taiwan, Hong Kong, Singapore. Its reason urges Hong Kong people to reject socialism after the territory wrongly handed over to the robber in the mainland.

Chinese people need to abolish socialism in the mainland, the utopian theory labeled Marxism-Leninist and renamed in China is Maoist, in Vietnam called Hồ Chí Minh's thoughts. Let's compare the living condition between South and North Korea, West and East Germany, actually, South Vietnam and North Vietnam. After winning the unpredictable war on April 30, 1975, the former overseas students of North Vietnam studied at Soviet-Union, East Germany confirmed by a saying: " *one year in East Germany equals 3 years in Soviet-Union but a moment at Saigon"*. Nowadays, the Vietcong regime continues to pauperize its people and the high profiles of the Vietnam communist party become the millionaire and billionaires, they sent the corrupted money to Western, purchased the assets, and sent their red seeds to Western countries. The most counter-revolution countries like the US becomes the dreamland of Vietnam communist's descendants and their family. Even the communist rejects their communist paradise, unfortunately, in the Western countries, the left parties and innocent people still favor socialism as Senator Bernie Sanders and the high profiles of the Democratic Party. The US people and the world knew the fallen communist paradise in Venezuela that shattered and pauperized the country by the crazy idea of Hugo Chavez and Nicolas Maduro. Socialism and communism **formulates 3 D= Deception+ Demagogy+ Destruction,** so when the left parties like the Australian Labor Party ruled Down Under by Prime Minister Bob Hawke from 1983 to 1991 and Prime Minister Paul Keating from 1991 to 1996, Australia's debt was $AU 96 billion and Prime Minister Kevin Rudd with Prime Minister Julia Gillard from 2007 to 2013, they spent $AU 42 billion of the surplus left by Prime Minister John Howard then the country started to sink down in the deficit./.

14. JIN YONG SENT THE UNTOLD MESSAGE TO CHINESE PEOPLE

The Fung Fu writer Louis Leung Yung has the pen name **Jin Yong** (*Kim Dung*) born on February 6, 1924, he is a well know author of Hong Kong and Asia countries as Vietnam, Taiwan…he wrote 15 books that fascinated a million readers and many books made movies. His books sold a hundred million copies and became among the best sellers. The reader and audience could enjoy Kung Fu's novel and movies and also could understand what the author wants to tell something inside for every story and the protagonist.

Author Jin Yong comes from a wealthy and intellectual family in China. Therefore, after Mao Ste Tung occupied the mainland in 1949, China communist party applied socialism. Obviously, the social purge carried out by the Landlord Reform campaign, the bloodshed spread throughout China, the genocide labeled revolution occurred in the mainland by the revolutionists, almost, they were illiterate and low educated peasant activated the crazy Maoist to kill the people and rob the asset. In the bloody massacre, Jin Yong's family to be attributed to the counter-revolutionary element, so Jin Yong lost contact with family in the mainland since 1950. As the most communist's victim, author Jin Yong has never forgotten the culprit, the mental wound has never healed, despite he didn't have an opportunity to revenge the inhumane regime, but, he has tried to do something. His effort carried out into 15 martial art books, those sent to untold message to Chinese people:

1-The orthodox gentleman Chinese: Author Jin Yong respects the honest, so his gentlemen's concern exposes morality and virtue. The heroes display the good behavior of the top-class martial arts recipient that reflects the righteous protection and eliminate the dishonest. The gentleman of Jin Yong is not as Chinese conqueror taught the people of the occupied land" *do not beat the people fell from the horseback*". The fake morality poisoned the native people when the invader defeated, the conqueror could return to homeland safely and next time, the invader will come back.

The orthodox gentlemen's concern of Jin Yong advised the Chinese people has to know how to revenge. Almost, his martial arts stories describe honest people's behavior, after the enemy defeated, they must fight for survival and finding the master to learn Kung Fu. When they have enough martial arts skills, they will find the enemy. The spiritual revenge could pass to the descendant if they failed to do.

After the nationalist failed at the mainland, the Taiwanese fought the" master" to learn Kung Fu from the Western. Honestly, the Taiwanese developed themselves the technology and the democracy, so nowadays, Taiwan is among the dragons in Asia. Japan fell in the Second World War, the Japanese gentlemen recognized the mistake in the past and they carried out the development the technology and Japan became the high technologic nation in the world.

In China, the mean persons in China communist party as Mao Tse Tung and now Xi Jinping covered the fake gentlemen's face is a fake gentleman name Yue Lingshan (*Nhạc Bất Quần*) in a book by Jin Yong. China communists didn't learn the" technologic Kung Fu" as Taiwanese and

Japanese, instead, China is keen to steal the technology and Intellectual Property from the Western. China communist is shameless, therefore, the dishonest prides the stolen technology develops the products as the ugly economic pattern" *free market is led by socialism"*. So China communist becomes the Den of thieves and the hub of counterfeit.

2-The Important Secret of Martial Arts: Author Jin Yong listed 82 Important Secret Martial Arts in his books, therefore, the **Heaven and Earth Great Shift's** secret martial arts (Càn Khôn Đại Na Di) is the lost wisdom of the Ming Sect in the West, nevertheless, the Heaven and Earth Great Shift's secret martial arts strictly learn and train. Totally, the Heaven and Earth Great Shift's secret martial arts has 7 levels, a normal person should spend at least 14 years for each level, but a top-class Kung Fu recipient could complete 7 years. In the record marked many Ming Sect's leaders killed when training this martial arts' skill, mostly, they have never completed 7 levels. Therefore, there is only Zhang Wuiji (*Trương Vô Ky*) just spent a night, he completed 6 levels because he succeeded the Nine Yang Manual's skill, and a year after, he succeeded the last level and becomes the 34th leader of the Ming Sect.

The Heaven and Earth Great Shift's secret martial arts based on the mind, if a learner mind complicated, it causes the self-harming the body and died. The essential metaphor's method is flexible the power in the body. The body force maximizes and also attracts the enemy's power then transforms to own power. When the Heaven and Earth Great Shift's secret martial arts pass to someone else and defeats any enemy, so its Important Secret Martial Arts are the top fun fu's skill.

Author Jin Yung sent the untold message to Chinese people, actually, his well-known novel" *The Heaven Sword and Dragon Saber*" (ỷ Thiên Kiếm và Đồ Long Đao) emphasized the Heaven and Earth Great Shift's secret martial arts has already in every Chinese in the mainland, actually the opponents as Wei Jingsheng is the famous democratic activist, he succeeded the book" the courage to stand alone" and awarded Sakharov Prize, Olof Palme Prize, and more awards, the famous artist Ai Weiwei and the others. The Western people need to know the cunning tactics and conspiracies of China communist than listen to the communist's accusers about the human rights violation happens in the mainland. The world and the major population knew the barbarous regime in Beijing, but the opponents didn't respond to the question that the Western wants to eliminate the evil communist and returning the democracy for the Chinese people. It is like a medical doctor warns of the deadly disease but doesn't show how to treat the illness.

Do not scare what the communist does

Let's do any what the communist fears.

There are not only Chinese opponents who fled the mainland and enjoy freedom in the US. The Vietnamese fake opponents are such as Cù Huy Hà Vũ, Điếu Cày (Nguyễn Văn Hải), Tạ Phong Tần…just accuse Vietcong regime, but they didn't show the US and the world know about the cunning tactics of Vietcong and the tactic to eliminate the Red evil./.

15. COMMUNISM HAS INSTALLED IN THE WESTERN

Communism and democracy radically conflict as water and fire, Good and bad, Satan and God, theism and atheism. Almost, the democratic countries are allergic to Communism, therefore, Western and democratic countries have been installed Communism for a long time with caution. The Western has paid the dire consequences after the wrong and negligent policies applied after China's communist regime silently developed Marxism-Leninist renamed Maoist (*or China stole it*).

Communism is like a deadly virus that often snoops in the human and it can cause the illness when the body is weak. On the other hand, the Communism pandemic has spread since Karl Marx released the evil bible. The human community knew Communism or Marxism-Leninist-Maoist-Ho Chi Minh pandemic killed more than a hundred million people and infected a billion people to be enslaved on the planet. Therefore, the innocent leaders, naïve politicians, profit love's businesses plus the traitors have created an opportunity for Communism to infiltrate the democratic countries.

From the early 1990s, the Communism vaccine of President Donald Reagan eliminated the viral Communism pandemic in Europe, the central Communism pandemic is Soviet-Union collapsed with the Eastern Europe Communist Bloc. Therefore, the viral Communism made in China called Maoist changed the form as lizard changes the color's skin to bluff the short mind leaders, the ugly economic pattern cheats" *the free market is led by socialism*" has deceived the world, so China grew faster from the negligence of Western, particularly, the Democratic Presidents of the United States of America (*Bill Clinton, Barrack Obama plus George.W.bush*) have helped the viral Communism installing its country and spread the world community since President Richard Nixon made the historic visit the den of Maoist pandemic in 1972. The Communism pandemic has silently infiltrated the Western, including the US with the soft army (*trade ties, trade agreement, diplomat*). The viral Communism installed the Western with the help of the domestic thugs to sow the deadly virus of Communism into the country.

1-The left parties are the same viral Communism, the tiger snake and Cobra are the poisonous reptiles, not the python. The Democratic Party in America, The Australian Labor Party, the UK Labor Party, the Greens party, and others are hidden communist parties, they created an opportunity for Communism pandemic installed into multiple fields:

-The negligent immigration policy to receive Chinese students inundated the Western university, particularly, the high-level thieves of stolen technology, so China does nothing but acquired the top technologies and the invention. China's Communist Party is the professional burglar targeting the top technologies in Western. Nevertheless, the espionage agents who disguise Chinese students infiltrated the university, Chinese researchers are the hardcore communists. Moreover, Chinese students are the red seeds, they propagate Communism to intoxicate the young generations in Western. It is the long term investment of China, Vietnam's communist as Ho Chi Minh's slogan:" *ten years to plant a tree, hundred years to plant the people*" (mười năm trồng cây, trăm năm trồng người). The viral Communism silently infected

Western education without the caution of the government, instead, the government welcomes Chinese students and other communists like Vietnam. The money drives the country in the wrong direction. Nevertheless, profit love's Vice-Chancellors have transformed from education to business. The naïve treasonous traitors are the national leaders and top academics who have opened the backdoor for China's Communist Party entering with the negligent policy plus the money. The Australian government and the universities worry the Covid-19 pandemic reduces Chinese Students. Even Drew Pavlov, a student of University in Queensland is expelled because he alerts the relationship with China at risk and human rights violation. It proved the university in Australia is controlled by China, so free speech applies in universities. Nevertheless, after the Australian government proposed the independent inquiry about the Coronavirus, China intimidates to stop the imports of wine, meat, barley, and tourists including students.

2-The legal system is rotten by Communism: the Western's legal system worsens the Constitution and humiliates justice when the dishonest lawyers exercise the job as the ROBBERS WITH THE PAPER KNIFE and the dishonest judges are the ROBBERS WITH THE WOODEN HAMMER. The Western countries granted too much power for the legal workers, the negative aspects create arrogant judges. It is dangerous when justice is infected by viral Communism. The 2020 presidential election debunked the judges, including Justices in the Supreme Court practiced justice is like the communist regime. From the local judges to Supreme Court expose the communist judges or the Wooden Hammer Terror Army to protect and legalize China's henchman Joe Biden who carried out the rigged election.

-The Special Counsel of legal thug Robert Mueller acted as the communist prosecute agency, he used $US 34 million of the taxpayers to impeach President Donald Trump with the fabricated dossiers.

-The People's court applied in the United States of America when the Democratic judge exploited the attorney power to harm Lieutenant General Michael Flynn, the prominent communist Barrack Obama is the perpetrator

-After 8 years ruled the US government, President Barrack Obama deployed the People's Courts in the US, it is the safety net to protect the traitors, corrupt persons like Hillary Clinton, Joe Biden, and the high profiles of Democrats.

-The first communist President Barrack Obama created the FBI is like the Public Security Guard force like Vietnam, China, and other communist regimes. So James Comey didn't indict Hillary Clinton about 32,000 emails and waived the cluster of crimes of Bill Clinton and others.

3-The Congress and Senate in the Western are led by socialism, particularly in America have applied the bush lawmakers like the sole parliament of communist regimes in China, Vietnam. The US Senate and Congress certified Joe Biden to win the rigged election, despite the US elected President Donald Trump but the global Deep State's boss China decided the election outcome as a slogan" *people vote but the communist party selects the candidates and decides"* (đảng cử, dân bầu)

4-The media becomes the propaganda machine of the communist, the most left stream media companies have propagated Communism, the left tech communication terror companies are Facebook, Twitter, Google censor the free speech.

5-The globalization is the hidden title of Communism, the demagogic label came from President Bill Clinton who brought the evil practices into the Western and the US. Globalization has deceived the people and the innocent leaders

The Western and the US have been threatened by Communism, China has exploited democracy, free speech to install the evil theory in society, including government, education. Communism has activated with the mongrel communists, they are the politicians, national leaders, wealthy persons, the academics. The democratic countries have slept a long time and now the time to wake up with the action.

After many decades to deploy the Deep State in the United States of America, China's Communist Party launches the crucial battle by using the presidential election in 2020 to rob the US government, an actual henchman Joe Biden to be used as a pawn, he is the presidential robber with the supports of the domestic thugs are Justice John Roberts (Supreme Court), Congress Speaker Nancy Pelosi and Vice President Mike Pence (Senate Speaker). Certainly, 74,000,000 people and the US patriotic President Donald Trump have never accepted the robber Joe Biden enters the White House. The inauguration of Joe Biden is sieged by 30,000 troops, the massive people protest, the national outrage. The US government doesn't transit anything to the presidential robber Joe Biden, instead, he faces treason and criminal charges.

Moreover, traitor Joe Biden vows to lead the US into Communism, so a former administration of Barrack Obama, now, Anita Dunn is going to take the White House's administration of Joe Biden, she promises Maoists will return to White House after Joe Biden inaugurated. The US alerts, China's Communist Party is going to colonize the country./.

16. THE US CANCEROUS POLITICS CAN NOT TREAT

The Constitution in 1817 transformed Americans to live in the new form of slavery from 150 years ago, the fake democracy and the political demagogy covered the truth of the United States of America is not a nation, the Deep State deceived the people, indeed, the wealthy land in North America has run as the **Corporation of the United States of America, the US president is like the CEO of Corporation, the US government is like a huge company to run the business**. The Deep State has been controlled by the financially powerful families, the potential CEO (*or the US president*) creates the deep debt to tie the people with the lenders and the people just pay the taxes, it is the CEO's job done properly. Some CEOs created wars to respond to the requirement of the big bosses in shadow, which means the administration borrows more money to carry out the ambition of the Deep State. Almost the wars reflected the willingness of the Deep State, the merciless rich components have made the money from the death of people and the destructive world. However, within four years, President Donald Trump created peace and making no war, so the Deep State has wanted to remove Donald Trump from office and after the presidency expired on January 20, 2021, with the second impeachment. Moreover, the Supreme Court aims the tax returns to stray, despite, the rigged election is the main function of Chief Justice John Roberts. The US people have confronted the Justices without the human minds, instead, the animal instinct exposes in the justice of the Supreme Court with the bush law and wild rules as a noble zoo in Washington D.C.

Eventually, the Deep State exploited the global hegemonic ambition of China's Communist Party using the biological weapon or China virus pandemic to attack the world, including the US. The China virus pandemic also helped the traitor, the mongrel ape Joe Biden to carry out the rigged election with the mail-in-voting. Therefore, the China virus pandemic hits hard China as a boomerang hits back the thrower, so China's economy disabled, Beijing must borrow more money to deal with the pandemic as a saying" *a sword made by China to stab Chinese*". Certainly, the Deep State makes a huge profit when all nations on the planet must borrow the money and spending on the vaccine. The presidential robber Joe Biden responds to the requirement of the Deep State, he destroys the economy, creates the massive jobless plus spending broadly, so Biden's administration must borrow the money and the US people have to pay at least 50 years.

Since 1871, the people have lived in a fake democracy, mostly, the politicians including the president must spend a lot of money. The wealthy persons or someone pouring the money to the candidates in the elections from the president, Congress, Senate, Governors, even the local government. Money drives politics, so democracy depends on the rich component, its reason explains the Deep State has cornered and controlled US politics from the grassroots. Nevertheless, the money can help foreign enemies to buy the politicians when a candidate does need the finance to run the expensive campaign. Particularly, the presidential candidate must spend a lot of the money from the nomination campaign to the White House race's campaign. China's Communist Party developed the negative aspect of US politics, China just spends a little monetary amount but getting a huge profit and the best interest. In the presidential election in 1992, China's super espionage agent John Huang provided the finance to Bill Clinton's campaign and another China's espionage agent Charlie Trie illegally financed the election in 1996. President Bill Clinton repaid the boon of China with the Most Favored Nation's policy, the hoax climate change to curb the Western industry while China freely releases the dioxide. Moreover, the hoax climate change currently creates mayhem in Western society with the supporters and opponents, and China could sell the solar power to make a profit. Despite China interfered in the presidential election in 1992 and 1996, therefore, Democrats and the left stream media companies waived the case of Bill Clinton, instead, they created fake dossiers to impeach President Donald Trump with the false accusation about Russia interfered in the election in 2016.

The fake democracy has cheated the US people since 1871, the Corporation of the United States of America has bullied the people with the rigged election. Moreover, the Constitution in 1871 deployed the dictatorial administration in the White House, Congress, Senate, and the Supreme Court. Particularly, the dishonest judges including the Justices of the Supreme Court are the robbers with the wooden hammer, the justice places for sale and turns thuggish with the bush law. The legal thugs appear everywhere at the courtrooms set the legal networks throughout the US. The victims of the robbers with the wooden hammer are plenty, even President Donald Trump is oppressed by the local judges at the swing states in the rigged election. Nevertheless, the Supreme Court is the highest legal thug, when six Justices rejected the lawsuits of Texas plus 30 states and 126 lawmakers. The fate of 330 million people is held by three persons are Chief Justice John Roberts, House Speaker Nancy Pelosi, and Senate Speaker Mike Pence who certified the 306 fraudulent electoral colleges of Joe Biden and Chief Justice John Roberts illegally presided over the unlawful inauguration of the presidential robber, Joe Biden. Now, the US people face the disaster with a million jobless, the economy plunged and the future turns dark. The Corporation of the United States of America is like a rotten building, the administration has been suffered political cancer that can not treat by Congress, Senate, the White House, and the Supreme Court. The corruption, treason, pedophile, and crimes come from the Constitution of 1871. The US Army, Police and FBI, CIA, and the intelligence agencies become the tools of the Democratic Party. Certainly, the Army, Police and FBI, and others are like the robots when the presidential robber Joe Biden holds the remote control in the White House, so the US Army, Police, the investing bodies plus the intelligence protect Joe Biden and the Democratic gang, moreover, they obey the orders of the robber. It is an ugly political form of the Corporation of the United States of America.

The Constitution of 1871 created mayhem and destroyed the democracy, so the system needs to eliminate as soon as possible. President Donald Trump failed to protect the outcome of the election despite Donald Trump won with a landslide victory right on the night of November 3, 2020. Therefore, Joe Biden robbed the results with the left stream media companies and the left tech communication companies to mislead the public. The Supreme Court legalized the rigged election and ignored the tribunal, the last stage was carried out by Vice President Mike Pence, the coward traitor, he exploited the job of Senate Speaker to certified the 306 fraudulent electoral colleges and Joe Biden becomes the first presidential robber in the US history with Chief Justice John Roberts presided on January 20, 2021. The malicious sitcom planned well although Donald Trump is still the 45th president and his term expired while Joe Biden is not the 46th president as the left stream media misleads the people.

The presidential election in 2024 will repeat the same situation, despite President Donald Trump or someone else getting the strong support of the people. Therefore, the rigged election with the Dominion voting system and the fraudulent counting to decide the Democratic candidate to win and Vice President Kamala Harris will certify the election outcome. Certainly, the Republican candidate will face the same problem like Donald Trump in the presidential election 2020 and Chief Justice John Roberts will legalize the rigged election then he will preside the presidential inauguration. The US politics face the deadlock, so the secession is the only solution to save America, the AMERICAXIT can reform the FEDERATION OF AMERICA, if not, Democrats with the Deep State control the US and Joe Biden, Kamala Harris, Barrack Obama applying the socialism like Maoist and Venezuela.

The communists have never prayed the evil bible of Karl

Marx, instead, the communists activate and propagate communism to intoxicate the innocent people in the Western and democratic countries. The left parties are the hidden communist parties to carry out the same function of China, Vietnam, Cuba, and other communist regimes. The theism followers always believe in God, the faith reflects the term" IN GOD, WE TRUST" and God bless America. Therefore, God just gives 50% and 50% is decided by the people

Can not use the praying to defeat the evil

Do not use the bible to win the enemy

Pope John Paul II prayed and also acted to save the people, he encouraged Polish people to unite under the Solidarity Movement in Poland, and the people eliminated communism. The Polish lesson wakes the US people and the other nations including China, Vietnam, Cuba, and Venezuela.

In the presidential election of 2020, a hundred million people in the US and around the world pray for President Donald Trump. Therefore, President Donald Trump didn't apply the EO-13848 to crack down the rigged election and accomplish the historic responsibility as President Abraham Lincoln, so the American people have been suffered the peril, America shattered by the bloody old mad, imbecile mongrel ape Joe Biden. The US people can not live with the hidden communist party when Democrats control the White House, Congress, Senate, and the Supreme Court. Even the 45th President Donald Trump can not confidentially play golf while Democrats and the Supreme Court denounce publicly to destroy his political activities and oppress the supporters. The cancer of rigged election has never fixed with the

Constitution of 1871, the US people choose between freedom or communism. The action needs to protect and save the country or AMERICAXIT. The AMERICAXIT avoids repaying $US 27.8 trillion and the debt of Joe Biden just created./.

17. AMERICAXIT IS THE ONLY SURVIVAL SOLUTION

Despite the controversy that occurred between Brexit and opponents plus the protests to support the European Union and they also used the Supreme Court to hamper the Brexit. Eventually, Prime Minister Boris Johnson got the support of Congress after the general election, and the British succeeded the Brexit after many decades joined the European Union. The different policies on the economy, illegal migrants, and other issues forced the people must get out of the complicated organization in Europe. The Brexit is the best decision of the British to escape the deadlock of the European Union, moreover, the United Kingdom still keeps their currency.

The second Constitution 1871 of America hides the new form of the colony after Britain gave up the wealthy territory in North America, the young nation was born with the Constitution 1776. Therefore, the colonial government was over yet but the money and the debt have tied America into the lenders. **The F.E.D controls the money with the families are Rothschild, Schiff, Warburg, Rockefeller, Morgan, Harriman, Lazarard Bros, Goldman Sachs, Brown Brothers, Henney Chrooer, Lehman Bros**, they are the Deep State to transform the United States of America into the

Corporation of the United States of America. Unfortunately, the people have not recognized the fake democracy, freedom, the free speech that have deceived Americans since 1871, indeed, the US people have become a new form of slavery. They have worked and pay the high taxes for the hidden bosses of the Deep State. A fair election is just a title, indeed, **the US presidents are like the CEO of the Corporation of the United States of America.** Most presidential candidates are wealthy persons or the rich people plus China who poured the money into the election, so the US presidents must serve the wealthy people and the foreign enemies like China's Communist Party, a circumstance of President Bil Clinton who received the illegal finance from China's espionage agent John Huang in the election 1992 and Charlie Trie in the election 1996, so Bill Clinton deserved the priorities for China, particularly, the Most Favored Nation's policy repaid the China's boon.

The CEO of a Corporation must do anything to keep North American ties with the Deep State. The mad mongrel Ape Joe Biden is not the US president, but the Constitution of 1871 cheated, indeed, Joe Biden is the CEO of the United States of America, the Deep State selected and their members are Chief Justice John Roberts, Mike Pence, Nancy Pelosi, and others legalized the illegal president of America is Joe Biden. Therefore, the Deep State can not deceive the people when they selected an old man, mental health illness, corruption, treason, pedophile to win the rigged election, so Joe Biden causes the Deep State to unveil and the people wake up after more than 150 years hid and concealed the truth. On the other hand, Joe Biden harms the Deep State, and the people must act for survival. The Deep State has the wrong choice, they must pay the consequences.

1-The Deep State aims to tie Americans by the debt, the lenders use the debt to control the country and squeeze the sweat of the people since the Second Constitution of 1871 affected the young wealthy nation.

The potential CEO or called the President of the United States of America to create the debt and America can not get out of the lenders and the people must work, pay the endless taxes, it is the new slavey's form. It is the common rule of China to deploy the debt trap to counterparts then China can use the debt to control the country plus setting one belt and one road.

-Australia is the victim of the left party, the **Australian Labor Party is the hidden communist party,** the policies are pro-China's Communist Party. After Labor won the election in 2007, Prime Minister Kevin Rudd, Julia Gillard with Fiance Minister Penny Wong, Treasurer Wayne Swan spent $A 42 billion surpluses of Coalition government leftover *(John Howard and Costello)* and the Labor government created debt, then China has used the debt to control the Australia government, nowadays, China treats Australia as the colony, the Australian people alert when Labor Party puts the comradeship above the national interest *(China often threatens the security in the region, but Labor Deputy opposition leader Richard Marles wants the Australia Army to collaborate with the People's Liberation Army)*.

-The US Presidents have done a good CEO of Corporation of the United States of America: President Barrack Obama, George. H.Bush, George. W.Bush created the debt through the wars in the Middle-East plus the inappropriate expenses on the hoax climate change, fake humanitarian programs of the United Nation, the World

Health Organization *(after the Chinese virus pandemic, W.H.O becomes the WORLD HELL ORGANIZATION)*, and other spendings despite the US is facing the deep debt, the CEO or the US president doesn't care about the debt because the lenders *(Deep State)* want to tie Americans with the debt.

2-The people can not suffer the devastation of the mad imbecile. Mongrel Ape Joe Biden: The rigged election in 2020 exposed the United States of America is just a corporation, so the lenders (*Deep State and China)* decided the US president Joe Biden although the people voted for President Donald Trump in the second term. Everyone knows Joe Biden robbed the election by stealing the ballots with multiple methods including the Dominion voting system. The presidential robbery of Joe Biden provokes the US people and waking up the patriotism, the people boycott Joe Biden everywhere because the US people didn't vote for him. Moreover, the crazy destructive executive orders of the mad imbecile, mongrel Ape Joe Biden to destroy the US economy and impoverish the people, including the broadly spending on illegal migrants, the hoax climate change (*Paris agreement)*, the abortion in the US and overseas, the corruption, and other lavish to create more debt. Certainly, the Deep State concerns a pawn Joe Biden has done a good job as CEO, but the US people anger and they can not suffer longer the control of the Deep State, so the Republican states can find the survival solution, if not, 330 million people have never afforded the freedom, democracy, free speech (*the Deep State's media and tech communication companies apply the formula 3 F = False poll +Fake news +Fabricated story and 3C =Cancel + Conceal + Censor to gag the free speech and transforming from the FREE SPEECH to SPEECH FREE)*

3- Americaxit is only the solution to survive and get

out of the Deep State after 150 years tied by the debt:

-The rigged election is the cancer of democracy: the Constitution in 1871 grants the license to rob including the election's robbery. The incident of the rigged election in 2020 shows the election system in the US can not fix, even President Donald Trump re-elected four more years, but the Democratic states *(swing states)* continue to apply the rigged election and they should win the presidency after Donald Trump. Moreover, after 4 years of Joe Biden-Kamala Harris, the rigged election develops more than 2020.

-The rotten Congress Senate and Supreme Court have never repaired, the Constitution 1871 mandates the absolute power for House Speaker, Senate Speaker, and Chief Justice. The Deep State does need to control three persons and leading the Corporation of the United States of America into the orbit of the lenders, they are the hidden bosses in America.

-The secession of Texas and the major Republican states are the primary solution to get out of the Deep State and reform the new country, it should be **THE FEDERATION OF AMERICA,** the concerned states including the Democratic States can join, the situation of the Corporation of the United States of America will be no longer to exist. Certainly, the rotten Congress, Senate, and the Supreme Court collapsed plus the illegal President Joe Biden ended. The Deep State can not revoke the debt of $US 27.8 trillion, the federal government borrowed, so 50 states have no responsibility for the debt, therefore, the last CEO Joe Biden take the responsibility to acquit the debt. The United States of America just changes the name and avoid paying the debt plus remove the mad, imbecile mongrel Ape Joe Biden from the top job, and the original Constitution of 1776 restores, the virtual nation revives after 150 years lost the independence, democracy, and freedom. No more Black Lives Matter and Antifa, the American slaves will be liberated, and the Federation of America can issue the court order to arrest Joe Biden, Mike Pence, John Roberts, Nancy Pelosi, Bill Gates, Bill-Hillary Clinton, Barrack Obama, and others who commit child sex trafficking ring, corruption, and serious crimes.

The secession easily to do, but the effect is great, the people can escape the new model of slavery and also revive the country. The Republican states must get out of the Deep State as soon as possible, do not wait for Joe Biden to wipe out the economy, and destroy the financial system within four years. Nevertheless, the Americaxit should avoid the bloodshed of the civil war when the major US people stand up to fight against the presidential robber Joe Biden and the Democratic super gang.

After the Federation of America was formed, the capital should be located in Houston (*Texas*) or Miami (*Florida*) and the new party of President Donald Trump will activate then politics with the fair election, no more Dominion voting system. The Democratic Party and Republicans lose the people's trust, certainly, the rotten Congress, Senate, and the garbage Supreme Court are no longer to remain, instead, the new Congress, Senate, and the Supreme Court apply the Constitution in 1776. The Federation of America can apply the political model like Singapore with the Patriotic Party because Democrats and Republicans betrayed the people, the corrupt politicians are plenty, no one trusts them. The Federation of America has impartial media, so the left stream media and tech communication companies will wither and facing bankruptcy, the world will change, the fake news will end./.

18. THE COMMUNISM HAS BECOME THE MOST HUMAN DISASTER

World with a million people in Venezuela rejected communism, they stand up and protest against the dictatorial regime of President Nicholas Madura continuing to apply the socialism carrying out by President Hugo Chavez imposed to its country from 1999 and now, the poverty causes the people to stand up against the obsolete economy's pattern. Karl Marx poisoned the world with his crazy idea. Therefore, Karl Marx's theory is as *a pie on the sky* as a former high profile communist of the Soviet Union Boris Yeltsin warned the innocent component, actually the young people. Communism suits the dishonest, Lenin who transformed the foolish theory of Karl Marx into reality from October 1917. The world is complicated by Karl Marx who is the mastermind of the most genocide on the planet.

Communism is the most human disaster since Karl Marx wrote the books teaching the killing, robber and enslave the people. He is considered as the mastermind of communism, and Karl Marx became the angel of communist, his statue and portrait placed into the solemn positions in the communist regime of China, Vietnam, North Korea, Cuba…

1-Karl Marx is dishonest: when someone has no food, accommodation, and money that you help. Therefore, the recipient has no gratefulness, instead, they want to kill and rob you, do you accept it? In England, Karl Marx and his family received income support from a wealthy man Frederick Engels, but Karl Marx wrote the books as Capitalism teaching the dishonest to kill the wealthy component. On the other hand, Karl Marx was the most traitor, the dregs in human society. Actually, everyone couldn't trust and listen to a dishonest, a robber, even a thief. There are only dishonest following the theory of Karl Marx. His books teach the dishonest have become the most human disaster, the Communist Manifesto, Capitalism, and Historical Materialism are the evil bibles

2-The genocide theory: The genocide theory labels under the title of revolution, socialism, and" a pie in the sky" is the communist paradise became the argument of the dishonest as such as Lenin in Russia, Mao Tse Tung in China, Hồ Chí Minh in Vietnam, Kim Il Sung in North Korea, Fidel Castro in Cuba, Pol Pot in Cambodia and the other massive killers on the planet have created the bloodshed since Karl Marx proposed his books

3-The practice: In reality, the communist has no right to tell about honesty, it is like a robber tells about morality and virtue or recently, a pupil of Karl Marx is Democratic Congresswoman Nancy Pelosi lies the border protection reflects the wall, she labeled" the wall is immoral"… Therefore, the communist has applied the malicious tactics to carry out the purpose:

-The propaganda sticks with terrorization: The communist advocates the lie, cheat and falsity. If the propaganda has no terrorization, Karl Marx's pupil couldn't succeed, indeed, the people boycott or kick the dishonest out from the society. In the communist regime, the killing, jail, or spiritual terror are the keys to remaining in the inhuman regime

-The label of People: Despite, the communist is

genocide, therefore, they always exploit the People's label as the curtain of the regime. Mostly, in China names nation is the People's Republic of China, North Korea is The Democratic People Republic of Korea, Laos is the Lao People's Democratic Republic....although Vietnam communist has not used the People for the national title, but they have the People's army of Vietnam.

-Karl Marx purposed to destroy human history: his evil book" Historical Materialism" concludes the human being derived from the Ape, indeed, Karl Marx and his followers have no evidence to support the claim. No one authorizes to impose the original human came from a kind of money, but there are only Karl Marx and the followers believe and forced the people living into the communist regime to comply.

-The class struggle: the communist always wants the social division, the hated campaign currently launches, mostly, whoever has a different stance, they are the enemy of the so-called counter-revolutionary. In the communist countries as China, Vietnam, North Korea, and the others, the class struggle carried out by the bloodshed, the social purge become the genocide campaign, actually, the landlord reform aim to the wealthy, landowner and intellectuals named the thugs, the victims killed and family suffered the three generations being treated as the second citizen or the enemy family of revolution.

In the Western countries, when the leftist as Barrack Obama leads the US, he couldn't raise the bloodshed as the communist regime, but Barrack Obama applied the class struggle forms as gender (the same-sex-marriage legislation), racial war revived between the Black and White. President

Barrack Obama brainwashed the US people in 8 years, he is the cause of the US division.

4-The dire consequence of communism:

-In the communist countries: Since Lenin transformed the crazy theory of Karl Marx into reality, communism causes the deaths of more than 100 million people and a billion people lost freedom. Despite the European Communist Bloc including Soviet-Union eliminated the inhumane regimes, but in Asia, China gathered the vestiges are Vietnam, North Korea, Laos. The communist's peril is not over yet, China leads the evil to attack the world into the Cool War.

-The leftist and left media in the Western: The left media has terrorized the people's minds by misleading the public, releasing fake news and fabricated stories. The left media terror is the domestic thug of the people, the democratic countries need to fight against the media terror has developed under the forms of media companies, the journalists without a brain, the reporters have no heart, they are the Karl Marx's pupils inserted into the mainstream.

Communism and socialism are the siblings, the dishonest advocate the genocide, robbery, cheat and lie. The social dregs promoted themselves the revolutionist in a communist country and progressive component in the democratic states. The left political parties are keen to apply socialism into democratic countries, they have carried out socialism in the wrong places, the propaganda without terrorization is like the tiger has no teeth. The demagogic policy just helps the left parties rule the government for a limited-term, therefore, the debt and the fallen national solutions are the disasters.

Communism is the most disaster of human history, so the world needs to eliminate evil. The people need to stand up in the communist regimes like China, Vietnam, North Korea, Laos, Cuba, and now Venezuela…in the democratic countries, the people boycott the left media terror companies. President Donald Trump quotes:" *From the Soviet Union to Cuba to Venezuela, wherever true socialism or communism has been adopted, it has delivered anguish and devastation and failure.*"

Karl Marl supported atheism, he considered religion as the enemy by a quote" *religion is the opium of the people".* Therefore, communist is the barbarous evil, the communism is like a cake picture painting the beautiful color, it is not really as Boris Yeltsin recognized" the pie in the sky", but in the Western, the innocent people believe it is real and wants to eat, unfortunately, the communist theory cheats. Nevertheless, Karl Marx's theory just fits for the dishonest, so the dregs of human society labeled themselves the descendant of the ape and raised the most genocide on the planet. The dishonest media, they are the left media destroyed the mainstream by the fake news and fabricated stories, they are the media terrorists attacking the people mind and misleading the people, poisoning the public. It is a form of brainwash that applies in democratic countries.

Venezuela's crisis signals the communism and Karl Marx's theory are going to end on the planet. The people live in communist countries learning the lesson of Venezuela to fight for freedom, democracy. The people's power is invincible, the evil couldn't win the God, the dictatorial regime couldn't remain forever, so the inhumane regimes have to eliminate from the human community. Actually, the left media to be unmasked after long term misled the public./.

1-The orthodox gentleman Chinese: Author Jin Yong respects the honest, so his gentlemen's concern exposes morality and virtue. The heroes display the good behavior of the top-class martial arts recipient that reflects the righteous protection and eliminate the dishonest. The gentleman of Jin Yong is not as Chinese conqueror taught the people of the occupied land" *do not beat the people fell from the horseback*". The fake morality poisoned the native people when the invader defeated, the conqueror could return to homeland safely and next time, the invader will come back.

The orthodox gentlemen's concern of Jin Yong advised the Chinese people has to know how to revenge. Almost, his martial arts stories describe honest people's behavior, after the enemy defeated, they must fight for survival and finding the master to learn Kung Fu. When they have enough martial arts skills, they will find the enemy. The spiritual revenge could pass to the descendant if they failed to do.

After the nationalist failed at the mainland, the Taiwanese fought the" master" to learn Kung Fu from the Western. Honestly, the Taiwanese developed themselves the technology and the democracy, so nowadays, Taiwan is among the dragons in Asia. Japan fell in the Second World War, the Japanese gentlemen recognized the mistake in the past and they carried out the development the technology and Japan became the high technologic nation in the world.

In China, the mean persons in China communist party as Mao Tse Tung and now Xi Jinping covered the fake gentlemen's face is a fake gentleman name Yue Lingshan

(*Nhạc Bất Quần*) in a book by Jin Yong. China communists didn't learn the" technologic Kung Fu" as Taiwanese and Japanese, instead, China is keen to steal the technology and Intellectual Property from the Western. China communist is shameless, therefore, the dishonest prides the stolen technology develops the products as the ugly economic pattern" *free market is led by socialism"*. So China communist becomes the Den of thieves and the hub of counterfeit.

2-The Important Secret of Martial Arts: Author Jin Yong listed 82 Important Secret Martial Arts in his books, therefore, the **Heaven and Earth Great Shift's** secret martial arts (Càn Khôn Đại Na Di) is the lost wisdom of the Ming Sect in the West, nevertheless, the Heaven and Earth Great Shift's secret martial arts strictly learn and train. Totally, the Heaven and Earth Great Shift's secret martial arts has 7 levels, a normal person should spend at least 14 years for each level, but a top-class Kung Fu recipient could complete 7 years. In the record marked many Ming Sect's leaders killed when training this martial arts' skill, mostly, they have never completed 7 levels. Therefore, there is only Zhang Wuiji (*Trương Vô Ky*) just spent a night, he completed 6 levels because he succeeded the Nine Yang Manual's skill, and a year after, he succeeded the last level and becomes the 34th leader of the Ming Sect.

The Heaven and Earth Great Shift's secret martial arts based on the mind, if a learner mind complicated, it causes the self-harming the body and died. The essential metaphor's method is flexible the power in the body. The body force maximizes and also attracts the enemy's power then transforms to own power. When the Heaven and Earth Great Shift's secret martial arts pass to someone else and defeats any enemy, so its Important Secret Martial Arts are the top fun fu's skill.

Author Jin Yung sent the untold message to Chinese people, actually, his well-known novel" *The Heaven Sword and Dragon Saber*" (ỷ Thiên Kiếm và Đồ Long Đao) emphasized the Heaven and Earth Great Shift's secret martial arts has already in every Chinese in the mainland, actually the opponents as Wei Jingsheng is the famous democratic activist, he succeeded the book" the courage to stand alone" and awarded Sakharov Prize, Olof Palme Prize, and more awards, the famous artist Ai Weiwei and the others. The Western people need to know the cunning tactics and conspiracies of China communist than listen to the communist's accusers about the human rights violation happens in the mainland. The world and the major population knew the barbarous regime in Beijing, but the opponents didn't respond to the question that the Western wants to eliminate the evil communist and returning the democracy for the Chinese people. It is like a medical doctor warns of the deadly disease but doesn't show how to treat the illness.

Do not scare what the communist does

Let's do any what the communist fears.

There are not only Chinese opponents who fled the mainland and enjoy freedom in the US. The Vietnamese fake opponents are such as Cù Huy Hà Vũ, Điếu Cày (Nguyễn Văn Hải), Tạ Phong Tần…just accuse Vietcong regime, but they didn't show the US and the world know about the cunning tactics of Vietcong and the tactic to eliminate the Red evil./.

19. THE INSUFFICIENT WATER IS THE DEATH OF CHINA

The global hegemonic ambition urges China's Communist Party to join the arms race, space race, and developing espionage networks around the world. Therefore, the Chinese dream of the ruthless regime surpasses the capacity of the obsolete political pattern while the communist or Maoists faced the deadlock after the bloody campaigns of Mao Tse Tung applied from 1949 to 1976 to kill a hundred million people, so the communist paradise becomes the hell of human society. On the other hand, the communist paradise just deserves for the members of the communist party, instead, the impoverishment plus obscurantism has enslaved more than a billion people in the mainland. Moreover, the brainwashing *(propaganda)* plus terror are the essential tactics of China's Communist Party to control the world's largest population.

The failure of Maoists solved by the stolen economic pattern of the capitalist called the *free market is led by socialism*. Despite China's Communist Party spread the Red-empire's hand everywhere with the global economic terror. The soft army has activated into the land of democratic countries, particularly, the US and Europe are the main battles with the business units, investment units plus immigration. The stolen technology responds to the insufficient invention, and research, so China creates from nothing to get many things from Western's technology.

The world extremely alerts the rapacious ambition with the plan of one belt and one road. China has tried to build the

Belt and Road by the debt trap, particularly, the waters of Indochina Pacific currently intensifies the tension while China often exposes the aggressive attitude, the security in the region being threatened by the People's Liberation Navy. Under the rule of the first Muslim and communist President Barrack Obama who flagged China illegally built and militarized the piratical stations to control the most important maritime transport estimates $US 5 trillion a year.

The world faces the real threat of China, nevertheless, after the presidential robber Joe Biden stormed the White House with the rigged election in 2020, the Deep State, Democrats, and China backed the bloody old mad, imbecile, mongrel communist Joe Biden to rob the White House with the accompaniment of the thuggish Chief Justice John Roberts and traitor Mike Pence. So China succeeded to create a pawn Joe Biden to control the White House and China's actual henchman Joe Biden eases the policies of President Donald Trump. Moreover, traitor Joe Biden pays the boon of $US 1.5 billion by the best policies to help China standing up and continuing to develop the global hegemonic ambition. On the other hand, Joe Biden eats America's bread but serves China's Communist Party.

However, China's Communist Party has committed suicide with their greedy power aiming to control the world. The China virus pandemic reflects the saying" *the sword made by China to stab Chinese* ". The China virus pandemic disabled its economy and crippled the financial system. China is isolated and sanctioned by its China virus, moreover, the foreign companies moved out from the mainland that aggravates the industry and employment of hundreds of millions of people. American author Peter Navarro wrote the book" *Death by China*" to alert the most dangerous enemy on the planet. Certainly, the US and allies can not defeat China by the war, but the suicidal policies of China's Communist Party cause the world's largest communist regime to collapse. China's ambition kills the most aggressive regime on the planet as a giant with the foot of clay being suffered cancer that comes from the greedy power.

In any nation, people do need the water, mostly, the big cities in the world built into the basin of a river. The role of rivers is a vital fact of a country, therefore, China's Communist Party and Vietnam's Communist Party ignore the water, as Vietcong destroyed the land with the crazy irrigation, and the illiterate government's officials gathered the people to dig the channels by hand to cut the land into the pieces as slogan:

" Nghiêng đồng, đổ nước ra sông

Vắt đất ra nước, thay trời làm mưa"

(Incline the farm pouring the water to the river

Squeeze soil to make water and replace the God making rain".

Mostly, Vietnam and China have been suffered the punishment of natural, annually, the severe floods cost the people's lives and the material damages. Nevertheless, the hydroelectricity aggravates the human's disaster, for many decades ago, China bribed the governments in the region of the Mekong River to build the dams, the insufficient water raises the grave concern of Thailand, Vietnam when the low basin of the Mekong River dried up, it affected the livelihood of ten million people in Vietnam, but China ignores.

However, the mainland in China has been committed the peril, the global hegemonic ambition causes 28,000 rivers in China to disappear among 50,000 rivers. Commonly, each river covers the basin about 60 square miles, so 28,000 rivers lost, which affects hundreds of millions of people. Moreover, annually, China has been suffered severe floods in the rainy season with 22,104 dams with the height are up to 15 meters including the Three Gorges Dam currently threatens the regime, therefore, the dry season, the water disappeared, the rash irrigation created the big and unsolved water's problem. China's communist government alerts the water of Yangtze River is drying up, now it becomes an urgent problem while 500 million people live on the water of Yangtze River. The livelihood of more than 1/3 population is threatened, certainly, the agricultural products can not survive without the water. Moreover, the industry grew cost 1,000 lakes disappeared, Yangtze River comes from Tibet and flows to Eastern China, the length is 6,300 kilometers. Since the 1980s, the level of the greatest river in China has fallen by 2 centimeters every five years, it marks China joined the world market after the historic visit of US President Richard Nixon in 1972. The dams and artificial channels swallow a lot of quantity of water when every local government has its own development. How can China fix the insufficient water problem? If the local governments return the water, the people's livelihood affected. It is the dilemma of China's Communist Party after more than 75 years built socialism.

The China virus pandemic plus the insufficient water in

the mainland become the vital problem of the world's largest communist regime. Moreover, Chinese people can not survive without water. For a long time ago, Chinese people currently face water problems, farmland, and industry plus the people do need water. Certainly, the foreign companies avoid China by the pandemics and now the water aggravates the situation. The nature is invincible general, the Winter General defeated the strong army of Napoleon Bonaparte in 1812 and Hitler withdrew after the **Winter General** attacked. Nowadays, the **Water General** has attacked China's Communist Party during the rainy and drying season. The hard resolution of water becomes the big problem in the mainland, certainly, Xi Jinping can not win the insufficient water with the slogan, the terror, and propaganda to nature. It is the dire consequence that comes from the global hegemonic ambition.

Despite China succeeded to create an actual henchman Joe Biden who robbed the White House with the support of thuggish Chief Justice John Roberts and traitor Mike Pence. Therefore, the insufficient water is the death of China, the communist regime can not carry out the global hegemonic ambition while the mainland faces the severe insufficient water, Yangtze River decides the livelihood of 500 million people. China can import the food, but they can not import the water. Nevertheless, the water problem deeply affects the products, food, economy, stock market, and other consequences. So the US and Western investors must consider carefully Chinese companies, investment in Wall Street, and the global market although Joe Biden deserves the facilities for China to dominate Wall Street./.

20. THE US SUPREME COURT TO SELL THE JUSTICE

For a long time ago, the US people doubted the function of the Supreme Court to place the justice for sale, the money and privileges have driven the justice into the wrong direction and conflicted the legal valuation including the basic lessons of a law school to condemn and reject the crime, illegal practices. When the judges place the justice for sale, the legal system collapsed, it is a disaster for the US judges including the highest judges in the Supreme Court. Certainly, the customers to buy the justice are China's Communist Party, the Deep State, and the Donkey super gang. The major Justices in Supreme Court joined the line of **the robbers with the wooden hammer with the commander in thuggish Chief Justice John Roberts** who is the most dangerous man in the US, and he is among the major enemy of the American people. Nowadays, the US people face the peril that comes from Chief Justice John Roberts after the presidential robber Joe Biden stormed the White House.

The robbers with the wooden hammer ruling the law and distorting justice when the **second Constitution in 1871 grants the license to rob for the Congress, Senate, Supreme Court, and the dishonest judges**. The bush law replaces the right and justice, so the US people have lived in the legal terror's country like the People's Court in China, Vietnam, and other communist regimes.

The Constitution of 1871 also deserves the absolute attorney power for the judges including the Justices with the term unlimited, and the court orders are not different from the decrees of the king in medieval. Certainly, the judges and

Justices are the senior lawyers and the senior public servants, the people have never voted for the judges, but the judges and Justices decide the presidency and force everyone must comply with the court orders. The legal system of Western and democratic countries went wrong, the dangerous legal practices should impose the bush law and the unfair order to the people, the robbers with the wooden hammer become the legal terrorists in the politics.

China's Communist Party and the enemies studied well the negative aspects of the Western legal system, almost, everyone can not ignore and oppose a court order, because every court order attaches the threat to fine or imprisonment to whoever doesn't comply with the statement issued from the courtroom, even a lawyer can issue the legal statement to threaten someone with a phrase" *taking the legal action*" when a client pays the legal fees. **So the money is the commander in a judge**

In Western and democratic countries, the wrong verdicts cost the life of the innocent victims, therefore, when the truth found, the legal system has no punishment for the judges, instead, the compensation comes from the taxpayers, so, the judges have no responsibility. The foreign enemies know about the court order and the obedience of the people, so the enemies just buy the judges and the Justices who issue the court order to accept the inhumane culture of the Sharia Law while it conflicts with the UN's Universal Declaration of Human rights, the Western society has not accepted the polygamy or impose to same-sex-marriage legislation, the abortion law as the US Supreme Court did under the rule of the first Muslim and communist President Barrack Obama despite the Supreme Court orders conflicted the religious faith, the major population. On the other hand, the Justices in Supreme Court are untouchable and sitting above the law, moreover, it is very hard to remove a Justice in the Supreme Court despite the felony Justice as Chief Roberts who admits the corruption and pedophile. The circumstance of John Roberts is like the king in medieval, no one can dethrone. The US kings of Justice control the country and bully the legal system.

The rigged election with the interference of China's Communist Party and 65 nations proved with the mountain of evidence and a thousand witnesses, moreover, the Dominion voting system changed the election outcome. Therefore, the legal team of President Donald Trump filed the lawsuits and won 2/3 cases, but the local judges, state judges rejected without the right reason, it is the bush law. Even Texas and 20 states plus 126 lawmakers filed the lawsuit against the swing states after the violation of the election. Unfortunately, six Justices of the Supreme Court including three conservative Justices are Neil Gorsuch, Brett Kavanaugh, and Amy Coney Barrett joined the line of robbers with the wooden hammer of Chief Justice John Roberts to reject the lawsuits although they knew the rigged election breaches the law. Nevertheless, the Supreme Court hated President Donald Trump, particularly, Chief Justice John Roberts, and his deputy didn't want President Donald Trump to win the second term. The US presidential election in 2020 is not different from China, Vietnam, and other communist regimes.

-In the communist countries, the deceitful election proceeds the election that the so-called representatives of the sole Parliament House that is a farce. The communist party selects the candidates and the people forced to vote,

the outcome is decided by the communist party, it is the rule of party selects and the people vote.

- In the US, the presidential candidate Joe Biden was chosen by Democrats, the Deep State, and China. The rigged election plus the left stream media and the left tech communication companies to give and propagate the results and the Senate Speaker Mike Pence certified the 306 fraudulent electoral colleges of Joe Biden and Chief Justice John Roberts who exploited the presidency expired on January 20, 2021, he illegal presided the inauguration of the presidential robber, Joe Biden. Indeed, the 45th President Donald Trump still remains the presidency, he is not the former president while the rigged election has not solved yet and 75,000,000 people voted. On the other hand, Donald Trump is the victim of the presidential robbery. The legal rule considers during the argument has not concluded, no one claims the winner, therefore, the thuggish Chief Justice John Roberts illegally presided the unlawful inauguration of Joe Biden. Certainly, Chief Justice John Roberts doesn't represent 75,000,000 people, instead, he behaved himself to impose the presidential robber Joe Biden ruling the country.

Possibly, the fair election in America is a farce, the US people voted for President Donald Trump, but Vice President and also Senate Speaker Mike Pence certified the fraudulent election colleges and Chief Justice John Roberts presided over the inauguration. It is a strong message sending the US people and the world about the fake democracy in the country decorated the Statue of Freedom.

The presidential election in 2020 shows the ugly democracy in America when the illegal President Joe Biden, Vice President Kamala Harris are the traitors, corruption. The cabinet of the bloody old mad, imbecile mongrel ape Joe Biden is like the animal farm of George Orwell. The world laughs and disdains the fake democracy in America, when the major members of the White House, Congress, Senate, and the Supreme Court are the social dregs. What is America look like? It is the shame of Americans.

The disgraced deception of the Supreme Court to open the files of the rigged election after the illegal president Joe Biden inaugurated and he destroyed the country with the destructive executive orders. However, the Supreme Court rejects the rigged election without the appropriate explanation, the people knew the Supreme Court continues to cheat the people and placing the justice for sale. The ugly objection of the Supreme Court to review the rigged election that revokes the people, even some Justices like Samuel Alito, Clarence Thomas, and Neil Gorsuch oppose. Therefore, the most hopeful Justices are Brett Kavanaugh, and Amy Coney Barrett betrayed the people. **The Supreme Court rejected the rigged election that is like a butcher shop refuse to sell the meats, Chinese restaurant rejects to cook fry rice, the Police force denies to fight against the crime.** The concerned Lawyer Sidney Powell posted on February 23, 2021:

"Thank you all! There are still important live cases. Irrefutable proof is coming soon. Keep educating everyone about the facts. Today's Supreme Court orders were disappointing but we are not done, and we will not let this fraud stand. We the people are supposed to run this country.

Our new Super PAC should be up tomorrow. WWW. DefendingRepublicPAC.com.

It's to amplify the voice of # WeThePeople across the country. We intend to expose corruption in both parties and support people with the courage to protect our constitutional rights and the rule of law. Sign up for updates. Join for as little as $ 10 a year. Contributors of $200 a year total or less are confidential ".

The situation of Corporation of the United States of America has never fixed, the rigged election is the professional tactic of Democrats, the Deep State, and China interferes plus the Dominion voting system. The Constitution in 1871 grants the license to rob for the Supreme Court, Congress, Senate, and the White House. After the rigged election in 2020 has not solved yet, even President Donald Trump has nowhere to protect, so the 45th President must move out from the White House on January 20, 2021, and the robber Joe Biden occupied. Unfortunately, the bullshit Constitution 1871 ties the US Army and the patriotism, so the presidential robber Joe Biden forces 50 states, the National Guard, Police, FBI, CIA become the robots to obey his orders to kill a million jobs and destroying America. The AMERICAXIT is the only solution to save the country, certainly, President Donald Trump will lose the election in 2024 although the major population support (it should be a hundred million people), and Kamala Harris will do the job as Mike Pence then John Roberts will preside a Democratic president in 2025, the old lesson will repeat.

The Supreme Court collapsed the people's trust, particularly, Chief Justice John Roberts is the pedophile and the corruption. On the other hand, the Supreme Court becomes the legal thug's den, not carry out the justice, instead, the Supreme Court is the culprit to help the presidential robber Joe Biden to storm the White House, so John Roberts is the main enemy of 75,000,000 people plus a million workers lose the job. The US people can develop the invincible power to get back the country as Russian, Eastern European people stood up to eliminate communism. The US people must choose between freedom or slavery, the mongrel communist Joe Biden applies communism in America./.

21. CHINA USED THE BRIBERY TO DESTROY WESTERN

Vietcong *(Vietnam Communist Party)* led by Ho Chi Minh ruled North Vietnam after the Geneva Conference signed on July 20, 1954, and after the last invasion carried out on April 30, 1975, in South Vietnam. The innocent Vietnamese people plus the domestic traitors caused the country to lose freedom and democracy. (*the domestic traitors were Four Stars General Dương Văn Minh, President Nguyễn Văn Thiệu and others).*

The Vietnam Communist super gang has applied socialism to the Vietnamese people, the prominent massacre was the Landlord Reform campaign. The bloodshed spread from the city to the countryside in North Vietnam. Genocide Ho Chi Minh and Vietcong super gang killed more than 200,000 people as Hanoi reported, therefore, the numerous victim was up to a million. In the barbarous campaign, Ho Chi Minh invited China communist advisors to watch and involve the Landlord Reform Campaign, China's advisors raped teenagers and killed the subjected components if they resisted, the motto used to purge the society was" *eradicating the intellectual, landlord and wealthy family*".

Nowadays, in the Western, despite there is no Landlord Reform Campaign but the top social class has been collapsed by themselves after China used the money to buy. The bribery is a sharp weapon of China's undercover activists and espionage networks arrayed in Western countries from China joined the free market. **The bribery tactic is a mighty weapon of China's Communist Party, the money created from the loss of Western countries and China has used the money to decay the top social class in Western countries and China also has robbed the inventions, intellectual properties by the dishonest academics sold**. On the other hand, China just spent a small monetary amount plus the privileges but Beijing got so many interests. Western money becomes the tool to help China corners the Western and also acquired high technologies. China succeeded a stratagem of Sun Tzu" *create something from nothing*". China's bribery uprooted the top social class in Western, Western, and democratic countries are slowly losing the national interest and sovereignty by the domestic traitors who have collaborated with China to colonize the country.

1-The left media has become the actual tool of China's Communist Party into the propaganda. China just paid some money and controlled the Western media companies, journalists, reporters, Columnists, T.V hosts. China eradicated the credit of Western media by money. China reported to the US Justice Department about the prominent media companies like The New York Times, The Washington Post, The Wall Street Journal received the money from China as a spy-saying:" *when a hunter recognizes its dog can not do the job properly, a hunter must know how to eat the dog's meat*". It is just an iceberg floating on the surface, indeed, the most left media companies in Western have fallen into the bribery trap. So the Western media has committed suicide by the fake news, fabricated stories, and false polls in the election. The suicide has processed from the Vietnam War, the Global Communist Bloc hired the left media, the commercial media companies applied the psychological warfare to propagate for Vietcong, the media business misled the public, the innocent component to be brainwashed, they became the human-robot protested against the allies sending the troop to help South Vietnam protecting the freedom and also prevented the communist wave spreading in the region. The Vietnam War to fight against a terror war like the Islamic. The US and allies with the South Vietnam government protected the people and keeping out the enemy, so the left media acted as treason. Nowadays, the left media completely lost people's trust. Nevertheless, after the US election in 2016 and recently the general election on May 18, 2019, in Australia to destroy the credit of the left media, the false polls collapsed and turned to garbage. Most news is fake often releasing from famous media companies are such as The New York Times, The Washington Post, CBS, MSNBC, CNN, and others in the US, in Australia with ABC, Channel Seven, Channel Ten...certainly, the people have no trust. The left media has involved the psychological warfare of China by releasing fake news about the death toll and infection of the Chinese virus in Western and concealed the death toll in China. The bribery of China assimilates the Western media as the propaganda machine in the mainland.

2-The dishonest academics are the left academics, the profit's lovers distorted the career for individual favor or the political purpose and destroyed the university's prestige. The dishonest academics have been involved in the hoax climate change that helps China curbs Western productivity, China is keen to pay for the dishonest academics to release the biased study about the hoax climate change, they drive the knowledge to appall the people about the dire consequence. Nevertheless, the dishonest academics represent 27 doctors of the famous universities are Harvard and Yale, 27 doctors turned dogtors after they dared to release and publicized the medical assessment to confirm President Donald Trump is the mental health illness despite 27 dogtors have never diagnosed President Donald Trump. On the other hand, 27 dogtors of Havard and Yale are based on the 25th Amendment to impeach President Donald Trump, not medical assessment. Eventually, Rear Admiral, Doctor Ronny Jackson debunked the dishonest dogtors. The top dogtors of Harvard and Yale exploited the medical degree to impeach President Donald Trump that matches China's conspiracy to take down the US potential commander in chief who leads the US and allies to fight against the global economic terror of China.

The dishonest academics cause the intellectual line to collapse, they sold the inventions and scientific researchers to China, so Beijing has not to need spending much money on research, the Western universities have carried out from the taxpayers but China got the outcome. China's communist regime focuses the Western universities, particularly the famous universities in the US like Harvard, Yale. The arrest of Doctor Charles Lieber, a Harvard professor who received the money and privileges of China that alerts the US.

Nevertheless, the profit lover-Vice Chancellors have downgraded the education to the business, so China and Vietnam communist students legally have penetrated the universities. Moreover, the skilled migrants helped the high level of technological burglars stole inventions and researches. In Australia, the intelligence discovered the stolen technological force called THE THOUSAND TALENTS PLAN that infiltrated more than 30 universities, the researchers paid by Australian taxpayers but China acquired, the treasonous academics sold the patents to China and the Australian's intellectual properties owned by China. The Australian intelligence and government must act while the country is threatening by domestic enemies and traitors. The betrayal academics must repay the finance and also face treasonous crimes.

China has treated Australia as the colony after the soft army controlled the national assets as Darwin port, Merriden Airport (Western Australia), particularly, Labor Premier Daniel Andrews signed *" one belt and one road"* with China in 2018 (*) so Beijing often raises the brazen attitude. On August 26, 2010, after the media reported the Thousand Talents Plan, Chinese Embassy representative Wang Xining told at Press Club about Australia to accept the foreign influence to earn the economic affluence. The Australian people are waiting for the reaction of the government, particularly Prime Minister Scott Morrison when a Chinese diplomat humiliates the country. The Australian people have not to trust the Australian Labor Party, the hidden communist party is like a branch of China's Communist Party, Senator Penny Wong is like the superpower in shadow, she commands Labor Party. Moreover, Labor's Deputy leader Richard

Marles announces the Australian army to collaborate with the People's Liberation Army while China raises the tension in the region and threatening Australia.

3-The left party and corrupt politicians: the dishonest politicians and the left party killed themselves by the demagogic policies are the hoax climate change, the same-sex-marriage legislation, and the asylum seeker covered the label of human rights. The corruption and China communist's donation contributed to the loss of credit from the public

The democratic country respects the academic, media, and politician, unfortunately, the people's icons collapsed, they sacrificed the people's trust and career for-profit and privileges granted by foreigners as China communists.

China communist has not needed to launch the Landlord Reform, therefore, China could use the undercover activists, espionage agents to pay the left media, dishonest academics, and the left parties plus the corrupted politicians. China could topple the high social class in Western by money. The money is as the bight of China carried out the function to support Beijing into the global hegemonic strategy and also eradicated Western society.

4-The international organizations collapsed the people trust: the global hegemonic ambition also carries out the bribery tactic to corner the international organizations:

-The United Nations lose the original function after China influenced the members, almost, the underdeveloped countries fell into the debt trap and government trap when the leaders received the hush money from China's communist regime or the undercover activists. The peace resolutions couldn't pass in the Security Council and General Assembly.

Circumstance of Mr. John Ashe, President of the United Nations General Assembly at its 68th session and President of UNICEF Executive Board in 2012, he received million dollars of the hush money from China's espionage agents. Nevertheless, the United Nations Secretary-General Antonio Guterres is a hardcore communist, he has driven the United Nations into China's orbit, so the world community distrust the UN.

-The World Health Organization becomes the WORLD HELL ORGANIZATION after Dogtor director-general Tedros Adhanom Ghebreyesus misled the medical information about the Chinese virus that causes the pandemic to spread worldwide. Possibly, the W.H.O has controlled by China's Communist Party, so the world loses the credit of W.H.O.

-The religions have fallen into the monetary method of China, the Vatican has kept quiet while China increases the human rights violation in the mainland, Tibet, Sinkiang Uighur. Moreover, Pope Francis signed a historic agreement with the atheism regime, so China can appoint the bishop and Rome accepts.

-China deeply influenced the UN's Human Rights Council, Beijing elected the member in Council, the rogue regime is a famous violation of human rights

-The International Court of Law of Sea has selected China's Communist Party judge Duan Jie Long while China illegally occupied and militarized into the disputed waters. The International Court falls it the bribery trap of China. The presentation of China's judge in the International Court of Law of Sea is like a pirate with a wooden hammer. Possibly,

China prepares to legalize the illegally artificial islands and the Nine- Dash Line that re-mapped by Beijing.

China's Communist Party is the global enemy, the rogue regime has used the soft army plus the bribery method to topple the top social class in Western and democratic countries around the world and also robbed the inventions, steal the technologies. The Western countries overhaul the communist students like China, Vietnam (*vassal of China*), let's eliminate Chinese pro-Beijing academics from the universities, the scientific research field favors China. The US can kick out the Chinese currency from the stock market, so China will no use the money, the trade to corner the world by bribery tactic. It is the better way to keep out the dangerous enemy from the country./.

Notes (*) citing news published from The Australian newspaper (27.08.20).

THIS IS THE BEST NEWS! AUSTRALIA IS DUMPING CHINA AND STOPPING FOREIGN INTERFERENCE.

Scott Morrison will legislate to tear up Victoria's multi-milliondollar Belt and Road Initiative agreement with Beijing, creating laws that will also ban a raft of other deals with foreign governments found to be against the national interest.

In an unprecedented move against Chinese interference and the protection of state secrets, the use of external powers under the Constitution to direct state, territory and local governments on national security issues will effectively kill dozens of agreements with foreign governments and institutions.

The Foreign Relations Bill, which will be introduced to

parliament next week, also extends to universities and captures any questionable agreements between Australian public institutions and foreign governments.

In a major flexing of its constitutional powers, the Morrison government will cast its net over all foreign relations agreements struck by lower tiers of government , amid fears that national security has been compromised by often secret deals between state governments and foreign powers.

The move could have rippling effects for the private sector, with the Foreign Minister given powers to review any private infrastructure contracts that a state government signed as part of a BRI agreement with China.

The list of agreements that could be scrapped under the proposed legislation will range from sister city agreements, popular with local governments, to memorandum of understanding deals and include all legally and nonlegally binding arrangements. ....

(thedawnmedia.com)

22. JOE BIDEN REFLECTS THE POLITICAL PARASITE

Almost, the viruses, and bacteria live in the human body, therefore, some kinds of bacterium threaten the people like Neisseria Meningitidis or Meninggocccus becomes a danger when it infiltrated the human brain, the patient should kill or paralyze, even amputate.

Joe Biden's family is among the most social dregs in America, the corrupt family's record publicized plus the treason of head's family Joe Biden, the corruption spread multiple nations, Ukraine government confirmed the corruption. Particularly, Joe Biden is a professional robber, he robbed the wife of Bill Stevenson who helped Joe Biden in the Senate campaign, and Jill Biden became espouse of Joe Biden. Moreover, Hunter Biden is the prince of the White House after the thuggish Chief Justice John Roberts presided the illegal inauguration for the presidential robber Joe Biden on January 20, 2021. Without Mike Pence and John Roberts, the illegal president Joe Biden has never inaugurated, so Mike Pence and John Roberts are the culprits of the presidential robbery. On the other hand, the national peril after the bloody old, mad, imbecile mongrel Ape Joe Biden storms the White House that comes from **Mike Pence and John Roberts, the enemies of America, million jobless and the dire consequences.**

The brazen deception's of Chief Justice John Roberts, Congress *(Nancy Pelosi)*, Senate (*Mike Pence*) proved the Corporation of the United States of America is the land of cheat, corruption, the hidden communist regime. The robbers appear everywhere from the normal criminals to the White Collar's robbers. The legal system in America is not different from China, Vietnam, Cuba, and others, despite the fake democracy is shielded by the Constitution of 1871, therefore, its Constitution grants the license to rob. **The dishonest judges are the robbers with the wooden hammer, the Black lives Matter, and Antifa is the terror and robbery organizations that have the untold license to loot the people, and Democrats promote, even the Black Lives Matter is nominated Nobel Peace Prize in 2021.** The land of opportunity unmasked the land of robbery, the dishonest components control the heads of government *(Joe Biden)*, Senate *(Chuck Schumer)*, the Supreme Court *(John Roberts)*. Unfortunately, **the US Army becomes the tool of the robbers who hold the remote control to order the world's most powerful army to protect Joe Biden from the inauguration, and now the US robot Army continues to protect the presidential robber Joe Biden in the White House. The world and allies disappointed the US Army has not responded to the national security, its army doesn't protect the country, instead, the US Army reflects a French saying** *"Le mouton de Panurge"*.

The political parasite or viral politician Joe Biden joined politics in 1973, he became the long term Senator, his political record is the sexual abuse plus the pedophilia ring, the corruption. So 47 years of Joe Biden served nothing for the country, people, he is the professional taxpayer's worm, he has lived in the people's sweat. The prominent political activity of Joe Biden was the presidential nomination of Democrats in 2008, but he and comrade Hillary Clinton were defeated by Barrack Obama, and he became the first black, Muslim, Communist-ruled White House from 2008 to 2016. Despite Joe Biden, Hillary Clinton, and Barrack Obama fought each other like enemies, therefore after Barrack Obama won the election, Hillary held Secretary of State and Joe Biden became the Vice President.

During 8 years to hold the Vice Presidency, Joe Biden exploited the position for corruption, China rewarded $US 1.5 billion for Hunter Biden and Biden family deeply involved the corruption, treason. Once again, political parasite Joe Biden becomes the first illegal president of the Corporation of the United States of America. The Deep State chose CEO Joe Biden to create the debt by devastating the economy with the record executive orders were 52 in 20 days. The political parasite Joe Biden entered the brain of America, he is like Neisseria Meningitidis, his orders conduct the massive jobless, the small businesses are on the brink of closing, the life of 330 million people are threatening. The political parasite Joe Biden targets 65 judges of President Donald Trump appointed and on February 11, 2021, Joe Biden's administration considers the travel ban restricts on Florida after the second impeachment failed and the world laughs. The US people are waiting for the political parasite Joe Biden to destroy America from the grassroots with the destructive executive orders, the disaster comes every day. The state's anger with the crazy executive orders of the political parasite, now the viral politician dominated the brain of America. The US people's outrage, the concerned politicians react against traitor Joe Biden as 20 Republican Senators oppose the executive orders of Joe Biden and some states like Texas, South Dakota's Representative Aaron Aylward introduced the bill HB 1194 to examine the executive orders of the illegal president Joe Biden. Certainly, 75,000,000 people didn't vote, and have never accepted Joe Biden as the 46th President, but Chief Justice John Roberts presided the illegal inauguration, so the executive orders of Joe Biden are unlawful, 50 states do not comply with the illegal decrees of the fake president. However, after the illegal inauguration, Joe Biden received $US 145 million in dark funds, his family members exploit the presidency of Joe Bide to do the business. The political parasite Joe Biden grabs every opportunity to make a profit, the Biden Cancer Initiative researched nothing, but they spent $US 3 million for salaries.

Despite the presidency is illegal, but the presidential robber Joe Biden acts like a king in medieval, he repaid China, the Deep State, and the supporters. The cabinet of Joe Biden recruited the political viruses of Obama's regime. The Corporation of the United States of America exposed the fake democracy, the corruption, the government, Constitution, and the legal system are not different from China. The people wake up after the rigged election legalized and the political parasite Joe Biden has an opportunity to broach the money. The country is endangered after the traitor Joe Biden stormed the White House and commands the most powerful country on the planet.

The Republican States and 75,000,000 people plus families must act for survival, the secession is the only solution to escape from the Deep State. The secession is the only rescue solution to disband the Corporation and reform the virtual nation, it should be **the Federation of America.** Certainly, the major Republican states are the strength to restore the Constitution of 1776. The Corporation of the United States of America is rotten from the Congress, Senate, Supreme Court, and the White House's swamp. The US people have the right to decide the future of 330 million people, not Chief Justice John Roberts and Democrats. The new nation nullifies the messy Constitution in 1871 and also eradicates the presidential robber Joe Biden with the political parasites, viruses, maggots in North America who cheated and squeezed the people's sweat for 150 years. Possibly, the parasites or viruses have no brain, it reflects the destructive executive orders of Joe Biden and his viral administration targets to ban the travel to Florida and Joe Biden can apply the travel ban to the Republican states. The US people have no way to live, the life is locked by Democrats, so the secession can save the nation and the people./.

23. PRESIDENT DONALD TRUMP IS THE GREAT ECONOMIC GENERAL

The United States Army pride Four Stars General George Smith Patton Jr had nickname is *Old Blood and Guts*. Therefore, General Patton who produced more outcome in less time with fewer casualties than another general of any army during the Second World War. General Patton was an excellent commander in the Second World War, his legacy becomes the legend of the US army.

In the Vietnam War, an untrained Four Stars General Võ Nguyên Giáp was the military genocide, he pushed more than a million lives of the People's Army of Vietnam killed from the Indochina to Vietnam War to exchange the victory by the bloodshed of his troop with the inhumane tactic called" *Human Wave*" devised by Mao Tse Tung. The communist ignores human life, so the victory means bloodbath of their army. Therefore, the South Vietnam Army (The Army of the Republic of Vietnam) admire the talented Lieutenant General Ngô Quang Trưởng who became the obsession of the People's Army of North Vietnam in the battlefield and adore the national heroes were Major General Nguyễn Khoa Nam, Brigadier General Lê Văn Hưng, Brigadier General Trần Văn Hai, Brigadier General Lê Nguyên Vỹ, all committed suicide after Vietcong occupied Saigon on April 30, 1975.

The war always creates bloodshed and the dire consequence is inevitable, the days of yore in China, Chinese ancient strategist Sun Tzu who wrote the book" *The Art of War*" plus 36 stratagems and it applied as the handbook of the war currently occurred between the ethnic nations in the region. Therefore, President Donald Trump wrote" *The Art of the Deal*" to avoid war and making the peace. Moreover, Sun Tzu was not the commander in chief, but President Donald Trump who commands the strongest army on the planet, nevertheless, President Donald Trump is a billionaire. However, the economic battle decides the military battle as a saying of Napoleon Bonaparte:" *an army marches on its stomach*".

President Donald Trump is considered as the Great Economic General despite he doesn't have the stars on the collar, but he is the potential commander in chief of the United States Army and President Donald Trump is also the commander in chief of the economist. He is in charge of the economic battle that occurs in the US and also offshore fighting.

The army generals command the military battle with the weapon, tactics, and casualties plus the injuries. However, the economic battle has never had the bloodshed but the enemies to be defeated or surrendered when the economy collapsed. The economic talent of economic general Donald Trump debunked the economic academics.

In the presidential nomination of Republicans in 2016, there were a group of 370 economists including 8 Nobel Laureates of Economy signed a letter to warn the Republicans do not to support Donald Trump, they labeled candidate

Donald Trump as" *a dangerous, destructive choice"*. A Nobel Prize-Winning Economist Joseph Stiglitz criticized the US economic protection of President Donald Trump facing several problems in Europe and concerns about the stability of China's growth. Therefore, the Nobel Economic winner Joseph Stiglitz ignored China bullied the US economy, and conspiring to colonize the US by the economic and financial tactics.

The other Nobel Economic Prize winner is Paul Krugman said the US economy will be engaged the recession in the next year (but it wrongly predicted as the hoax climate change appalls the people)…moreover, after President Donald Trump getting the office, Janet Louis Yellen, the chair of the Federal Reserve criticized the economic policy of President Donald Trump, certainly, Janet Yellen was pointed by President Barrack Obama, so the people have no surprise the hostile behavior of this factional economist. The academics plus the Nobel Economic winners have never made billion dollars if they have the talent, why didn't they make the billionaire like Donald Trump, instead they earn the income from the salary? Certainly, the economic academics and the Nobel Laureates of Economy Prize winners are able to tell about the economic theory as the economic parrot in universities or the institutes, actually, the excellent economists teach the people how to make the money in the seminars, in the media, and the universities. But why don't they keep the secrets to make the money? they are the economic clowns while on the battlefield, the army needs the fighting soldiers than the parade soldiers on marching with the colorful uniform. The economic field needs the experiences than the economic theory, so the people laugh when the economic academics and the Nobel Laureates of Economy winners criticized President Donald Trump on the economic policies. Instead, they must learn from President Donald Trump and calling him is the economic master. Unfortunately, the economists plus Nobel Laureates of Economy winners above are arrogant, their qualifications and the economist's title have nothing for the country, except working for individual favor and personal wage.

The Nobel Prize Committee made many mistakes awarding the most valued prize on the planet, the committee may be influenced by the political stance, faction, and bias, so the people doubt Nobel Prize winners:

-The Nobel Peace Prize in 1973 wrongly awarded the multiple doctoral degree Henry Kissinger and the mogul terrorist of Vietcong is Lê Đức Thọ. The Nobel Peace Prize that cost the loss of South Vietnam on April 30, 1975, after the Vietcong terrorist broke the Paris Peace Agreement signed on January 27, 1973. Vietcong applied the dried bloodbath policy, Vietcong's regime centralized more than 800,000 members of the South Vietnam Army and public servants in the hell of a prison. The worst treatment killed more than 165,000 political prisoners and 90,000 Vietnamese people lost freedom and a million Vietnamese people died on the way to find freedom after Vietcong invaded South Vietnam. The consequence of the Nobel Peace Prize in 1973 still remains in Vietnam. The Nobel Peace Prize in 1973 is an accomplice with Vietcong terrorist, genocide, and human rights violation in Vietnam.

-The Nobel Peace Prize in 2000 awarded to the leftist South Korean President Kim Dae Jung who used $USD 500 million of South Korea's taxpayers to finance North Korean leader Kim Jong Il, but the missile launch and bomb test continued threatening the region.

-The Nobel Peace Prize in 2007 awarded former Vice President Al Gore who has exploited the hoax climate change for business, now Al Gore is the climate change's billionaire. Moreover, the hoax climate change helps China develops and selling Solar Power.

-The Nobel Peace Prize in 2009 awarded President Barrack Obama despite he didn't have a peace-making record. Therefore, President Barrack Obama became the global warmaker, he ignited the gender war (the same-sex-marriage legislation), the racial war in the US, and spreading to Africa. President Barrack Obama created an opportunity for Islamic State founded after he ordered the US army to withdraw from Iraq, President Barrack Obama also provided the weapon, military training, and financed for ISIS. His double cross war game putting the life of the US soldiers at risk, actually the 4 deaths at Benghazi (The US ambassador and 4 servants), and the debt reached $USD 19.84 trillion.

President Donald Trump makes the peace in the Korean peninsula, he is the first US president forced North Korean leader Kim Jong Un who volunteered to stop the missile launch and bomb test then the summit in Singapore on June 12, 2018, following the meeting at Hanoi on February 28, 2019, and on June 29, 2019, President Donald Trump is the first US president stepped in DMZ after the Korea War ended in 1953.

The peace record and economic success of President Donald Trump are eligible for the Nobel Peace Prize and

Nobel Laureates of Economy. Actually, the economic doctrine" *Make America Great again"* **conducts the US growth, the Dow Jones increased from 17,000 of Barrack Obama's era, now the Dow Jones reaches nearly 27,000. Within more than two years, Dow Jones grew about 10,000 points, it is incredible.**

Since China's communists joined the global market, actually, China entered the WTO, the rogue regime in Beijing has carried out the global hegemonic dream, the global economic terror is the sharp tool to transform the world, including the US to be China's vassal. President Donald Trump wakes the world as President George W.Bush did after the event on September 11, 2001. The war fights against the den of thieves, the hub of counterfeit and the center of a cheat created the potential damages of China, so Beijing should hire the left media, the dishonest (or left) academics have attempted to stop the economic war by the propaganda, therefore, the phony psychological warfare is obsolete after the outcome exposes the winner is the US.

The 370 economists plus 8 Nobel Economic Prizes are the shame, after two years, the US economy restored and grows, the unemployment is 3.6 % hits the lowest record since 1969, the debt reduced from $USD 19.84 trillion to $USD 16.17 trillion.

The commander in economy Donald Trump succeeded the economic weapon, the sanction causes North Korea leader Kim Jong Un who volunteered to stop the missile launch and bomb test then Kim Jong Un who accepted to attend the summit at Singapore on June 12, 2018, and Hanoi on February 28, 2019, and recently, on June 29, 2019, it was a first time, the US incumbent President Donald Trump stepped in DMZ to meet North Korea leader Kim Jong Un since the Korea War ended in 1953.

The Intercontinental Ballistic Tariffs Missile of the **great economic General Donald Trump crippled China's economy.** The global market lost, actually, President Donald Trump granted the death certificate to the giant telecommunication Huawei and 70 affiliates, so Huawei becomes the ghost telecommunication company. The economic weapon affects multiple hundreds of millions of jobless in the mainland, the inhumane regime panics the collapse is possible. The economic weapon can eradicate the grassroots of China communist. Nowadays, China communist regime faces the mountain debt, from $USD 23 trillion to $USD 34 trillion and now, the debt is $USD 40 trillion or 400% GDP, certainly, China must spend at least 50 years to pay the deficit if China economy is like the US. The Intercontinental Ballistic Tariffs Missile of the Great Economic General Donald Trump crippled China's economy and ruined the financial system. The debt is like terminal cancer to kill the rogue regime in Beijing. The economic weapon affects the rogue regime in Teheran, the sanction ruined Iran, the economic missile can destroy the enemy's tummy without the war.

China can challenge the arms race and global hegemonic strategy by the money, actually, the rapacious ambition called one belt and one road plus the illegally artificial islands built and militarized into the disputed waters must carry out by the money. Therefore, the Intercontinental Ballistic tariffs Missile of the great economy General Donald Trump shattered China's hegemony and transforming the China dream into a nightmare. The economy is the death vulnerability of China communist, so Beijing fears the new tariffs of $US 300 billion can impose any time. China doesn't care about the war, because the communist snubs human life, but communist fears the money as the materialism. The communist has no money that is like the engine without petrol, the show has no audience./.

Do not fear what the communist does

Let's do what the communist fears./.

24. THE TOILET BATTLE STRUGGLES BETWEEN GENDERS

Obama lies matter, an iconic evil, a global thug and global war-maker, he just ruled the White House in 8 years, but the US nearly destroyed and the world is complicated. His dire consequence has remained in the US and the world. Barrack Obama helped Islamic State founded, he used the taxpayers to play the double-cross war game. During holding the power, President Barrack Obama called to fight against the terror, indeed, he provided the weapon, money, and training Islamic State. Before leaving the second term, the **BLACK LIVES MATTER** appeared and it spread worldwide. The protests with riot have spread from the US to Europe, Australia, Canada, the culprits are Democrats, hidden China's Communist Party, and the domestic thugs after the suspicious death of an idol of felony George Floyd who has a dozen criminal record, he was arrested and resisted the police officer after using forgery $US 20. Black Lives Matter has applied the tactic of communists in the Vietnam

War, the protests with violence, looting to pressure on politics and justice. On the other hand, the Black Lives Matter sits above the law because the death of George Floyd must carry out the legal process, with the forensics, and coroner needs to apply the justice while George Floyd was a drug addict and he contracted Coronavirus before arresting, so he couldn't breathe that shouldn't police officers fault, therefore, the left media distorts the career, so the protests spread despite Coronavirus outbreak.

The Black Lives Matter discriminates against the white, the **BLACK SUPREMACIST** has created mayhem in the Western. Moreover, Barrack Obama advocated and promoted homosexuality and it becomes a global movement. **HOMOSEXUALITY LIVES MATTER** marks the mayhem's record of President Barrack Obama, yes he can harm the world

President Barrack Obama is considered as the Pope of the homosexual movement or HOMOSEXUALITY LIVES MATTER, the homosexual movement globalized as a religion has the global adherent, flag, but the homosexual religion has no bible, nor temple, neither church, instead, they have the slogan" *love is equal*" as Catholic has" *amen*", and Buddhist prays" *Namu Myōhō* **Renge** *Kyō*". On the other hand, the homosexual religion based on the practice of the bible. The sexually personal practice publicizes and politicized when the First US Muslim and communist Barrack Obama ruled the White House in 8 years (2008-2016).

Homosexuality is an untold religion of unnatural sexuality influencing worldwide and the taxpayers spent for

135

the rallies plus the plebiscite, the politicians spent a lot of time debate. In Australia, Prime Minister Malcolm Turnbull who carried out the postal survey cost taxpayers $AU 122 million. The prominent homosexual politician in Australia is Senator Penny Wong, she expects as a preacher and cleric of Homosexual religion.

The Homosexual religion politicalized by the left parties and Greens Party (*Garbage Party*), they use love is equal to gain the ballot of minor homosexuality and also legalizing same-sex marriage targeting worldwide. Nowadays, there are 30 countries that legalized same-sex marriage, the United Nations have not hung the Rainbow flag yet but the UN respects homosexuality. Therefore, founder Barrack Obama changed the white's color of the White House by Rainbow and he destroyed the US Army to permit homosexuality and transgender.

The crucial battle that occurs between the major natural couple, and the minor homosexual couple still conflict into society, the same-sex-marriage won over the religions and multiple million years of human history. The gender battle is unrest, particularly, the toilet battle has struggled in public and the national budget spending the money to build the toilet deserves for the homosexual components and transgender. President Barrack Obama signed Executive Order 13672 on July 21, 2014, the reason cited" *it prohibited discrimination in the civilian federal workforce on basis of GENDER IDENTITY and in hiring by federal contractors on basis of both SEXUAL ORIENTATION and Gender identity"*.

In 1969, the US succeeded the space program with Apollo 11 marked the first human landed the moon.

Therefore, nearly a half-century later, President Barrack Obama conducted the US people to enter the toilet, it is not a normal restroom in public, but the toilet deserves for transgender. **The toilet revolution** activated by the first communist and Muslim President of the United States of America being controversial, the national budget spending for the special people decided their gender by themselves and doctors carrying out the transgender.

The restroom became the crucial battle occurring in the US, the transgenders have the right to choose their gender's status and the taxpayers' spending, therefore, the transgender's toilet using confuses the public. The law is not clear about the toilet users, so the transgenders can use the public toilet based on the physical body that clarifies males and females by a doctor. However, the transgender's toilet can be exploited by the sex predators disguised as the female and entering the restroom. It is an outstanding's achievement of President Barrack Obama who had the demagogic slogan" *yes we can*" including" *Yes we can have the transgender* ".

The homosexual movement deeply influences the politics, the left parties woo to support from the LGBT, the hungry ballot's politicians need to win the election or retain the seat in parliament, so the homosexual movement becomes the political force in the Western countries, they often rallied and promote the love is equal and the left parties support as Black Lives Matter's rally. Somewhere else, the homosexual force pressures the government to build a special toilet for homosexual people in the public and the government plus private buildings. In Russia, the Ape Revolution in October 1917 succeeded by Lenin, and the Red flag globalized plus the bloodshed with more than 100 million people killed. The toilet revolution activated in Singapore, the WTO (*World Toilet Organization*) briefs as the World Trade Organization. The World Toilet Organization founded in 2001, initially, the WTO had 15 members and now they have 151 member organizations in 53 countries. The WTO requires the United Nations to consent to the World Toilet Day is November 19.

China joined WTO (*World Trade Organization*) but the rogue country has exploited the free market to carry out the global hegemonic ambition. China also favors the World Toilet Organization called the Toilet Revolution. Xinhuanet published an article on November 11, 2018:" CHINA FOCUS: CHINA'S TOILET REVOLUTION BRING BETTER SANITATION TO RURAL SCHOOLS"

However, communist countries are such as Vietnam, China and the other communist paradise are keen to use human excrement into agricultural products. In Vietnam, the great leader Hồ Chí Minh of its communist party and also the icon of Jane Fonda, John Kerry, Joe Biden, Bill-Hillary Clinton, the left media...Hồ Chí Minh concerned the people is precious assets, so Vietnam communist encourages the people using the excrement on farmland and feeding the fish. In Vietnam, the common economic model of Uncle Ho's Fish Pond popularized, the family has an **Uncle Ho's Fish pond** to feed a kind of fish called" *Cá Vồ*" and also solves the toilet's problem. The fish fillet's Basa export overseas including the Western countries. In Vietnam, the excrement is precious so the burglar focuses that causes a saying" *the toilet in socialism needs the enclosure".*

The excrement becomes the fertilizer in the communist paradise, the people who live in the communist paradise appall their agricultural products. Its reason conducts Chinese people favor the US agricultural products as soybean despite China's communist regime imposed retaliatory tariffs on US products. Despite, Ape Emperor Xi Jinping calls Chinese people do not to eat the US, Australia's meat, soybean, but Chinese people do like the agricultural products of the capitalist than socialist food.

The toilet's battle silently occurs in the Western, the transgender and homosexual movement require the special restroom for them, moreover, the Black Lives Matter currently activates in the Western as cancer, it outbreaks when the left parties, the dishonest politicians, and the foreign as China incites./.

25. THE CRUCIAL BATTLE OF FREE SPEECH VERSUS FREE FAKE NEWS

Democratic countries respect free speech that is an important activity in society, the people in Western can expose free speech by multiple reactions as a personal protest, rally (*but a rally must apply the Police is due to social order and public security*) including the media can reflect the opinion by the articles and releasing the news (*not fake news*) and impartial information to the public. While the communist regime expects free speech is the dangerous enemy, the dictatorial government gag the people, whoever lives in the communist paradise must obey the order and speaking comply with the government's decision. So free speech in communist countries is led by socialism. In Vietnam, the people react Vietcong regime by saying:" *eating is like a prisoner, sleeping as a monk and talking is like the national leader"*. The propaganda machine pilots the people to repeat the government's policies like the parrot and chanting the genocide leaders, even Hồ Chí Minh, Mao Tse Tung died, but the people must adore as the order of government. It is a farce of the communist's free speech as the stolen economy's pattern of capitalism called" *the free market is led by socialism*". The free speech of communists means SPEECH-FREE as a sign" SMOKE-FREE" in Western countries displayed the public places or offices, restaurants. Certainly, the leftists in Western knew communist countries have no free speech, but they support the inhumane regimes while they always advocate human rights and free speech. Nevertheless, the leftists excited by the communist paradise, therefore, no-one wants to choose the living style in China, Vietnam, North Korea...the hypocritical leftists couldn't hide the face. In the US, Jane Fonda does love Vietcong, but she denied the communist paradise in Vietnam although she prides the nickname is Hanoi Jane, she doesn't want to live in Vietnam. Australian Labor Party's Senator Penny Wong always stands and serves for China's interest, but she seems not interest to live in the communist paradise in mainland China. The communist's supporters in Western eat the democratic hamburger but adore the evil communist. The communist's supporters are the domestic thugs in Western, the dangerous enemy of democracy.

In Western countries, the left media has exploited free speech for business and political purposes. The dishonest media's workers transform communication into propaganda. **Free speech has distorted to free fake news,** the public misleading is a form of fraud, it expects as a crime that conducts the social mayhem. From the Cold War, the left media was the culprit of the violence and social disorders. The left media is a form of terrorist, the weapon is fake news, fabricated stories have struck the people's mind and the victims act like a robot, so the rallies with violence come from the propaganda of the left media. The innocent people have been misled by the fake news and fabricated stories that cause the currently social war or domestic war in Western countries. So the lawmakers in Western countries need to make a law punishing the fake news's conviction as the terrorist. It is a crime against society, the mastermind is the perpetrator of a crime. **The left media's conviction has not prosecuted yet by law, therefore, a common case calls defamation that is an individually legal argument and lawsuit. But, the left media harm the country, their crime is serious than defamation.**

Any job and career must respect the rules and law because every field has the dishonest distorts the career or exploits the job for individual favor. Unfortunately, democratic countries have deserved the priorities for the media, so the dishonest media's workers have distorted the communication to propaganda. The left media becomes arrogant, they expect themselves as the kingmakers and sitting above the country, commanding the President, Prime Minister. The left media is the cause of the national crisis, political mayhem, and social disorder.

The US's presidential election in 2016 exposed the evil face of left media in Western. The evil media maximally developed the cunning tactics contained in the essential formula is **3 F=False polls +Fake news +Fabricated story**. Actually, the False polls are the form of a rigged election that can influence undecided voters. In Australia, most media are leftist, the television companies are ABC, Channel Seven, Channel Ten, Channel Nine, SBS, and the newspapers applied the false polls to help Liberal turncoat Malcolm Turnbull toppled Prime Minister Tony Abbott in the coup 2015. The left media companies in Australia caused the political crisis since the inappropriate coup. Once again, the left media in Down Under lied the public and snubbed the Australian people in the federal election's campaign held on May 19, 2019, by the false polls guaranteed opposition Bill Shorten will be Prime Minister and Senator Penny Wong will drive Australia into China's vassal when she holds Foreign Affairs Minister and she vowed to permit Huawei to operate 5G in Australia while the national security threat by China's cyber spy unit 61389. The people believe behind the left media is China's espionage agent and China's communist-backed comrade Labor Party to win the election. Eventually, the Australian people defeated the Labor Party and debunked the malicious polls of the left media companies on night May 19, 2019, Prime Minister Scott Morrison claimed the landslide victory.

Nowadays, the left media becomes the FAKE NEWS THUG, the enemy of people, the foe of the public, and the garbage of mainstream media. The prominent media companies like CNN, The New York Times, The Washington Post…and the left media companies in Australia lost the people's trust.

The media is like any career, whatever, national security

and national interest are the most important issues in the country. The media must respect the nation and people, so the classified information is not the field of media because of the information linking national security. There is no one sitting above the law and national security, so Australian Federal Police raided the office of the prominent fake news ABC in Australia (*the fake news ABC funded by the taxpayers, they misused the money to oppose the national interest*). The incident is like strong stuff of pesticide sprayed, so all kinds of insects physically react. Obviously, ABC tried to use the taxpayers for legal action against the Australian Federal Police. Therefore, the lawsuit was not successful and all kinds of fake news made the people laugh by releasing the blacked-out text on the left media's newspapers and the left television networks chimed. Nevertheless, the left media backed by the hidden communist party in Australia that labeled the Australian Labor Party.

Certainly, journalism is not a crime as the Media Freedom Act. Therefore, free speech can not surpass the national security and national interest as the left media protects the illegal migrant being advocated under the **title of human rights, but it turns the human wrong, actually, it becomes the human fraud when the people smuggling rings made money from the Australian's taxpayers**. Free speech is not free fake news, free false polls, and free fabricated stories to mislead the public. For those who commit crimes and fraud, Western lawmakers need to have the law to limit the field of media as any job and career. The media's loopholes have become the room of media's dishonest using free speech for money and political purpose./.

26. THE SHADOW OF PHILANTHROPIST BILL GATES

The people just based on the contributed financial record of Microsoft billionaire Bill Gates and praise the generous heart of the US philanthropist. Therefore, time can prove the reality of Bill Gates that reflects a stratagem of Chinese strategist Sun Tzu" *hide a knife behind a smile*". Mr. Bill Gates has a close relationship with President Barrack Obama, on November 22, 2016, President Barrack Obama awarded the Medal of Freedom to Bill and Melinda Gates.

After President Donald Trump inaugurated on January 20, 2017, the US fights against the global economic terror of China, the US companies and investors moved out or repatriated the homeland to avoid the tariffs, therefore, Bill Gates ignored it. Since January 2019, Bill Gates planned the Nuclear Power Plant in China, but it halted, and in November 2019, once again, Bill Gates re-tried the Nuclear Power Plant in China and the US thwarted it. The US government recognizes billionaire Bill Gates often interests the business with China. After China's Nuclear business failed, on March 13, 2020, Bill Gates announced to step down from the Microsoft company's board and he told to spend more time on charity.

China's Communist Party launches global biological warfare terror, the world including the US rise the death toll, infected population and economy being recessed. During the US, President Donald Trump and its people are fighting against the Coronavirus, Bill Gates exposes the hypocritical face, he cleverly criticizes President Donald Trump's response to the pandemic, and recently, Bill Gates urges to call the world leaders to fight COVID-19 with the personal protection equipment and vaccine. Democrats, particularly, the heartless Governor Cuomo have exploited the Coronavirus for the presidential election in 2020.

Everyone recognizes the Novel Coronavirus is the biological weapon of China's Communist Party to launch the crucial battle aiming for multiple purposes, possibly, the inhumane regime uses the virus to reduce the population and stop Chinese people from standing up after the massive jobless, solved the democratic movement in Hong Kong and destroy the US economy, a stone kills many birds. Whatever, China has never confirmed the Coronavirus is their biological warfare, instead, China strays the Coronavirus comes from the bat, wild animal meat at Wuhan's fish market. Indeed, Chinese people have eaten the bat and wild animal meat for a long time but Coronavirus didn't happen. Moreover, Asian countries like Vietnam, Indonesia, East Timor, and others have eaten those, but no Coronavirus. Beijing lies about the Coronavirus that comes from the US, and the socialist Pope Francis drives the Coronavirus causes climate change. China's sophistication can not convince the world, instead, the massive compensation increases from the victim nations, the global lawsuit can file against China to pay more than a hundred trillion US dollars for compensation, so China faces bankruptcy when two hundred countries take China to the international court.

Certainly, the Coronavirus appeared at Wuhan where is near the first biosafety level 4 Laboratory of China (*Jiangxia district, Hubei*). Therefore, the US billionaire Bill Gates-funded the Wuhan Laboratory, so Bill Gates was a member of China's Academy of Sciences and China awarded the highest honor.

China's communist regime attacks the world by biological warfare terror, and China also exposes the hypocritical morality by sending the false test kit and the contaminated mask to Europe, Asia, and the US. The malicious tactics of China to be debunked as former Speaker of Australian's House Representative Bronwyn Bishop warns the medical supplies from China to Sydney*:" flight from Wuhan is a part of a propaganda wa*r", she said*:" the Chinese let that virus out, brought the free world to its knees and now are going around saying they are a superior system of government, have cleaned up the problem in China and now they are going out to help the rest of the world have done the damage in the first place"*. The US philanthropist Bill Gates who financed Wuhan's laboratory and also calls the world leaders to fight against the Chinese Virus comes from Wuhan's Laboratory. It is like President Barrack Obama called to fight against terrorism but in the shadow, he used the US taxpayers to finance, provide the weapons and training for Islamic State.

The Coronavirus wakes up the world and unmasked the traitors inside the Western countries. The charity of Billionaire Bill Gates should be reviewed, his contributions created problems in India, the amount was $US 1.2 billion to vaccinate the Polio causes more than 496,000 paralyzed children from 2000 to 2017. Moreover, the other charity programs of Bill Gates becomes a disaster in Asia, Africa, so the US people doubt Bill Gates who promises to find the

Coronavirus vaccine. Nevertheless, Bill Gates has a long term relationship with China, the charity has hidden behind the business, China spread everywhere, China's agent is Yinuo Li labeled a non-profit activates on global health praises Bill Gates:

" Most people in China have heard of Bill Gates. They know him as a technology industry leader and a co-founder of Microsoft. But fewer people are aware of the foundation that he and his wife, Melinda, created in 2000 to reduce poverty and improve health around the globe.

Our vision for China is ambitious. While we continue to support development within China in areas such as poverty reduction, HIV, tuberculosis, tobacco control, and philanthropic development, we are also committed to supporting China as a stronger development partner for the rest of the world. By tapping into Chinese resources, innovation, and expertise, we aim to replicate China's remarkable success in addressing health inequity and poverty in some of the poorest regions of the world. China's domestic reforms, increasing global engagement, and emerging capacity for innovation reinforce our faith in China's potential as a catalyst for development worldwide.

As the director of the China office, I hope you will explore the work we do and join us in our effort to ensure that everyone in China—and the world—has the chance to live a healthy, productive life.

Yinuo Li

Director, China Office "./.

27. THE PATRIOTISM IS THE BACKBONE OF COUNTRY

Certainly, a bird must have the nest, a person needs the house, a country promotes the history is the national originals, the national spirit contains in history and reflects the patriotism. On the other hand, patriotism and history are like shape and its shadow. The country has no history that is like a man without the backbone, the tree has no roots. The motive of the country exists and develops that comes from patriotism. Japanese prides the history that derives patriotism and nationalism, despite, Japan has not many national sources but its country becomes a wealthy nation in Asia and the world. Jewish people lost the country for thousands of years, but they always have kept the national nuance and the patriotism, eventually, Jewish people returned to the homeland and rebuilt the country.

The country is the common house of a people when a person loves its house, its place makes better. The patriot always puts the country above the individual favor, so patriotism is the key to develop the country. Education is a place to keep the patriotic treasure, the futuristic country belongs to the young generations, certainly, the multiple levels of the national school do need to promote the history, it is the backbone to develop the country. History conducts patriotism and nationalism.

Communism conflicts with patriotism and becomes the enemy of nationalism. The communists abolish patriotism, it causes the people to lose the national spirit, so the people who live in the communist paradise lose the invention like China, so the rogue regime solves the inventing shortage by stolen technology to carry out the global hegemonic ambition. The pupils of Karl Marx reflect the most dishonest component on the planet, the communist governments pull back the human history, it is just a dynasty in the democratic era but it worsens more than the monarchy. On the other hand, the communist regimes are the same kind of dynasties in medieval. Almost, the dynasties in the days of yore drove patriotism to serve the royal family, and the loyalty distorted to serve the king.

The communist wants to destroy the national history, abolishes the patriotism. National loyalty drives into loyal socialism, so the army, police, and government in the communist countries protect and serve the communist party, not the country, nor the people. Under communist rule, all the national valuation and history are threatening as communist regimes like China, Vietnam, and others. The malicious conspiracy of communists to eliminate history and be replaced by the communist party's history. After many decades ruled by the communist party, the people forget the national history and patriotism distorts to socialism. The Vietnam Communist Party propagates the slogan" *patriotism is led by socialism*". In the communist regimes, the national heroes replaced by Communists, particularly, Karl Marx, Lenin are the great heroes. In China has great hero Mao Tse Tung, Vietnam has Hồ Chí Minh, Cuba has Fidel Castro, North Korea has Kim Il Sung. The young generations easily brainwash in the education's system, Hồ Chí Minh quotes:" *ten years to plant the tree, a hundred years to plant the people*" (Mười năm trồng cây, tram năm trồng người". Vietnam Communist Party has intoxicated many generations of Vietnamese people since the communist party founded on February 3, 1930. Nowadays, the major Vietnamese people have not known the national history, instead, they learned

149

well the history of the Vietnam Communist Party, so they have not acted when the Vietnam Communist Party and Hồ Chí Minh gave the Spratly islands and the lands at the border to China. Instead, the North Vietnamese people prided when Prime Minister Phạm Văn Đồng issued the diplomatic statement to offer the Spratly islands for China on September 14, 1958. The patriotism of the Vietnamese people lost while Vietcong sold the country to Soviet-Union and China. The patriotism is led by socialism that cost tens of thousand lives of Vietcong troop in the Điện Biên Phủ battle and 1,500,000 Vietcong lives plus 300,000 troops went missing in the Vietnam War.

The Western countries have neglected the education, the major purposes of science, technology to be promoted. History concerns as a secondary subject, so patriotism fades, even the graduate students are illiterate in history. The important facts have forgotten for a long time, it created an opportunity for communism to infiltrate Western education. Moreover, the ill-concerned and profit lover's Vice-Chancellors put the business above the education and training. The students who come from communist countries like China, Vietnam have exploited the negligent education system to penetrate. Every communist student is a propaganda activist and a high technological burglar, moreover, the skilled migrant's policy opened the gate for the red seeds that inundated the universities in the Western. They climbed higher and dived deeper into the top technological universities, so Chinese researchers stole the technologies and handed them to China. Nevertheless, the Western students were intoxicated by China's communist students and the left parties endorse imposing communism or socialism into the universities plus high schools. It causes the major students including the graduate students are leftists, so they have been brainwashed by its education. The left parties like Democrats in the US, the Australian Labor Party, the U.K Labor Party flag the communist development into the schools. The political ambition causes the Western's education to be poisoned by communism and the patriotism travels into the demagogic propaganda of the left parties, so the students of multiple school levels become the leftists. A circumstance of Facebook's CEO Mark Zuckerberg came from Harvard University where is a den of communism that alerts Western education is rotten.

China and comrade Democrats have tried to abolish patriotism, the conspiracy has fed a long time into the US's education, now the time to act. The US patriotic President Donald Trump recognizes the country being threatened by communism and the domestic thuggish Democrats. The US president establishes a commission to promote PATRIOTIC EDUCATION that highlights history. President Donald Trump announced a federal 1776 Commission to carry out the education reform. It is the key to restore patriotism after many decades went in the wrong direction and the enemy infiltrated, the US education being poisoned by the leftists plus China's propaganda activists ambushing into the education system. Nevertheless, US education needs to reform from the grassroots, the maggots hid into universities can not activate the counter-patriotism, the US young generations will restore the patriotism, the history can help the country grows and protect the sovereignty. The domestic thugs react when the education reform of President Donald Trump released, it is the physical reaction of all kinds of insects struck by the insecticide. Democrats and its tool are Liberty worrying the important place will be no longer to activate and intoxicate the young generations, they oppose the patriotic education. The Black Lives Matter and Antifa are the tools of Democrats, the protests with riot, loot, killed the police officers, burned down the businesses, destroyed and vandalized the historic statues, monuments including the statue of Jesus and Maria that reflect the communism in the US, the domestic thugs focus to destroy the historic relics and abolish the patriotism./.

28. THE TRAITOR REJECTS THE PATRIOTISM OF PRESIDENT TRUMP

Patriotism is the backbone of any country, it reflects the national protection and the national spirit. The treason conflicts with the patriotism that is clear to distinguish between two forms of the full opposition, fire, and water have never the integrated.

The left parties and leftists advocate against patriotism, they deny national protection including the national interest. In 2018, French President Emmanuel Macron exploited the First World War's commemoration to attack patriotism:" *patriotism is the exact opposite of nationalism. Nationalism is a betrayal of patriotism. By putting our own interests first, with no regard for others, we erase the everything that a nation holds dearest, and the thing that keeps it alive: its moral values".*

French President Emmanuel Macron is the worst

rhetoric, he confused between patriotism and nationalism, both are not opposite, instead, nationalism derives from patriotism. The nationalism without patriotism is like the fish without water, a medical doctor without a degree, the cheese without fat, a cheque has no money in the account, the music has no sound...

It is very hard to believe a French President couldn't understand and distinguish between patriotism and nationalism. The patriot always puts the nation first and the nationalist serves the country, both cling to each other as the shadow and body, there is not a nationalist without the patriotism contains in the mind. Socialism ignores patriotism and nationalism, the communist and the left parties demote the patriotism despite they often cheat the people by the nationalism, it is the demagogic propaganda as the communist regime deceives the nationalism is led by socialism, even the ugly economic pattern tricks:" *the free market is led by socialism"*...certainly, the genocide, corruption, the cruelty, human rights violation..are led by socialism. On the other hand, the left parties and communists have used the label of nationalism to cheat the people, indeed, they are the traitors.

French President Emmanuel Macron drives the country into the disaster, he supports the illegal migrant and the hoax climate change applies to the fuel price hikes that created the public outrage, it causes a hundred thousand people have protested with the Yellow Jacket movement, the economy lost a billion US dollars and the situation seems unrest, now the protest continues to the week tenth. The worst situation of France that worries the concerned people, among them, a group of French General wrote a letter to President Mr.

Emmanuel Macron, they accused Mr. President is committing treason by signing the UN migration pact. The essential policy of the left parties including the Socialist Party of Emmanuel Macron put the party and faction above the national interest and security, so they want more migrant and illegal migration to arrive, they would have more ballot in the elections.

In the US, the left party Democrats have not respected the patriotism, certainly, the Donkey's Head Party demotes the nationalism, they want to open the border, and the illegal migrant invaded under the era of President Barrack Obama. President Donald Trump who is a patriot puts the nation first, the wall reflects border protection. Therefore, Democratic Congresswoman Nancy Pelosi and Senator Chuck Schumer abandon the wall cost $USD 5.7 billion, instead, they increase $USD 12 billion for foreign aid. The US people recognize the treasonous action of Democrats, actually, Nancy Pelosi and Chuck Schumer distort the lawmaker's function to lawmaker terrorists. The lawmaker terrorists storm the taxpayers and threatening national security including nearly a million government workers are suffering the blackmail of Democrats.

Australian Labor Party has not escaped the leftist tradition, they have no patriotism and nationalism. The left incumbent or retired leaders as former Prime Minister Bob Hawke, Paul Keating, Kevin Rudd putting the comradeship above the national interest and security, they often insisted the Coalition government stand alongside with China communist and distance the long term mateship the US. The lacked patriotism and nationalism of Labor caused more than 50,000 asylum seekers to invade within 6 years of Kevin Rudd and

Julia Gillard's government, the taxpayers wasted tens of billion dollars but the problem is not over yet, actually, the boxing kangaroo opposition leader Bill Shorten promised to give the second chance for thousands of asylum seeker will resettle in Australia if Labor wins the next federal election. Actually, the asylum seeker and the people smuggling are waiting for Labor wins the next federal election.

The incumbent shadow cabinet of the Australia Labor Party has no patriotism as senior Senator Penny Wong who rejected Trump's idea of patriotism over globalism. Labor ignores patriotism, instead, socialism hid inside the demagogic policy. IN the US presidential election in 2016, almost the left media companies as ABC (Australian Broadcast Communist), Channel Seven, Channel Ten...propagated and promoted their beloved comrade Hillary Clinton. Actually, almost, the total Labor Party hated candidate Donald Trump, opposition Bill Shorten used the low-class language to Donald Trump" *barking mad*". Mr. former Union boss Bill Shorten unfits the national leader and a politician, indeed, any concerned politician must keep a neutral attitude in the US election. Whoever elected in White House, Australia must have the trade ties, security share, and other bilateral issues. Senator Penny Wong was the same attitude in the US election, she raised the dislike candidate Donald Trump in the election's campaign, now he is the US president.

Senator Penny Wong or PENNY WRONG was responsible for the national economy's decline. The Finance Minister Penny Wong and Treasurer Wayne Swan of the Labor government caused $AUD 42 billion surpluses of Coalition government was gone, instead, the debt increased.

Nevertheless, the NBN also contributed by Penny Wong and Communication Minister Stephen Conroy, the obsolete technology that conducts the taxpayers wasted $USD 65 billion but it made the profit for China including the national security risks. Moreover, Senator Penny Wong deserved the most political time for the same-sex marriage legislation, she is Lesbian, so she works for her gender's status than national services. Now, Senator Penny Wong is the shadow minister of Foreign Affairs and she also is the leader of Labor in the Senate. If the next election, Labor wins, Senator will be Australian Foreign Minister, it is dangerous when Penny Wong drives Australia into a hostile policy with the US and Australia will fall into the orbit of China communist.

Senator Penny Wong's position is very important in Australia, therefore, she rejects patriotism, what does she serve for? Where is her country? Nevertheless, the incident of Senator Sam Dastyari (now he retired) is not simply a corruption but it links to the national intelligence. During holding Senator, Mr. Sam Dastyari supported China occupied the islands into the disputed waters while the piratical stations of China threatening the security in the region including Australia. The people question the role of Labor Senate leader Penny Wong, she should be the boss of Senator Sam Dastyari?

The patriotism does need for the nationalism, Japanese raises the high spiritual patriotism that derives the nationalism, so Japan developed and become among the wealthy countries on the planet although Japan has not many natural resources. There is only the traitors reject the patriotism./.

29. THE PATRIOTISM UPROOTS ALL KINDS OF VIRUSES

Every country already obtains patriotism, it is the potential immunity system like the human body has the immune system to protect the viral invasion and fighting illnesses, diseases. The country remains independent, development and sovereign originate from the strength of patriotism. On the other hand, patriotism is a strong antibiotic to kill all kinds of treasonous viruses inside and outside. The communist countries like China, Vietnam, North Korea, Laos, Cuba, the national immunity system changed the patriotic gene, and **patriotism is led by socialism or communism**, particularly, in China, Chinese patriotism has shifted to viral Maoist. Chinese patriotism is infected by viral Maoists since 1949, it causes Chinese patriotism was destroyed by viral Communism, and the Chinese national immunity system disabled, its reason explains the people in the communist paradise lose the patriotism and the ruthless regimes remain although the people know the democratic loss, free speech gagged, even, Chinese people in the mainland have not reacted enough the heartless regime killed a hundred million people. The Viral Maoists destroyed the national patriotism by brainwash plus the terror policy. The viral Maoist causes the obscure syndrome, the patriotism effected.

Thousand years of Vietnamese history proved the strong patriotism, Vietnamese ancestor defeated Chinese dynasties invaded. Unfortunately, Vietnamese patriotism has been infected by viral Hồ Chí Minh and its viral communist party. Nowadays, in Vietnam, people have not reacted to Vietcong's regime while Vietnam becomes the actual vassal of China.

The viral Communism infected North Korea from viral leader Kim Il Sung imposed the totalitarian regime while South Korea rejected the viral Communism and the country is among the Asian dragon. Therefore, viral President Kim Dae Jung attempted to impose viral socialism into South Korean people, despite Kim Dae Jung couldn't destroy the national patriotism of South Korean people, but South Korean taxpayers wasted $US 500 million by the fake peace of Kim Dae Jung.

The democratic countries respect freedom and democracy, certainly, patriotism always installs into the national spirit. Therefore, the domestic viruses gently ruined patriotism and collaborated with foreigners to destroy the national immunity system. From 2008 to 2016, viral President Barrack Obama imposed viral socialism, so the US patriotism infected by the syndromes of the hoax climate change, the same-sex-marriage legislation, and illegal migrants.

The Coronavirus or Chinese Virus devastated the nations on the planet, the death toll is up to 200,000 and the infected cases rise more than 3,500,000. The global economy is recessed by China Virus. However, the Chinese Virus arouses spiritual patriotism and the domestic viruses appeared with the Chinese Virus (*). The viral billionaires like Bill Gates, Andrew Forrest, Kerry Stokes protect China and opposing the country to investigate Coronavirus. Moreover, the World Health Organization appeared viral Dogtor Tedros Adhanom Ghebreysus who helped the Chinese Virus spread by the medical misleading and delaying the pandemic outbreak. In the US, the viral politicians join the Chinese Virus attacking the US people, viral lawmaker Nancy Pelosi attacks President

Donald Trump who fights against the Coronavirus. The viral Governor Andrew Cuomo exploits Chinese Virus to play the dirty game, he encourages New York residents to use Personal Protection Equipment (PPE) made in China, the den of Chinese Virus. Nevertheless, viral Governor Andrew Cuomo received 1,000 ventilators from China, he ignored the dire warning of British senior doctors and he also hid the medical supplies provided by the US's federal government, so the death toll and infected case in New York are highest in the US. In California, on April 14, 2020, viral Governor Gavin Newsom spent $US 1 billion of taxpayers to buy China's face mask while the US, Europe, and somewhere else knew China's medical supplies are poor quality, the test kits giving 80% wrong results and the face masks attaching virus and contamination. However, the domestic viruses in the US like viral Governor Andrew Cuomo, viral Governor Gavin Newsom support viral Xi Jinping to develop more death toll and infection by using China's medical supplies. When patriotism wakes up in the US, the next election in 2020, the viral politicians will be vaccinated by the people and they will be retired.

Chinese Virus arouses national patriotism and the national immunity system activates after a long time cheated by the viral businesses, the viral politicians of the viral leftist's parties. The national patriotism stands up after the Chinese Virus attack and the domestic viruses appeared the treasonous face. Whoever tries to stray the Chinese Virus comes from somewhere else or opposing the investigation on Coronavirus, they are the domestic viruses. Certainly, the national immune system recognizes the domestic viruses, and the patriotism antibiotic can destroy the domestic viruses plus the Chinese Virus. The domestic viruses have hidden a long time in democratic countries, therefore, when the Chinese Virus outbreak, the domestic viruses company with the Chinese virus. Patriotism is like the pesticide to kill all kinds of viruses, including the domestic viruses uprooted with the Chinese Virus./.

Notes: (*)

THE PATRIOTISM WAKES UP EVERYWHERE (Below, there is a patriotic reaction from a concerned Australian)

State Premiers need to allow Scott Morrison to get Australia moving on from coronavirus

For the first time in decades, Australia faces real hardship. To get through it, we can't afford the indulgent thinking – or state bureaucracy – that's held us back in the past, writes Peta Credlin.

Peta Credlin

Subscriber only

May 2, 2020 9:00pm

When the deputy chief health officer of Victoria calls Captain Cook an invader and likens him to COVID-19, we have a history problem.

When two of our leading business figures oppose an inquiry into the origins of the coronavirus because it might hurt our trade with China, we have a self-respect problem.

And when the same Premiers that demand we must all "heed the science on climate-change" reject the science on children going back school, we have a credibility problem.

Recovering from a corona crisis that will kill off tens of thousands of businesses, hundreds of thousands of jobs and hundreds of billions in national wealth will demand a comprehensive reset in the way we approach our country's problems.

For the first time in decades, <u>Australia faces real hardship</u>and, to get through it, we can't afford any more of the indulgent thinking that's held us back.

All <u>credit to the Morrison government</u> for protecting Australia from the many thousands of deaths that this virus has caused in Britain, Europe, the US and elsewhere.

I'm not one of those who want to criticise them for locking us, and the economy, up in order to save lives; it's lousy to want to punish our country's success. But getting the economy back on track is likely to make the health effort look easy.

The Morrison government deserves commendation for protecting Australia from the thousands of deaths that coronavirus has caused in other countries.

Last week, Roy Morgan estimated a staggering 10.5 million Australians have had a change to their employment due to this virus: 3.8 million have had their hours reduced, 2.7 million have been stood down, 1.4 million have had their pay cut and almost 700,000 have been made redundant.

The PM said on Friday that restrictions can now start to ease but it will be a long time before this virus has worked its way out of the economy. And that's why the sooner we stop focusing on "First World problems" and get Australians back to work, the better.

Key in all of this has to be rebuilding manufacturing in this country — and, given high power prices are making the few industries we have left more and more marginal, fixing our energy mess remains an urgent priority.

For all the billionaires like Twiggy Forrest demanding the Prime Minister let China off the hook over this virus, let's not forget it's these same business types who contracted out to China all the things we used to make here for ourselves — putting balance sheet profit ahead of national security.

Yet there was Forrest last week, holding another dubious press conference to crow about importing goods from China that we used to manufacture here, then stinging the taxpayer hundreds of millions to reimburse him.

Andrew "Twiggy" Forrest has raised concerns about the timing of an inquest into the origins of coronavirus.

Is it any wonder people are angry about how economically dependent we have made ourselves on China — how much of our farming land, energy and water companies, ports, roads, agricultural processing plants and heaven knows what else we have sold off?

While big business might have turned a blind eye to the Chinese Communist Party's longer-term agenda, the ordinary public are awake to it. Last year, only 32 per cent of Australians told a Lowy Institute poll they trusted China to act "responsibly" — a 20-point fall on a year earlier, and this was before the coronavirus. And 74 per cent agreed Australia was "too economically dependent" on China too.

Convincing Australians we need to make more here won't be such a challenge. But it might be more difficult to get them to understand that, in order to achieve this, we must get rid of stifling rules and regulations that make operating a business here so hard.

So much of our green and red tape comes from bogus international agreements and bodies that politicians sign up to strike a pose without properly understanding the impact.

By all means, we must have laws in this country to protect our magnificent environment but those laws should be a reflection of what Australian voters decide is appropriate to strike the balance between new dams, power stations and development with whatever local frog is at risk, or the farce of punishing us for emissions caused overseas by our coal being burned there.

Our economy will feel the effects of COVID-19 for years to come.

With well over a doubling of unemployment and a 10 per cent drop in GDP likely, persisting with the regulatory delays that have typically held up major projects looks like economic self-harm.

The federal government knows (even if the states mostly do not) that a strong recovery from this coronavirus crisis means lower taxes and less regulation, as well as a much more hard-headed approach to foreign investment, and self-reliance in strategic manufacturing.

A concern, though, are signals out of Canberra wanting a "consensus" on reform and suggesting the so-called National Cabinet might be the best way to achieve it.

The National Cabinet has worked well when the PM signs a big cheque but not so well when he doesn't. So far, the National Cabinet hasn't even been able to achieve a consensus on sending kids back to school, let alone hugely contentious issues like tax reform.

If everything has to be achieved by agreement with Labor premiers, then the bar is set low.

We might end up with a tougher line on foreign investment and maybe government intervention in strategic industries, but there's no way we'll get the greater economic reforms needed to get our economy back on its feet, and to start paying back the trillion-dollar debt left over from this crisis.

The National Cabinet works well when the Prime Minister signs a big cheque but not so well when he doesn't

It's leadership, not consensus, that's needed to make a difference on hard issues. We only have a consensus now on border protection, for example, because the Coalition was prepared for a colossal fight to stop the boats. And this was only possible because orders could be given to the Navy that didn't first require legislation in the Senate or the agreement of the states.

As things stand now, dams, power, planning, infrastructure, environmental regulation, public schools and public hospitals are all the legal responsibility of the states even if they are increasingly the political responsibility of the Commonwealth. Yet who really holds the states to account? Beyond maybe the premier, who can name relevant state ministers or even the opposition leader and how many of us actually understand how deeply in debt our states really are?

Since 2007, according to the Australian Election Study, our "satisfaction with democracy" has dropped 27 points to just 59 per cent. Much more than the revolving door prime ministership, my sense is that this is due to our national inability to get things done.

Of all the things that must change after COVID-19, this is No.1../.

30. THE CHINA PHOBIA MADE BY CHINA COMMUNIST

Chinese people are not China's communist, neither Maoist nor any kind of Marxism-Leninist. Therefore, the Ape super gang robbed the authentic government of Chinese people in 1949, the Communism labeled Maoist is like the deadly pandemic has infected in the mainland, the Maoist epidemic killed more than 65 million Chinese people from 1949 to 1976 by a superbug Mao Tse Tung and the deadly pandemic infected 1.4 billion people in the mainland. Moreover, the viral Maoist has spread worldwide by the infected overseas students to study in Western countries. Mostly, China's overseas students come from the Red noble class in China, their families infected by viral Maoist, so China's student could transmit the deadly viral Maoist to the students in Western universities, high school, and society. The Western countries need to quarantine strictly the overseas student come from the infected states like Vietnam, China, Laos, Cuba... business education helps viral Maoist spread into universities in the Western.

In the mainland, the viral Maoists spread into multiple stages of Great Leap Forward, Hundred of Flowers, Landlord Reform, Culture Revolution. Moreover, in the viral stage of Deng Xiaoping, there were tens of thousands of Chinese people killed in Tiananmen Square in 1989. The viral Maoists spread worldwide with the Maoist rebels in India, Nepal, South America, the Philippines. Unfortunately, the United Nations ignored the deadly pandemic called Maoist. Nowadays, the victims of viral Maoists estimate a hundred million people killed in China. So viral Maoist is the most dangerous pandemic on the planet.

China's mainland becomes the viral Communism or viral Maoist, moreover, China also the paradise of epidemics as SARS, Bird flu, Swine flu, and recently the Novel Coronavirus outbreak to threaten Chinese people and the world.

The viral Communism or viral socialism, viral Maoists in China are the *" comrades "* of deadly pandemics. Since viral Maoist has appeared in China, Chinese people become the victims, moreover, the viral Communism or viral Socialism products to create for the deadly viruses, because the communist paradise is keen to use the human's excrement as the essential fertilizer on the farm plus the unhygienic food that conducts the pandemics thrive. Nowadays, the world has **CHINA-PHOBIA** that comes from viral Maoist and deadly pandemics.

-The viral Maoist silently has infiltrated the world, including the Western and the US, although Western countries are not the land of viral Communism or Communism free but the trade trap, debt trap, the government trap to help the viral Maoist developed and harming the national security, national interest. The viral Maoist is a sibling with viral Socialism that brings by the left parties and left media and infecting the innocent people, actually, the young generations easily be infected by viral Socialism.

The viral Socialism has transmitted from innocent people to the naïve persons in Western and infected society, the Socialism pandemic silently outbreaks, it conducts the social mayhem. The socialism patients lose the mind, they become human robots, so the socialism patients often protest, actually, the hoax climate change highlights the socialism syndrome in the Western. The prominent patient of socialism's hoax climate change is the Swedish teenage Greta Thunberg who talks and acts without concern as a human-robot. The socialists steal the future of Greta Thunberg, unfortunately, her parents didn't recognize it, instead, they are proud.

-The viral Maoist hides the global hegemonic ambition, it develops into the disputed waters in Indochina Pacific and one belt-one road's plan.

-The viral Maoist has attacked the world's economy by the global economic terror since Maoists joined the free market and later WTO.

-The products made in viral Maoist harming human health, mostly, the products made in China matched the unhygienic process, poor quality, poison contamination, and short life. The world has China-phobia for a long time with China's products and food. The profit lovers in the Western helped viral Maoists spread the harmful products to their people, they are the innocent traitors. China succeeded in the trade trap by the profit lovers *(the companies, businesses)* in the mainland and offshore China's companies share with the Western companies.

The viral Maoist eliminated by the democratic vaccine in

Taiwan, Hong Kong, therefore, some infected patients appeared like Hong Kong Executive Leung Chun-Ying, Carrie Lam failed to develop the viral Maoist. In the US, Senator Bernie Sanders is the patient of viral socialism, but the US people quarantine.

In Australia, the viral Maoists penetrated into multiple government levels, actually the House of Representatives and Senate (*federal and state*). The ASIO, the Australian government may quarantine some infected viral Maoists as Senator Penny Wong and MP Gladys Liu, and the politicians do the business or working with China's companies. When the people see any politician protects as Australian Labor Senator Sam Dastyari, certainly, they are infected by viral Maoists. The corruption helps viral Maoists corners the counterparts after the politicians infected.

The infected Communism exposed on the left media, the major infected patients are The New York Times, The Washington Post, CNN, NBC, MSNBC,…and in Australia has ABC, Channel Seven, Channel Nine, Channel Ten, SBS…in the United Kingdom has The Guardian, BBC…even Vietnamese language's media being infected by the viral Communism like Người Việt News, Việt Báo in South California, Cali Today in San Jose, SBTN…Vietnamese people overseas quarantine the left media in their language and boycott them. The movie stars and pop singers in Hollywood have struck by viral Communism, so they lose the mind and blinding to follow the viral Democrats. The US people have phobia on the left entertainment workers.

The world has no phobia of Chinese people, but

strong phobia against China's Communist Party, the viral Communism transmitted from the Ape of Karl Marx to human-like the world has no Islamophobia, but the Sharia phobia threatening to wipe out the culture, social valuation in the Western countries. The people suppose the Novel Coronavirus comes from the bats and wild animal's meat or China's failed to create the biological warfare and Coronavirus leaked to kill Chinese people before attacking the US and Western. Whatever The Novel Coronavirus derived from viral Maoist.

The viral Communism brought by the Ape and renamed Maoist. So Bird flu, Swine flu, and the recent Novel Coronavirus made in China. Chinese people need to quarantine the viral Maoist that is the master of deadly pandemics in the mainland. The countries deeply infected by viral Maoists in the trade, free trade agreement, the currency swap agreement have received the dire consequences after the Coronavirus outbreak that comes from viral Maoists. The world rushes to find the vaccine to stop the Coronavirus, but Chinese people acquired the democratic vaccine to expel the viral Maoists, so Chinese people can apply to save themselves and the country. The Maoist vaccine was all ready to use./.

31. THE SLOGANS CAN NOT WIN NOVEL CORONAVIRUS

The Novel Coronavirus made in China and threatening the world. Almost, the global consumer has never trusted all products made in China to meet the poor quality, poison, contamination, and short life, the cheap prices conflict the standard quality, so the global consumer obsess China made, actually, the epidemics made in China is terrible.

Most pandemics made in China as SARS, Bird flu, Swine flu, and now the Novel Coronavirus outbreaks without control that adds more fear about China. It is **China's phobia** made by the Ape super gang that has ruled China since 1949. The communist party transformed China's mainland to be **the den of thieves, the hub of counterfeit, the center of a cheat, and the paradise of the pandemic.** So Chinese people have been ruined by the Ape super gang. On the other hand, the Ape rule killed a hundred million Chinese people, certainly, the Ape has no human's minds, instead of the animal instinct, so the most communist regimes are barbarous, the humanity completely absents in the communist paradise. There are some theoretical proposals the deadly pandemic called COVID-19 by the World Health Organization should come from:

–**The bats and wild animal meat sold in Wuhan's seafood market**. The information released from China's communist authorities about the cause of the deadly virus, therefore, do not list to what the communist talk, let's watch what the communist did.

–**The unhygienic food derived from socialism**, because China's communist regime advocates and encourages the people in the communist paradise to use human excrement as the major fertilizer on the farm. The frozen Berries exported from China fear Australian consumers after the illness appeared by China's frozen fruits. In Vietnam, after the Geneva Conference signed on July 20,

1954, in North Vietnam, the communist regime has promoted human excrement as the strategic fertilizer on the common farm running by the government. Once again, after Vietcong invaded South Vietnam on April 30, 1975, the communist regime has activated the nationally economic pattern called" *Uncle Ho's Fish Pond*", every family has a little pond to solve the toilet's problem and also feeding a kind of fish called Vồ, it does live the human's excrement. The Vồ fish's fillet processed Basa to export to Western countries. The most Vietnamese refugee fears Vietnam's Basa, they knew the original as Chinese people fear China's infant milk powder after six babied died and 300,000 were poisoned.

-China should create biological warfare to wipe out the US and Western plus allies. This suspicion is reasonable because the Coronavirus has appeared after China signed the phase 1 agreement with the US, it exposes the surrender statement of the rogue regime. Moreover, China also failed to use Iran to deceive the war in Middle-East by attacking the major oil facilities of Saudi Arabia, fired the oil tankers, shot down the US drone, and launched a dozen missiles into the Iraq bases where were the US soldiers stationed including shot down Ukraine's passenger plan to attack the US's economy (*if the US intelligence didn't have the evidence, Iran could claim the Boeing 737 and require the compensation as two accidents in Indonesia and Ethiopia*). Nevertheless, the close comrade with China is Democrats completely disappointed the unconstitutional impeachment after Senate acquitted President Donald Trump (*the cunning impeachment conspired more than three years that failed*). Moreover, there are the people of some Asian countries who have eaten the bat's meat but the Coronavirus has not appeared. China's communist regime is the most barbarous government on the planet, the ruthless Maoists killed more than a hundred million Chinese people on the mainland since 1949, so China can create biological warfare to kill the enemy called capitalist without pity. Normally, after an epidemic appeared, the world quickly responded to contain and found the vaccine. Therefore, the Coronavirus has activated since December 2019, but the world can not find an effective vaccine, even the World Health Organization urgently conferred at Geneva with 400 top scientists, but they could not guarantee the vaccine, instead WHO predicts at least 18 months to have the vaccine. The people suspect the Novel Coronavirus created by China's scientists. China's communist regime can do anything to carry out global hegemonic ambition. There is evidence that proved China conspires to create the biological warfare released from the US media:

" *Virus-hit Wuhan has two laboratories linked to Chinese bio-warfare program*

Virology institute there has China's only secure lab for studying the deadly virus

By Bill Gertz – *The Washington Times Friday, January 24, 2020"*

The Coronavirus pandemic overtook the borders, obviously, the deadly pandemic appeared at Wuhan where is near China's biological laboratory. Possibly, the Coronavirus should leak from the laboratories and China's government concealed to avoid the damages, actually, the investigation of the world, the Western can find the original virus. Its reason, China denies the US help. Unfortunately, the Novel coronavirus develops quickly spreading without control, now, the deadly pandemic spread to at least 25 countries, certainly, China received the dire consequence as a saying quotes" *the sword made in China that stabs Chinese*".

Since the Novel Coronavirus outbreaks, the death toll and infected people skyrocket, despite China has tried to reduce the massively numerous deaths and infections but the high technological communication debunked the concealment. China's communist regime panics but they have not enough money and a weak health system that can not deal with the massively infected population. **There are more than 500 million Chinese people unwelcome the deadly virus but the Coronavirus reaper visits the communist paradise and the massive population occupies more than 1/3 of the mainland locked down.** Nevertheless, the poor and low-income earners are the majority in the communist paradise, they have suffered difficulties while China's government has no social security facility to help. What can Chinese people do?

The Coronavirus pandemic deeply ruined China's economy and financial system, almost, the transport disabled while at least four provinces infected, more than 60 cities locked down and become ghost towns. The public transport suspended that affected 80.41 million people who can not use the bus or train to go somewhere. The supermarkets plus petrol stations were closed.

The other businesses as the tourism industry, hotels, restaurant chain deeply affected. China's Cusine Association reported 500 billion Yuan lost during Lunar New Year with 93% of restaurant shut down. Apple at Shanghai must close 42 stories *(in 2019, the revenue of Apple earned 17% from China market, so Apple intended to open more stories, now Apple must run away by coronavirus)*. Starbucks in Shanghai closed 2,000 shops, even Crown Casino and Resort in Macau shut two weeks *(certainly, Australian billionaire James Packer gets more bad news after China robbed $AU 4.2 billion by the bush law issued by Red Emperor Xi Jinping)*. The anti-communist experts warned about the bush law, the malicious business, the trade trap, the debt trap, the government trap, the global hegemonic ambition, the global economic terror of the largest communist country on the planet, however, the innocent leaders, naïve politicians and the profit lovers *(business)* ignored. Therefore, the Novel Coronavirus says nothing but the world strictly complies, actually, profit lovers as Apple, Starbucks, and other foreign companies see the coffin and cry but it is too late. The potential damages are inevitable. Certainly, China's economy paralyzed and damaged the foreign's profit lovers by Coronavirus.

Red Emperor Xi Jinping fears his throne risks, after the Coronavirus struck a month, eventually, on February 15, 2020, Xi Jinping has to visit a place at Wuhan with the blue face mask and the white gown, his visit becomes the propaganda to defuse the panic state in China, he added more 2,600 military medical personnel to Wuhan, total medical officials reached 4,000.

However, the action of the number one leader in China is too late, the death toll, infected people and the massive population locked down, the economy paralyzed and the Western countries order the travel ban the people from China plus evacuated their citizens out from the communist paradise. Valentine 2020 in China is abnormal, a romance affair fears the virus, so the people avoid to hug and kiss each other. Moreover, China cargo ships have fallen into a standstill status at the foreign ports because of the Coronavirus fear. The Western people also fear Chinese restaurants and Chinese groceries, it is the untold China phobia developed when the Coronavirus outbreaks in Wuhan and spreading throughout China's mainland, so the Western people don't know who is infected deadly virus.

It is the manner of the communist regime that faces the low tide of revolution or the disaster to carry out by the psychological warfare that applies to defuse the worst situation. Red Emperor Xi Jinping released the slogan:" **Race against the time- Fight the virus"** and he also said*:" The results are not hard-won progress made by all sides"*. Certainly, the Coronavirus can not hear and see the slogans and China's communist leader talks. Fighting against the invisible enemy without the ear- the eye is impossible by propaganda, so the slogans can not win the viral war, instead, the medicine, vaccine, and money are the potential weapons to expel the deadly pandemic. Moreover, Red Emperor Xi Jinping calls the nation to get back the business while the pandemic outbreak and the government locked down the huge areas. What can Chinese people do?. The Red Emperor Xi Jinping is nervous, he has no solution to stop the deadly pandemic, his panic attitude proved Xi Jinping loses confidence and lacks the leadership capacity./

32. THE MULTIPLE FACES OF DOCTOR ANTHONY FAUCI

Mr. Anthony Stephen Fauci was born on December 24, 1940, in Brooklyn, New York, Italian-American. Mr. Anthony Fauci attended Cornell Medical College, he is an infection expert, not a medical doctor, so the medical treatment shouldn't his field. Since 1984, Dr. Anthony Fauci has served as Director of the National Institute of Allergy and Infectious Disease. However, the head of Infectious diseases becomes the national and global figure when China's Communist Party attacks the world with a biological weapon. Therefore, the Director of the National Institute of Allergy and Infectious Disease conflicts with the effective treatment's medicine Hydroxychloroquine that is referred by President Donald Trump and 6,277 medical doctors of 30 countries support Hydroxychloroquine including Yale Epidemiology Professor, Dr, Harvey Risch who confirmed Hydroxychloroquine can save a hundred thousand lives. Doctor of infectious diseases Anthony Fauci distorted the career to politics, he ignores the lives of people. Nevertheless, the inappropriate attitude of Dr. Anthony Fauce matches the conspiracy of Democrats and China to rob the US government by the rigged election. The mail-in voting is the essential static of Democrats, so the role of Dr. Fauci is very important, he exploits the directorial position of the National Institute of Allergy and Infectious Disease to support the mail-in voting. Unfortunately, the US people recognized Doctor Anthony Fauce becomes DOGTOR (*) after his distorted medical career debunked, the conspiracy of mail-in voting failed.

The heartless plan of Democrats and Dogtor Anthony Fauci to use the lives of people into the political game with the propaganda of the left media companies that collapsed.

Moreover, the merciless attitude of Dogtor Anthony Fauci reflects the long-term relations with the Billionaire Bill Gates. In the record, Billionaire Bill Gates provided multiple million dollars with Dr. Fauci's researches, and Bill Gates invests the vaccine to make a trillion dollars to respond to the Chinese virus, so Bill Gates opposes Hydroxychloroquine despite he knew the effective medicine. Billionaire Bill Gates's interest influences Dogtor Anthony Fauci while the patients of the Chinese virus being endangered, initially, the patients do need effective medicine to save a life, but Bill Gates and Dogtor Anthony Fauci ignore and prevent. The merciless attitude of Dogtor Fauci and rogue billionaire Bill Gates creates public outrage, particularly, the families of the dead people raise questions about the conscience of Dogtor Anthony Fanci. Nevertheless, Dogtor Anthony Fauci seems to match the fake news and Democrats, they want Covid-19 perpetuates as longer as good, the malicious conspiracy focuses to destroy the US economy and taking down President Donald Trump, so the Coronavirus pandemic transmits to propaganda pandemic, the economic pandemic, and the election pandemic.

China's Communist Party, Democrats, and the left media have used the Chinese virus to support Sleepy Joe Biden who makes the journey to the White House. However, the US people show strong support ever in history to the patriotic President Donald Trump with the massive rallies throughout the country that worries Democrats, Joe Biden, and China. Recently, Dogtor Anthony Fauci changes the attitude because he knew the vaccine is underway to release and the people recognized the real face of billionaire Bill Gates who has a close relationship with President Barrack Obama, the medal of freedom was awarded by Barrack Obama to honor Bill Gates and his wife Melinda Gates that proved the comradeship. Moreover, Chinese virologist, Dr. Li Meng Yan defected, she provided the needed information about the original Chinese virus was made in a laboratory, it is the blatant evidence to confirm the Coronavirus is the biological weapon of China's Communist Party and the commander in viruses Xi Jinping. The witness Dr. Li Meng Yan destroyed the prestige of the World Health Organization transformer to the WORLD HELL ORGANIZATION after Director-General, Dogtor Tedros Adhanom Ghebreyesus drove the most medical organization to help China spreading pandemic worldwide with a biological weapon, so Dogtor Tedros Adhanom Ghebreyesus becomes the medical terrorist, the world needs to take Dogtor Tedros Adhanom Ghebreyesus to the International Court for genocide.

Dogtor Anthony Fauci of Infectious expert is not a medical doctor, but he is a Dogtor like Tedros Adhanom Ghebreyesus who is not a medical doctor but becomes the head of W.H.O. The rumor of **the original Coronavirus spreads about the deep conspiracy of President Barrack Obama, billionaire Bill Gates, and China's Communist Party's leader Xi Jinping**. In 2012, Billionaire Bill Gates financed a group of scientists at North Caroline University to study the Coronavirus and President Barrack Obama approved. After two years, the Coronavirus was completed, Bill Gates stopped the fund, and some Chinese researchers brought the Coronavirus to China. Facebook provided the details:" *Back in 2014, the Obama administration prohibited the U.S. from giving money to any laboratory, including in the U.S., that was fooling around with these viruses. Prohibited. Despite that, Dr. Fauci gave $3.7 million to the Wuhan laboratory. And then even after the State Department issued reports about how unsafe that laboratory was, and how suspicious they were in the way they were developing a virus that could be transmitted to humans, Obama never pulled that money.* "

The incident of Coronavius suspects the deep conspiracy of Xi Jinping (China), Billionaire Bill Gates, President Barrack Obama with the involvement of Dogtor Anthony Fauci. Nevertheless, President Barrack Obama destroyed the United States of America, within 8 years, from 2008 to 2016, the US shattered and became a colony of China. The people suspect **the biological warfare should plan by" Three Amigos" Xi Jinping, Bill Gates, and Barrack Obama** after the essential plan to control the world in 2025 failed. Nevertheless, Billionaire Bill Gates has a close relationship with China, on November 22, 2019, he planned to help China builds a nuclear reactor, therefore, the trade war to stop Bill Gates. Moreover, China gave Bill Gates the highest academic honors.

The heartless offense of China to attack the world with biological weapons and the domestic thugs in the US created economic damages, the death toll, and infected cases worldwide. Chinese virologist, Dr. Li Meng Yan unveiled the top secrets about Coronavirus, certainly, the perpetrators appall and the blatant evidence that forces China's Communist Party to face the genocide and the lawsuit applies to seek the massive compensation estimates a hundred trillion dollars, China fears.

Dogtor Anthony Fauci exploits the infectious diseases expert to help Democrats and Sleepy Joe Biden in the rigged election, he stabs in the back of the US people, and democracy, so President Donald Trump calls Dogtor Anthony Fauci is a DISASTER./.

Notes: (*) DOGTOR is the word of write to define an academic distorts the career by using the doctoral degree to serve individual favor and political purposes. The people need to know who is a doctor and a dogtor../.

33. CORONAVIRUS TRANSMITS TO DEMOCRATIC PANDEMIC

Chinese virus or Coronavirus pandemic purposes to destroy the US economy and the world, moreover, China's Communist Party also uses the deadly virus to kill Chinese people, it is the heartless plan to keep the ruthless regime remain and China's communist government should avoid the collapse when the major population plus hundred million jobless in the mainland rush to fight the pandemic. The Ape Emperor Xi Jinping and China's Communist Party have never cared about Chinese people, instead of the animal dynasty remains.

The COVID-19 develops flexibly into multiple purposes in the US and the allies, the Coronavirus pandemic transmits to the economic pandemic, the political pandemic, and the Democratic pandemic. The Chinese virus becomes the black magic of evil, the Satanic Democrats and China's Communist Party conspire to use the biological weapon to destroy the great economic achievements of the US patriotic President Donald Trump and take down the commander in chief, the Coronavirus also paves the way for China's actual henchman Joe Biden to win the election in 2020. Nevertheless, the Coronavirus pandemic also conspires the mail-in-voting, the malicious plan to rig the election that is the only way helping Joe Biden to win the election. Therefore, the Constitution has not accepted, the mail-in voting just deserves special circumstances, the US people voted in the two World Wars. Certainly, the Black Lives Matter, Antifa, and Democratic fan protested with riots since the death of felony George Floyd and recently, the lawmaker terrorist Nancy Pelosi arrived at a salon in San Francisco without a face mask, so the mail-in-voting failed.

Democrats, China, and the left media companies

maximally mislead the public and perpetuate the pandemic as longer as good. So domestic thugs are Democrats, the dishonest doctors *(the write defines Dogtor who exploits the doctoral degree to makes a profit or political purpose),* the left media have tried to prevent the effective medicine Hydroxychloroquine despite thousand medical doctors and the concerned medical professional confirmed Hydroxychloroquine save the life and reduce the death. The heartless Democrats, the left media, and the Dogtors couldn't conceal the truth when many patients recovered after treatment by Hydroxychloroquine (*). Nevertheless, the **WORLD HEALTH ORGANIZATION** turned to the **WORLD HELL ORGANIZATION** after W.H.O director-general Dogtor Tedros Adhanom Ghebreyesus appeared the actual henchman of China. The World Hell Organization misled medical information and cheated the medical advice that is led by socialism, so the global death toll reached more than 25 million and 600,000 died. The world rushes to find the vaccine, there are 76 countries with 168 researchers who have the trials and underway to apply. Therefore, the World Hell Organization propagates the vaccine will take at least two years while the reliable researchers in the United Kingdom, the US, Europe raise the new hope to eliminate the Chinese virus. **Do not listen to the World Hell Organization talk, let's watch what the W.H.O cheated.** Certainly, the US can not trust W.H.O, if the vaccine hands over to the World Hell Organization, China doesn't need to send the hacker stealing the vaccine, W.H.O helps China and the den of counterfeit will produce the vaccine of US or Europe and sell around the world. The US, Europe, and the world community don't trust the World Hell Organization, so they have not provided any information about the vaccine, and W.H.O knows nothing, certainly, the world boycotts W.H.O, it is the tool of China's Communist Party.

In the Vietnam War, the left media companies just released the casualties of the US soldiers, instead, they concealed the massive casualties of the Vietcong. The misled information discovered after the Vietnam War ended on April 30, 1975. It was too late, the last democratic land of the Vietnamese people lost. The left media waived 1,500,000 Vietcong troops killed plus 300,000 went missing. There was only the Tet offensive battle in 1968, Vietcong lost a hundred thousand troops, but the left media concealed.

Nowadays, the left media companies and Democrats have applied the Vietnam War, they just released the death toll and infection of Coronavirus in the US, India, Brazil, the United Kingdom, France, Italy, Spain, and others. Instead, the left media conceals and waives the massive death toll and infected population in China. Unfortunately, the phony propaganda debunked when high technological communication, social media, and multiple information sources publicized the truth. The fake news companies, Satanic party Democrats, and its dogtors can not cheat the US people. The obsolete psychological warfare completely collapsed after the **Centers for Disease Control (CDC) reported the death of Coronavirus is just 6% among 165,000 deaths**. During the Coronavirus pandemic outbreaking, Dogtor Anthony Fauci appalled the US people and White House, he based on the false report to guess shutting down the economy (*Anthony Fauci is the infectious experts, he is not a medical doctor, so he matches the Dogtor*). The US economy damaged by the medical fraudsters, possibly, Dogtor Anthony Fauci takes responsibility as W.H.O Dogtor Tedros Adhanom Ghebreyesus misled the medical information.

The Satanic party Democrats, the evil left media, and its dishonest Dogtors can not escape the responsibility. The

Coronavirus pandemic transmits to the Democratic Pandemic, the cheat reports, and the misleading public that aggravates the deposed candidate Joe Biden and Kamala Harris. The prestige of media companies like CNN, The New York Times, The Washington Post, and others plus in Australia like ABC, Channel Seven, Channel Nine, Channel Ten, SBS, BBC, the Guardian in the United Kingdom…all collapsed the people trust.

The Coronavirus death toll is just 6%, it is the worst medical cheat and the garbage media propagates. Initially, the Democratic Dogtors, Health officials, and the insurance companies must take responsibility. They must refund the medical bill to the government and the dishonest persons will face criminal charges, certainly, the medical license should be revoked plus the heavy fines, and the left media companies must share the crimes, the Justice Department can prosecute Democrats, the murders by medical deception to be upgraded. Once again, Democrats convict the crime opposing human rights. They have exploited the people's lives for political purposes and help China destroying the US economy.

The Satanic party Democrats can not change the loss of Joe Biden, the Coronavirus pandemic transmits to Democratic pandemic hits back the Donkey Party. The election day comes closer, but Democrats receive more worst news, the **Centers for Disease Control (CDC)** advises the states to prepare the vaccine that will be available on November 1st 2020. The vaccine will have before the election day November 3, 2020. The economy enhances, the Dow Jones rises to 29,100 (*higher than before Coronavirus*), S & P increases to 3,580. The Chinese virus vaccine is going to stop the pandemic and the US people will eliminate the Democratic pandemic on November 3, 2020./.

NOTES (*)

In Australia, Labor Premier of Victoria state Daniel Andrews signed one Belt and One Road with China, he becomes an actual henchman of China's Communist Party. The Victoria state (*capital city Melbourne*) becomes the hottest spot of COVID-19 in the second wave, its state refuses using Hydroxychloroquine so the death toll rose. The Australian Labor Party and Democratic Party in the US are the siblings../.

34. TECHNICAL MEDIA BUSINESS TERRORIZES FREE SPEECH

The businesses, companies, clubs including political parties must comply with the law and the code practice that applies for every job, function, and field. Therefore, the dishonest component can exploit the career to make a profit or political purposes, the democratic countries deserve the law to punish the wrongdoers.

The left media companies have breached the law since the Cold War, particularly the Vietnam War, the fake news, concealment, mixed the truth and fake news, false polls created the national damages, the election rigged that causes the social disorder. The fake news released that matches the criminal. However, Western lawmakers have not issued the law while the high level of crimes has attacked free speech, abused the democracy and Constitution. Certainly, free speech is not free-fake news, free false polls, free misleading the public, free-propaganda, free distortion of truth, and free terror of the public.

The communication companies like Facebook, Google, Twitter, and others have exploited technical communication to censor free speech, it is the crime opposing democracy. A censor is a form of media terror, the rogue communication businesses have terrorized the free speech and the users. Certainly, the US government can not deserve the space for self-promotion's kingmaker. Nevertheless, technical communication companies are not media but they have practiced the businesses are like the state media's department in China, Vietnam, Cuba, North Korea. The arrogant CEOs like Mark Zuckerberg who ignores the law and free speech, instead, Facebook declares war with the US government. The left stance conducts Mark Zuckerberg opposes the national interest, free speech, and targets the US commander in chief Donald Trump who cracked down on the global economic terror of China and fighting against the culprit of Coronavirus. Moreover, Facebook has become the propaganda firm of China, CEO Mark Zuckerberg has helped China's Communist Party to conceal the Coronavirus and mislead the public, so between April and June 2020, Facebook took down at least 7,000,000 posts linking to the information about the Chinese virus, Facebook also deleted the posts of the US government about the pandemic. Recently, Mark Zuckerberg threatens to ban Australian users if the government requires to pay for the news. Certainly, Facebook terrorizes Australian users as China terrorizes Australia's economy after the government proposed an independent inquiry about Coronavirus. On the other hand, Facebook becomes the enemy of users and the foe of free speech.

The previous US presidents deserved too much power and priority for the left media companies, so the left media overrode the career, they have terrorized free speech and democracy. Therefore, President Donald Trump reforms the mainstream media and returning free speech to the US people. The appropriate action of President Donald Trump is like the strong stuff of pesticides, all kinds of viral media react physically before falling into the motionless state.

The executive order of President Donald Trump to social media radically has affected the thug of people, the foe of the public, so Facebook, Google, Twitter filed a lawsuit against the US President Donald Trump, they sophisticate about the executive order curtails and chill constitutionally protected speech during the presidential election. Therefore, Facebook, Google, and Twitter deleted the information about the human rights violation of China, Vietnam. Certainly, those technical communication companies above have practiced the businesses that are led by socialism, they transform free speech to serve China's communist regime. Before Huawei filed the lawsuit against the executive order to ban the telecommunication company owned by the People's Liberation Army, the well-known cyber spy unit 61389 threatens the national security of the US and the world community. Therefore, Huawei and the cluster of companies linking China that disabled, the legal action was nothing, instead, the lawyers were happy with the legal fees. Once again, on Monday 27, 2020, Tik Tok filed the lawsuit to block the executive order of President Donald Trump, certainly, the court has no power to nullify the order of the US President including the Congress of Nancy Pelosi. However, the Tik Tok ban raises the concern of Mark Zuckerberg, because Facebook links to China's communication company. On July 24, 2019, the Federal Trade Commission fined Facebook $US 5 billion that caused privacy violations. TikTok also filed a lawsuit against the executive order of President Donald Trump, China's company will do nothing to stop the order. The legal actions of Facebook, Google, Twitter, Huawei, and Tik Tok are like an egg-throwing stone wall.

CEO Mark Zuckerberg ignores the law and free speech,

so Facebook must pay the dire consequences. Initially, Facebook lost more than 160 major companies advertising that cost billion of US dollars. The advertising plunge continues to pursue Facebook, on August 28, 2020, Apple blocked a Facebook app update that aggravates the future of Facebook, possibly, the CEO Tim Cook of Apple recognizes Facebook being faced the trouble. Recently, on September 2nd, 2020, Facebook has suspended the operation in Russia that deals with the election. Nevertheless, the US government and the White House's administration, and President Donald Trump can file the lawsuit against the rogue technical communication companies that have exploited the technological devices to gag the free speech, breaching the democracy, and terrorize the users. The serious crimes that conflict with the democratic valuation and constitution will apply to force Facebook, Google, Twitter, and others including the media companies must respect the law and people. Those media companies and technical communication companies will face heavy charges if the justice is found guilty, moreover, the presidential order represents the national interest but the businesses focus the profit. Most companies fear license revocation, so Facebook, Google, and others should lose the license, it is a strong message sending to the arrogant CEOs./.

35. THE FREE SPEECH IS NOT FREE PROPAGANDA AND RELEASING THE FAKE NEWS

The democratic country respects free speech and permits the demonstration but anything must accord to the law. Whoever exploits free speech for propaganda as exciting the riot, terrorism, social hatred, and the protest plus the violence, they break the law. Someone distorted the free speech to defame, they would face legal action.

The left media has exploited the free speech from the Cold War, actually, the Vietnam War was among the hottest spot in the Cold War. The left media's journalists and companies as CNN, The New York Times, The Washington Post…in Australia had ABC, Channel Seven. The media companies distorted the communication to propagate for Vietcong, it was an early terror after the Second World War. The left media biased the news and has misled the public, now the toxic propaganda of the Vietnam War still remains in Western society. The left media's tactic could recognize by the forms below:

-Releasing the fake news

-The Fabricated story

-Publishing the haft true and half lie.

-Mixing between the true and false

-Concealment the truth.

The left media's formula is 3 F (3 Frauds)=False poll+Fake news+Fabricated story. On the other hand, the left media in Western performs the career as a communist's propaganda, but they disguise under free speech. The Golden time of the lies and cheat in the Vietnam War is no longer exists after Vietcong claimed the unpredictable victory on April 30, 1975. The real face of the inhumane regime of Vietcong and the genocide of Ho Chi Minh couldn't hide anymore. Therefore the bullshit media has tried to survive while the people have no trust **the thug of people and the enemy of communication**.

The US presidential election marks the worst time of the left media. President Donald Trump is the first US president to unmask the evil media, the fake news seals the truth could not deceive the public, so the garbage media companies have lost the people support plus the advertising. **The left media is the domestic thug attacks the free speech and national interest**, the journalists without patriotic concern to burn themselves by the biased article and the untrue reports.

As the arrogant attitude, the left media promotes themselves as the most powerful component in the Western countries, they corner the public, actually the election, the biased reports and articles conduct the vote, so the left media makes the profit in the elections from federal, state and local government. Therefore, the US presidential election in 2016 overturned, the left media's hated candidate Donald Trump, they often released fake news, fabricated stories, and false polls confirmed Hillary Clinton wins the election, some media companies predicted Hillary advanced Donald Trump 12 points. Ultimately, the outcome unmasked the cheat of the left media, almost, the propaganda completely failed, President Donald Trump transformed the first US female president Hillary Clinton's dream into a nightmare. Certainly, the left media companies plus the bullshit Journalist, the garbage T.V hosts lost the credit, some left media icons to be sacked but the media companies couldn't restore the prestige, the damage control takes a long time to mend. Therefore, the garbage reporters, bullshit T.V hosts are shameless, they still appear in the media, the disgraced clowns may find an asshole to hide the ugly faces. Unfortunately, their faces are thick as crocodile's skin. The people don't want to see the liars anymore, so the media companies lose more readers and viewers.

The people are no longer to trust the left media after many decades lied and misled the public. Nevertheless, technologic communication has not allowed the left media to poison the propaganda, so every time when an article publishes from the left media like the New York Times, the readers doubt the truth level.

The left media becomes the domestic thug, they snub the people, insult the free speech, and damage the mainstream. Moreover, social media and impartial information are helpful than the left media, actually the television. On the other hand, the left media has been defeated by the people boycott and the advertising declined that cause of the bad time for telling a lie media. President Donald Trump twittered*:" The fake news media is the opposition party. It is very bad for our great country..but we are winning"*.

The democratic government may have the law to prevent the media exploit free speech for propaganda, if a media company releases fake news or fabricated the story, they will be fined or revoked the license. It is a possible tactic to bring the media back in the right direction./.

36. HOW COULD THE SOUTH VIETNAM LOSE WITHIN 55 DAYS? AND THE OBAMA'S LESSON

The Army of Republic Vietnam (ARVN) was considered the strongest force in South East Asia, it was founded in 1954, after Geneva Convention signed by Vietnam communists plus the master Soviet Union, China with France delegation. According to the convention confirmed, Vietnam divided into two parts: North Vietnam dominated by the dictatorial communist regime, and South Vietnam managed by the democratic government. However, after the Geneva convention, the North Vietnamese communist obeyed the order from their great master Soviet Union and China, so the Vietnam war was created by the communist's ambition. The propaganda title to be raised by the Vietnamese communist party was:" fighting against American empire" while the US and allies had not come to help South Vietnam yet, nevertheless, since May 1959, the Vietnamese communist party set up a special task force, code 559, then congregated 100,000 laborers repaired the abandoned road linking to 3 nations Vietnam, Laos, and Cambodia, it was Ho Chi Minh trails, the main transportation of international communist bloc to carry multiple infantry divisions, armor units (the sorts of the tank such as T-54, PT-76 Russia built), the heavy artillery units (level regiment used missile 122, 107, howitzer 130 and late had anti-aircraft missile SA-7, SA-10).

The ARVN had grown up in the war that fought against the international communist bloc, its army had more than 1,000,000 soldiers being into the 4 Army Corps with the good fight units below:

1- The 11 infantry divisions dispensed into the territories:

-The First Army Corps: 1, 2, and 3 division.

-The Second Army Corps: 22 and 23 division.

-The Third Army Corps: 5, 18, and 25 division.

-The Fourth Army Corps: 7, 9, 21 division.

2- The well general reserved units:

-Airborne division,

-Marine corps division,

-The brigade of 81 special airborne rangers, each army corps had at least a ranger regiment and a special force camp, actually at central Vietnam, there were many Ranger regiments confronted the invaded divisions from the North.

3- The regional force located in the province:

– Every province had many regional battalions and independent companies.

– Every village had at least one village, a soldier platoon.

4- Air force: every army corps has one air force division located at the military airports.

5- The armor had a tank brigade for each army corps with tank M-41, M-113 and later had model M-48 provided by the US.

-Navy had strong coast guard ships and the river had fighting boats.

6-The artillery: each division has an artillery battalion with the howitzer 105, 155, and 175, supporting the battlefields into the territory.

Exclusive of the civilian self-defense force for every hamlet and region in the city, the numerous fighters reached multiple million, mostly the weapon using from the second world war as the carbine, Garant, Thompson...but they could fight well and self-defend the territory.

The ARVN defeated the Vietnam communist invaded from Ho Chi Minh trails into the well-known battlefields as

Binh Long, Quang Tri…actually in the Tet offensive 1968, during the ARVN had about 30 % of military personnel being on holiday, the weapon was not updated, mostly the from the second world war, meanwhile, communist used A.K 47, B-40… However, the ARVN pushed out the numerous troopers from the well fighting North communist divisions and local guerillas. The communist had been disabled with more than 100,000 troopers killed. However, in March 1975, it was just 55 days, the ARVN lost, it was incredible. South Vietnam loss that was not caused by:

-The ARVN had not potential fighting: they still had enough ammunition at least a year, despite the president Nguyen Van Thieu raised the fake lacking of ammunition after the Paris treaty signed on January 27, 1973. After Vietnam War ended, communists took the South Vietnam arsenal to fight with Khmer Rouge for 4 years, however, they were still in stores and the arsenals exploded at Long Binh, and somewhere else proved the ARVN had enough condition to fight. Some rumors talked about the lacking of ammunition that wasn't right, the question to be raised here:" why didn't president Nguyen Van Thieu sell 16 tons of solid gold from national treasure for buying the weapons? Therefore, he left over for the communist after fled to Taiwan and later resettled in the U.K, he then died in the US in September 2000.

-The key ally the US stopped supporting, it wasn't true, because, in Saigon, a US D.A.O (Defense Attaché Office) was still there until the last president, a Vietcong penetrated, General Duong Van Minh expelled within 24 hours. On the other hand, the US didn't know president Nguyen Van Thieu, who was also a commander in chief ordered the withdrawal at the 1st Army Corps. Lieutenant General Dang Van Quang revealed before passing away: The US didn't want to accept General Quang resettled a new life in the U.S, because he didn't report about the withdrawal orders of president Thieu, so General Quang had to live in Canada and he just came to US few years before deceased.

Therefore, president Nguyen Van Thieu acted like a double agent, he destroyed the 1st Army Corps by the unclear and unmilitary orders, he also dispensed the good fight Airborne division and Marine Corps, all disabled. So his destructive orders helped Vietcong occupied south Vietnam's territory so quickly, plus the surrender order of General Duong Van Minh on April 30, 1975, if not, the Vietcong had faced the potential damages as the Tet offensive 1968.

In the world military history, there is no such strong army as South Vietnam lost within 55 days, there is not any strong army that survives if the highest commander wants to disband and surrender. The Vietnamese communist didn't win the war as they propagandized, even though the Ameri-Cong didn't win the war as a book title of author Roger Canfield…but south Vietnam lost by president Nguyen Van Thieu, now after 39 years, end of the Vietnam war, people have recognized president Thieu who is the Vietnamese's national criminal, he couldn't escape the history judgment.

President Nguyen Van Thieu's withdrawal orders cost 160,000 lives, the bodies spread on the road, that named the Horrible Highway. The surrender order of Duong Van Minh on April 30, 1975, caused 800,000 ARVN and Public servant jailed by the drying blood bath hidden under the nice title "re-education", then the political prisoners being worst treatment: bad living condition, starvation, sickness without treatment, execution, torture, forced hard labor, and there were more than 165,000 killed in the re-education camp.

There is nobody who could know as well as the Vietnamese, actually the soldier of ARVN, I wrote the cause of South Vietnam lost in my book number 2″ GOOD EVENING VIETNAM", I believe someone, actually the foreigners could find the genuine document there.

South Vietnam lost on April 30, 1975, that is a circumstance of the 44th US president Barack Obama, his action is like the president Nguyen Van Thieu in the Vietnam War. In 8 years, President Barack Obama applies the brainwash policy to the US people, he destroyed the army by consent homosexuality and he gave the withdrawal order in Iraq that created convenience for the extreme Muslim, so the Islamic State founded. Moreover, as the accusation of Donald Trump in the presidential campaign and Wikileaks, President Barack Obama provided the finance and Hillary helped the weapon for ISIS, all money comes from the taxpayer. It contradicts the US policy, while Obama helped ISIS, but he appealed to the UN an ally fighting against ISIS. How could the US lawmakers ignore and the constitution kept quiet? Obama's circumstance is like the Ho Chi Minh, he secretly invited the French returning by the Sainteny treaty at La Fontainbleau on June 3, 1946, but when the French army landed on the Vietnam shore, Ho Chi Minh appealed to the national resistant fighting against the colonial French.

In 8 years the US was ruled by Obama, the US army is weak, he allowed homosexuality in the armed force that destroyed the most potential army in the world. The behavior of Obama is like South Vietnam's President Nguyen Van

Thieu, but luckily the US has a strong constitution, the army, police force are independent despite the president is the commander in chief, so president Barack Obama couldn't destroy the country as the South Vietnam President Nguyen Van Thieu did. However his top advisor is Valerie Jarred, the hardcore of communists in the US and the other 6 key advisors are Muslim, so the US received the damage after 8 years, if not the US would collapse as the South Vietnam government./.

37. VIETCONG PRIME MINISTER NGUYEN XUAN PHUC VISITS USA

Statement from the Press Secretary releases Vietcong Prime Minister Nguyen Xuan Phuc will come to the U.S On May 31, 2017. The Vietnamese community in the U.S prepares to protest against a high profile of inhumane regime, the cause of poverty, human rights violation.

In the passage of time, Hồ Chí Minh, an actual hand of the Global Communist Bloc, founded the communist party on February 3, 1930. The Vietnam Communist party has the Vietnamese skin but the organ is communist, hence this communist super gang appeared in Vietnam, the bloodshed has occurred, actually, since the Geneva conference signed on July 20, 1954, that divided the North and South Vietnam by the conspiracy of French and Global Communist Bloc. In this period, the communist had lost the potential Korean war, so they had to leave South Vietnam for the nationalist with the democratic government from 1954 to 1975.

After the Geneva treaty, North Vietnam was ruled by the communist regime, it was so-called the Democratic Republic of Vietnam. The land-reform campaign massacred more than 200,000 people, imprisoned a million and its regime pauperized North Vietnamese people for 20 years. Vietcong is the genocide, on May 19, 2013, the Polka newspaper of Poland released a list of the most massacre in the 20th century, and Hồ Chí Minh killed 1,700,000 people.

However, Vietcong also was an early terrorist as Al Qaeda and ISIS today, but the US and the world had no mention about it, because Vietcong killed their people, therefore Vietcong regime has never changed the terrorism on Vietnamese people, and they badly violates the human rights at the moment.

The loss of South Vietnam on April 30, 1975, and Vietcong a domestic Conqueror imposed the barbarous policy on South Vietnamese people, a high ranking cadre Nguyen Ho told his comrades in Saigon: "their houses, we occupy- their wives, we take- their children, we enslave".

After Vietcong invaded South Vietnam, obviously they centralized 800, 000 members of ARVN and public servants into the hell of re-education camp. They took revenge by dried bloodbath with the worst behaviors as execution, starvation, forced laborer, torture, illness without medicine to kill 165, 000 people. Moreover, Vietcong robbed the asset of South Vietnamese people and the regime causes more than 1 million Vietnamese people to flee for freedom and became refugees in democratic countries, including the U.S. The Vietcong is the same as Pol Pot, but the tyranny regime still remains because they are malice, pretending to open the door, cheating the western countries by an ugly economic pattern "socialism leads the free market" to save their regime after Soviet Union collapsed and also the tricky renovation policy that created about 300 millionaires and billionaires worth in US dollar, all monies have made from the corruption and the foreign aid. The Vietnam regime is the same as North Korea, Pyongyang threatens neighbor countries by the nuclear ballistic missile test and Hanoi provided sand for the great master China to build the artificial islands within the disputed waters and unofficially offers Vietnam's waters as the maritime springboard for China in order to raise the tension in the region and challenging the US.

Prime Minister Nguyen Xuan Phuc was selected by the communist party, not by people's vote, so he doesn't represent the Vietnamese people. Moreover, the position of Nguyen Xuan Phuc is just a butler of a communist party, indeed the power being held by Secretary-General Nguyen Phu Trong. The appearance of a Vietcong high profile Nguyen Xuan Phuc in the US digs up the deep sorrow of million victims, the Vietnamese refugees in the US, and also 58,000 US soldiers sacrificed in Vietnam War plus multi-million Vietnam veterans and their families. Nguyen Xuan Phuc, a member of the Vietcong super gang, an early terrorist organization, and human rights violation./.

38. VIETCONG REBUILT CU CHI TUNNEL FOR MAKING MONEY AND CHEATING THE TOURIST

After winning the war, Vietcong promoted Củ Chi Tunnel as the outstanding underground military base. Therefore, do not listen to the communist talk, let's watch and review what they did. As the experience, whoever mentions about the communist, let's imagine" when a communist is born, obviously the midwife sees the mouth". The so-called Củ Chi Tunnel is the worse cheat of Vietcong, but it could deceive the foreign tourist, even the Vietnam people who have never lived in Củ Chi region, they could be the victims of the tricky propaganda. However, the truth defeats the lie, the question about Củ Chi Tunnel has the answer and testimony from the witnesses.

The Củ Chi tunnel is the underground network that combined many parts as the commanding station, hospital, stores, dwelling for guerrilla and other facilities. Củ Chi Tunnel belongs to the Củ Chi district, outskirt of Saigon, the capital of South Vietnam. In the Tet offensive 1968, Củ Chi was a base of Vietcong.

The US and South Vietnam Army recognized it was a den of Vietcong, so few operations launched as Operation Cedar Falls, actually, Operation Crimp began on January 7, 1966, with B-52 dropped 30 tons bomb with high explosive, mostly the tunnels collapsed. The US army had 8,000 troops from the US 1st Infantry Division, 173rd Airborne Brigade Combat Team, and 1st Battalion of Royal Australian Regiment. In a tactic region as Củ Chi, Vietcong couldn't carry out the biggest project during the war, actually, the South Vietnam army controlled the territory and the allies helped with the air force, artillery supported. If Vietcong had not the interior activities being laid inside the South Vietnam government, so Vietcong couldn't perform the Củ Chi Tunnel.

Major Lê Xuân Sơn, chief district Củ Chi who flagged

Vietcong digging the tunnel. Major Lê Xuân Sơn was born in North Vietnam, the family fled to the South after the Geneva treaty signed on July 20, 1954. Obviously, his family resettled at Bình Chính, a suburb of Saigon. In 1966 he graduated from the Army Academy at Dalat. His first career was as the reconnaissance company commander of infantry division label 25. The company located at the boundary of Cambodia and Vietnam, its region was the intersection of smuggling, including drugs. He met a woman named Mười An, a financial cadre of Vietcong at the eastern provinces in South Vietnam, she held a smuggling ring to supply the food, medical, and other needs to the Vietcong secret bases in the area. Miss Mười An offered her daughter named Vàng for Lê Xuân Sơn, despite she married with 2 children. Miss Mười An also established contact with Lieutenant General Đỗ Cao Trí, commander in chief of the Third Army Corps, so Lê Xuân Sơn quickly promoted, it just was in a short time, he became Major and also transferred to the Củ Chi district. The role of Miss Mười An was important, so Mr. Stephen Young suspected. In the book" Khúc Quanh Định Mệnh" written by author Lê Hữu Cương, pre-chief Củ Chi district, he graduated from course 16th of Army Academy, on page 282 confirmed Miss Mười An was a mogul of smuggling between the boundary of Cambodia and Vietnam.

During the period in charge of the Củ Chi district, Major Lê Xuân Sơn colluded with Vietcong in the region, so the Củ Chi tunnel carried out easily. At night, Major Lê Xuân Sơn ordered the regional force to stay away from the digging area, then Vietcong could dig the tunnel safely. When the day breaks, Major Lê Xuân Sơn ordered the engineer corps took the soil away to make the road.

After Vietcong won the unpredictable war on April 30, 1975, Major Lê Xuân Sơn spent a short time in the re-education then he came back Củ Chi with the asset while the most ARVN members were castigated and imprisoned long term. In 1994 Major Lê Xuân Sơn resettled in the US under the Orderly Departure Program (ODP), he lived in San Diego. The witnesses and Củ Chi residents alleged about the tunnel, at last, Major Lê Xuân Sơn came back Vietnam and he founded a website" http://www. Haingoaiphiemdam.com" in Vietnam, he used many ten names as Nghiêm Võ, Nguyễn Trọng Hoàn, Lê Vũ, Nguyễn Tiến Đạt, Lính Dù, Đồ Biển, Zuyên Hồng Trần.... Major Lê Xuân Sơn published the fake news, created stories, the target aims to the anti-communist activists overseas.

Vietcong strongly pushes the propaganda of the Củ Chi Tunnel after the Vietnam War for making money and attracting foreign terrorists, including the Vietnam people. However, Marine Corps Colonel Tôn Thất Soạn who was high commander of multiple battalions, his last position was chief of Hậu Nghĩa province. He spent 13 years in the re-education camp after South Vietnam lost, now he lives in Iowa City (US).

Former Marine Corps Colonel Tôn Thất Soạn shared the experience about Củ Chi Tunnel to everyone on the Hậu Nghĩa, Special Magazine published in 1999. The most linking tunnels disabled in the rainy season and tiger snakes, insects, scorpions fled to tunnels. Many Vietcong guerrillas were killed by the tiger snake, the most Vietcong being struck by skin diseases. In the war, a high-ranking cadre Võ Văn Kiệt hid in Củ Chi Tunnel in few months, at last, he moved to Cambodia territory because of the worse living condition (Võ

Văn Kiệt who recruited the South Vietnam girls then sending to the North for sexual service for Hồ Chí Minh and his comrades, he did a good job so Mr. Võ Văn Kiệt was promoted the Prime Minister from August 1991 to September 25, 1997, he was a billionaire too). Moreover, the tunnels had no ventilator system, so the air was a problem, actually, the cooking could cause suffocation.

Marine Corps Colonel Tôn Thất Soạn released the truth about Củ Chi Tunnel: from the period of US Major General Weyan commanded Division 25, the most Vietcong secret bases as Đồng Dù, Củ Chi, Hố Bò were paralyzed by multiple sorts of artillery 105, 155, 175 and bombarded by B.52. A rumor told the US Army released a kind of Africa ants that could bite the guerrilla in the tunnels.

In January 1972 Lieutenant General Weyan (former commander of Division 25), was in charge as the head advisor of the Third Army Corps. He launched the campaign Rom Plow with heavy 12 machinery vehicles, the most tunnels to be eradicated and destroyed. Therefore, after the Vietnam War ended, Vietcong rebuilt the Củ Chi Tunnel that aims to make a profit and cheat the tourist and also propaganda../.

39. VIETCONG AND EXTREMIST HAVE EXPLOITED THE HUMAN BEING IN TERRORISM

In the Korean War, the China communist replaced the lacking weapon with the **human wave tactic**, therefore the inhumane idea devised by Chairman Mao Tse Tung that barbecued a million troop of the People's Liberation Army. This tactic also repeated in the Điện Biên Phủ's battlefield, the puppet General Võ Nguyên Giáp pushed 10 thousand lives for the victory over colonial France, instead, the French loser lost a thousand soldiers and in the Vietnam War, Vietcong lost 1,500,000 troops plus 300,000 missings but the Vietnam communist's government has not sought the missing troops instead Hanoi regime is keen to find the US soldiers missing in the action for money, it is the real face of Vietcong, the **Karl Marx pupil's character is throwing the lemon skin after emptied juice**. In the Western, the innocent people must learn the lesson of 300,000 troops missing.

In the US election 2008 and 20012, black candidate Barrack Obama succeeded the Racial Shield tactic in the White House race, the black skin's shield exploited the racist's accusation that stopped the attacks of Republic candidates John Mc Cain and Mitt Romney, so the debates were unfair. In the US election 2016, Hillary Clinton applied the **Woman Shield tactic** by using the women in the smear campaign, but Hillary Clinton failed and she lost the election.

However, the Human being tactic is not obsolete with terrorism, in the record it applied from the Vietnam War but the left media concealed about Vietcong exploited the children and women for the human shield. The psychological warfare also developed maximum in the Western, actually, the countries sent the army to South Vietnam to prevention the communist wave in South East Asia. The domestic thuggeries in Western covered the face under the free speech, those are the left media companies currently published and broadcast the biased articles, the fake news to mislead and poison the public. The communication has been distorted to propaganda, that cause of the mainstream received the damage control and losing the people's trust.

The left media became the actual tool of Vietcong in the Vietnam War, the fabricated stories lied the allies army killed innocent children, women, and innocent civilians and the toxic propaganda has poisoned the Western people, the public has been misled long term. In Vietnam War, Vietcong exploited the children and women for the terror's mission. In this period, Hồ Chí Minh awarded two heroic titles were" **The Victorious Knight**" for whoever killed at least 5 soldiers of South Vietnam and" The **Killing American Knight**" which honored whoever killed at least 5 US soldiers. At Huế province, a 12 year- old teen guerilla Nguyễn Văn Hòa, the nickname is Cu (Vietnamese means Penis), he born at Nguyên Thủy village, Hương Thủy District, the teen terrorist has honored both knight titles of Hồ Chí Minh. The Mỹ Lai village was among the stronghold of Vietcong in the Fifth Inter-regions consisted the provinces were Quảng Nam, Quảng Ngãi, Bình Định, and Phú Yên, so the **Mỹ Lai village was a place of the Knight's title of Hồ Chí Minh in Vietnam War, everyone in Mỹ Lai, including children and women could kill South Vietnam and the US soldier. After the Vietnam War ended on April 30, 1975, the Mỹ Lai village had many heroes and the villagers became communist government officials. The massive massacre at Huế in Tết Offensive 1968 to be concealed by the Western left media, although the victims were up to 7,200 people as the Tiananmen Square in China 1989, therefore, they often repeated the Mỹ Lai impact as the disgraced propaganda.**

Nowadays, the Islamic extremist applies the human tactic, mostly the children and women have been favored into the terrorism, including the suicide mission. The Western countries ignore the role of children and women in the anti-terrorism, but the teenagers and women could carry out the terror.

Terrorism develops the mind commands the action, **so**

psychological warfare is the key to terrorism. In Vietnam War, the Vietcong cadres propagated to the low or illiterate peasant into the terror mission, so the guerrilla came from the rural region. In the terror war, the extremists are the bigots, the radical clerics propagate the hatred to the Muslim adherent at the offshore community, the mosque, actually the youth.

The anti-terrorist could eradicate from the root, the hunting terrorist after the bloodshed is negative anti-terrorist. The national security, intelligence agencies could open the battlefield right on the bases where are the Muslim community and the mosque. The Extremist always hides in the community and the mosque. Let's stop the religious hatred's propaganda and having the toughest law to whoever exploits the religion of terror.

The Western government seems negligent in the human tactic of terror, actually, the woman and young people including the teenager should be recruited the terrorist. In the Western countries, the Allah adherent's family could send their children returning to the den of terror in the Middle East for study but some states granted the money support the child under the social beneficiaries. The young Muslim could access easily the hated propaganda from the bigots, extreme clerics and become the terrorist. The government has to control the Muslim families sent the children to the homeland, they are the seeds of terror./.

40. CHINA HAS BECOME THE GLOBAL ENEMY FROM COLD WAR

After the Second World War, the Cold War continued, China and Soviet-Union were the perpetrators. The hot spots were North Korea, West-East Germany, actually, theZ Vietnam War became the crucial battle. South Vietnam's government, actually the Army of the Republic of Vietnam (ARVN) bravely fought against totally Global Communist Bloc and later, the US with its allies were South Korea, the Philippines, Australia, Thailand, and Taiwan came to South Vietnam to help its territory to fight against the global communist while the Global Communist Bloc was escalating, actually, China and the Soviet Union were the key's support the weapon, advisers to command the war, and China sent the troops to North Vietnam. The US and allies came and helped South Vietnam to prevent the spread of communism in the region if not, the Marxism-Leninist wave would invade the neighboring countries including Australia, New Zealand. Vietcong or North Vietnam's communist was the actual vanguard of the Global Communist Bloc, Hồ Chí Minh, and its party propagated the fighting against the American, indeed, Hồ Chí Minh served for his great master China and Soviet-Union. On the other hand, Hồ Chí Minh and its communist gang exploited the blood of Vietnamese people to serve the Global Communist Bloc. Vietcong also was an early terror organization like Al Qaeda, the Islamic State, and others. In the Vietnam War, Vietcong shelled into the crowded population's area, Vietcong didn't discriminate the schools, churches (*on March 9, 1974, Vietcong shelled by mortar 82 mm into Song Phú's Primary School at Cai Lậy District, Định Tường province, 32 students killed and 55 injured*). Vietcong killed Vietnamese people by barbarous methods: using the machete beheaded, broke the skull with a sledgehammer. Therefore, the left media, the left parties just slammed the US troop and allies and concealed the cruelty of the Vietcong.

Instead, they have never accused China, Soviet-Union and totally Global Communist Bloc poured the weapon and military equipment to the Hanoi regime. Certainly, the People's Army of Vietnam (*Vietcong troop*) couldn't fight with the machete, hammer, and the bamboo's sharp cutting head. Instead, North Vietnam troop (or Vietcong) used the rifle AK 47, CKC, B-40, B-41, Rocket 107 mm, Missile 122 mm, machine gun 12.7 mmm, mortar 61 mm, mortar 82 mm, anti-aircraft missile SA-7, SA-10, artillery 130 mm, Tank T-54, Tank-PT 76 (*Soviet-Union built*).

China grew as a Nazi, so Australian Representative Andrew Hastie, the chairman of the Intelligence Committee in parliament house, compares China is like the Nazis. Certainly, China slams and some innocent politicians plus the politicians or high profiles in Australia should have the business or working for China as former Prime Minister Paul Keating (*he is an advisor of Development Bank of China*), Senator Penny Wong to attack MP Andrew Hastie.

After the Second World War, the global hegemonic ambition has urged China to spread the han*d everywhere.* Actually, China was the great master of the Vietcong *(Vietnam Communist Party)*. Responding to the expansion of communism in Asia, China controlled Vietnam Communist Party from the Điện Biên Phủ's battle. Hồ Chí Minh promoted his actual hand was Võ Nguyên Giáp to Four Stars General, Ho explained": *Who defeats a general, who would be a general",* the commander was not a boxer in the arena. The Four Stars General Võ Nguyên Giáp had never attended a military academy, but he commanded the most well-known battle at Điện Biên Phủ. It was a farce, therefore, it happened and the left media plus the innocent and illiterate historians praise the Four Stars General Võ Nguyên Giáp as the potential commander, it is the garbage history of the biased historians. Indeed, the untrained Four Stars General Võ Nguyên Giápb was a puppet, Mao Tse Tung sent the Chinese Military Advisory Group led by General Wei Guoqing, General Chen Geng was as Scholar General and 281 military expert officers held the commanding of Hồ Chí Minh's people army. The People's Army of Vietnam became the human-robot, the commanders were China plus the inhumane tactic called" **the Human wave**" barbecued more than tens of thousands of Vietcong troops in Điện Biên Phủ's battle while France lost about a thousand soldiers. The human wave tactic caused a million troops of the People's Liberation soldiers killed in the Korean War and in the Vietnam War, Four Stars General Võ Nguyên Giáp and Văn Tiến Dũng exchanged the unpredictable victory on April 30, 1975, by more than 1,500,000 troops and 300,000 missings.

The left media and the Vietcong's supporters like Jane Fonda (*Hanoi Jane*), Joe Biden, Bill-Hillary Clinton, and the others couldn't lie to the public, actually, the victims of Vietcong. Therefore, they have never repented and trying to protect the wrongdoings as Ken Burns and Lynn Novick lied to the public, Vietnamese people, Vietnam veterans the world about the film" *the Vietnam War*".

However, the Chinese Army in the Vietnam War is Xiao Bing Li is going to release the book on January 9, 2020" THE DRAGON IN THE JUNGLE" to debunk the hidden secrets of China in the Vietnam War. According to Oxford University Press (Academic) refers:

" The Dragon in the Jungle

The Chinese Army in the Vietnam War
Xiao-Bing Li

- •*A previously untold story of China's intervention in the Vietnam War against the U.S*

- •*Access to newly available Communist sources in China, Russia, and Vietnam*

- •*Personal interviews of Chinese, Vietnamese, and Soviet officers and veterans*

- •*A new conclusion that China shifted its security concerns from the U.S. to the Soviet Union, and that the Sino-Soviet conflict collapsed the communist alliance"*

On Amazon wrote:" *Western historians have long speculated about Chinese military intervention in the Vietnam War. It was not until recently, however, that newly available international archival materials, as well as documents from China, have indicated the true extent and level of Chinese participation in the conflict of Vietnam. For the first time in the English language, this book offers an overview of the operations and combat experience of more than 430,000 Chinese troops in Indochina from 1968-73. The Chinese Communist story from the "other side of the hill" explores one of the missing pieces to the historiography of the Vietnam War.*

The book covers the chronological development and Chinese decision-making by examining Beijing's intentions, security concerns, and major reasons for entering Vietnam to fight against the U.S. armed forces. It explains why China launched a nationwide movement, in Mao Zedong's words, to "assist Vietnam and resist America" in 1965-72. It details PLA foreign war preparation, training, battle planning and execution, tactical decisions, combat problem solving, political indoctrination, and performance evaluations through the Vietnam War. International Communist forces, technology, and logistics proved to be the decisive edge that enabled North Vietnam to survive the U.S. Rolling Thunder bombing campaign and helped the Viet Cong defeat South Vietnam. Chinese and Russian support prolonged the war, making it impossible for the United States to win. With Russian technology and massive Chinese intervention, the NVA and NLF could function on both conventional and unconventional levels, which the American military was not fully prepared to face. Nevertheless, the Vietnam War seriously tested the limits of the communist alliance. Rather than improving Sino-Soviet relations, aid to North Vietnam created a new competition as each communist power attempted to control the Southeast Asian communist movement. China shifted its defense and national security concerns from the U.S. to the Soviet Union. (Amazon)"

After Geneva Conference signed on July 20, 1954, by French Prime Minister Mendes France and communists with China's delegator Zhou Enlai, Soviet-Union's delegator Molotov and henchman Phạm Văn Đồng. ***However, since 1959, Hồ Chí Minh launched the campaign to fight against the so-called America Emp***ire. Hồ Chí Minh ordered Major General Bùi Xuân Đăng founded the Special Task Force, code 559 with 100,000 laborers to repair an abandoned road linking Vietnam-Laos-Cambodia, so the Ho Chi Minh trails started in 1959, therefore, the US and allies just came to South Vietnam to help from 1965. After the Vietnam War,

Secretary-General Lê Duẫn confirmed the truth:" **we fought against Empire America for great master China and the Soviet Union**". (*)

China is the global enemy and the most threat the peace in the world. The global hegemonic ambition has grown into the arms race, the space race, actually the global economic terror that China has carried out after joining the free market and WTO. The silent invasion of the soft power army of China trapped the counterparts from many decades ago and now China arrayed the debt trap, trade trap, government trap that applied into the bribery, political donation and inserting China's spy into the Congress, Senate, and multiple governments' level. NATO has named China as a new enemy alongside Russia in a summit on November 20, 2019. It is too late but it is better asleep from China joined the free market. After the Soviet-Union collapsed in the early 1990s, China gathered the vestiges of communist countries in Asia are Vietnam, North Korea, Laos, and the vassals like Cambodia. The Cold War is not over yet, but China and its vestiges have applied the lizard changes skin's color tactic to cheat the world and bluffing the innocent politicians in Western. Indeed, the Cold War transforms into the COOL WAR and China continues to spread communism, actually the Maoist./.

_____**Notes:** (*) the books wrote about the Vietnam War of author Hoa Minh Truong published in 2010, 2011, 2012, 2015 provided the secrets of Vietcong as the Ho Chi Minh's embalmed body, the cause of the Vietnam War, the espionage networks in South Vietnam (code A22, A 26, A 54, A-4, T-10). Actually, the first book" The Dark Journey is chosen by the library of US Congress:

The dark journey: inside the reeducation camps of Viet Cong / Hoa Minh Truong. LC Control

Number: 2013376006Brief Description:Truong-Minh-Hoa.

The dark journey: inside the reeducation camps of Viet Cong / Hoa-Minh-Truong.

238 pages : illustrations ; 23 cm ISBN:9781609111618 (pbk)LC Call Number:HV9800.5 .T78 2010Dewey Number:959.704/37 23The Library of Congress is open to researchers and the public for in-house research only. Researchers must register in person at the Reader Registration Station; the Library cannot accept register strations via mail, telephone, or electronically./.

41. JOHN KERRY HAS THE HISTORICALLY TREASONOUS RECORD

The veteran has no strange Mr. John Kerry who was the traitor in the Vietnam War, his betraying saga in the USA, and nowadays, his treason goes further. On the other hand, Mr. John Kerry represents the component of *eating democratic bread by adoring the communist evil.*

In the Vietnam War, the name of Mr. John Kerry listed with the high profiles of Vietcong terrorist's supporters as Jane Fonda (Hanoi Jane), Joe Biden, Bill-Hillary Clinton, and the others plus the left media. Mostly, the traitors joined Democrats, the undercover communist party in the US.

During the Vietnam War was occurring, the US people, government, and allies were fighting against the global communist Bloc in Vietnam's battle. The Vietnam communist party seized the power at North and established a nation co-called The Democratic Republic of Vietnam, the rogue state led by Ho Chi Minh who was the genocide, he killed 1,700,000 people, raped a 15-year-old girl named Tuyết Lan in Thailand in 1929, and pedophile, therefore Ho Chi Minh is the icon of the left media, left author, John Kerry and his Democratic comrades. The domestic thugs in Western were communist undercover activists, espionage agents and the domestic traitors opposed the warfighting against the communist, they activated the anti-war movement, the protests with violence often carried out in the cities, capitals and on the street, actually, the rallies focused the countries were sending the troop to help South Vietnam protect the freedom. However, after the Vietnam War ended, the world knew the inhumane regime of Hanoi and the real face of Ho Chi Minh but the anti-war movement and the prominent anti-war movement's faces have never repented. Moreover, the Vietnam War's traitors became powerful persons in the US government, Congress, Senate, and the legal system. When Democratic President Bill Clinton ruled the US, in 1994, he lifted the embargo for Vietcong's regime, despite Hanoi has never changed the human rights violation, actually, John Kerry, Hanoi Songbird John McCain endorsed Bill Clinton.

Mr. John Kerry went too far in his political life, a time he was the presidential candidate in 2004 but Goerge W. Bush won the election. Therefore, John Kerry held the Senator of Massachusetts from 1985 to 2013 and he became the 68th United States Secretary of State. **Mr. John Kerry represents the treasonous line in the US, he contributed to play the double-cross war game with President Barrack Obama and Hillary Clinton, they used multiple trillion dollars of the taxpayers to fight the terrorist and also provided the weapon and finance to the terrorists.**

The article was written by Jay Solomon and Carol E. Lee published on September 6, 2016, on the Wall Street Journal that revealed the domestic thugs in the White House:

" *The U.S. Transferred $1.3 Billion More in Cash to Iran After Initial Payment*

First, $400 million coincided with Iran's release of American prisoners and was used as leverage, officials have acknowledged

The Obama administration followed up a planeload of $400 million in cash sent to Iran in January with two more such shipments in the next 19 days, totaling another $1.3 billion, according to congressional officials briefed by the U.S. State, Treasury, and Justice departments.

***The cash payments—made in Swiss francs, euros, and other currencies—settled a decade- (Wall Street Journal) million coincided with Iran's release of American prisoners and was used as leverage, officials have acknowledged*"**

And President Donald Trump accused:*" The nuclear deal gave Iran "$150 billion, giving $1.8 billion in cash — in actual cash carried out in barrels and in boxes from airplanes. " —* Donald Trump *on Thursday, April 26th, 2018 in an interview on "Fox & Friends"*

Despite Mr. John Kerry is no longer hold authority in the US government, therefore, he still in contact with the evil regime in Teheran and stabbing back the policy of the US. President Donald Trump scrapped Iran Nuclear Deal and called the Iranian military unit is a terrorist. The Vietnam War's lesson repeats, during the US people, government with allies fought against Vietcong terrorists but the traitors supported the enemy. Nowadays, Mr. John Kerry supports and contacts Iran, the enemy of America. Mr. John Kerry always opposes the US interest, he breached the Logan Act as

President Donald Trump said during a White House Press:" "*John Kerry violated the Logan Act*" and Mr. President emphasized:" *He's talking to Iran and has had many meetings and many phone calls and he's telling them what to do. That is a total violation of the Logan Act.*" The Logan Act enacted in 1799, is a federal law that criminalizes negotiation by unauthorized persons with foreign governments having a dispute. It is a clear reason that President Donald Trump proposes to prosecute traitor John Kerry as the US law. The US people, victims of Vietcong believe Mr. John Kerry who has a historically treasonous record in the US, should be indicted by the legal system. Nevertheless, the other traitors are still remaining in the silence as Hillary Clinton, Bill Clinton, Barrack Obama, and many high profiles Democrats. Although, justice has not come yet, therefore, the people are the judges to condemn treason, serious crimes, and corruption./.

42. JOHN Mc CAIN, WAR HERO, TRAITOR OR HANOI'S SONGBIRD?

Foreword: the writer is an ex-lieutenant of ARVN, after Saigon lost, Vietcong centralized 800,000 members of the South Vietnam Army and public servants into the barbarous prison camp's system. The worst treatment of Vietcong that killed 165,000 by the dried bloodbath revenge's policy. A former political prisoner, a survivor after 6 years in 9 Hells of re-education camp. I would like to share the bloody experience and the circumstance of the POW as Senator John Mc Cain.

The so-called re-education camp or the prison camp of

Vietcong are the same kinds. In the camp, the prisoner's administrative system set up the spy networks being laid into the interior prisoner line, because the guard force, staff couldn't control the prisoner and also prevent jailbreaking the riot. Actually, the prisoner of war and the political prisoner are the dangerous elements for the regime.

In most prison systems of communists, the prisoner currently being starved, so the shorted food could drive some spiritually weak prisoners to become traitors. The prison camp staff could use some facility benefits are available in the camp for deploying the domestic spying network between the prisoners, it is the prisoner controlling inmate's policy of Vietcong. The South Vietnam POW named the betrayers as a hunting dog or antenna, but Vietcong titles the traitors are the progressive prisoners. The Vietcong cadres use little beneficiaries as provision more food, special for a family visit or the other needs, then the weakly minded prisoners could become the hand of Vietcong, they inform the inmate's situation to the staff, report the personal behavior, even the speeches, thinking. The South Vietnam political prisoners were killed by many bloodshed revenge methods, among there were the betrayal informers.

Senator John Mc Cain wrote his book" Faith of My Fathers", he confessed the collaboration with the enemy while imprisoning. Like the routine, a Prisoner of War or a political prisoner who just releases the personal details are the full names, army rank, function, and the military record. A concerned prisoner could mislead the enemy by the fake information and deny any further questions with the answers: don't know, don't see, and have never known. Certainly, the enemy couldn't know further, actually the intelligence to be concealed. Unfortunately, Mr. John Mc Cain provided the military secrets that helped the Vietcong's anti-aircraft force reduced the damages of the US bombarded and also more airplanes shot down. Mr. John Mc Cain plunged into the betrayal, he appeared on the Vietcong broadcast, it was the psychological warfare that covered up and defended the worst treatment of communist to the prisoner and also attacking against the accusation of the US government about the POW being held in the hand of Vietcong, so during detaining in the prison camp, John Mc Cain became a tool of Hanoi into the propaganda's campaign. A son of Admiral who early turned the face against the US and POW, he acted as a songbird for the enemy after Vietcong regime deserved some beneficiaries, the inmates nicknamed John Mc Cain is Prince. POW John Mc Cain was the precious war booty of the Vietcong regime into the long term of the political investment. Probably, the Vietnam Communist party could use John Mc Cain as a tool in the US government, actually, his position is a senior politician and a time he was a presidential candidate in 2008. Moreover, Vietcong kept the dossier of POW John Mc Cain during detaining in the prison camp. It is the blackmail being followed by Mr. John Mc Cain from the POW's period and whole life. Certainly, Vietcong always applauds General Võ Nguyên Giáp as the greatest hero, so Mr. John Mc Cain behaved as a parrot, he praised General Võ Nguyên Giáp as the top Vietnamese army commander, indeed General Võ Nguyên Giáp is the military genocide, he was the responsibility of million troops killed during he was in charge. The guilty complex being obsessed Mr. John Mc

Cain, actually often fears of the POW in Hanoi Hilton (Hỏa Lò) should reveal his betrayal's record and the missing in action if still alive, they could accuse the cowardice behavior of Senator John Mc Cain being detained in the prison camp. The Vietnamese POW after Saigon lost, Vietcong hates the intellectuals so they killed the brilliant prisoners as Lieutenant Colonel Nguyễn Đức Xích, captain Quách Dược Thanh at Vườn Đào camp in 1979. Besides there were the cowards are such as captain Bùi Đình Thi who killed some inmates by the Vietcong's order. A musician Vũ Thành An, despite resettled in the US but he collects money sending to Vietnam under the title of charity. A Judge Nguyễn Cần (pen names are Tú Gàn and Lữ Giang) who became a journalist of Vietnamese language in the US, but he often writes the articles endorse Hanoi regime and China, nevertheless in 2000 while a traitor (fake refugee) Trần Văn Trường hang the red flag of Vietcong and Hồ Chí Minh portrait at his Hi-Tech shop that caused of ten thousand Vietnamese refugees in Garden Grove (California) protested in 60 days, but Mr. Nguyễn Cần stood alongside with the traitor, he wrote the articles protected Trần Trường on the Saigon Nhỏ News. In the presidential election 2016, Nguyễn Cần wrote a lot of articles that attacked candidate Donald Trump and now he still does the job as the left media. Captain Phạm Tín An Ninh who received some food of Vietcong cadre Nguyễn Văn Thà in the re-education camp, so he wrote the books appraise, it may be the syndrome of Stockholm. The Orderly Departure Program (ODP) in The US helped the South Vietnam political prisoner resettle the freedom life. Therefore, every ODP recipient had to sign a statutory form to confirm no involvement any anti-communist organization offshore; some former prisoners have complied because they could return to Vietnam (the US government may eye on the ODP recipients who have returned to Vietnam without a problem, they should be the Hanoi songbirds), but the most former prisoners couldn't come back, instead, they keep fighting for the democracy of Vietnam people.

The circumstance of Senator John Mc Cains is not an exemption, the blackmail of prison record that pursues whole life and effected into the politics. Senator John Mc Cain has turned the face with the Vietnamese nationalist in the US, instead, he interests the leftist or communist Vietnam in the US. Likely Mr. Đoàn Văn Toại, a Vietcong's supporter in South Vietnam, was a member of the university's student staff at Saigon in the 1960s. After Vietcong won the war on April 30, 1975, Đoàn Văn Toại became an official. Therefore he pretended opposite against the Vietcong, then the tyranny regime should arrange Mr. Đoàn Văn Toại who fled to French and later on resettled in the US. Senator John Mc Cain sponsored Đoàn Văn Toại in the fake democratic organization with the US taxpayer, but Mr. Toại pushed the embargo lift for Hanoi. Moreover, Mr. Đoàn Văn Toại has returned many times Vietnam, he is a fake anti-communist face. In the election 2016, the left media of Vietnamese language as Việt Báo or VietUSA/news with journalist Hạnh Dương, Người Việt news, and the others. Nevertheless, the Hanoi regime wanted Hillary to become the US president because Bill Clinton is the central left rival of the Democrats. Moreover, in the passage of time, Mrs. Hillary Clinton visited Vietnam 4 times, she was welcomed by the Vietcong government as a very special guest, she met some of Vietcong's high profiles as Prime Minister Nguyễn Tấn Dũng. So Senator John Mc Cain has attacked and often abused President Donald Trump because Hanoi dislikes the 45th US president. In an interview, the presidential candidate said Senator John Mc Cain is not a hero, but it is not important that Hanoi supports Hillary Clinton, so John Mc Cain has to follow as a French saying:" le mouton de Panurge". The blackmail of Vietcong has pursued Senator John Mc Cain for life, Vietcong is malice then Hanoi uses John Mc Cain as a lure for the Vietcong interest. Nevertheless, Senator John Mc Cain behaves as a decoy of democracy but has done anything that is suitable for Hanoi's policy. In the Vietnam War, the bastards are Jane Fonda (Hanoi Jane), John Kerry, Joe Biden, Bill and Hillary Clinton…and John Mc Cain (a Hanoi Songbird). President Donald Trump has done the wonderful presidency within 100 days, instead of in 8 years President Barrack Obama did nothing, his motto" Yes we can" therefore it is" no we couldn't" so the US being plunged into the deep deficit ever and Obama leftover many Obama-Scares as Obama care, Obama mess, Obama failure the offshore, Obama vacation (taxpayer spent multiple hundred million dollars for his family's enjoyment), Obama mouthful President…However, Senator John Mc Cain said:" American leader was better under Obama than Trump". Certainly, Obama is the first communist President in the White House and also a comrade of the Vietcong, so Senator John Mc Cain has to appraise Barrack Obama. Senator John Mc Cain sold the soul for evil by using the national interest exchanges the betrayal record in a prison camp../

43. FIGHTING AGAINST THE AGING AND KEEPING HEALTHY BY YOURSELF

*F*OREWORD: The writer spent the life experiment into the battle against the illness and survival during imprisoning 6 years into the hell of re-education from 1975 to 1981. The prison camp of Vietcong is quite different from the prison camp of the democratic country. In the re-education camp of Vietcong, the political prisoner to be treated like an animal, the food always lacked (the daily ration was a bowl of rotten rice with a worm, I ate with rocky salt), accommodation was zero, mostly in 6 years I slept on the wet soil with a nylon mat (my family provided), forced laborer, illness without medication and treatment, Vietcong always brainwashed and spiritual terror (the antenna-network was the inmates would report anything to the camp's administration), torture, execution without court's order. The life of a prisoner is like an ant.

I faced terrible adversity while detaining in the re-education camp. After Vietcong won the unpredictable war on April 30, 1975, the beloved comrade of Jane Fonda, John Kerry, Joe Biden, Bill-Hillary Clinton, and the anti-war-pro-communist movement is Vietcong, the inhumane regime congregated 800,000 members of ARVN (South Vietnam soldier) and public servant into the re-education camp. The barbarous revenge policy called **dried bloody bath** that killed 165,000 prisoners, the survivors have never healed the trauma, it is the psychological scar.

In the re-education, the worst treatment of the enemy plus the lost spirit could kill the prisoner. During living in the hell of communist paradise, I believed in survival and I did. The strong spirit helped me took over the adversity and self-learning English for my-self promise while living in the prison camp:" If I survive, I will write the true story". In the re-education camp of Vietcong, English was the counter-revolutionary language or the Empire America's language, whoever tried to learn English, the life to be risked if Vietcong discovered. I used at least 30 years writing a first book" The Dark Journey" and now I had 5 books published in the US.

The survival experiment shares in my fourth book, the science-fiction" **NICK MORROW:** *AFTER A HALF CENTURY, A MISSING MAN RETURNS*" (*) published by Strategic Book Publishing and Rights Co in 2015. Its book classified as a top book by New Book Journal after it was released and in 2017, once again, Pinterest classified a top book. This book contains health concerns, I believe my work helps everyone finding happiness and reduce illness.

"Congrats Hoa Minh Truong on the #newrelease "Nick Morrow" | Newly ...

https://www.pinterest.com.au/pin/25494602888250660 4/

1. Cached

Congrats **Hoa Minh Truong** on the #newrelease "Nick Morrow.

I would like to share the health experiment, nevertheless, in the hell of re-education camp of communists, the prisoner has to fight both battlefields: the worst accommodation and spiritual survival. The fighting against aging and keeping healthy by yourself is a vital concern. My life experiment could help everyone challenge yourself against the aging and illness, the key is in your hand, everyone can do it. Thank you for your reading, well being, and best wishes

Hoa Minh Truong.

(Founder & Editor of thedawnmedia)

When you get sick, normally the G.P (General Practioner) could help you. Therefore, everyone is a self-doctor, obviously, you are the first one to recognize the illness as chest pain, stomachache, headache... and a medical doctor is second. The doctor based on your health status's provision declares and finding the illness on pathology. The medical treatments come from the patient provides the syndromes appear and the doctor or specialist could apply the knowledge plus experience for treatment.

The psychiatrists come from Harvard and Yale University or cardiologist of Cripps Research Institute have never heard President Donald Trump declared some things relate to his health, but the doctors above dared the conclude President Donald Trump is mental health illness and heart problem. Those doctors destroyed the career, insulted the medical field. Before the doctors diagnose, obviously the self-doctor Donald Trump must know his health then Rear Admiral, Doctor Ronny Jackson based on" self-doctor" Donald Trump provided the details and Dr. Ronny qualifies to release the medical statement.

As **the self-defensive reaction's body**, when you fall down or something hit, obviously you feel sore for a while and after then you feel better and late the pain is gone. It is not a miracle, but your self-defensive reaction's body releases a substance that opposes the concussion. For multiple thousand years, the people knew the self-defensive reaction's body and applied to multiple fields, as the infighting, when someone hit, you must react naturally.

The acupuncture of ancient Chinese originated from the war that occurred between the ethnic nations. The early acupuncture's discovery began from the Chou dynasty (103-220 BC), during the fighting, the injured soldiers struck by arrows, therefore, before they had suffered some chronic illnesses. After the arrows took out, the diseases were gone and the Chinese started to study acupuncture with the nervous system. The original needle made of animal bone and later the metal replaced. Acupuncture is not a miracle because when a needle contacts a point of the body, the human's nervous system reacts and releases a substance against the strange thing.

Japanese has Shiatsu (acupressure) founder by Tokujiro Mamikoshi (1905-2000), from 1940, the first Shiatsu College built to train the physician. The ancient Vietnamese people knew the self-defensive reaction's body and applied the Cạo Gió from 5th century AD. The treatment for the common cold was the traditional medical practice. Every Vietnamese is a doctor who just uses a piece of ginger or coins to rub skin (back or chest or some places in the body). The body reacts and releases a substance that opposes the concussion and after Cạo Gió, the patient feels better. Under thousand years invasion of Chinese in Vietnam, the conqueror colonized the occupied land and also stole the Vietnamese's treatment, they changed the name is Gua Sha. The cupping and massage based on the self-defensive reaction's body, so after treatment, the people feel better.

The political prisoners could live longer than the

criminal conviction because the political prisoners believe in the future if survival with the strong spirit and the nervous system released the suitable substance, a circumstance of Nelson Mandela could prove the self-defensive reaction's body worked.

When you are happy, your nervous system releases the beneficial substance that helps you fight against aging and illness. Therefore while you are upset or despair, your nervous system releases the harmful substance that could make you sick or get old before age. Happiness and strong belief are the best medicine to fight against aging and illness.

President Donald Trump strong believes in himself and also he does what he believes to makes America great again with the patriotic heart that conducts the nervous system releases the benefit substance, so he has excellent health as White House's physician, Rear Admiral, Doctor Ronny Jackson, actually, President Donald Trump is looked young than his age. While former President Bill Clinton and his wife Hillary being withered because they are worried about the consequence of the wrongdoings those will repay anytime. Believe in yourself and happiness are the best medicine to fight to age and keeping healthy. If you didn't do something wrong, you have no worry and your nervous system releases the benefit substance that helps you keep young.

The self-defensive reaction's body is a natural law, the supreme lawmaker is the universal creator. Its law has no document, neither lawyer nor judge and government but whole the planet including the universe has to comply without complaining. The law of self-defensive reaction's body affects and influences all. On our planet, there are some symbol aspects that naturally comply with the law of the universal creator:

1-The natural phenomenon:

-The sunlight contacts the water's surface, water self-reacts by evaporation the steam.

-The hot and cold air contact, both self-react and making wind, storm, or tornado.

2.The tree: the tree recognizes the weather changes and it self-defends the reaction for the reasons. When the winter comes, the tree knew the sunlight reduces so the leaves drop and the spring makes the tree's happiness and it releases a substance so the flower and fruit thrive. When a tree damaged, it self-reacts by releasing a latex, later the wound healed.

3-Animal: the animal has a self-defensive reaction, the hunger comes from the nervous system releases a substance from the stomach demands and conducting the hunting food.

4-The Human: the dirty, criminal and dishonest mind affects the nervous system, and its self-defensive reacts by releasing the harmful substance:

-Karl Marx disappointed the living's situation and anger the incumbent society, his nervous system released the harmful substance that causes him wrote books teaching the robbery, killing, and enslaving the people.

-Most communist's brains struck by the crime, the nervous system self- defensive reacts to the harmful substance and they become cruel. China, North Korea, Vietnam, and the other communist regimes gathered the dishonesty.

-China communist regime dreams the global hegemony, the Maoist teaching plus the rapacious mind affects the brain and conducts the nervous system, the harmful substance released so China currently shows off the aggressive attitude and stolen the technology, the Intellectual Property (IP).

-The rapacious mind affects, the nervous system's self-defensive react and the harmful substance releases that conduct the corruption. Hillary and Bill Clinton deceived the people with the hoax charity Clinton Foundation

-Senator John Mc Cain struck by the betrayal mind, his nervous system has the self-defensive react and he did against the national security, now the harmful substance affects and he has been engaged the brain cancer.

-The left media affects the dirty mind and their nervous system self- defensive react with the harmful substance that causes the fake news, fabricated stories, biased polls released.

-The psychiatrists come from Harvard and Yale University or cardiologist of Cripps Research Institute have the dishonest mind, their brain, and nervous system self-defend reaction by releasing the harmful substance, so they distorted the career by releasing the fraud medical report about President Donald Trump.

The self-defensive reaction's body is a natural law, everyone on the planet couldn't live outlaw, instead, to comply absolutely. The honest, stable, and transparent mind affects the nervous system and it releases the benefit substance as the self-defensive reaction's body and the honest people could fight against the aging and keep healthy by its mind, otherwise the dishonest could get old before the age and the facing bad health ./.

(*) Notes: Doctor Paul Johnson, Vice-Chancellor of the University of Westen Australia wrote about the book Nick Morrow:

"I have no doubt that you once had an incredible yet very very difficult life, but I am happy to see that you have now been able to build a positive and happy life here in Australia. You are obviously a very strong person with the resilience to live through some of the world's most horrific events.

I will ensure that this book is placed in the UWA library so that everyone may have access to your work"./.

44. THE BARBAROUS REVENGE OF VIETCONG AFTER HANOI WON THE WAR

After the black day or mourning day of the Vietnamese people on April 30, 1975, the world has never known what happened the fate of the multiple million people who lived in South Vietnam, actually, the anti-war movement and the prominent faces as Jane Fonda, John Kerry, Joe Biden, Bill, and Hillary Clinton...the left media have kept the mouth shut, they are shameless and coward although they knew all the truth.

The Great Uncle of Vietcong and leftist, including the left media was a rapist (victim was Ms. Tuyet Lan, 15-year-old at Thailand), Ho Chi Minh was the well-known pedophile and genocide, he killed more than 1,700,000 people. Despite, the Vietcong's supporters have concealed the truth, therefore, after 1975, the world knew Vietcong is an inhumane regime as the most communist countries in China, North Korea, Laos, Cuba, and the former Soviet-Union.

After winning the unpredictable war on April 30, 1975, Vietcong applied the dried bloodbath policy, they didn't kill straight away as Khmer Rouge in Cambodia, instead the killing carried out gently. Obviously, the Vietcong regime centralized more than 800,000 members of South Vietnam's armed force (ARVN) and public servants, the political prisoners sent to the hell of the prison camp that camouflaged under the nice title" re-education camp". The worst treatments plus the cruel revenge policy that killed more than 165,000 political prisoners by starvation, execution, torture, spiritual intimidation, sickness without medicine, forced laborer, worst accommodation. Vietcong or the other communist regimes has never respect human rights, unfortunately, a time, Vietcong regime and China became the members of UN Human Rights Council, it is the farce, UN insults itself, the shame of the United Nations. The Democratic President Bill Clinton embargo lifted the Vietcong regime in 1994 with the happiness of John Kerry and John Mc Cain (Hanoi Songbird) despite the Hanoi regime has never changed the human rights violation and also remaining the hostile policy the South Vietnam soldiers, including allies, so the annual anniversary the so-called" Victory Day" April 30 in Vietnam, Vietcong leaders condemned the America empire as the period in Vietnam War, they display the museum. Nevertheless, from August 2016, the Vietcong regime hampered the Australian government commemorates Long Tan's battle in Vietnam and now the Cross repatriated to Australia. Why does the Western country aid to Hanoi regime while Vietcong always concern as the enemy?

The Vietnam Communist Party's high profile is Mr. Đỗ Mười who held the most important positions in Vietcong government: in 1940, he was elected General Secretary of the Central Committee, Congressman of sole parliament, Deputy Prime Minister, Prime Minister, and Secretary-General, but still held an advisor of Central Committee from 1997 to 2001 because the advisory council disbanded. Mr. Đỗ Mười was low-educated, his job was the pig's sterile (in Vietnam, the pig's sterile is not veterinarian as Western). Therefore, a low educated person became the big boss of the Vietnam communist party, including the top job, the national leader. Mr. Đỗ Mười said:" *Giải phóng miền Nam, chúng ta có quyền tịch thu tài sản, trưng dụng nhà cửa, hãng xưởng, ruộng đất chúng nó. Xe chúng nó ta đi, vợ chúng nó ta lấy, con chúng nó ta bắt làm nô lệ. Còn chúng nó thì ta đầy đi lao động khổ sai vùng Kinh tế mới vào nơi rừng sâu nước độc. Chúng nó sẽ chết lần mòn...* " (South Vietnam's liberation, we have the rights to castigate their assets, house, factory, farmland. We take their vehicle, we take their wife and their children enslaved. We force them hard labor at the new life e zone in the deep jungle with toxic water, they will die gently". Nevertheless, after Saigon lost, the pig sterile's Secretary General Mr. Đỗ Mười who planned to send more than 3,000,000 family members of South Vietnam to the deep jungle at Thanh Hóa, he wanted to ruin the life of the enemy's family, but his plan didn't apply.

After South Vietnam lost on April 30, 1975, once again, at Saigon town hall, Mr. Nguyễn Hộ, the central committee told his comrades:" We castigate their house, their wife, we take and their children enslaved". Vietcong applied the revenge policy to the losers despite South and North Vietnam are the Vietnamese people.

The American Civil War occurred from 1861 to 1865, the bloody war ended when General Robert Edward Lee surrendered. The winner didn't revenge, instead, they opened arms, everyone had free to live, the government also set up General Robert Edward Lee's statue and all the dead soldiers of both sides to be treated equally in a national cemetery and somewhere else in the US.

However, Vietcong avenged, the solder of South Vietnam to be imprisoned, their family has been faced discrimination in society, they are the counter-revolution component, the children to be kicked out from the education system, actually, the university and overseas student always deserve the priority for communist's family, so the Western countries made the terrible mistake to grant the scholarship for Vietcong, almost the scholarship recipients are the Vietcong's children. The statues of South Vietnam's soldiers knocked down and Vietcong dug the cemeteries, including Biên Hòa's national cemetery. Vietcong is malicious, they also planted the trees in the cemetery and the roots destroyed the graves, even whoever escaped and lived overseas, Vietcong still applies the hostile policy. (*)

However, Vietcong always raises the mouthful reconciliation, it is like a robber, after took money, assets and killed the family members, the dishonest raise the nice voice to appeal the victims forget the crimes, it is the fake morality of robber. Nevertheless, Vietcong exploited the political prisoner's scheme for exported the Vietcong's decoys. Under the era of President Barrack Obama, the hoax anti-Vietcong regime settled in the US such as Mr. Cù Huy Hà Vũ, Trần khải Thanh Thủy, Điếu Cày (Nguyễn Văn Hải), Tạ Phong Tần...while South Vietnam captain Nguyễn Hữu Cầu imprisoned 37 years, but Obama and Amnesty International ignored, he still lives in Vietnam under the probation of regime.

Vietcong has never changed the hostile policy to the losers and the allies, the so-called reconciliation is a farce, Vietcong cheats the Western, therefore they couldn't deceive the Vietnamese people. The barbarous policy deeply left sorrow in the Vietcong's victims ever. Do not trust communist talks, let's watch they did.

Karl Marx is the great, great master of Vietcong and the other communist regimes. Karl Marx's theory confirmed the people derive from the ape (a kind of monkey), therefore, in the jungle, the zoo has many kinds of monkeys, why don't they drop the hair and become human beings? However, the communist recognizes their ancient is a monkey despite they have the human body. The communist concern themselves as a monkey, they badly treat the people as animal treats the people. On the other hand, the communist has a human body with the monkey's brain, mostly the animal is wild and they have not to brain as a human being. Its reason causes the communist to kill the people in cold blood. From Karl Marx's theory applied, there are more than 100,000,000 people killed and a billion people enslaved. The animal has not recognized right and wrong, so communist and the left media are the same kind, all telling a lie and cheat, it is the character of animal's behavior./.

Note: (*) The writer is a former of South Vietnam army (ARVN), after the war, I was imprisoned 6 years, I survived and escaped for freedom by small boat, I settled a new life in Australia from 1983, I have never returned to Vietnam because Vietcong could kill and arrest if I return, even my 88-year-old mother deceased on February 14, 2016, I couldn't attend her funeral. In 1994, twice, I sponsored the tourist visa for my mother, I wanted to meet her before she dies, but the Vietcong regime didn't grant the visa for my mother../.

45. THE US LEFT ACADEMICS AND VIETCONG REWRITE THE VIETNAM WAR HISTORY TO ESCAPE THE GENOCIDE

FOREWORK: All the communist is the same cruelty, the Karl Marx's pupils created the greatest massacre in human history with more than 100,000,000 killed since Lenin succeeded the October Revolution in 1917 in Russia and the communist movement spread like a deadly catastrophe.

There was just China communist party that killed more than 65,000,000 people, and Soviet-Union massacred 30,000,000....Within 4 years (1975-1979), Khmer Rouge killed more than 2,000,000. Vietcong is a similarity, after winning over South Vietnam on April 30, 1975, Vietcong revenge by the dried blood bath policy, obviously, they congregated 800,000 thousand members of the Army of the Republic of Vietnam and public servant into the hells of re-education camp. Vietcong killed 165,000 political prisoners, not including multiple hundred thousand soldiers and government servants to be killed in central Vietnam after President Nguyễn Văn Thiệu (Commander in Chief) abandoned by the unconditional withdrawal order of two Army Corps in March 1975. Cambodia has Khmer Rouge, in Vietnam is Vietcong Rouge. The Vietnamese people and history have never forgotten the Vietcong genocide despite the supercriminal gang Vietcong and the leftist in the Western country try to rewrite the Vietnam War history.

After the Vietnam War ended on April 30, 1975, Vietcong claimed the unpredictable victory with the pride of a conqueror, the tyrannical regime in Vietnam has applied the cruel policy to the occupied territory (South Vietnam).

Despite Vietcong is Vietnamese but they treated their people as a foreign invader in medieval. The barbarousness reflected by a speech of a high profile Vietcong member of the Vietnam communist party, Mr. Nguyễn Hộ who told with his comrades at Saigon:" their house, we occupy-their wife, we take-their children, we enslave". The robbery, killing policy caused multiple million Vietnamese people to flee for freedom bid.

The victory of Vietcong in 1975 unmasked the ruthless regime, Hồ Chí Minh is no longer the national icon, indeed Hồ was the rapist (in Thailand, in 1929, he raped a 15 years old girl name is Tuyết Lan), Hồ Chí Minh was a serious pedophile and he was a genocide with 1,700,000 people killed. The espionage agent and the pro-Vietcong component overseas plus the leftist in the Western countries have tried to re-polish Hồ Chí Minh's symbol, the Town of Newhaven honored and placed the statue of Hồ Chí Minh that created the anger of the Vietcong victim in the UK and the British media's criticism.

The Vietcong regime lost the world credit and Vietnam people, its regime in Hanoi is similar to Khmer Rouge, and so Vietcong has conspired to rewrite the history of covering up the genocide against humanity. After Vietnam War ended, Vietcong secretly cooperated with the leftist academics in Western countries, it is likely the William Joiner Center's Director. Dr. Kevin Bowen activated" for the study of war and social consequences". It's a studying body that belongs to the University of

Massachusetts in Boston, Massachusetts (UMass). Nevertheless, in 1999, UMass was sponsored by Rockefeller Foundation Humanities Fellowship for a study's theme was" the Constructing Identity and Place in Vietnamese Diaspora" and the William Joiner Center carried out within 3 years and after the endeavor achieved, it would release broadly, the Vietnam War history to be driven by the Vietcong's view. While the Vietnamese refugee could provide the impartial document, therefore the William Joiner Center invited two cultural propagating cadres from Hanoi were Mr. Nguyễn Huệ Chi and Hoàng Ngọc Hiển. They would rewrite the Vietnam War history as nowadays Beijing wants to impose communist education on Hong Kong's people. The conspiracy of Willian Joiner Center at the University of Massachusetts faced the strong reaction of the Vietnamese community overseas, actually in the US and Vietcong failed to re-write the history.

However, Vietcong has not given up the conspiracy to rewrite the Vietnam War history. In 2012, Vietcong published a propaganda book" Bên Thắng Cuộc", its meaning is the winner. Author Trương Huy San, pen name is Huy Đức, he was born in 1962 at Hà Tĩnh Province (North Vietnam). The author didn't join the invasion of North Vietnam's communist troop to terrorize the southern in the Vietnam War. Certainly, it is like an untrained doctor who couldn't cure the patient, so Author Huy Đức who didn't know about the battle in South Vietnam but he wrote about the field that he has never known. Most documents provided by Vietcong, so this book is just propaganda, not impartial, it is a garbage book, unfortunately in the US, from 2005 to 2006, the Vietcong regime sent Huy Đức to study the University of Maryland under a Hubert. Humphrey Fellowship and in 2012 he received a fellowship from the Nieman Foundation for Journalism to study at Harvard University in Cambridge, Massachusetts. The left academics in the US promoted their comrade Huy Đức studied at the universities.

The garage book" Bên Thắng Cuộc" is a worse drama that turns to comedy. Certainly, it is a propaganda product" made in Vietcong, packed by the US left academics" and exposing broadly. Therefore, this book is a product made in China, so the reader has no interest. It is the shame when the shoddy writing of Huy Đức has been praised and supported by the US academics and universities, including the Vietnamese academics graduated from the US universities and also South Vietnam's refugee as Dr. Trần Hữu Dũng, Dr. Nguyễn Mạnh Hùng, Dr. Đinh Xuân Quân, and the Vietnamese Journalist Đinh Quang Anh Thái and the other left Vietnamese refugees.

Nevertheless, the Người Việt News (the left media of Vietnamese in California) promoted the propaganda book" Bên Thắng Cuộc". Journalist Mặc Lâm of RFA (Radio Free

Asia funded by the US taxpayers) and Journalist Nguyễn Giang of BBC applauded and advertised this book. On the other hand, the Vietcong book" Bên Thắng Cuộc" published and also unmasked the left academics of the US plus the left Vietnamese overseas.

Most Vietnamese knew this book made in Vietcong and many victims of Vietcong and the vital witness discovered the book" Bên Thắng Cuộc" lied. There was a week released, a former Lieutenant Colonel Lê Quang Liễn, Marine Corps division of ARVN displayed the truth, he attended the military operation in the region, so author Huy Đức had to write an apology's statement.

During the US left academics, some Universities and the Vietnamese leftist hidden under refugee's cover praise the propaganda book" Bên Thắng Cuộc" but a former Vietcong high profile, former People's Army Colonel Bùi Tín confirmed author Huy Đức was just true 33%, it means 67% lie...Bùi Tín is a hoax defector, in 1980's he exiled by the domestic rival's fighting and lives in Paris. Although he slams the Vietcong he tried to protect Vietcong massacred more than 7,000 people in the Tet offensive at Hue in 1968. Nevertheless, former Colonel Bùi Tín served as the Vice Chief Editor of the People's Daily (Nhân Dân Nhật Báo), the most important media of the Vietcong regime. He was a great master of Huy Đức into the propaganda field.

The book" Bên Thắng Cuộc" is like a general self-criticism's statement of Vietcong, they confessed the negatives as killing, robbery the people, but author Huy Đức who performs the propaganda mission always prides of the winner. As the same circumstance of a gang, after killed, robbed, and created the crimes, the bandit members confessed the wrongdoing but also praise the gang as honest. Nowadays, everyone knows Vietcong is barbarous, so any effort rewrites the Vietnam War history has not convinced, instead of the leftist academics to be eradicated as the left media couldn't deceive the fake news, bogus polls and created stories./.

46. THE CULPRIT OF HUẾ MASSACRE IS HOÀNG-PHỦ -NGỌC-TƯỜNG WHO HAS DAUGHTER LIVES IN THE US

Geneva Accords was the collusion between colonial France and Global Communist Bloc. France exhausted the competence after Second World but they wanted to keep the Indochina colony, so the war occurred in South East Asia. Therefore France lost Điện Biên Phủ battle while the Global Communist Bloc had lost the crucial battle in Korea 1953.

In Geneve's conference, French Minister Mendes France versus Zhou Enlai (China), Molotov (Soviet Union), and Mr. Phạm Văn Đồng (Vietnam Communist party). Both sides were facing difficulty, actually, the Global Communist Bloc had not enough strength to keep the total territory in Vietnam, so the Geneve Accords signed on July 20, 1954, reflects the weakness of France and Communists in this stage. It reason helped South Vietnam founded the democratic government during North Vietnam controlled by the communist party, the dictatorial regime led by Hồ Chí Minh.

As the annual routine self-declared the truce from North

and South, the Lunar New Year held the ceasefire in 3 days. However, in the New Year 1968 (Tết Mậu Thân), Vietcong exploited a part of the soldier and government public servant was on holiday, they launched hundred thousand troops plus the guerrilla at South Vietnam in the crucial battle, Vietcong attacked totally South Vietnam's territory. South Vietnam and allies defended, the Mậu Thân's battle occurred fiercely, ultimately Vietcong was defeated, they faced more than a hundred thousand casualties and the numerous injuries were not accountable. Among the furious battle, Huế began on January 31-1968, North Vietnam communists plus the guerrilla and undercover activities occupied Huế in 26 days. The Tết Offensive 1968 left the black spot of Vietnam history and the human rights disaster, therefore, the culprits and perpetrators are Vietnam communist party has not indicted yet. Vietcong acted like the terrorist, within 26 days occupied Huế, the North Vietnam communist troop and local communist killed more than 7,000 civilians (including men, women, children, and infants), it was from 5 to 10% of the total population of Huế, among were the foreigners worked here. The numerous victim could compare the Tiananmen Square. Huế's massacre is the genocide, but the left media and Vietcong have concealed it. The victim's body buried in dozens of mass graves after Vietcong to be wiped out by ARVN and allies.

The actual killer at Huế was Vietcong's undercover activist Hoàng Phủ Ngọc Tường, he born on September 9, 1937, at Bình Khê hamlet, Triệu Long village, Triệu Phong district, Quảng Trị province. The genocide criminal Hoàng Phủ Ngọc Tường lived at Huế, he gained the education of South Vietnam's government from primary school to university. From 1966, he left the city and joined the Vietcong's terrorists. In The Huế battle, he was the key to the massacre because he knew the resident well and conducted the North Vietnam troop to kill the civilians.

After Vietcong controlled Huế, **Hoàng Phủ Ngọc Tường and his younger brother Hoàng Phủ Ngọc Phan, comrade Nguyễn Đắc Xuân involved the Huế's massacre**. They knocked the door to the house to house and congregated at public places as school, government offices. The Huế's massacre carried out the order of the Vietnam communist party because all Vietcong units to be controlled and commanded by the political officers from company to army corps. Therefore, **the Vietcong fake defector Colonel Bùi Tín** (now lives in Paris), weaseled out the crime of the Vietnam Communist party, he told the massacre at Huế was not communist party policy but some units did. In Australia, **Mr. Nguyễn Quang Duy, the head of 8406 Bloc at Melbourne,** its organization relates to the Vietnam Reform Party (PBS Television, Frontline unmasked on" the terror in Little Saigon" showing the Vietnam Reform Party with terror unit K9 involved in the massacre of 5 journalists in the US),

Mr. Nguyễn Quang Duy strays and dodges the serious crime of Vietcong at Huế in 1968, he wrote China did it, indeed at Huế, there was not China troop involved, he also appeals the family's victim and Vietnamese people do not tell and remind the massacre story for unification's reason. The Holocaust and Tiananmen Square have never forgotten by the annual commemoration. Therefore, after creating the genocide at Huế, Vietcong and its hand appeal to the victim's family and Vietnamese people forget it.

The Huế's massacre has never forgotten the Vietnamese people, actually the victim's families in Vietnam and overseas. In Vietnam, Vietcong celebrates the so-called Mậu Thân's victory while the Vietnamese people condemn the genocide crime to oppose humanity and commemorates the victims. If Khmer Rouge still rules Cambodia as Vietcong controls Vietnam government, every year, Khmer Rouge's government celebrates the liberation day and prides the massacre more than 2,000,000 people, and the statue of Pol Pol will place somewhere as in the Western countries as Hồ Chí Minh's statue appeared at Town of Newhaven (UK), Paris…

The massacre culprit Hoàng Phủ Ngọc Tường and his comrades are the heroes of Vietnam communist regime. He becomes the propaganda's high profile and married with the so-called Poet Lâm Thị Mỹ Dạ. In the communist regime, the writers are the propaganda tool of the regime as North Korea has Kim Jo Jong who is the head of the propaganda machine, therefore, she is the icon of the left media as CNN in the Winter Olympics 2018 at Pyongchang.

The genocide criminal Hoàng Phủ Ngọc Tường and his wife have two children are Miss Hoàng Thị Dạ Thư works at the Trẻ's publisher, actually, his last daughter is Hoàng Dạ Thi (writer) who migrated to the US by the spouse sponsoring of a Vietnamese refugee turns asylum seeker, that man returned safely to where he escaped for freedom and now he is the son in law of the genocide criminal Hoàng Phủ Ngọc Tường.

The Huế's massacre is the genocide crime as Tiannan Square, Holocaust, but the international court has not taken the culprits for the tribunal, indeed a time, Vietcong selected in UN Human Rights Council, what is going?. After Vietcong took over South Vietnam, the Huế's massacre becomes the victorious event of the regime, after April 30, 1975, at Huế, almost the undercover activists appeared, among was Mr. **Trần Kim Đoàn**, now he lives in Sacramento (US), some Huế's resident recognized his face and his role after South Vietnam lost./.

47. TRAITOR JANE FONDA WHO ACTS AS JUDA DEFENDS THE FAITH

In Vietnam War, movie star Jane Fonda's story is a saga while the democratic countries including the US were fighting against Vietcong, the early terror organization after Second World War. Nevertheless, Vietcong is barbarous than Al Qaeda, Islamic State, or any terrorists, therefore Jane Fonda traveled to Hanoi and celebrated with North Vietnam's troops during the US soldier, allies were confronting with Vietcong. Certainly, Jane Fonda stood alongside with Vietcong terrorist is like the Islamic State's supporters nowadays. On the other hand, Jane Fonda is a traitor, she stabbed at back the democratic countries and the US national security because the Vietnam battlefield was the sharp arrow of Vietcong attacking the peace and also threatened the security in the region and the US-led allies battled against the Vietcong.

Jane Fonda was shameless and no brain while the US soldiers detained in the prison camp called Hanoi Hilton where was the hell of Prisoner of War (POW). Vietcong treated the prisoners as an animal, but Jane Fonda prided her activity and nickname Hanoi Jane. The comrades of Jane Fonda in the Vietnam War were John Kerry, Joe Biden, Bill, and Hillary Clinton...the left media as CNN, The Washington Post, The New York Times....concealed the trust in Vietnam War, instead they propagated for Vietcong. They have misled the public for a long time, moreover, after Vietnam War ended on April 30, 1975, Jane Fonda and her comrades knew the inhume regime in Vietnam, Vietcong congregated more than 800,000 members of ARVN and public servant imprisoned in the hell of re-education camp of Vietcong, the worst treatment killed more than 165,000 people in the dried bloodbath policy. Nevertheless, multiple million Vietnamese people risked the life trying to escape the paradise of communist in Vietnam. The Vietnamese survivors who live in democratic countries told the world about the barbarous regime, therefore Jane Fonda and her comrades have never shown remorse, they have kept quiet as a stone.

The people always fight against the crimes, therefore Hồ Chí Minh was the rapist, in 1929 in Thailand, he raped a 15 years old girl named Tuyết Lan (she was pregnant). Hồ Chí Minh was a famous pedophile in North Vietnam, he also was the genocide with 1,700,000 people killed during his rule. However, Hồ Chí Minh is the beloved comrade of the anti-war movement and the high profiles as Jane Fonda, John Kerry, Joe Biden, Bill, and Hillary Clinton...and the left media. They are the dregs of the democratic country.

Jane Fonda has never removed the title Hanoi Jane, even after she died, the US people and the world stuck Jane Fonda with Vietcong. Despite the real face of Vietcong unmasked, but the communist vestiges are still remaining the wrongdoing, so **Ken Burns and Lyn Novick recycled the Vietcong's propaganda documentary in the film The Vietnam War and film The Post, those are like Juda defends the faith,** the wrongdoers have tried to escape the historical criticism, their conscience travels into the deception. When a dog did something wrong, it knows how to show remorse by waving the tail, but the anti-war movement in Vietnam War has never regretted it. Under Democratic President Barrack Obama, once again, Jane Fonda to be honored although the Vietnam veteran strongly reacted and condemned. The US people recognize **Barrack Obama as the worst president in history, he is the homosexual revolutionist and father of the toilet for transgender. Obama also is the pioneer of using taxpayers for vacation** (Obama and his first lady spent more than $USD 100 million on private travel), so the people have no surprise when Obama honored Jane Fonda, they are the same kind.

Jane Fonda has lived on the lie, it is the leftist's manner and the traditional traitor, so she endorsed comrade Hillary Clinton in the US election 2016, even President Donald Trump inaugurated on January 20, 1917, Jane Fonda and her comrades showing the hostility a man who makes America great again.

After a year of getting the office, President Donald Trump achieved the most promises although Democrats and some turncoat Republicans as Senator John Mc Cain have tried to thwart and attacking a man who sacrifices his wealthy life for the country. The fake news lies about Russia meddled the US election that has never helped Hillary Clinton enters the White House without the election. The impeachment carries out by the malicious conspiracy that failed, the actual punters like James Comey and now Robert Mueller do nothing with the investigation based on the fake news and fabricated story, instead of the investigation based on the fake fact that insults the FBI. Nevertheless, the stronghold of Democrats is Hollywood struck by the harassment's bomb and more than two dozen of Hollywood's icon disabled, their reputation ruined after many years built up.

Recently she proved her comments attack President Donald Trump that is the worst of the worst because of the patriotic heart and the great achievements of President Donald Trump that wiped out the lies and deception. Whoever attacks President Donald Trump, terrorizes the national interest, so Jane Fonda rarely shows remorse for a while as Juda defends the faith, but the people have never trusted a treason. However, Jane Fonda and her comrades have never confessed the treason in Vietnam War, they supported the Vietcong's terrorist./.

Nobody trusts Jane Fonda

Who did against the democracy and national interest of the USA

Hanoi Jane has never removed the nickname.

In her life and even after she died.

History has no tolerance.

But President Barrack Obama honored the treason

Jane Fonda lines up behind Hillary Clinton

She attacked President Donald Trump

As she did in Vietnam War.

She acts as Juda

The remorse exposed for a while.

But her character has never changed

Juda defends the faith.

Liar .../.

48. JANE FONDA IS THE SERIOUS TRAITOR AND MURDER SHE DID IN VIETNAM WAR

As the law, whoever links with the enemy, attacks the national interest, they face treasonous crime. Therefore, Jane Fonda who committed serious treason during the US government and allies were fighting against the Global Communist Bloc on the Vietnam battlefield, actually, Vietcong was an early terror organization and also the genocide. Nevertheless, Jane Fonda has adored Ho Chi Minh as a great leader of the Vietnam Communist party, therefore, Ho Chi Minh did many things that the people condemn:

-In 1929, during hiding from the hunt of France and Chiang Kai Shek's government, Ho Chi Minh escaped to Thailand, he raped a 15-year-old girl named Tuyết Lan. The victim was pregnant, her mother discovered then Ho Chi Minh ran away to China.

-Ho Chi Minh was a well-known pedophile, he forced many teen girls for sex.

-Ho Chi Minh was the genocide, he killed 1,700,000 people, his name listed on the most genocide in the 20th century.

However, Ho Chi Minh is the adorable icon of Jane

Fonda, Joe Biden, Bill-Hillary Clinton, John Kerry, the left media (CNN, The New York Times, The Washington Post...). Particularly, in Vietnam War, Jane Fonda carried out psychological warfare for Vietcong, she had photographs with Vietcong troops and her life has never removed the nickname is **Hanoi Jane**. She stabbed in back the US government, the democratic countries, actually the soldiers who sacrificed the life to fight against Vietcong's terrorist. Nowadays, whoever stands alongside, support, propagate and finance for terrorist, they must be punished by the anti-terrorist law. Therefore, Jane Fonda and his comrades have not indicted although everyone knew they endorsed Vietcong's terrorist. The treasonous crime stuck into Jane Fonda's record, moreover, in Vietnam War, she colluded with Vietcong to kill the US soldiers detained at Hoa Lo's Prison camp. The traitor Jane Fonda enjoyed when seeing Vietcong killed the POW. The survivor is Colonel Larry Carrigan who spent 6 years in Hanoi Hilton, but three men were beaten to death.

The witness is Ronald Sampson who recounted Jane Fonda walked with a cameraman in Hoa Lo's prison camp, she shook the hand of each POW and asked:" *Aren't you sorry you bombed babies*" and:" *Are you grateful for the humane treatment from your benevolent captors?* " (*) and the prisoners of war handled their sliver of paper.

Mr. Ronald Sampson wrote:" *She took them all without missing a beat. . . At the end of the line and once the camera stopped rolling, to the shocked disbelief of the POWs, she turned to the officer in charge and handed him all the little pieces of paper...*

Three men died from the subsequent beatings. Colonel Carrigan was almost number four but he survived, which is the only reason we know of her actions that day"

When President Barrack Obama ruled the White House, he honored" beloved comrade" Jane Fonda despite he knew Hanoi Jane is serious treason, President Obama insulted the US army and the democratic valuation. Certainly, President Barrack Obama exploited the US's presidency to praise the felon and challenged human rights. Barrack Obama stood alongside traitor Jane Fonda, it is like evil praises Satan. The honor's Jane Fonda hurts 58,000 US soldiers sacrificed in the warfighting against Vietcong's terror and millions of Vietnam veterans plus the family.

The murder she did in Vietnam War still carved deeply into the memories of the POW. Despite the Vietnam war was over from April 30, 1975, but Hanoi Jane has no changed, she and her comrades have never shown remorse. Nowadays, the victims and witnesses are still alive, they told stories about Hanoi Jane, the lucky treason has not indicted yet, instead, she listed in 100 years of great women. What is going on?. The Human rights turn Human wrong, traitor becomes a patriot and national hero. The people need justice applies to the felon, actually the treason.

The US to be vulnerable by the ill-concern people, almost they are the leftists in media, academics, the bullshit Democrats, and the garbage persons. As communist's ancestor Karl Marx title the communist originated the ape (a kind of monkey). Certainly, the monkey is an aminal, the action based on instinct, not mind. The animal doesn't recognize right and wrong, so they honored Jane Fonda is among the great women as honored as the serious traitor./.

(*) **The references**: the writer is POW after Saigon lost on April 30, 1975, I was arrested on May 2nd, 1975. Vietcong sent me to 9 hells of the prison camp. I was among 800,000 members of ARVN (Army of the Republic of Vietnam) and public servant to be concentrated and treated in the dried bloodbath's revenge policy of Vietcong, so the so-called" *Are you grateful for the humane treatment from your benevolent captors?"* of Jane Fonda is a farce, lie. In the prison camp, Vietcong treated POW lessens than an animal, the food always shorted, the starvation currently occurred, the worst accommodation, illness without medicine and treatment, forced labor, torture, execution (by the bush law, without justice), actually, Vietcong applied the brainwash's method plus the currently spiritual terror. I was a survivor among 165,000 POWs killed in the prison camps of Vietcong. I understood how the POW suffered, actually, the psychological wound has never healed. Therefore, Jane Fonda and her comrades including the left media have never apologized, instead, they pride the treason. I wrote my personal experts in the first book" the dark journey" published in New York in 2010./.

49. HO CHI MINH WAS THE BOSS OF DRUG LORD IN VIETNAM

In the Vietnam War and nowadays, Vietnam Communist Party's founder Ho Chi Minh has become the icon or" *Uncle Ho*" of left media, the prominent leftists are Jane Fonda, John Kerry, Bill-Hillary Clinton, Joe Biden, and the other high profiles of Democrats. The libraries in the US and Western countries have many books that glorify Ho Chi Minh as a great leader, the left authors didn't know about the traitor Ho Chi Minh but acclaimed, it conflicts with the professionals in Western's valuation. The concerned person just supports something if they knew well, as the social routine, a customer buys some products if they knew the original. Therefore, in the Vietnam War and nowadays, the left media and leftists have not repented after supported the Vietcong Ape supper gang in the Vietnam War despite Vietnam War ended on April 30, 1975, the Vietnamese refugee and victims of Vietcong told anything about the ruthless regime, unfortunately, the left media and leftists keep quiet as a stone.

Ho Chi Minh was a genocide, he killed more than 1,700,000 people, the role of Ho Chi Minh in the Vietnam War was the terrorist leader as Osama Bin Laden, but the leftists praised him as the great leader. Uncle Ho Chi Minh raped a 15-year-old girl named Tuyết Lan in 1929 in Thailand, actually, after Vietnam communist's Ape super gang occupied Northern of Vietnam, Ho Chi Minh was a famous pedophile. On the other hand, Ho Chi Minh was a serious felon, his crimes oppose humanity, but somewhere else as Town of Haven in the United Kingdom honored Ho Chi Minh's statue and on November 24, 2017, the UNESCO office in Hanoi honored Ho Chi Minh by the UNESCO Resolution 24C/18.65. The world went wrong, actually innocent people couldn't recognize the wrong and right, so the evil activates in the democratic countries.

After the Geneva Conference signed on July 20, 1954,

between French Prime Minister Mendes France and communist representatives were Phạm Văn Đồng (Vietnam communist party), Zhou Enlai (China communist), and Molotov (Soviet-Union). Vietnam divided into two parts with different governments. North Vietnam controlled by the communist party, and the communist government wanted to take control of all territory including the ethnic groups. So the People Army had tried to occupy the Hà Giang's territory where was the Opium field operating since the French colony in Đồng Văn district. The territory controlled by Meo (Miao) King Vương Chí Xìn(*Miao ethnic is the Hmong people live in East and South-East Asia.)*

However, Miao king Vương Chí Xìn had a strong troop to protect the Opium field, the numerous member was as a battalion with the modern weapon. The military commander of Hà Giang province couldn't take the land after sending a regiment and they met strong resistance. Eventually, the local government's committee reported to Ho Chi Minh to find the solution. Therefore, Ho Chí Minh ordered the local government to stay away and he silently sent an invitation letter and later Miao King Vương Chí Xìn to Hanoi. Eventually, Miao King Vương Chí Xìn became the Representative of Hà Giang in the sole parliament of Vietcong.

Miao King provided the Opium for Ho Chi Minh and the people believed Ho Chi Minh secretly commanded the drug syndicate. Therefore, Ho was an Opium addict, he used drugs a long time. So Ho Chi Minh deserved the facilities for Miao King Vương Chí Xìn, even the mother in law of Miao King Vương Chí Xìn who was a Chinese widow named Xíu, the local government didn't touch her business, and the Public

Guard force supported while the assets of wealthy families confiscated and imprisoned.

Uncle Ho of the leftists and left parties in Western was a boss of the drug lord, certainly, the propaganda machine of the Hanoi regime has never unveiled the incident of Hà Giang province and the secret story between Miao King Vương Chí Xìn and Ho Chi Minh, instead, they acclaim Uncle Ho is the great leader ever. The late generations of Vietnamese people including the young communist members have never known the truth, so they believe Ho Chi Minh is the patriot, instead, he was the traitor, he sold Vietnam country for China and Soviet Union's interest, Ho Chi Minh was a genocide, his crimes oppose humanity as Pol Pot in Cambodia. Moreover, the Vietcong regime canonized Ho Chi Minh as the successful Buddha, his embalmed body placed in Mausoleum at Hanoi and the Buddhist temples placed Ho Chi Minh's statue alongside the Buddha at the altars in the main halls of temples in Vietnam./.

50. GEN. VO NGUYEN GIAP: THE GREAT COMMANDER IN CHIEF OF THE PLACENTA'S BATTLEFIELD.

The world knew well a Vietnam communist 4 stars General Võ Nguyên Giáp, also known as the military icon of the Global Communist Bloc and the symbol of the innocent people, the leftist in the western country. His life is circled and curtained by the legend and also anecdote. Mostly, his brilliant record being launched likely the propaganda promoted by the Vietnam communist party which attaches the victories in the conflicts from 1945 to 1975. Moreover, the names of General Võ Nguyên Giáp's personality being stuck throughout Vietnam history, but the communists praise only plus the innocent people in the western country's adoration. Certainly, the Vietnam communist party extremely honored Võ Nguyên Giáp with the hero's title, a great man and the invincible general in the so-called Vietnam people army. In the record, it founded on December 22, 1944, at Trần Hưng Đạo Jungle's region, district Nguyên Bình, Cao Bằng province. Previously, the people army began with small troopers, the numerous militant was as an infantry platoon with 34 persons, it called Military Propaganda Group, the common weapon was the bamboo cut the sharp head and few rifles left by the French and Japan army.

The first combat operation launched on the evening August 16, 1945, at a Banian tree in Tân Trào village, district Sơn Dương, Tuyên Quang Province. General Võ Nguyên Giáp read the first military order and the next day, the unit formally celebrated for entry the battle. The title Tân Trào Banian tree (Cây Đa Tân Trào) became the historic event of the Vietnam communist party, actually the people army, the local resident respect this tree, they call" Sir Banian".

The Vietnam communist founded on February 3, 1930, while the communist party was weak, a small group of nationalist parties as Việt Nam Quốc Dân Đảng (Vietnam Nationalist Party) founder is the patriot Nguyễn Thái Học who executed by France after the uprising failed, Đại Việt Quốc Dân Đảng (Đại Việt Nationalist Party) founded by Trương Tử Anh who killed by the communist. However the

Vietnam communist party was cunning, leader Hồ Chí Minh trained in Russian in 1924, he was an activist of Soviet Union, the mission aimed to Asia. Hồ Chí Minh received strong support from the Soviet Union, including finance (salary) and later on, China contributed after 1949. Moreover, in prime time, in Vietnam, the scholars, academics, and the innocent intellectuals didn't recognize the danger and the real face of the communist, so they lined up behind Ho Chi Minh because they were wrongly concerned and expected Hồ Chí Minh was the patriot but after Genève treaty on July 20, 29154, Hồ Chí Minh controlled North Vietnam, the supporters knew Ho Chi Minh was treason, but it was too late, among of them, many were killed or imprisoned.

The Vietnam communist party is malice after the nationalists doubted the relationship between them and the communist. In 1944 Hồ Chí Minh pretended to disband the communist party, he changed the brand was The Study Marxism Club, when the date the communist party changed the name, Hồ Chí Minh had 5,000 members. Therefore in 1946 the number of members increased by 15,000 and continued to add more: in 1947 had 50,000 and in 1948 had 700,000 last in 1951, Hồ Chí Minh revived the communist party with another name was The Vietnam Workers' Party.

After the Geneva Convention 1954, the communist party sent the cadre and trooper to the Southern, they called the People Revolution Party (Đảng Nhân Dân Cách Mạng Việt Nam) because of the peasant allergies with the communist.

Ultimately, after winning the war by the unpredicted victory on April 30, 1975, they restored the real name, is the

Vietnam Communist Party (đảng Cộng Sản Việt Nam). Nowadays, they have more than 3,000,000 members and rules Vietnam with the dictatorial regime. The Vietnam communist party always prides itself on three victories:

1-Crushed down Fascist Japan: In reality, Japan surrendered after the US dropped two atomic bombs on Hiroshima and Nagasaki. The Vietnam communist had never won over the Japan in Second World War.

2-Won over the colonial French: It was not true because the US rejected the air force support in the Điện Biên Phủ's battle. The US recognized the colonial French was rapacious, they ruled Vietnam for nearly a century by the barbarous treatment of the native people. French pressured the Global Communist Bloc in the Geneva Convention and they forced to sign the treaty on July 20, 1954. The communists gave up because they just lost the crucial battle in Korea, if not they occupied the whole of Vietnam.

3-Defeated the Empire America: It is fully fun and comedy, the US releases the involvement in Vietnam after the Paris Convention on January 27, 1972. South Vietnam lost by the traitors as president Nguyễn Văn Thiệu who destroyed the South Vietnam army, so the North Vietnam armed force with 20 division took 55 days, not spent more than 2 years as the predict of the communist General Văn Tiến Dũng, the highest commander in the Hồ Chí Minh Campaign from March 1975. Moreover, General Dương Văn Minh, an infiltrator of Vietcong who served for the strategic espionage agency code T-4 since 1962 and A-10 in the decade of 1970, ordered the surrender on April 30, 1975. The US didn't lose the war, but

South Vietnam lost by the traitors, unfortunately, they held the top jobs in government, the presidency and also commander in chief. In the historic war, when the top commander wants to surrender or destroy the army, surely there is not any strong-armed force survives, so South Vietnam failed by the betrayal commander in chief.

However, Vietcong regime has never titled defeated the China despite from 1975 Vietnam and China conflicted, both sides lost tens thousands of troopers because Vietnam communist and China are the brotherhood, the bloodshed conflict to be expected as the domestic crisis, not fight against the foreigner.

General Võ Nguyên Giáp is famous in the Indochina and Vietnam War, but it is communist propaganda. Therefore General Giáp's biography being biased, the Vietcong and the left media in the western country have poisoned the world, so the misunderstandings conceal the truth. Likely an American broadcast journalist, best known as Anchorman (CBS Evening News from 1962 to 1981) Mr. Walter Leland Cronkite, also the senior reporter of many international events as Second World War, Vietnam War, Watergate…but he wrongly concern about General Võ Nguyên Giáp, his writing completely buries the reputation and the life record of a senior journalist of the media mainstream:

"General Vo Nguyen Giap

General Giap was a brilliant, highly respected leader of the North Vietnam military. The following quote is from his memoirs currently found in the Vietnam war memorial in Hanoi:

'What we still don't understand is why you Americans stopped the bombing of Hanoi. You had us on the ropes. If you had pressed us a little harder, just for another day or two, we were ready to surrender! It was the same at the battle of TET. You defeated us!

We knew it, and we thought you knew it.

But we were elated to notice your media was helping us. They were causing more disruption in America than we could on the battlefields. We were ready to surrender. You had won!'

General Giap has published his memoirs and confirmed what most Americans knew. The Vietnam war was not lost in Vietnam — it was lost at home. The same slippery slope, sponsored by the U.S. media, is currently underway. It exposes the enormous power of a Biased Media to cut out the heart and will of the American public.

A truism worthy of note: . . . Do not fear the enemy, for they can take only your life.

Fear the media, for they will distort your grasp of reality and destroy your honor."

Mr. Võ Nguyên Giáp a 103 years old who returned to the communist paradise and reunited with Karl Marx, Lenin, Stalin, Mao Tse Tung, Hồ Chí Minh, and the other iconic communists at 18 pm on October 4, 2013, at Hanoi.

Mostly, the general has to be trained from a military academy at West Point in the US, they served the long term in an army and had the experience. But General Võ Nguyên Giáp was unusual, he had never attended any military academy, however, he commanded multiple million troopers from the Indochina War to the Vietnam War. Certainly,

General Võ Nguyên Giáp had no military knowledge, he also knew nothing about the tactic, strategy, weapon using… but he just learned how to throw the hand grenade from Mr. Ernst Frey, a defected corporal of the French army.

An untrained soldier couldn't fight well in the battle, but an unqualified general is a military disaster, so General Võ Nguyên Giáp is the military genocide, his commander killed multiple million communist troopers.

Hồ Chí Minh nominated the 4 stars General Võ Nguyên Giáp that based on his quote:" who defeats a general, who would be a general". As Hồ Chí Minh said, the General doesn't need to be trained, but it is like the boxer, who beats the foe, to be the champion. The Điện Biên Phủ's battle had many untold stories, but the Vietcong hid all, therefore the witnesses unveiled the battle didn't run well as the communist propaganda's machine misled the public. For the preparing the battle at Điện Biên Phủ's valley, in April 1950, Hồ Chí Minh requested Mao Tse Tung helped and China dispatched the Chinese Military Advisory Group led by General Wei Guoqing, General Chen Geng was as Scholar General and 281 military expert officers held the commanding of Hồ Chí Minh's people army.

China's high profile advisors recognized the Vietnamese communist army being lost the fighting spirit while seeing many Vietnam trooper fearing, they deserted or self-destructive body by the individual weapon, so China's advisors warned Hồ Chí Minh had to fix the problem as soon as possible. Obviously, Hồ Chí Minh created the stories of unreal heroes were Phan Đình Giót and Bế Văn Đàng who used the bodies barred the wheels of artillery for saving the falling into the abyss. Likely in the Indochina War, a high-profile cadre. Mr. Trần Huy Liệu (former culture minister of Hồ Chí Minh's era) made up an imagined story about hero Lê Văn Tám who set alight body as the human torch to illuminate a unit while attacking the French's ammunition depot at Thị Nghè (Saigon). The fake story of hero Lê Văn Tám has been teaching into the Vietcong's education system and the lie became the real from the Indochina War, the late generations believe and adore the national hero Lê Văn Tám.

In the Điện Biên Phủ's battle, General Võ Nguyên Giáp was a puppet, whole combat operation was decided by China's delegator. The outcome wasted the blood of the Vietnamese, more than ten thousand lives exchange one thousand of French armed force. However, the Điện Biên Phủ's victory to be exaggerated by the propaganda machine. In the Điện Biên Phủ's battle, Vietnam communist spent the blood of its people, the weapon provided by the Soviet Union and China (the howitzer 105 mm left by Chiang Kai Shek's army) and the combat decision held in the hand of China's advisors.

Following the Vietnam War, General Võ Nguyên Giáp applied the Human wave tactic of Mao Tse Tung likely at Điện Biên Phủ's battle, but General Giáp received the heavy losses in the Khe Sanh battle 1966, 1967, he barbecued ten thousand lives of the North Vietnam troop. Therefore the Tết Offensive 1968 had a disaster, there were 100,000 casualties excluding the highly numerous injuries, it disabled the Vietcong people army.

General Võ Nguyên Giáp was disgraced, moreover, in this period the rival fighting between the pro-China and the Soviet Union purged many high profiles of the Vietnam communist party. Among was the Võ Nguyên Giáp wing, despite his comrade trimmed a lot his fan, but they still used General Giáp as a puppet. Therefore he was a coward, not behaved as a general's attitude, he was shameless by the acceptance of the new job, but this job harmed his reputation ever. Therefore the leftists in the western countries as Jane Fonda, John Kerry, Joe Biden, Bill Clinton, Hillary Clinton, and Walter Leland Cronkite…CNN waived, they concealed as the cat hid the shit.

After the Tết Offensive lost, Hồ Chí Minh, replaced Võ Nguyên Giáp by General Văn Tiến Dũng who commanded the people army. General Võ Nguyên Giáp downgraded to the Mother and Child's Protection Committee, his assistant was Miss Đinh Thị Cần, a chef of Hồ Chí Minh, and she was a fellow country with Hồ Chí Minh.

The Committee's duty was abortion, the unborn baby plus the placenta were the economic patterns. The dead body of the unborn baby to be used for pig fed or organic fertilizer. But the placenta was useful, the communist party encouraged the people to use the placenta replaced the protein because North Vietnam had been facing insufficient meat, fish. The placenta has become the favorite food of the shorted food population, they fried the placenta with a kind of vegetable called" Lá Mơ". The legacy of General Võ Nguyên Giáp is still remaining, nowadays somewhere in North Vietnam, the placenta being sold in the market as the meat. Mostly the placenta provided by the hospital.

The death of Placenta General Võ Nguyên Giáp being controversial, mostly the Vietnamese people condemn a military genocide, but the communist party and rare Vietnamese as former the South Vietnam ambassador Bùi Diễm glorifies. However, the innocent people, left media praise General Võ Nguyên Giáp, because they know nothing about the man who killed multiple million communist troopers from the Indochina War to Vietnam War.

General Võ Nguyên Giáp completely lost respect from the Vietnamese people since he served in the Mother and Child's Protection Committee. The North Vietnamese diffused the common verses:

"Hoan nghinh đại tướng Võ Nguyên.

Giáp xưa thắng trận, Điện Biên anh hùng.

Ngày xưa đại tướng cầm quân.

Ngày nay đại tướng cầm quần chị em".

Translated:

Applaud four stars General VÕ NGUYÊN.

GIÁP won the Điện Biên, he is the hero.

Before General commanded the army.

Today General holds the female's pants.

Or:

"Ngày xưa đại tướng công đồn.

Ngày ni đại tướng bịt L...chị em"

Translated

Before the General commanded the army,

Today General gags the pussy.

The inexperienced people and innocent element the communist in the western countries, likely the US, all became the eating the democratic bread but serving for the communist as the saying quotes. They are the domestic thugs, the worms in the free speech country. The famous faces are Jane Fonda (a nickname is Hanoi Jane), Joe Biden, John Kerry (a traitor in Vietnam War), Bill Clinton, Hillary Clinton...they have puffed the propaganda toxic into the western people since the Vietnam War and they praised the military Genocide Võ Nguyên Giáp, it is the shame. Nowadays, the leftists lost the credit and their reputation buried into the tricky record.

There is only the Vietnam War, Vietcong paid 1,500,000 lives and still missing about 300,000 troopers, therefore the Vietcong regime has no policy for finding their missing comrades, instead, they are keen to find the US soldiers who were missing in the action for money. While the loser is South Vietnam lost about 300,000 soldiers in the fierce battle from 1954 to 1975. However after Vietcong won the war on April 30, 1975, they killed about 165,000 members of the Republic Army of South Vietnam and public servants in the re-education camp by the execution, starvation, illness without medication and treatment, the currently spiritual intimidation, the forced laborer... The leftists and the left media don't want to see the barbarous treatment of the Vietcong tyranny regime, but they are keen to glorify the communist, actually the military genocide as General Võ Nguyên Giáp./.

51. DEMOCRATS APPEARED THE REAL FACE OF COMMUNIST

Obviously, the US just had the left party *called the Socialist Party of America* but from 1919, its party split and established the **Communist Party USA (CPUSA)**, the impact occurred after Lenin transferred the crazy theory of the dishonest academic, Karl Mark, to reality on October 1917, it also called the October Revolution 1917.

The CPUSA ties closely with the American Labor Movement and later on, CPUSA has influenced US politics. The growth of the Soviet-Union developed the strength of the Communist Party USA, actually, from the 1960s, the US Communist party affected the society, the party also secretly collaborated with the Soviet Union into the intelligence on the US soil until the Soviet Union collapsed in early 1990. The prominent leader of CPUSA was Mr. William Z. Foster born on February 25, 1881, in Taunton, Massachusetts, he died on September 1, 1961, in Moscow, Russia. He held the CPUSA president in 1924, 19128, and 1933. William Foster was an aggressive communist leader, at a general conference, he declared to kill 2/3 US population if communist takes over the US government.

Almost, the Western people have never known the barbarous policy and the cruel character of communism, they just read the books written by the leftist authors and listen to the propaganda. The Vietnamese people have never forgotten a story of a wealthy woman named Nguyễn Thị Năm, she dedicated a lot of money to Ho Chi Minh and the Vietnam Communist party into the period fighting against Colonial France from 1945 to 1954, she gave away 20,000 Indochina

Piasters were worth 800 lạng vàng (1 lạng vàng=37,8 gram pure gold), nevertheless, she couraged two sons joined the Viet Minh's troop. In the Indochina War, Ho Chi Minh promoted Nguyễn Thị Năm was the president of a woman in Thái Nguyên Province and Northern inter-region. She took care of the food and accommodation at her place for the hight profiles of the Vietnam Communist Party were as Trường Chinh, Hoàng Quốc Việt, Lê Đức Thọ (Nobel Peace Prize with Henry Kissinger), Phạm Văn Đồng (Prime Minister), Hoàng Hữu Nhân, General Võ Nguyên Giáp, General Nguyễn Chí Thanh, Hoàng Tùng, Vũ Quốc Huy, Hoàng Thế Thiện, Lê Thanh Nghị.. However, when Ho Chi Minh took over North Vietnam after Geneve Conference signed on July 20, 1954. Ho Chi Minh founded the Democratic Republic of Vietnam, the bloodshed spread throughout North Vietnam, it was the Landlord Reform, so woman Nguyễn Thị Năm to executed on July 9, 1953, at Đồng Bẩm, Thái Nguyên Province.

If the **Communist Party USA (CPUSA)** controls the US, obviously, billionaire George Soros will be executed first for the sample as the circumstance of the wealthy Vietnamese woman Nguyễn Thị Năm and following, 10.2 millionaires will be killed and the assets to be castigated.

After Vietcong claimed the unpredictable victory on April 30, 1975, at Saigon town hall, Mr. Nguyễn Hộ, a member of the center communist party told his comrades:" *their house, we occupy-their wife, we take and their children, we enclave"*.

The communist, left media, socialist are the siblings, they have the common great master Karl Marx who

labeled the advanced component as the communist derived from the Ape in his book" Historical Materialism". Certainly, the Ape is not a human being, so almost the communist and leftist ignore human rights and having the demagogy, lie, cheat…After Karl Marx declared the communist manifesto, the communist movement spread worldwide. Actually, since 1917 and after the Second World War, the communist occupied China, Vietnam, Laos, Cambodia, Cuba, and Eastern Europe. The Cold War conflicted between the Global Communist Bloc and the democratic country is led by the US. The communist was not only developed into poor countries, even the wealthy countries as the US, Europe, Japan, and Australia too.

In the Down Under country, the Communist Party of Australia (CPA) founded in 1971, most, the members came from the Socialist Party of Australia. Until 1991, CPA dissolved, the communist members merged In the Vietnam War, the Communist Party of Australia, Labor Party **Australian Labor Party (the writer calls Australian Leninist Party).** In the Vietnam War period, the undercover activists and the communist espionage network protested with violence to support Vietcong terrorists and opposed Australian troops fighting against the communist in Vietnam's battle.

Most of Karl Marx's pupils in democratic countries, actually the US and Western have never known communism, but they blindly have followed and activated. The innocent and honest component easily becomes the leftist or the communist in the Western. Despite the leftist, left media and the left parties are such as Democrats in the US, ALP in

Australia, the Socialist Party in France, UK Labor Party knew the communist movement killed more than 100 million people and enslaved the other a billion people. They always condemn the cruelty, dictatorial regime and respect the human rights, therefore, they have followed the communist, it is a contradiction. In the US, the major people recognize the communist movement as the most genocide on the planet. However, Democrats always keep communism as the backbone of the party. Author Trevor Louden published an article on February 8, 2019, titled:

Democrats Allow Communists to Infiltrate There Party Across the Nation

The opening wrote:

"The Communist Party USA (CPUSA) is infiltrating the Democratic Party across the country. Communists, some openly, some secretly, are working in Democratic campaigns, holding Democratic Party leadership positions, and even running for public office on the Democratic Party ballot line. The communists also are pushing their policies inside the Democratic Party, to the point that it's almost impossible to distinguish between the CPUSA and Democratic Party programs. Many comrades also work closely with influential Congress members or U.S. senators.

The CPUSA supports China, Cuba, Venezuela, and the Russian Communist Party—all enemies of the United States. The CPUSA still <u>advocates</u> *for the "overthrow of the capitalist class" in this country, yet the Democrats do absolutely zilch to keep the communists out of their party."*

President Barrack Obama followed communism since he

attended law school, author Aaron Klein and Brenda. J. Elliot published the book on May 3, 2010:" **The Manchurian President: Barack Obama's Ties to Communists, Socialists and Other Anti-American Extremists"** on Amazon referred: *The book uncovers a far-leftist, anti-American nexus that has been instrumental in not only helping build Obama's political career but in securing his presidency. Klein details with shocking precision how this nexus continues to influence Obama and the White House and is involved in drafting policy aimed at reshaping our country. Highlights of The Manchurian President:*

-Obama's mysterious college years unearthed

-Shocking details of Obama's relationship with Bill Ayers and other Weathermen terrorists

-Obama's ties to Islam and black liberation theology

-Startling facts about Obama's eligibility to serve as president

-Obama's membership in a socialist party probed

-How Obama's hope & change slogans stem from communist activism

-Radical socialists involved in drafting stimulus bill, ObamaCare

-Communists, socialists and other radicals on team Obama, including an expose on Obama's top guns in the White House

*-Never-before-revealed depth of Obama's relationship with ACORN (*The Australian Cybercrime Online Reporting Network)

President Barrack Obama is the first black president, the first Muslim and Communist-ruled the White House in 8 years. He recruited Miss Valerie June Jarrett held the top advisor, she served as a Presidential Assistant for public engagement and intergovernmental affairs from 2009 to 2017 (two terms of president Barrack Obama). Mis Valerie Jarrett is the hardcore communist in the US, despite FBI investigation but President Barrack Obama hampered. Moreover, President Barrack Obama had 6 Muslim advisors (mostly the Muslim Brotherhood). President Barrack Obama applied socialism in the US, he brainwashed the people, destroyed the economy, pauperized the people, created the social mayhem that replaces the class struggle in the communist regime by:

*The gender struggle: the same-sex-marriage legislation has become the conflict between the natural couple and the homosexual couple, it causes social division.

*The racial fighting: President Barrack Obama dug up the ashes of Civil war, he exited the Black discriminates the White. His racial discrimination influenced Africa, actually, the White farmers in Zimbabwe, South Africa were the victims of killing, robbery, and confiscate the assets

*President Barrack Obama pauperized the US people and helped comrade China controlled the US economy. It is the debt trap that Obama created in 8 years.

President Barrack Obama also helped Vietcong's fake anti-government persons as Điếu Cày (Nguyễn Văn Hải), Cù Huy Hà Vũ, Tạ Phong Tần, Trần Khải Thanh Thủy migrated to the US while the South Vietnam captain Nguyễn Hữu Cầu who was imprisoned 37 years didn't afford the humanitarian policy. Actually, the Amnesty International and the other human rights organization are an accomplice with President Barrack Obama to get the fake anti-communist recipients migrated in the US.

The most Democratic presidents as Jimmy Carter closed with comrade China, so China became a member of the UN Security Council and the UN eliminated Taiwan. President Bill Clinton helped China grew faster with the Most Favored Nation's policy and using the hoax climate change to curb Western productivity. President Barrack Obama transformed the US to be China's colony. In 2016, he demeaned the US presidency by using the stairway that replaced the red carpet and 21 gunshots apply for the national leader.

It is like the Communist Party of Australia (CPA) after it disbanded, the members merged into the Australian Labor Party. In the US, Democrats being faced difficulty after the loss of the election in 2016, so the leftists united and Democrats favor the Communist Party for the USA's access and stay. Nevertheless, communism's stance appeared with senior Senator Bernie Sander and fresh Congresswoman Alexandria Ocasio Cortez's vow to lead the US into socialism. However President Donald Trump confirmed the socialism has no way to exist in the US, nevertheless, the people recognized Venezuela pauperized after President Hugo Chavez and Nicolas Maduro applied socialism.

Democrats and communists have the same character as the common formula are 3D=Demagogy+Deception +Destruction./.

52. JANE FONDA, A VIETCONG TERRORIST'S ACCOMPLICE

If in the Cold War, the Global Communist Bloc raised the terror in the soil of the US or somewhere else likely September 11, 2001. Certainly, the domestic thugs as the anti-war movement, the left media, and the innocent people in the western country couldn't launch the fake peaceful love campaign attacks the allies by the protests plus violence and they couldn't mislead the public by propaganda. Actually, the within thugs aimed to act the countries were sending the troop to help the South Vietnam fighting against the communist.

In the reality, Vietcong is an early terror's organization, the terrorist is their tradition and has never changed. In the Vietnam War period, every day the terrorist Vietcong killed the Vietnamese people in the countryside with the cruel practice as beheaded by the machete, execution, buried still alive….but Vietcong is proud the barbarous killing its people, in the Museum at Mỏ Cày district, Bến Tre province where displays the Sledgehammer and below appraised Mr. Nguyễn Văn Thắng, vice district Mỏ Cày who used it to break the skull of 10 people. Therefore in a western country like Australia, the media and the animal protection firm claimed the cows import to Indonesia, Vietnam to be killed by the sledgehammer, but they have never known in the Vietnam War, Vietcong broke the human head with this hammer. They also shelled into the crowded residential region, no exception the school, church. The Vietcong terrorists set up the bomb in the city, like Saigon capital to be targeted as the famous terrorists Nguyễn Văn Trỗi, Trần Văn Đan…now, the names of Vietcong's terrorist placed the street.

The anti-war, pro-communist movement, and the left

media as CNN are the domestic thugs, who eat the bread of democrat but adore the evil communist. The traitors have not shown remorse yet, despite the Vietnam War was over and they knew the Vietcong is a terrorist more than ISIS or Al Qaeda. As the news from Polska of Poland released in May 2013, Ho Chi Minh's name listed among the most massacre in 20th, he killed 1,700,000 people, but the anti-war movement waived the genocide against humanity.

A million Vietnamese people died on the wayfinding freedom and the other few million survivors live with the anti-war element that is enough to wake up, but they keep motionless as stone.

The famous faces of anti-war, pro-communist are Joe Biden, John Kerry, Bill Clinton, Hillary Clinton...and Vietnamese are Zen master Thích Nhất Hạnh and his Buddhist fellow Võ Văn Ái (now they live in French). All ignore the victims of Vietcong, they are shameless.

Among them, the case of Jane Fonda is the brilliant face. Her spouse is Ted Burned, who founded CNN, the most famous left media in the US launched the propaganda, misled the public, poisoned innocent people in the western state since the Cold War. The propaganda's toxic of the left and pro-communist as Jane Fonda, John Kerry...have remained into the society.

Likely the terrorist, Al Qaeda, ISIS....the suicide bomb person will come to heaven and honored by Halal, in the Vietnam War the terrorist titled the hero. Launching the terror campaign, chairman Ho Chi Minh encouraged the killing, he granted the titles:

-The Victorious Knight: the criteria is killing at least 5

soldiers of South Vietnam.

-America's killing Knight: the criteria is killing at least 5 US.

Therefore, the Ho Chi Minh's medal is the top one, but Jane Fonda honored as Hanoi Jane, her name has become the global title that is more valuable than any Honor's title or the top medal of Vietcong. Despite Jane Fonda, John Kerry, Bill Clinton, Hillary Clinton....killed not anyone, but their consequence affected the lives of millions of Vietnamese people; particularly after Vietcong claimed the unpredicted victory, the super gang communist in Vietnam congregated more than 800,00 members of the South Vietnam army and public servant, the revenge policy that also calls the dry bloodbath killed 165,000 by the worse treatments: execution, starvation, illness without medical, currently spiritual terror, torture, forced laborer. The crimes against the humanity of Vietcong and whose helped the terrorist Vietcong succeeded is the genocide likely. Therefore the culprits have not paid for their crimes, moreover, Jane Fonda or Hanoi Jane honored by the 44th US president Barack Obama. The US people, actually the Vietnam veteran anger the president but they couldn't change the president's order. On the other hand the first black US president, an undeclared Muslim and communist in the White House applied the brainwashing method into the US people in 8 years, among the communist practice, president Obama imposed the unfair as honor Jane Fonda is like the communist regimes in China, Vietnam, North Korea, Cuba...promote the genocides as Mao Tse Tung, Ho Chi Minh, Kim Il Sung, Fidel Castro are heroes, the national symbols./.

53. THE LEFT PARTIES AND COMMUNIST ADVOCATE THE VIOLENCE

The real face of the Democrats party exposed to the public, the communist parties in China, Vietnam, North Korea, and the other communist countries are the siblings of Democrats, the violence is the character of Karl Marx's pupil. On the other hand, communists and the left parties in Western are like the tiger snake and cobra. The innocent pest lovers could make the wrong judge when they consider the kind of venomous snake called NUA (Vietnamese people call), it is like the python but its venom can kill the people as a tiger snake. The Western people wrongly believe the left parties as Democrats, Labor party are progressive parties, indeed, those are the communist parties call the different title. Therefore, the left parties couldn't hide the communist character when inside the parties have the left-wing, central left-wing (Bill Clinton is the central left-wing).

The so-called class struggle has applied flexibly into multiple circumstances, whatever, the class struggle couldn't hide the violence despite the communist regimes, and the left parties in the Western have used the demagogic tactic to cheat the people.

1-In the communist countries: violence becomes the backbone of most policies to remain the authoritarian government ruled by the Ape super gang. The so-called revolution, class struggle, socialism, social reform, communist paradise are just a pie in the sky. The communist parties expose the super gang's character. Communism is the culprit of the most genocide that occurred on the planet with

273

more than 100 million people killed more than a billion people enslaving. Therefore, the communist pride and enjoy the serious crimes opposing humanity. On the other hand, communist has never repented instead they consider the killing, robbery and enslaving the people are the morality. In Vietnam, Ho Chi Minh and its communist party killed 1,700,000 people into the landlord reform campaign, beaten the capitalist campaign and social purge campaign, but Vietcong praises the title of revolutionary morality.

2-In the democratic countries:

-The left parties couldn't apply the inhumane policies as the communist regime, therefore, the left parties apply the demagogic policy to win the election and control the government. The common formula of the left parties is **3D=Deception+Demagogy+Destruction**. The left parties have no policy on national security, border protection, and national interest, so they cover the fallen policies by the same-sex-marriage legislation, the hoax climate change, actually the human rights has exploited to support the asylum seeker or illegal migrant that helps the left parties gaining the ballot from the ethnic. Its reason, the left parties are such as the Australian Labor Party, the UK Labor Party, Democrats Party in the US, Socialist Party in France, Greens Party always endorse asylum seeker despite they knew the illegal migrant conflicts against the law and national security. (the asylum seeker is the illegal intruder into the other country).

-The left media is the culprit of social complication. Since the Cold War, actually the Vietnam War, the left media knew communist is an inhumane regime, but the left media has transformed the communication to business, the media career belongs to the payment, so China and the other communist countries should hire the left media into psychological warfare to propagate into the Western countries. The Vietnam war misled by the left media, the innocent people in the Western to be brainwashed and became the human-robot. The protests with violence to support Vietcong terrorists and distorted the war to fight against Vietcong terrorists of the South Vietnam government, the US, and allies. After the Vietnam War ended with the unpredictable victory of Vietcong on April 30, 1975, the world recognized Vietcong regime caused a million Vietnamese people to flee for freedom and more than 90,000,000 Vietnamese people lost the freedom.

Nowadays, the left media has continued to mislead the public, actually, after the loss of the presidential election in 2016, Democrats and the left media have excited the fan, the innocent Democratic supporters to protest with violence against the US President Donald Trump. So the left media is the thug of people, the foe of communication. The left media has never changed the character with the common formula is **3F=3Frauds=False poll+Fake news+Fabricated story**.

Democrats and the left media just excite the people creating the violence, but when their tool arrested or getting the legal trouble, the perpetrator hides and escape the responsibility. The coward could abandon the supporters as a saying:*" throwing the lemon skin after the juice emptied"*.

Senator Tim Kaine (D-VA) raises the aggressive speech:" *"What we've got to do is fight in Congress, fight in the courts, fight in the streets, fight online, fight at the ballot box, and now there's the momentum to be able to do this"*. The

US people have no surprise Mr. Tim Kaine who was the vice-presidential candidate of Hillary Clinton in the election 2016.

Since President Donald Trump getting the office on January 20, 2917, Democrats always attack the commander in chief with cunning tactics. The impeachment failed after the legal terrorist Robert Mueller concluded the report and resigned the head of Special Counsel. Obama's judges issued court orders to block the travel ban's executive order and border protection orders, the Democratic thug is led by the lawmaker terrorist and commander in the Nancy Pelosi currently opposes the national security policy of the government and recently, the legal thug failed to block $USD 2.5 billion of the defense fund to complete the wall. Senator Tim Kaine excites the violence on the street, what does he do for the country? /.

54. PRESIDENT BARRACK OBAMA IS THE HOMOSEXUAL REVOLUTIONIST

Lenin expected as the first Communist revolutionist after he transformed the crazy dream and deadly theory of a dishonest man, Karl Marx, into reality. Following the most human massacre on the planet originated from Russia in October 1917. The super gang communist's catastrophe spread worldwide with the **Red Flag**, almost, the continents appeared the iconic communist revolutionists as Mao Tse Tung in China, Ho Chi Minh in Vietnam, Kim Il Sung in North Korea, Fidel Castro in Cuba, Pol Pot in Cambodia and the other evil revolutionists, they are on the list of the most genocide in the 20th century, the crimes oppose against the humanity have never forgotten on the planet. However, in the Western, the left media dodges to talk about communist genocide and the supporters are such as Jane Fonda, Joe Biden, John Kerry, Bill-Hillary Clinton, and the other Democratic high profiles have not shown remorse after they knew well Vietcong in Vietnam War.

The dishonest components covered the revolution's label, they killed more than 100 million people and enslaved a billion people. Nowadays, the toxic radioactivity of Karl Marx still affects the world including the democratic countries represents the left media, they destroyed the mainstream's prestige by the fake news and fabricated story. The hoax revolution of communists insults the French revolution in 1789.

The hoax communist revolution destroyed the society, mostly, the revolutionists were the illiterate or low-educated peasants exploited the label of revolution to revenge the intellectuals and wealthy components, so after the so-called proletarian unmasked the evil face is the thug of the people. Most communist countries fell into poverty as Vietnam, North Korea, Cuba, China (the government is rich but the major population is poor), and others. While the poison of communists still remains, in the US, the **Homosexual Revolution** has started the movement, and somewhere else, actually, the US, President Barrack Obama was among the pioneer of the Homosexual Revolution, the movement expects Obama is prominent of the same-sex-marriage legalization. Nowadays, there are 21 countries legalized same-sex- marriage.

The Homosexual Revolutionist Barrack Obama had the slogan" *Yes we can*" in the US presidential election 2008, but" *Yes he could*" change the true color of the White House to Rainbow. Yes, he allowed the US army to practice homosexuality, he cornered the Supreme Judges to impose the same-sex-marriage legislation into 50 states. Homosexuality globalized, in Australia with revolutionist Penny Wong, Bill Shorten, and almost the Labor party's high profile support. The same-sex-marriage legislation in Australia spent a lot of time, actually, the Labor Party's politicians wasted the time on the same-sex marriage debate in parliament house and taxpayers cost $AUD 122 million for the postal survey. Nowadays, the Rainbow flag becomes a global symbol, it populates than the United Nations flag.

The communist hoax revolution pauperized the people, genocide, therefore, the Homosexual Revolution destroyed multiple million years of human history, wiped out the religious faith and social valuation.

Former President Barrack Obama is the Homosexual Revolutionist as Lenin is the Communist Revolutionist. Both changed the world, the consequence has leftover on human history. The Homosexual Revolutionist Barrack Obama ignites the gender war between the natural couple and homosexual couple, he also the racial activist war between the black and white in the US (the racial war spread in Zimbabwe and somewhere else as in Africa). The most achievement of Obama is the toilet serves for the transgender in the US, but the economy is nothing, he left over the US the deep debt estimates $USD 20 trillion.

The worst record of President Barrack Obama

Who destroyed the economy and social value of America?

He is the homosexual revolutionist

And declares worldwide the gender war../.

55. THE MIND TERROR IS THE SERIOUS CRIME AGAINST HUMANITY

The mastermind is the perpetrator of the serious crime including the genocide, mostly, the culprits are malicious, they excite the public, actually, the innocent components to carry out the ambition or the political purposes. The psychological tactic applying as French quotes" le mountain de Panurge" becomes the essential rule using in the propaganda. The Vietnamese people concern:" *A doctor wrongly treats, a patient could kill-A national leader applies the wrong policy, a general killed-A teacher taught the wrongs, many generations killed"*. The left media has misled and poisoned the people by the fake news, fabricated stories since the Cold War, it conducts the world including Western society being disordered, the people hated each other, so the left media is the most dangerous, the invisible terrorist hides into the labels of media and the free speech. The people need to fight against the left media terrorist in any way, including pressure, the lawmakers decide the anti-media terrorist law.

In the Second World War, Hitler was the mastermind of more than 6 million Jewish massacres, the victims concentrated into death camps and killed by cruel methods. The man who carried out the mastermind Hitler was Dr. Paul

Joseph Goebbels held the Reich Minister of Propaganda of Nazi in Germany from 1933 to 1945. Under the rule of Hitler, the hatred propagated to excite the people involved in the movement and created the war.

Karl Marx was the mastermind of the communist movement, his books taught the dishonest components the methods the killed, social purge, robbery, enslaved the people labeled the revolution.

Mind discrimination is dangerous than racial discrimination or the religious discrimination of the Muslim's bigot and the arrogant clerics. The mind discrimination destroys whoever has a different concern, thinking from the communist party including family, parent, and relatives. The communist ignores the moral, family and human being, the **propaganda transformed the human body to human-robot after the mind being controlled by the communist party**, so communist killed their parent without pity, instead, they pride to be the revolutionist. Karl Marx's evil theory applied in Vietnam, its country divided into two parts after the Geneva conference signed on July 20, 1954. At North, the government so-called the Democratic Republic of Vietnam led by genocide Ho Chi Minh and the communist party (disguised as the Vietnam Workers Party) launched the Landlord Reform Campaign. The bloodshed spread everywhere, Ho Chi Minh and his comrades killed more than 200,000 people to be labeled" landlord, wealthy component and intellectuals", indeed, the numerous victim estimated a million people. In the massacre campaign, at Hương Sơn's village, Dr. Nguyễn Khắc Viện who became a human-robot, was very happy to clap the hand while seeing his father was a well-known intellectual named Nguyễn Khắc Niêm being confined in a wooden cage, his father was waiting to appear at the people court, certainly, the death sentence was inevitable. Karl Marx mastermind is the most human disaster on the planet, every communist regime always performed psychological warfare to excite the people hate each other, it calls the" *class struggle*", so the regime created the genocide and the human-robot carried out the policies, almost, the massacres came from the mastermind was Karl Marx or Marxism-Leninist. The communist movement killed more than 100 million people and enslaved another billion people. Unfortunately, the left parties adore Mastermind Karl Marx. The human robots of communism have never recognized the serious crimes against humanity, instead, they pride themselves to be the revolutionists, so the left media has never confessed the mastermind of the social disorder in Western.

The terrorist struck somewhere else, the bloodshed or materials damaged, but the police and government just condemned or arrested the terrorists. Therefore, the perpetrators are the bigot clerics and preachers plus the arrogant Muslim community leaders who propagated the hatred into the Allah adherent in the mosques and communities. Psychological warfare is the key to conduct terrorism, they extremists exploit the faith of Allah to propagate hatred and urging terrorism.

The left media carries out the psychological warfare, the fake news, fabricated stories, and the false polls are the mind terror as Dr. Paul Joseph Goebbels of the Hitler regime and the propaganda machine in the communist regime did. The mind terror has originated the social disorder, the people division, the nation shattered.

The communist propaganda could recognize, but the mind terror is invisible in the Western. The media terrorists label the free speech and communication worker, certainly, every job and career couldn't avoid the dishonest. The legal services have dishonest lawyers, they practice the lawyer's career as the robber with the paper-knife, the dishonest judges are dangerous, they are the robbers with the wooden hammer. The media line has the honest, but dishonest media workers are the terrorist have used the psychological warfare as the sharp weapon to transform the mind of victim belongs to the fake news and fabricate stories.

The world always complicates, the society divided, the people misunderstand each other which causes conflicts and war. The propaganda misleads the public and controls the people's minds is a crime against humanity. In Vietnam War, the left media terrorists propagated to support Vietcong terror, so Vietnam communist party gained support from the innocent people, actually, they adored Ho Chi Minh, instead, the left media concealed the truth about Ho Chi Minh is the genocide, he killed 1,700, 000 people, in 1929, Ho Chi Minh raped a 15 years old girl named Tuyet Lan at Thailand, nevertheless, Ho was the famous pedophile. The left media terrorists and the supporters are Jane Fonda, John Kerry, Joe Biden, Bill-Hillary Clinton, and the others have never confessed the truth. The left media terrorists are the culprits of the riots on the streets after President Donald Trump getting the office including the inauguration's day celebrated on January 20, 2017. The left media terrorists exited the innocent people protested for every national security and border protection's order of President Donald Trump. The left media terrorists and the media terror bases CNN, The Washing Post,

The New York Times, CBS, NBC, MSNBC…and in Australia has ABC, Channel Seven, Channel Ten…currently attack the people mind and the public being disordered, the society falling into the mayhem. The toxic mind terror remains a long time in the society as the nuclear radioactivity.

The people believe the left Western journalists and the left media companies are the intellectuals, they know the wrong and right, but they activate the propaganda for the evils and become the enemy of the people. They know the fake news and fabricated stories are the lies and cheats. Therefore, the money conducts the dishonest in the mainstream selling out the soul to the evils, actually, the left media companies should receive the finance and privileges from the offshore enemies as China communists, the terrorist organizations and the others then the left media companies pay the left journalists. Nevertheless, the offshore enemies could link the financial chain into the Western companies, so the advertising influenced the left media companies into the communication.

Every nation applies the law anti-terrorist, why didn't they have the anti-media terrorist law? Nevertheless, the left media is the most dangerous terrorist than any form of terror. The lawmakers need to create the law in media to prevent the media terrorist. The journalist, reporter, Radio operator, T.V host must comply with the law, so whoever released the fake news and fabricated stories to be punished by law. Actually, the pollsters must have the license and the code of practice as any job, career, whoever conspires the false poll, it is the rigged election and they will face the criminal charge as the terrorists.

The honest media must act as soon as possible to protect

the mainstream's trust, the Committee to Protect Journalist Prestige (CPJP) will restore the mainstream's credit. The left media terrorists have destroyed the mainstream's fundament since the Cold War. Now the time to eliminate the mind terrorists is a serious crime against humanity./.

56. THE TURMOIL OF THE DEMOCRATIC STRUGGLE IN VIETNAM.

The democratic struggle in Myanmar and Vietnam started at the same time, but Myanmar approached the target, the movement leads by Miss Aung San Suu Kye succeeded, and the country steps toward democracy, now they will have a president, Mr. Htin Kyaw who was nominated for Myanmar presidential position.

Unfortunately, in Vietnam, the most democratic movements are the scam and cheat, mostly the communist has used the decoys, they pretend to fight for democracy, therefore in the reality, they have driven the movement to stable for the Vietnam communist party. The most famous face is the senior Venerable Thích Quảng Độ, a member of Ấn Quang temple. In the Vietnam War, Ấn Quang Temple is the den of Vietcong carries out undercover activities in South Vietnam territory. After Vietcong claimed the unpredicted victory on April 30, 1975, the monks and nuns of this temple appeared the real faces, they are the Vietcong. The senior venerable Thích Quảng Độ cheats and collects the money many decades the Vietnamese patriot overseas. Likely a needle hid a long time in the bag, a day it would be discovered,

284

on April 29, 2009, the senior Venerable Thích Quảng Độ, chief of the monk and nun of his religion form, he declared the struggle tactic:" protest at home" that means to stay at home, no demonstration at the street, from this time, the Vietnamese people stayed away from a decoy.

There are many liars as Cù Huy Hà Vũ, a prince of the communist party, he confirmed:" I have never opposed the communist party". A pretending opponent the communist is Điếu Cày (Nguyễn Văn Hải) to be promoted as the democratic fighter by the Amnesty International and the Vietnam Reform Party, a fake democratic affiliate in the Vietnamese community overseas, it founded by admiral Hoàng Cơ Minh, but this illegal organization is the culprit of the massacre 5 Vietnamese journalists from more than 3 decades ago and the terror in the community. A fake democratic fighter Điếu Cày came to the US in 2015 as a political prisoner, the US president Barack Obama welcomed and met him at the White House. Mr. Điếu Cày was not a political prisoner, indeed he was convicted the tax evasion....Amnesty International and the US government made the terrible mistake, they were being alongside Điếu Cày and helped him resettled in the US. It is a sample of a scam political prisoner, during living in jail, he had properties for rent and his daughter was an overseas student in Canada. In 1975, most of the soldiers of South Vietnam and public servants were incarcerated in the re-education camp, their families had to sell cloth, jewelry, and anything to buy the food...

The democratic movement in Vietnam to be driven by the communist party with the fake fighters above, so Vietnam couldn't reach the target as Myanmar. On the other reason, every year, the Vietnamese refugees turn asylum seeker have returned safely to where they fled for freedom and condemned, they provided to the tyranny regime about $ USD 20 billion/ a year, so the communist regime couldn't collapse.

While Myanmar turns to freedom, but Vietnam is still sinking down into the dictatorial regime. Moreover, Vietnam's situation worsens than Hong Kong, but like Tibet, Sinkiang Uigur, because the Vietnam communist party becomes the vassal of Beijing, they provided the sand for China to build the artificial islands in the disputed waters.

Moreover, the people in Vietnam were brainwashed by the Pavlov method, mostly they lost the national spirit when history gently wiped out and replaced by communist history. The national spirit is the key to the country's development, likely Japan, its people promotes the highly of the history, so everyone tries to do something for the homeland, then Japanese is proud about the country has not much the natural resources but rich the patriotic heart.

Most Vietnamese people are proud of 4,000 historic years, but now history destroyed by the communist. The democratic stage in Vietnam being dipped into turmoil, the Vietcong regime is malice, they recognize the collapse of the Soviet Union and the Eastern Europe Communist Bloc, so they prevent the loss of the inhumane regime by the decoy of the democratic fighter. Since the fake democratic movement has started, the Vietcong's faces as Nguyễn Hộ, an author of the famous speech:" their house, we occupy. Their wife, we take. Their children, we enslave", Hoàng Minh Chính, a high profile of communist, General Trần Độ, Dr. Nguyễn Thanh

Giang, Dr. Nguyễn Đan Quế, Dr. Nguyễn Quang A, Dr. Lê Đăng Doanh...all are liars. The decoy of democratic fighter act like the fire brigade, they have the prevention fire and the bushfire would be avoided.

The world, actually the human rights firms have to be careful about the fake democratic movement in Vietnam. The most democratic struggles are the decoy, they cheat the people, therefore driving the people into the rival fighting in the communist party, not for freedom, so the communist rival will replace the defeated rival and the democratic status in Vietnam has no change./.

57. THE COMMUNIST EXPLOITS BUDDHISM COVERING GENOCIDE

The theoretical Buddhism calls CAUSE and EFFECT fortifying the REINCARNATION's rule that can apply to multiple circumstances by the different components and circumstances. The Police Force and armed force can use the gun to protect the society and country, therefore, the gun can help the robber, killer creates the crimes. A knife is helpful for a housewife in the kitchen, but a knife should become the weapon of murder or bandit. The wrong practice of Buddhism becomes a disaster for people and society. So the generous opening heart of Buddhism reflects the theoretical Cause and Effect plus the Reincarnation that become the shield and argument to protect the serious crimes of the dishonest including the genocide. Any bank can loan anyone, but the bank requires conditions like income, job, guarantor, and others before approval. The tolerance without condition that feeds the crime, the dishonest can exploit to escape the crime.

` After South Vietnam lost on April 30, 1975, Vietcong applied barbarous policies into the occupied land. The ruthless regime of founder Hồ Chí Minh treated South Vietnam as the foreign invader that reflects a famous phrase of high ranking cadre Nguyễn Hộ (*the senior communist member as Prime Minister Võ Văn Kiệt*). Mr. Nguyễn Hộ told to his comrades at Saigon Town Hall:" *their houses, we occupied-Their wife, we take and they children, we enslave*". Vietcong freely robbed the assets, killed the people, actually, Vietcong applied the untold revenge policy called" *the dried bloodbath*" to the people served in South Vietnam's government. The Ape super gang in Vietnam centralized more than 800,000 members of the Army Republic of Vietnam (*South Vietnam's Army*) and public servants into the hell of prison camp's system was like the death camp of Nazi in the Second World War. The worst treatment applied by the cruel revenge methods was execution, torture, starvation, sickness without medical and treatment, forced labor, currently spiritual intimidation, so Vietcong killed about 165,000 political prisoners. Unfortunately, the bamboo curtain closed after Vietcong claimed the unpredictable victory, the Western and the human rights organizations have never known the serious crime of Vietcong's regime did after April 30, 1975. Actually, the left media didn't want to know their comrade Vietcong killed the people without pity, instead, they concealed the bloodshed after Vietcong won the war. Moreover, the families of South Vietnam's prisoners sent to the jungle and the recess of the mountain's region called the

New Economic Zone. The discrimination policy ruined many families of South Vietnam people and cause many deaths in the worst-living condition. Nevertheless, Vietcong applied the pauperization's policy by 3 times changed the currency. In the Vietnam War, every day, the people who lived in South Vietnam faced the fierce war by Vietcong terrorists, the massive killing weapon provided by China and Soviet-Union plus total Global Communist Bloc. Certainly, Vietcong couldn't fight with the machete and bamboo's head sharp cut, but the left media didn't tell about the sources of the weapon. Nevertheless, the Vietnamese people witnessed the bloodshed occurred everywhere and at any time, but no-one wanted to leave the country. Therefore, after Vietcong occupied, there were million Vietnamese people fled for freedom bid with small boats. Vietnam refugees killed at sea estimates a million, and the United Nations helped.

However, the boat people feared the piracy in Thailand's gulf, the barbarous pirates were Thailand's fishing boat, but the fisherman turned pirates. The pirates killed, robbed, and raped female Vietnamese refugees including the teenagers without pity. Nevertheless, the pirates justified the serious crimes with theoretical Buddhism by misusing the Reincarnation and the Cause and Effect's rules. The pirates concerned the Vietnamese refugees had the previously bad life, so pirates helped them to pay for the debt of the before life by killing and raped the female, helping them to pay quicker. Therefore, who can know the previous life? Certainly, the pirates were not Buddha or God, no-one mandated the pirates acted the serious crimes that labeled Buddha's will. The pirates in Thailand's gulf obsessed the Vietnamese boat people, the traumatization has become the mental wound of victims who have suffered for life. Vietnamese refugees have never forgotten the crime of pirates in Thailand's gulf. Therefore, the pirates have never repented, instead, they felt happy to help the previously bad life's people to pay the debt. The pirates granted the boon for the victims as their concern, certainly, the Vietnamese boat people have never committed the previously bad life's debt *(* the information wrote in the book " The Dark Journey" published in 2010 at New York)*.

Vietcong is the same practice of pirate, despite communist respects the atheism, but Karl Marx's pupil has exploited the theoretical Buddhism to protect the crimes by covering the genocide based on the Cause and Effect's rule and The Reincarnation. Vietcong has propagated to Vietnamese people by Buddhism that is led by socialism in Vietnam and overseas.

-165,000 political prisoners have a previously bad life, so they must pay the crime of before life. That means Vietcong helped them repay the crimes by killing but who authorizes to know the previous life.

-The high-ranking cadres, communists have the previously good life, so they can earn the benefit that they made from the before life. Its reason, the communists feel free to kill the people and corruption as the Rule of Cause and Effect and the Reincarnation of Buddhism.

-Almost, Vietcong has titled themselves having the previously good's life, so Vietnamese people must obey the order as the Buddha's will. The distorted Buddhism theory has helped Vietcong, China, Laos, North Korea remaining the ruthless regime when the major Buddhist population accepts the adversities created by the dictatorial regime. Its reason explains the major population in the communist countries accepted the Buddha's will and their fate while Europe's communist states eliminated Marxism-Leninism from the early 1990s.

The communist countries have developed Buddhism for preventing the people stand up. The major Buddhist population in the communist countries has been intoxicated by the distorted Buddhism theory. The obscure and low-educated Buddhists become the victims of the religious deception, they accept the inhumane regimes, actually, they blindingly believe 100,000, 000 people killed by the global communist movement since Lenin succeeded the Ape Revolution in October 1917. China communist massacred more than 65,000,000 Chinese people, and tens of thousands of Chinese people killed at Tiananmen Square in 1989. In Vietnam, there were about 1,700,000 people killed by Hồ Chí Minh and ten thousand people massacred at Huế in the Tết Offensive 1968, more than 200,000 Vietnamese people killed in the landlord Reform at North Vietnam after the Geneva Conference signed on July 20, 1954...all victims have a previously bad life, so they paid the consequence and the victims and families are grateful the communists helped them repay the debt of the before life as the communist's propaganda that exploits from Buddhism by the false monks are the communists inserted into the temples.

Buddhism has distorted by the dishonest and communists. When a robber concerns the victim has a previously bad life, so the robber becomes the helper and victims must thank the robbery who granted a boon to help the victim repays the debt of their previous life.

The distorted Buddhism theory prevents sexual harassment victims to speak out because they believe to repay for the previously bad life and accepted to pay it while the sexual harassment victims of Catholic, Christian accused the priests, the priests jailed as Cardinal George Pell in Australia. Therefore, Buddhist victims kept quiet, nevertheless, from multiple thousand years ago, the false monks and nuns intoxicated the Buddhists by the distorted faith, whoever including a monk did wrongly, the Buddha knows and punish, so the Buddhists often shut the mouth and the victims of sexual harassment tolerate the monk's sex-predators. A case of Senior Venerable*Thích Chánh Lạc (names Nguyễn Ngọc Quang)* rarely occurred, he raped two Buddhist girl teenagers, but he dealt with the victims and paid $USD 480,000 at the US court (*the money contributed by the Buddhist adherent*). Moreover, the monks feel free when having love affairs with the female Buddhists because both believing they had a relationship from the previous life.

Buddhists occupied the major population in Vietnam, so Vietcong has exploited Buddhists from the Vietnam War. The famous den of Vietcong in South Vietnam was Ấn Quang's temple at Saigon with Senior Venerable Thích Trí Quang (*leader*). After Saigon lost, the Vietcong's Buddhist monks appeared the real thugs of Vietcong's undercover activists as Thích Trí Quang, Thích Minh Châu, Thích Quảng Độ, Thích Hộ Giác (*he vowed to fight against South Vietnam's government and the US to the last drop of blood, but after 1975, he migrated to the US and built a big Buddha's temple in Texas, he died in 2012*), nun Huỳnh Liên, chief of monks Thích Huyền Quang, Thích Đôn Hậu and the others the monks were the undercover activists of Vietcong, in France with Zen master Thích Nhất Hạnh, Mr. Võ Văn Ái activated the anti-war movement in Western. Moreover, senior Venerable Thích Quảng Đức who burned himself to death in 1963, the monks of Ấn Quang Temple canonized Thích Quảng Đức (*real name is Lâm Văn Tuất*) who became the successive Buddha. Nevertheless, Vietcong honored his statue at the corner of Phan Đình Phùng and Lê Văn Duyệt street because Vietcong recognizes this monk contributed to the so-called Revolution.

Vietcong has exploited the theoretical Buddhism calls Cause and Effect and Reincarnation to curb the people to stand up while Hong Kong people have protested for democracy, but Vietnamese people in Vietnam and Chinese people in the mainland have not any action, the obscurantism policy-based on the theoretical Buddhism that works. The atheist communist transforms the religious faith of Buddhism into superstition. In Vietnam, Vietcong trains the Buddhist monks and Catholic priests at The People Police Academy. Actually, the monk's covered police officers easily occupied the temples in Vietnam, and the Vietcong regime promoted the positions like Venerable and Senior Venerables. Almost, the Buddhist temples in Vietnam become religious propaganda institutions, and the regime controls the Buddhist temples. Moreover, Vietcong also expanded the temples overseas, actually, the Western countries may watch out the Buddhist temples of the Vietnamese community when the monks and nuns easily migrated from Vietnam, almost, they are the religious propaganda's agents of Vietcong. Nevertheless, the monks and nuns have the background of An Quang Temple, almost the Vietcong. The Buddha temple of Vietnamese overseas also is the den of spy and tax evasion.

Moreover, Vietcong has exploited the negligent immigration policy of the Western country to infiltrate the espionage agents through the Buddhist temples. There are many monks and nuns who migrated from Vietnam to Europe, the US, Australia, the Vietnamese people doubt their background, so the intelligence may eye on the monks and nuns.

The world and Western countries do not trust the monks and nuns in Vietnam, mostly, the Vietcong regime controlled the religious Buddhist. A circumstance of a high ranking police's officer wearing the frock and promoted himself the Buddhist Venerable named Thích Chân Quang who is a nephew of Hồ Chí Minh. The fake Venerable Thích Chân Quang is head of a Buddhist temple at Bà Rịa, Vũng Tàu, he uses Buddhism to propagate the communist and praises China communist as a big brother of Vietnamese people. The fake Venerable Thích Chân Quang often preaches the innocent Buddhists in Vietnam and he also made the video to propagate the Buddhists overseas.

The Sa. avataṃsakasūtra's bible wrote about Buddha said:*" in 49 years, I have never spoken a sentence, a word"*. Possibly, Buddha predicted his theoretical Buddhism will be distorted by the dishonest, so Buddha denied anything that taught in 49 years. The fable's Buddhism describes a lion's story in the jungle as vincible, even after the lion died, no animal dares to eat its meat but the worm can. The worm destroys Buddhism and Buddha is communist and the false monks. Despite Karl Marx hates the religions, he concerned" *religion is the opium*" but his pupil as Vietnam, China communist have used Buddhism for survival and also delude the innocent Buddhists believe the Cause and Effect plus the

Reincarnation are led by socialism, actually, the communists behave the Buddha's will to mandate the killing, robbery and enslaving the people./.

58. THE LEGAL BUSINESS DISTORTS CAREER TO FEAR JUSTICE

Commonly, a business serves for-profit, actually, the legal services are not free, the so-called human rights lawyers make a profit from the taxpayers based, not human rights protection. The legal servants including the private sector can distort the career for pocket and political purposes. So when a lawyer talks, the people examine carefully, actually, the high-level lawyers and the judges can exploit the position to serve a client, political party, or foreign interest. Sharia law completely conflicts with human rights, the Universal Declaration of Human rights has never accepted gender discrimination. Certainly, the lawyers and judges respect human rights, actually, gender discrimination with violence is a crime, therefore, some judges in the Western recognized Sharia law in the legal system, the judges sit above the law and acting as the king in medieval. Unfortunately, the Western countries deserved too much power of the judges, so the people and government know some court orders conflict with the law, but the court orders are like the decrees of the king, everyone must comply without a condition, there is the only way to appeal to the high court level, but when a high court or supreme court-ordered, everyone, including the president, the prime minister must obey. The people have never voted the judges, instead, the president, prime minister, and the politicians elected by the people. Unfortunately, the judges are just the senior legal servants but they have the power over the national leaders. It is a de-democratic form that has applied in democratic countries.

-The major natural couple in the US obeyed the Supreme Court imposed the same-sex-marriage legislation into 50 states, despite the people knew it is the Obama justice cornered Supreme court

-In Australia, everyone recognizes the asylum seekers are not refugees, the intruders breached the law, but Justice Cameron Macaulay ordered the government to compensate $AU 70 million for illegal migrants and also paid $AU 20 million of legal fees for Slater & Gordon law firm.

-In the US, the law professors from Harvard university exploited the degree and legal career to attempt the impeachment of President Donald Trump although they knew the Constitution defines the presidential impeachment must meet the treason and high crime. Therefore, President Donald Trump does nothing wrong, instead, he makes America great again.

There are many cases of the legal servants of the public and the private sector distorted the career that fears justice. The law school permits a lawyer can stand with a defendant or a plaintiff, so the lawyers can have a flexible career, actually, the dishonest lawyers and dishonest judges have no loyalty, the money and privileges put above the justice and national interest.

The terrorists are dangerous, while the world welcomes the deaths of three top terror commanders of Iran, actually,

Major General Qassem Soleimani who was the terror mastermind and commander of the elite force of Iran is the Islamic Revolutionary Guard Corps. Therefore, the International Review of Law Agnes Callamard, the UN special rapporteur distorted the career by a twitter released on January 3, 2020:" *The targeted killings of Qassem Soleimani and Abu Mahdi al Muhandi most likely violate international law including human rights law. Lawful justifications for such killings are very narrowly defined and it is hard to imagine how any of these can apply to these killings"*. The UN's excellent human rights Agnes Callamard (*French citizen*) turns the human wrong's protection, she ignores the victims of terror, the hostages to be executed by beheading, cutting the throat, and the barbarous methods. Certainly, the terrorists have never applied the law, including the international law of the United Nations, instead of the bush law. The people don't know what does Agnes Callamard doing in the United Nations?. Actually, the law fighting against terrorism can apply to eliminate or reduce the bloodshed by killing the terrorists. Whatever, a terrorist killed that saves many lives.

Human rights lawyers always call to help the asylum seekers, it is not humanity concern, but the profit call. If the government cuts the legal aid fund for asylum seekers, the appeal can not apply and the human rights lawyers lose the cases. The world has been complicated by dishonest lawyers and dishonest judges, they practice legal services like robbers with paper-knife (*dishonest lawyers*) and wooden hammers (*dishonest judges*). The people need honest legal practitioners to protect justice, unfortunately, the dishonest components in the legal field have distorted the career for profit and political purpose. The lawmakers and Justice Department of the democratic countries need to overhaul the legal system, actually, the tough punishment applying to the dishonest lawyers and dishonest judges. The legally distorted career causes social disorder and harming justice. Nowadays, people doubt when a top lawyer, a judge, and a law firm tell somethings, actually, the politics. It is not judicial talk, but the profit talks./.

59. AL GORE IS THE FALLEN CLIMATE CHANGE PSYCHIC

Former Vice President Al Gore is an opportunist, he understood the climate change is a hoax, nevertheless, the hoax climate change has activated and promoted worldwide by his comrade Bill Clinton who repaid the illegal finance of China's communist espionage agent John Huang in the presidential election 1992 and Charlie Trie in the election 1996. The hoax climate change is the deep conspiracy of Bill Clinton-Al Gore aiming to curb the Western industry including the US, so China freely releases dioxide while the Western fears the pollution. Nevertheless, the **Most Favored Nation** of Bill Clinton helped China grew faster in 8 years of Bill Clinton who served as China's executive in the White House. China also makes a profit from selling solar power and nowadays the electric car. Moreover, the hoax climate change causes mayhem in the" *capitalist countries*" or counter-revolutionary states" with the minor hoax climate change activists and major opponents that cause the current protests and clash between the supporters and opponents. The hoax climate change is like stone kills two birds, China's communist regime does like it.

Most climate change activists are not scientists like Prince Charles, Prince Harry, Pope Francis, Bill Clinton, Al Gore, 150 religious leaders in Australia, Sir. David Attenborough, Secretay-General Antonio Guterres, actually a **Swedish teenage girl Greta Thunberg becomes the global thug or a model of Khmer Rouge's teacher reflects on the film Killing Field**. The US people and the world watched the ugly scenes of Democratic high profiles as Joe Biden, Nancy Pelosi, and her Congressional gang knelt to pay the respect of a serious felony George Floyd who convicted dozen of crimes and the people also saw the academics, politicians of the left parties including traitor Jane Fonda to adore Greta Thunberg, a teenager has not graduated the high school, therefore, Greta Thunberg becomes the guru of the hoax climate change, it is the shame of the top social class in Western. Certainly, Mr. Antonio Guterres, the hardcore communist, Secretary-General of the United Nations who brainwashed the world successfully, the hoax climate change's obscurantism that worked. Certainly, the hoax climate change activists have no qualification to tell about climate change, it doesn't their field as a mechanic talks about pathology, cancer, diseases. There are more than 30,000 scientists who confirmed that climate change is not real.

Former Vice President Al Gore is malicious, he exploited the label of former US Vice President to call climate change while the well-known climate change activist was Dr. David Suzuki went around the world to tell about it. The Nobel Peace Prize Committee awarded Al Gore in 2007, therefore, Dr. David Suzuki disappeared a long time, possibly he recognized that climate change is a deception. Former Vice President Al Gore has developed climate change's business and now he becomes the billionaire of climate change. The Nobel Peace Prize committee in 2007 was wrongly awarded a climate change businessman and 2009 awarded the global war-maker Barrack Obama. In Australia, the well-known climate change activist is Dogtor Tim Flannery who had a good job from the taxpayers, he was an icon of Labor Minister Kevin Rudd (*or Kevin Thug*), Julia Gillard, and the Australian Labor Party. Therefore, Dogtor Tim Flannery wrongly predicted climate change in Australia. After Labor lost the federal election in 2013, Dogtor Tim Flannery was no longer to have the idle job, he disappeared on the television many years ago.

Former Vice President Al Gore, the dishonest academics, the left parties, the left media have launched psychological warfare to appall the world about the dire consequence of the hoax climate change, the left media has used the communication to frighten the people by the untrue facts and biased pictures. The hoax climate change is the religious climate change, they have an incantation:" *The Sky is falling! The Sky is falling! Wake up before it's too late* ". However, the hoax climate change to be debunked by an article below:

" Al Gore's 10 Global Warming Predictions, 12 Years Later — None Happened!

January 1, 2018, by Edward Morgan

Gore's Predictions Fall Flat

12 years after Al Gore's "Inconvenient Truth" guilt/fear-

producing predictions, let's close by examining just how accurate his "science" proved to be on his way to the bank.

   1. *Rising Sea Levels – inaccurate and misleading. Al was even discovered purchasing a beachfront mansion!*

   2. *Increased Tornadoes – declining for decades.*

   3. *New Ice Age in Europe – they've been spared; it never happened.*

   4. *South Sahara Drying Up – completely untrue.*

   5. *Massive Flooding in China and India – again didn't happen.*

   6. *Melting Arctic – false – 2015 represents the largest refreezing in years.*

   7. *Polar Bear Extinction – actually they are increasing!*

   8. *Temperature Increases Due to CO2 – no significant rising for over 18 years.*

   9. *Katrina a Foreshadow of the Future – false – past 10 years, no F3 hurricanes; "longest drought ever!"*

   10. *The Earth Would be in a "True Planetary Emergency" Within a Decade Unless Drastic Action Taken to Reduce Greenhouse Gasses – never happened.*

A while back, the Washington Post stated in an expose' that, "Al Gore has thrived as a green-tech investor."

Coincidental?"

Every natural disaster becomes an opportunity for the hoax climate change propagates to appall the people, moreover, the climate change business making a profit without a drop of sweat. The annual bush-fire in California and Australia is not the cause of climate change. However, bush-fire history has occurred for millions of years ago. **Recently, the bush fire in the US is slammed as the cause of climate change, the disgraced presidential candidate Joe Biden uses the bush-fire to woo the ballot.** Therefore, the police arrested the arsonists who ignited the fires and claimed climate change, it is the worst sitcom of the hoax climate change's movement, the arsonists come from Antifa, they fired the bush at Washington State, Oregon, and California, it is the PEACEFUL CAMPAIGN of Joe Biden and Democrats, is it?. The scientifically illiterate activist of the hoax climate change like Al Gore, Greta Thunberg, and the left politicians, the left parties, the left media couldn't deceive the world after the confirmation of former Vice President Al Gore predicted from 12 years later, now all failed. Certainly, Al Gore is the fallen psychic, his prediction turned to garbage and bullshit, the cheat is no longer exist, the people know the hoax climate change's perpetrators have exploited the ebullient character of the primary-school students as the Red Guard of Mao Tse Tung in the Culture Revolution *(1966-1976)*. The Green Guard, the Extinction Rebellion, and Vegan are the trouble makers in Western. The hoax climate change has stolen the future of the young generations to make a profit from the deceived climate change's perpetrators. The professional fortune teller and a psychic are based on the details provided by a client and develop the predictions. In the same circumstance, the hoax climate change psychics just based on the storms, bush fires, and distorting the public for business. Former President Al Gore represents the fallen psychic of the hoax climate change./.

60. THE WESTERN PAYS CLIMATE CHANGE BUSINESS FOR CHINA

The hoax climate change is the most deception on the planet, it is the deep conspiracy of Democratic President Bill Clinton and Vice President Al Gore. Both US leaders exchanged the national interest for individual favor. In the presidential election 1992, China's super espionage agent John Huang provided the finance for candidate Bill Clinton and in the second term's presidential election in 1996, China's espionage agent Charlie Trie illegally financed for Bill Clinton. The intervention of China in the US's presidential election that concealed as a cat hides its shit after defecated, but the Donkey's Head gang and left media have carried the greatest witch hunt in the US history. Everyone knows Russia didn't intervene in the US election 2016, therefore, Democrats used the fake dossiers to impeach President Donald Trump, and now, they continue to use the fake news plus the fabricated stories, the designed witnesses to remove President Donald Trump into Ukraine's incident.

President Bill Clinton and Vice President Al Gore were the unofficial Executives of China in the White House, they repaid the boon for China throughout 8 years, the US damaged and leaving the long-term consequence worldwide. The malicious climate change helped China freely released dioxide while the Western curbed. Moreover, the left parties (*Democrats in the US, Australian Labor Party, UK Labor Party, Socialist Party in France, Greens Party, and the others*) frequently activate the hoax climate change. The Green Guard appeared as a form of Mao Tse Tung's Red Guard in the Culture Revolution. The Green Guard has the

Extinction Rebellion, Vegan, the innocent component in Western. Actually, the hoax climate change's perpetrators exploit the ebullient character of the young people including the primary-high school student to protest plus the violence, mostly, the Green Guard often locked the traffics or occupied the public places, the Green Revolution revives the Culture Revolution in China in Western. Climate change is a hoax, former Vice President Al Gore becomes the climate change's billionaire and he also won the Nobel Peace Prize in 2007 featured the hoax climate change. However, there are more than 30,000 scientists confirmed that climate change is not real. Nevertheless, the hoax climate change activists have no knowledge about a field that they endorse as a mechanic tells about the pathology and diseases. Indeed, the hoax climate change is a business of China and the demagogic policy of the left parties because they failed the economic policy and national security. In an election, the people easily recognize any political party or politicians use climate change, the same-sex-marriage legislation, and support the asylum seeker as the essential policies, they are the leftists. The hoax climate change purposes:

-Curbing the Western industry, but China freely released the dioxide. President Bill Clinton and Vice President Al Gore paid a priceless for China and the hoax climate change has continued to harm the Western economy.

-It makes the profit for China selling solar power and equipment.

-Western society divided, the civil war currently occurs between the hoax climate change activists and the major population. China just uses domestic thugs *(climate change activists and the left parties)* to attack and complicate the Western country, the social mayhem.

China has made a profit from the climate change activists in Western, so Beijing is keen to endorse climate change and China should hire the left media to propagate, despite China is the number one state releasing dioxide. China has activated global climate change, it is a farce. On June 29, 2019, Chinese State Council and Foreign Minister Wang Yi, French Foreign Minister Jean Yves Le Drian, and United Nations Secretary-General Antonio Guterres reaffirmed their strong commitment worldwide about climate change that backs the Paris Agreement. Actually, UN Secretary-General Antonio Guterres is the hardcore communist from the Cold War, he has exploited the United Nations serving for China's business and the demagogic policy of his comrades (*the left parties in the world*).

Mr. Secretary-General promoted the hoax climate change at General Assembly on September 23, 2019, he snubbed the United Nations by admitting a 16-year-old Sweden mental health girl Greta Thunberg to teach the world about climate change, he acts as Pol Pol in Cambodia using the children lectured the adult. The United Nations focus to raise $USD 100 billion a year as the Green Climate Fund (GCF). France ruled by Socialist Party, so French President Emmanuel Macron advocates the hoax climate change, its reason conducts France urges United Nations and China to co-operate with the Paris Agreement. The collaboration carries out between China, France, and United Nations Secretary-General Antonio Guterres is like evil unites with Satan. The hoax climate change applied in France that sparked the Yellow Vest movement, the protests cost the

French economy. In Australia, the electric car was among the causes conducts the potential loss of the Australian Labor Party in the federal election on May 19, 2019. Under the rule of President Barrack Obama, climate change damaged the US's economy and the job, the factories closed and the mining industry ruined.

President Barrack Obama led the US to join Paris Agreement and he also used the taxpayers for the hoax climate change. In April 2016, before the second term expired, President Barrack Obama signed the Paris Agreement and he issued ab executive order in September 2016. According to the commitment, President Barrack Obama contributes $USD 3 billion to the Green Climate Fund, its fund has to focus to raise at least $USD 100 billion a year by 2020. If Hillary Clinton elected in 2016, the US taxpayers would waste the money for China's business.

On June 1st, 2017, President Donald Trump announced the US would cease all participation in the 2015 Paris Agreement, he warned: " the Paris Accord will undermine the US economy and puts the US at a permanent disadvantage". Nevertheless, the US paid for the hoax phenomenal facts.

On November 5, 2019, President Donald Trump pulls out of the Paris Agreement that saves the US taxpayers. Moreover, the so-called Corporation Renewable's former Vice President Al Gore proposes at least one trillion US dollars. Certainly, Al Gore does nothing but becomes a billionaire by cheat.

The hoax climate change has made a profit for China but the US and the other Western countries paid. President Donald Trump is rights, hopefully, the other countries like

Australia, United Kingdom, Europe wake up and staying away from Paris Agreement or any hoax climate change organizations. China is the most dioxide releasing state but they activate the hoax climate change to sell solar power. The left parties, China and the UN's Secretary-General is the communist, they drive the world in the wrong direction./.

61. FEDERAL RESERVE IS THE BASE OF DEEP STATE (*)

The second Constitution in 1871 grants the license to rob for the white-collar, the noble robbers have deceived the people with the demagogic propaganda, particularly, the fake democracy covered the fair elections applying into multiple levels, actually, the presidential election just is the cheating game to deserve for the wealthy persons or the rich people invest the political businesses for a candidate who secretly promises to repay the boons after winning the presidential election. There is only the US president has two terms, each term is four years. Therefore, the Congress, Senate, and Supreme Court are unlimited terms, those are the powerful places that the Deep State needs to keep control of the country. The deceitful Constitution in 1871 has driven the wealthy land in North America to be the major center of the Deep State. The main base is **Federal Reserve or F.E.D** to launch the maliciously financial tactics to dominate the global finance including America.

The money is the key to tie the white-collar robbers with the Deep State, although the United States of America called as a nation. Indeed, it is the Corporation of the United States of America hides the fake nation, so the US president is like

307

the CEO, the lenders in the shadow hold the power and command the CEO, the lenders are the supreme commanders in chiefs, so the policies of the US's administration reflect the Deep State's interest.

The US people have no control over the currency, the US dollar belongs to the Federal Reserve or F.E.D to control the central banks, the major owners are Rothschild and Rockefeller family plus the other magnates are the financial bosses. Monetary domination is the key to control Americans and the country, the Deep State has exploited the wealthy country, the military strength, and the abundant talent of the young nation to develop power throughout the world. The US dollar becomes the potential weapon to force the counterparts to use for trade, so the Euro and Yuan are not the foes of US currency. The Federal Reserve has used the paper currency called the US dollar to loan America and the world. Between December 2008 and October 2014, the Federal Reserve printed $US 3.7 trillion bill notes to loan America and other countries with the long-term interest rate. The China virus pandemic created an opportunity for Federal Reserve to make a profit, in 2020, F.E.D printed $US 1.87 trillion, almost, the Federal Reverse spends about $US 700 million for the cost of printing a year, but they make the great profit with the paper's bill notes. The paper's US dollar becomes the global currency, so the most banking system bases their currency on the US dollar. On the other hand, F.E.D has invested the paper to control the world as a stratagem of Sun Tzu:" *great something from nothing*". **The Federal Reserve becomes the currency terror's base** in the US and the world by using the paper notes to control America and the countries using the US dollar.

The Deep State activates the monetary power with the

malicious tactics to print the paper currency and also controls the central stock market in Wall Street, so the powerful bosses in the shadow could create the economic crisis, depression, or recession by increasing the interest or creating the stock-market disorders. Every time Wall Street shaking, the Deep State creates more debt to the countries, while they can issue the currency to buy the bond, to loan, create the debt increases and the world has never escaped the hand of the Deep State. Whoever touches the exclusive monetary position of the Deep State, who would face the danger as President Kennedy and nowadays, the 45th President Donald Trump wants to get back the currency for the people, so the Deep State has applied the terror methods to stop. Its reason explains the actual henchman of Deep State is Democrats have attacked President Donald Trump since he stepped into the White House on January 20, 2017, therefore, the impeachment of legal terrorist Robert Mueller failed, and recently, the second impeachment didn't succeed.

Nowadays, American people wake up and recognize the hidden enemies cornered the Congress, Senate, the Supreme Court, and the White House, the supreme commander is the Deep State with the Federal Reserve's base. The Deep State controls the Corporation of the United States of America, actually, **the bloody old mad, imbecile mongrel ape Joe Biden** drives the country to disaster. Therefore, Joe Biden is the potential CEO of the Deep State, he creates massive jobless and broad spending in the US and overseas. Before the first Muslim and communist President Barrack Obama did a good CEO's job from 2008 to 2016, Obama created the deep debt, he created an opportunity for Islamic State founded, then provided the finance, weapons, training to the major terror organization, and Barrack Obama also called to fight against the terror. The doubt cross war game of Barrack created the debt reached $US 20 trillion. Moreover, CEO Barrack Obama bribed Iran $US 152 billion to conceal the secret death of Osama Bin Laden. Certainly, Barrack Obama doesn't pay the debt, instead, the US people pay for the Deep State. The Deep State ties the US people with the debt and its country can not escape the hand of the Deep State. America is endangered, the people have to fight for survival:

-Standing up to eliminate the ape's regime of Joe Biden: the dictatorial and communist regime can not confront the invincible power of people. In the early 1990s, Soviet-Union, the Eastern European communist countries collapsed when the people stood up, so the US people have enough condition to pull down the presidential robber Joe Biden, the animal cabinet, and the Ape Congress, ape Senate plus the ape Justices in the Supreme Court. Moreover, the US Army can wake up and arrest the traitors.

-The secession is the best solution to escape the claws of Deep State: Texas and 28 Republican States can secede and reform the FEDERATION OF AMERICA, and the Corporation of the United States of America will collapse, CEO Joe Biden will lose the job and declare the bankruptcy, and 50 states waive $US 27.8 trillion of debt, certainly, the lenders can not require the states to repay because the federal administration borrowed. The secession and reform of the Federation of America also eradicate the Federal Reserve, which means the Deep State will not control the money and printing the paper bill notes to create the debt with the interest. Certainly, the Federation of America can issue the virtual currency of the American people, it can call **American**

Dollar ($AMD) to replace the US dollar. Otherwise, if the states accept to live with communism, the people must pay the debt at least 50 years and the slavery continues to squeeze the people's sweat with the taxes, the Federal Reserve continues to print the currency paper to loan America. Moreover, the secession avoids the pay the debt, the dishonest lenders must return the money to American victims. The people can not suffer the ugly policies of mongrel ape Joe Biden including the states of Democrats like Oregon has five counties voted to leave the state and join Idaho, the north-western state of America, the 11th largest state in land area and 14th largest in total area (*land and water*) despite the population is about 1.7 million (*39th largest state by population*). It is the appropriate action must take after Joe Biden destroyed the country with the crazy executive orders and the social purge of the hidden communist party to apply in America.

The Deep State gathers a small numerous rich component, plus the henchmen, the left stream media, and the left tech communication companies while a hundred million people can destroy the enemies by the power. So the Deep State and henchmen always pall the people's power, its reason conducts the presidential robber Joe Biden, and its Donkey gang to remain the National Guard in the Washington D.C with the high fence and razor wire after storming the White House. The people consider Joe Biden doesn't represent America, he always fears to contact the people, and Kamala Harris returns the homeland at San Francisco with a few old people welcome, where are 80 million voters?

The Federal Reserve is the central culprit of economic crisis, so the investors doubt about Wall Street's operation, the people versus the Federal Reserve and the staff currently is investigated by the FBI with the corruption plus the illegal services for many decades ago. On February 24, 2021, the Federal Reserve's banking system went down in several hours, the electronic services disabled, and 537,000 transactions per day suspended, the money estimates $US 2.7 trillion. The incident signals the problem of Deep State and the central finance has started to face the people oppose against the illegal banking operation in the US./.

62. PRESIDENT DONALD TRUMP IS THE JOBLESS EXTERMINATOR

The US people favor the job, the living standard improvement, social safety, border protection, actually, the major population have never wanted to live on the food stamps. Therefore, President Barrack Obama succeeded in the great policy on the food stamps, he is **the food stamps president**. **Yes, he can** create more people joining the food stamps line plus homeless (*the major homeless people gathered at the Democratic states*). During the era of Barrack Obama, the unemployment was high, a time, it reached 10% in October 2009, that year, the Nobel Peace Prize awarded Barrack Obama. On the other hand, Yes, President Barrack Obama can do, there are some Obama did while his consequences are plenty after Barrack Obama expired the second term:

-He can destroy the US from A to Z.

-He can create a deep debt after 8 years

-He can help the Islamic State founders and he can provide the weapon, finance, and training for ISIS.

-He can flag China illegally built and militarized the artificial islands into the disputed waters

-He can help Iran bluffing the Nuclear Deal and provided the finance.

-He can brainwash the US people in 8 years

-He can shift the job to China

-He can use $USD 100 million of the taxpayers to enjoy the luxury trips

-He can unleash the border for illegal migrants to invade and he can spend a hundred billion dollars a year on the taxpayers for the asylum seekers.

-He can tell a lie and cheat the US people

-He can activate the racial war between black and white.

-He can sparkle the gender war between the major natural couple and a minor homosexual couple, he can use the Supreme Court imposed the same-sex-marriage into 50 states.

-He can make the US becomes China's vassal

-He can make the heap of mess in the US.

-He can flag ISIS killed four US servants including Ambassador Christopher Stevens in Benghazi to destroy the key witness of terror linking between Barrack Obama's administration and the Islamic State.

The US's presidential election will be held a year while Democrats seem to face the deadlock, mostly, the candidates have debated as the clowns perform, the US people have not interested the unpopular politicians, actually, the hopeful candidate Joe Biden has struck the scandal of corruption in Ukraine and his son Hunter Biden received $USD 2.1 billion from China. Speaker Nancy Pelosi and her Congressional gang have tried to impeach President Donald Trump by Ukraine's incident. Unfortunately, the solo resolution in Congress is garbage. President Donald Trump and Republicans easily campaign in 2020, when the unemployment is 3.5%, it hits the lowest record since 1969 that guaranteed the landslide victory. Instead, Democrats will face big losses in the White House race, Senate, Congress, and state government (*the numerous governors will reduce*). Moreover, the strongholds of Democrats change the support by the low unemployment, the Democratic fan wakes up. According to PoliData reports the swing states will decide the ballot on the job:

Unemployment in WI:

3.2% Sep 2019
3.9% Sep 2016 (Pre-Trump)
6.6% Sep 2012 (Pre Obama Reelection)
5.2% 2008 (Pre-Obama)

Michigan:
4.2% Sep 2019

5.1% Sep 2016
9.1% Sep 2012
8.4% Sep 2008

Pennsylvania
4.00% Sep 2019
5.4% Sep 2016
7.9% Sep 2012

5.6% Sep 2008.

The left media always released the bad news and false polls for President Donald Trump. Nevertheless, the fake news has misled the public by the bullshit prediction about Donald Trump while the impeachment is just a dream of the losers. The daydreamer's Nancy Pelosi, Adam Schiff, and the Democratic gang in Congress saw the coffin but they have not cried yet. The lowest unemployment decided the ballot, even the false polls rig the election, but the US people vote for the job and national interest. There are not only the swing states, the other strongholds of Democrats like New York, and California will also change the electorate colleague when the Democratic fan recognizes President Donald Trump who is the jobless exterminator and helping the people getting out from the food stamps. However, the Minnesota Muslims are food stamp recipients, the Muslim community wants the government to grant $USD 150,000 for a pork-free food giveaway (*Somali-Americans community call no-pork-zone at the shells of food banks*). Muslim religious leader Imam Hassan Mohamud said:" *It's about human rights also-Basic human rights to get the proper food and also healthy food*". Human rights turn Human Wrong, even Human fraud (*people smuggle*), certainly, the US is not a Muslim country as Somali, moreover, the US people have never forced whoever comes to get the free food, so the Muslims in Minnesota goes too far, they require Allah certified the food banks. If President Barrack Obama still rules the US, the request of Minnesota Muslims would carry out. The Community activist, Mr. Fartun Weli said*:" Some food shelves are trying to meet the need, but some of them already got canned beans that already been mixed with pork — and there is a literacy* *issue here,"*.

The SATAN'era of Barrack Obama is gone, now the SANTA's era of President Donald Trump makes America great again. In God we trust, Donald Trump, we vote, Democrats we trash, Marxism, we eliminate./.

63. BARRACK OBAMA EXPECTED THE PRESIDENT OF FOOD STAMPS

In the record marked about SATAN's era of President Barrack Obama who created the high jobless rate in US history. Therefore, President Barrack Obama raised the demagogic slogan" *Yes we can*" in the first presidential election campaign in 2007. However, after the United States of America ruled by Barrack Obama for 8 years, the US people really recognized the first communist and Muslim president in the US as the rhetorical activist as a saying of the communist experts' quote" *when a communist a born, obviously, a midwife sees the mouth*". The slogan*" yes we can*" that meant" *yes we can*" make the high unemployment rate. Currently, the jobless was about 5%, but the high tide in October 2009 was 10%, it coincided with the Nobel Peace Prize Committee awarded the most valuable prize on the planet for the global warmaker Barrack Obama.

President Barrack Obama also named the president of food stamps, former House Speaker Newt Gingrich said on CNBC on December 2011 while the second term of Obama was campaigning:" *We are going to have the candidate of food stamps, the finest food stamp president in*

American history, in Barack Obama, and we are going to have a candidate of paychecks."

However, after President Donald Trump inaugurated on January 20, 2017, all predictions of 370 economists including 8 Nobel Prize economy winners turned to garbage by writing and signing a letter to pressure Republicans do not to nominate candidate Donald Trump. The bullshit predictions warned about the US economy will worsen if Donald Trump becomes the US president, therefore, the warnings totally went wrong. The well-known economists distorted the career and placed for sale the knowledge, actually, China communist is keen to hire and pay money and privileges to whoever serves for Beijing interest despite they knew China is the most barbarous communist regime on the planet. Dishonest academics are dangerous than low educated dishonest. The dishonest academics easily deceive and mislead the public by the doctoral degree and social position.

SANTA's era of President Donald Trump boomed the job, in August 2019, there were 157,878,000 jobs and the unemployment rate is 3.7% hit the lowest record since 1969. Moreover, President Donald Trump cut the taxes for workers and companies, so everyone is happy, except Democrats and China don't want to know about the US bonanza exposing on the economy. Moreover, President Donald Trump achieved the major promises in the election 2016 including the wall and he will win the second term while Democrats struggle to find a candidate including the recycled candidates as Bernie Sanders and Joe Biden. Nevertheless, President Donald Trump makes America great again, the enemies fear and allies restored the truth while the domestic thugs ruined the cunning tactics to impeach the patriotic president in the US.

The great achievements did after more than two years that defeated and debunked the left media, profit lover's academics, all domestic enemies failed the phony psychological warfare to frighten the US people about the recession if President Donald Trump continues to impose the tariffs on China products and goods.

The garbage propaganda hits back the henchman of China in the Western, the public has no trust in the left media and also doubts the honesty level of academics after they appalled the people by the recession. However, when the job boomed, economic growth and the US currency stabilized while China faces the mountain debt escalating without control, China currency devalued over the alert level that conducts the inflation in the mainland. Moreover, the massive jobless comes from the loss of the offshore market, actually, the tariff weapon of commander in chief and the great economic general that eradicates the den of thieves.

President Barrack Obama was the worst leader in US history, he was the president of jobless and food stamps. Certainly, under the era of President Barrack Obama, there were multiple million US people who fought so hard to stay away from the food stamp, but they had no choice while president Barrack Obama created the job for China and abandoned American. Therefore, President Donald Trump helped at least 6.2 million people getting out of the food stamps, they got a job and returning the normal life.

President Donald Trump who volunteers to serve the country without salary, his presidential wage donates the public interest, while former President Barrack Obama still earns an annual pension is $USD 207,000 and in 2018, his office's request cost the taxpayers $USD 1,153,000 although the former President Barrack Obama has the assets are worth $USD 40 million (the people question about the sources of money). Recently, former President Barrack Obama purchased the property was $USD 14.85 million on Martha's Vineyard included the weathered-Shingle house is set on 29 acres with a private beach. It is the glorious life of the President of food stamps in the US./.

64. BARRACK OBAMA BECAME AN ILLEGAL PRESIDENT OR TREASON

The birthplace of the first Muslim and communist President Barrack Obama has raised the long-term controversy since a man who joined the Democratic nominee's campaign and throughout two presidential terms with the mouthful slogan" *yes we can*". The blind fan, naïve component, and the Democratic donkey's voters supported and helped a man who destroyed the US from A to Z. Certainly, the supporters share the responsibility of the shattered country. A French proverb quotes" *It faut tourner sept fois sa langue dans sa bouche avant de parler* " that failed in the circumstance of Barrack Obama. The irresponsible voters didn't study carefully before voting, so the US ruined in 8 years and nearly facing the brink of collapse after the wrong ballots endorsed Barrack Obama. In the presidential campaign in 2008 and 2012, *President Barrack Obama went high and the innocent voters went low.* Moreover, President Barrack Obama was the global thug, his legacy leaving the long-term disaster in the world. Unfortunately, the Nobel Peace Prize Committee wrongly awarded Obama in 2009.

There are many sources and rumors released about President Barrack Obama's background. Moreover, the mysteries covered by Democrats including the outside enemies. The case of President Barrack Obama is not different from viral meningitis infiltrated the human's brain, the life risked or paralyzed. The outside enemies, domestic thugs, actually, the communist and terrorist arrayed Barrack Obama *climbed higher and dived deeper* in White House, certainly, the enemies always want to destroy the United States of America, but they couldn't defeat the US by the war, economy or any tactics, so it is the best way to annihilate the US by its president and politicians as a Buddhism's fable describes the lion is invincible in the jungle, even after lion died, no animal dares to eat the lion's meat, therefore, the worm can. President Barrack Obama could destroy the US as the worm of Buddhism's fable, so *yes we can* make the US collapse. On the other hand, President Barrack Obama didn't represent the US people although they elected and also believed Obama would develop the country as his mouthful speech. Instead, President Barrack Obama served for communist and terrorist through 8 years in the White House, he strayed the commander in chief to commander in cheat and commander in thug, even commander in terror.

Certainly, President Barrack Obama always protects himself about Kenya's citizenship. He always denied any clue and accusation about citizen fraud. Despite, Mr. Barrack Obam is no longer rule the White House from January 20, 2017, therefore, the birthplace of Obama still discussing, the question has no answer, actually, the fake news and Obama's fan have never revealed his birthplace in Kenya. **Article Two of the Constitution requires the US president must be a natural-born citizen of the US**. Moreover, Barrack Obama's birth certificate was a forgery as some theories proved. Therefore, the life of Barrack Obama covered the mysteries, the people believe Barrack Obama was not born in Hawaii, instead, he is Kenyan. Certainly, Barrack Obama his their childhood in Indonesia, he was an Indonesian citizen. President Barrack Obama succeeded to apply the Racist shield to protect the citizen fraud and also gag the presidential candidate Republican in the campaign's debated 2008 and 2012.

After 8 years ruled the US, President Barrack Obama made the worst America ever, the consequences Obama can recognize on few consequences:

1-The domestic: Obama destroyed the economy and financial system, ignited the racial war and gender war. President Barrack Obama is the culprit of social division and digging up the civil war in the US. Nevertheless, President Barrack Obama brainwashed the US people in 8 years.

2-The International issues: President Barrack Obama created an opportunity for the enemies to besieged the US from Middle-East and Asia.

-Barrack Obama created an opportunity for Islamic State founded and he provided money, weapon, and training to the terrorist by the US taxpayers. Formally, President Barrack Obama called to fight against the terror and using the taxpayers to play the double-cross war game.

-Barrack Obama flagged" *comrade China*" built and militarized the piratical stations in disputed waters at Indochina Pacific.

-President Barrack Obama and Secretary of State John Kerry fed the rogue regime in Teheran, they also gave multiple billion dollars of the taxpayer to Iran.

3-President Barrack Obama represents corruption, he left the swamp in the White House, now President Donald Trump drains out.

-Barrack Obama lavished $USD 100 million of the taxpayers by his family's trips.

-The US people question about the assets of Obama reached more than $USD 40 million, he also purchased a luxury mansion in the US, and recently, Obama has bought the vineyard is worth $USD 14.85 million. The US people doubt the money that Obama got and become multiple millionaires after leaving the White House in a few years.

Former President Barrack Obama put the US soldiers and national servants at risk by his double cross war gam, actually, 4 deaths in Benghazi have not investigated yet. President Barrack Obama is eligible for treason, his suspicious crimes are plenty. If the court found former President Barrack Obama convicted the treason as the Consitution, he will escape by the birthplace in Kenya that means Barrack Obama will confess he was a false president. Former President Barrack Obama is clever and also avoids treason. If former President Barrack Obama confessed to the Kenyan, that means he born in Kenya, so Democrats and Democratic National Convention lied and deceived the US people, they breached the Constitution, actually, Democrats helped the enemy infiltrated the White House in 8 years. So, Democrats are treason.

Almost, the US people and the world, actually Wikileaks recognized Barrack Obama as a Muslim and communist. However, Miss Valerie Jarrett, a hardcore communist in the US, former top adviser of Barrack Obama, guested Americans owe Obama a debt of gratitude. Miss Valerie Jarrett exposes the true character of a communist, she snubs the US people and honored Barrack Obama as Nobel Peace Prize Committee awarded a global war maker the peace prize. Miss communist Valerie Jarrett snubs the public and the world, she told like a million victims of the Landlord Reform's campaign in North Vietnam. The landlords and intellectuals must shout" *bravo uncle Ho great*" or" *long life chairman Ho Chi Minh*" before execution by fire-arm, the machete beheaded, and the other barbarous methods. Certainly, the victims and families have never owed the genocide a debt of gratitude for the killers. So Miss communist Valerie Jarrett applies the tactic as Ho Chi Minh and the communist party killed the people and forced victims to praise the culprit.

Whatever, former President Barrack Obama is treason. If he was born in Kenya, he will escape the treasonous conviction, but he will be charged with frauds and the US government will force Barrack Obama to refund the president's salary paid in 8 years, $USD 100 million's vacation plus the privileges (*Secret services, the office budget of retired president cost the taxpayers a million dollars a year*) and deport Obama to Kenya./.

65. BARRACK OBAMA DEVASTATED A PROMISED LAND

The first Muslim and communist US President Barrack Obama ruled the White House in 8 years. However, there were just two terms from 2008 to 2016, the United States of America shattered, the society divided, the untold civil wars of gender, racist, the hoax climate change, and illegal migrant have complicated the US and leaving the long term damages in the US and the world. The slogan" *yes we can change*" sending the wrong message to the innocent component and the shorted mind people when the rhetorical man or a con-politician named Barrack Obama who lied and cheated the US people, and the terrible mistake cost the dire consequences, the world complicated, particularly, the Black Lives Matter and Antifa are the domestic terror organizations in the United States of America to terrorize the people by the protests with riot, loot and vandalized the historic monuments, statues including the statue of Jesus, Maria. The Black Guard and Antifa of Barrack Obama and Democrats reflect the Red Guard of Mao Tse Tung activated the bloodshed campaign called Culture Revolution in China from 1966 to 1976.

In the presidential election of 2008, the rhetorical candidate Barrack Obama cheated the people about the demagogic policies. Indeed, President Barrack Obama changed the world's most wealthy country of the US to be China's colony, he used the taxpayers to finance the Islamic State and provided the weapons plus training, therefore, Barrack Obama also called to fight against the terror. President Barrack Obama changed the US in the deep debt, jobless, the ghost towns, thousands of factories shut down and the other terrible changes, all changes worsened. President **Barrack Obama did nothing for the country but got anything for his family**. Nevertheless, four deaths at Benghazi including Ambassador john Christopher Stevens have not investigated the hidden conspiracy of Barrack Obama-Hillary Clinton to destroy the victims. The death of Al Qaeda leader Osama Bin Laden doubts, therefore, the death of Bin Laden helped Barrack Obama in the election 2012. Moreover, the Navy Seal team was mysteriously killed in action, possibly, they were the victims of the cheat to destroy the witnesses. The people don't know Osama Bin Laden died or not, the secrets still cover. Nevertheless, President Barrack Obama and Secretary of State John Kerry cheated the world with the nuclear deal with Iran, and they also financed the rogue regime in Teheran.

President Barrack Obama's circumstance matches a saying of Vietnamese" *a mouse falls in the sticky rice pot*" (*chuột sa hủ nếp*). Any family in Vietnam hates a mouse infiltrates a pot of sticky rice, that mouse enjoys the food and also devastates anything inside. President Barrack Obama is the same case as the Australian Labor Party's Premier Daniel Andrews, he is the hidden's face communist, he signed one Belt and One Road with China in 2018. Victoria's state becomes the hottest spot of Coronavirus in the second wave, therefore, Premier Daniel Andrews lavished the taxpayers:

" *DAN'S TAXPAYER-FUNDED LIFESTYLE It has been revealed that Premier Andrews and his team are spending more than $1 million dollars on food and drink each year. The Department of Premier and Cabinet has doubled its food, drink, and entertainment costs since the Premier were elected, including $9,000 of taxpayer money on a "boozy"* *office party for staff. This is in addition to other massive costs, like $30,000 on morning and afternoon teas in just one month, splashing over $400,000 of your money in the first 6 months of 2019. Premier Andrews is spending your money to support his lavish parliamentary lifestyle!* (from Facebook)"

The US president Barrack Obama made America worsens ever, he lavished the taxpayers, $US 100 million spent for the luxurious trips overseas and domestic. Every time to play gold, the taxpayers spent at least $US 2.7 million. Moreover, before leaving the office, Barrack Obama planned to spend billions of dollars on the taxpayers for the overseas trips of the former US president in a decade, therefore, President Donald Trump scrapped it. The stories of Barrack Obama and Michelle Obama are saga, however, after leaving the White House, former President Obama often attacks President Donald Trump and also earns the pension plus the presidential privileges despite he is a millionaire. Where did the money come from?

On November 17, 2020, former President Barrack Obama published the book" A PROMISED LAND: THE PRESIDENTIAL MEMOIRS VOL 1" by publisher Crown, the price is $US 68 with 700 pages. The introduction of publisher wrote:" *In his own words, Barack Obama tells the story of his improbable odyssey from a young man searching for his identity to the leader of the free world, describing in strikingly personal detail both his political education and the landmark moments of the first term of his historic presidency—a time of dramatic transformation and turmoil.*". Certainly, former President Barrack Obama self splurges the record but everyone knows Obama did nothing for the US, instead, he devastated the country from A to Z, and

Obama also is the global war maker but awarded the Nobel Peace Prize in 2009. His promised land (*) conflicts with the record of the worst president in US history. Despite Barrack Obama left the White House on January 20, 2017, therefore, the people obsess over the SATANIC era of Obama who made America worsened. Former Vice-President and the Democratic candidate Joe Biden reflects the policies of Barrack Obama, its cause conducts the US people including the concerned Democratic fans endorse patriotic President Donald Trump. A Promised land of former President Barrack Obama is the same book" *What Happened"* of Hillary Clinton, so the readers know what Barrack Obama wrote, but the left media companies polish it. It is the manner of a man who destroyed the US and writing a book to acclaim himself, a cat praises its long tail. The book of Barrack Obama is a farce, he lied about the memoirs and concealed the truth as a thug wants to prove the patriotic heart, a traitor talks about national protection, a corrupt politician promotes purity, the communist regime tells about democracy, the fraudster praises the dignity. Nowadays, the global thug Barrack Obama is among the world's hateful faces as Meghan Markle, Joe Biden, Kamala Harris, Michelle Obama, Bill-Hillary Clinton, John Kerry, Jane Fonda, Xi Jinping...The people's abhorrence proved Netflix lost the profit when its entertainment business has Barrack-Michelle Obama and recently, a young deposed royal couple Harry-Meghan Markle signed contract is worth $US 150 million. It causes the television channels to lose more audience by those faces appeared on the screen./.

by Barack Obama (*)

A riveting, deeply personal account of history in the making-from the president who inspired us to believe in the power of democracy

In the stirring, highly anticipated first volume of his presidential memoirs, Barack Obama tells the story of his improbable odyssey from young man searching for his identity to leader of the free world, describing in strikingly personal detail both his political education and the landmark moments of the first term of his historic presidency-a time of dramatic transformation and turmoil. Obama takes readers on a compelling journey from his earliest political aspirations to the pivotal Iowa caucus victory that demonstrated the power of grassroots activism to the watershed night of November 4, 2008, when he was elected 44th president of the United States, becoming the first African American to hold the nation's highest office.

Reflecting on the presidency, he offers a unique and thoughtful exploration of both the awesome reach and the limits of presidential power, as well as singular insights into the dynamics of U.S. partisan politics and international diplomacy. Obama brings readers inside the Oval Office and the White House Situation Room, and to Moscow, Cairo, Beijing, and points beyond. We are privy to his thoughts as he assembles his cabinet, wrestles with a global financial crisis, takes the measure of Vladimir Putin, overcomes seemingly insurmountable odds to secure passage of the Affordable Care Act, clashes with generals about U.S. strategy in Afghanistan, tackles Wall Street reform, responds to the devastating Deepwater Horizon blowout, and authorizes Operation Neptune's Spear, which leads to the death of Osama bin Laden.

A Promised Land is extraordinarily intimate and introspective-the story of one man's bet with history, the faith of a community organizer tested on the world stage. Obama is candid about the balancing act of running for office as a Black American, bearing the expectations of a generation buoyed by messages of "hope and change," and meeting the moral challenges of high-stakes decisionmaking. He is frank about the forces that opposed him at home and abroad, open about how living in the White House affected his wife and daughters, and unafraid to reveal self-doubt and disappointment. Yet he never wavers from his belief that inside the great, ongoing American experiment, progress is always possible.

This beautifully written and powerful book captures Barack Obama's conviction that democracy is not a gift from on high but something founded on empathy and common understanding and built together, day by day./.

66. SATANIC OBAMA HAS INTOXICATED THE WORLD

The enormous evidence proves Coronavirus originated from Wuhan's Biosafety Level 4 Laboratory, it is the biological warfare of China's Communist Party to attack the world, the culprit is commander in viruses, Ape Emperor Xi Jinping. Black Lives Matter appeared under President Barrack Obama's rule, before leaving office, Obama advocated the racism movement by using the Black racial shield and the Black racist against the White's movement spread worldwide. It is the BLACK LIVES

MATTER'S PANDEMIC that creates the mayhem in Western despite the Coronavirus outbreak, but the Black Lives Matter pandemic ignores the lives, the innocent components have been exploited by the hidden perpetrators, they are the domestic thugs.

It is the first time in US history elected a black president, it proved the US people have no racist, if not, the United State of America didn't elect the first communist, and Muslim President ruled the White House in two terms. Whoever claims the US people racist, it is the propaganda of the enemy and communist. Commonly, the Western countries have no racist, the government promotes multiple cultural policies, so the black people, Asians, Muslims migrated. Nevertheless, the Western government treats equally to everyone, so the black, Asia politicians elected to multiple levels of government.

However, from the period of the first black President Barrack Obama who ruled the White House (2008-2016), racism has spread and developed in the US and worldwide. Initially, President Barrack Obama dug up the ashes of civil war, he advocated the **BLACK discrimination against WHITE,** his Black racist against the White has spread worldwide, and the countries in Africa like Zimbabwe, South Africa have responded to the Black racist of Barrack Obama by robbing, killing the farmers of white people. Therefore, the white people, the victims of Black racists have not protested worldwide with the slogan" **WHITE LIVES MATTER**", and the left media avoided releasing the Black discrimination against the White people. Instead, the left media supports and propagates the Black discriminates against the white by distorting the conflicts between the ethnicity, particularly the black and white.

President Barrack Obama has intoxicated the US people and the world despite he left office on January 20, 2020, but his consequence remains in the world community, it causes the Western countries are complicated by Barrack Obama. The **BLACK LIVES MATTER** is the dangerous vestige of Barrack Obama left in the US and the Western countries. **On the other hand, Black Lives Matter is internal cancer, the culprit is Barrack Obama. The cancerous Black Lives Matter can outbreak anytime when an incident or a conflict occurs between the black and white and the left media excites**. The sensible concussion happens between the Police and black persons that incite and sparkle the protests with riots, certainly, Democrats, hidden China's espionage networks including the domestic thug plus the Muslim extremists develop the incident and inciting the innocent components to rally with riots.

The incident of a black man named GEORGE FLOYD who was arrested by the Police, but he resisted, the struggle conducts the death. Therefore, Mr. George Floyd is a drug addict, moreover, he was contracted by Coronavirus before arrested, so his death being suspicious. Certainly, the US government investigates and forensic needs to find the truth, and justice follows after the coroner confirmed. It is the legal process in a democratic country like the US. Therefore, the Black Lives Matter perpetrators exploit the death of a black man to launch the protests with riots, they sit above the law by using the protests to pressure justice.

However, Democrats, China's communist regime should

have stood behind, the domestic thugs have exploited the death of a serious felon to politicize by the protests with riots. The actual forces are Antifa and Black Lives Matter activate in the rallies, the domestic thugs have spread **George Floyd Pandemic** and the Black Lives Matter becomes the racist shield in the US, Europe, Australia, Canada. The protests outbreak in Western despite the Coronavirus pandemic is not over yet. Democrats, Barrack Obama, and the domestic thugs ignore the lives of the protestors, they exchange the lives of innocent people for political purposes. Moreover, when the protestors arrested and charged by breaching the social distance law, curfew and riot, certainly, Democrats, Barrack Obama help nothing, even they stay away from the conviction.

The communist countries like China, the genocide Mao Tse Tung killed more than 65 million Chinese people, but China's communist government promotes Mao as a great hero and he becomes an angel" *Mao goes to Pope*". Vietnam is the same, Ho Chi Minh killed 1,700,000 Vietnamese people, he raped a 15-year old girl named Tuyết Lan in 1929 in Thailand and he also was a famous pedophile, therefore, Vietcong promotes Ho Chi Minh as a great hero and he also becomes the successful Buddha. It is the method of communist regimes, therefore, the left media, Democrats, and domestic thugs have applied the same method with the communist countries in the Western.

Mr. George Floyd has a long criminal record, he convicted of more than a dozen crimes of drug traffic, burglary, robbery, property intrusion, and $USD 20 forgery caused the arrest. He spent 5 years in prison by robbery. Mr.

George Floyd has a notorious criminal history, but Democrats and domestic thugs plus the left media promote the idol. Therefore, the brilliant felony icon has been used for the political purposes of the shadow enemies.

It is incredible when the death of felony George Floyd sparkled the protests with riots, looting in the US, Europe, Australia, Canada. **The portrait of George Floyd appeared in the US, Europe as the statue of Mao Tse Tung in China, Ho Chi Minh in Vietnam, Kim Il Sung, and Kim Jong Il in North Korea.** Certainly, former President Barrack Obama strongly supports his Black Lives Matter, he and comrade Joe Biden attended the funeral of a former felon George Floyd with pathetic emotion. However, the family of George Floyd collected more than $USD 8 million of fundraising. The death of a serious felony George Floyd focuses on multiple purposes, unfortunately, the innocent components have not recognized yet the deep conspiracy of Democrats, China's communist regime, and the domestic thugs.

The left media contributes actual propaganda, they just broadcast the death of George Floyd but conceals the truth while the protestors killed the Police officers, two black Police officers are David Dorn and Patrick Underwood killed by the rioters while they protect the people. A 77-year-old retired police captain shot dead by looters while he tried to protect the business. According to the record in the last 50 weeks, there were 38 Police officers who have been shot dead in the line of duty. **The so-called justice for George Floyd turns terror**, the Black Lives Matter's supporters are 32-year-old lawyers Colinford Mattis and 31-year-old Urooj Rahman threw the firebombs to Police vehicle in Brooklyn, both Black Lives Matter's supporters bailed $USD 250,000, they should face 20 years in the prison. Certainly, Democrats, Barrack Obama, Joe Biden, Nancy Pelosi, and the other high profiles of the Donkey Party will not help two stupid lawyers escape the conviction.

It is the shame, the innocent components in the US, Europe, Canada, Australia have fallen into the racism movement of the global thug Barrack Obama who has intoxicated the Western countries. It is incredible when a felony George Floyd is idolized by Democrats, the domestic thugs, and former President Barrack Obama is the hidden perpetrator of the protests with the riots throughout many states in the US and spread to Western countries. Somewhere else, Black Lives Matter turns LOOTER MATTER, the looters have free plunder's goods, among of them, Chinese students pride the free goods by posting on Facebook. In Chicago, a Nail saloon's owner Johny Pham shot the Vietnam overseas students while they were looting, a looter named Kaity Vo injured and rushed to the hospital. The US police reported 300 Vietnam overseas students arrested by looting.

Satanic Barrack Obama is the global thug and global war-maker, therefore, the Novel Peace Prize Committee in 2009 awarded, it is a farce. On the other hand, Novel Peace Prize's Committee downgraded the most valuable prize on the planet. The demagogic slogan "yes we can" of Barrack Obama conflicts what he did. Yes he can help Islamic State founded, yes he can create Black Lives Matter, yes he can waste $US 100 million of the taxpayers for the luxurious trips, yes he can destroy the US, and "yes" he could intoxicate the world from 2008./.

67. FROM BLACK LIVES MATTER TO BLACK SUPREMACY

The major population of western countries is white people, nevertheless, the world's most humanitarian programs including refugees have supported finance, immigration and others contributed by the White people. Unfortunately, the generous heart of white people has responded by the label racist, Supremacy, right-wing, far-right. The multiple cultures have a negative aspect when the ethnic groups want to impose their culture and religion into an adopted country, it causes social conflict and becomes the ethnic war, the untold civil war has never ended. So the multiple cultures divided the country into a hundred tiny nations, the unification's signification overturns, **multiple cultures become multiple troubles**. The patriots expose the concern about national security, border protection, particularly the illegal migrants, but some ethnic groups claim racism, indeed, patriotism and nationalism are not racist. It is unfair, the multiple ethnic groups have misunderstood, even the dishonest component, the ill-concerned politicians have propagated the hatred to the White people, it causes the mayhem and social division. The misunderstanding created by dishonest politicians, the religious bigot, the malicious propaganda of left media companies plus the evil journalists, the Satanic reporters, **so the title racist has stuck to the White people, they become the victims of Black racism against the White.**

If western people are racist, the Black, Asian and Muslim migrants couldn't accept to stay. Indeed, the immigration policy always opens the door for everyone can come under the immigration criteria by law. Nevertheless, western

335

governments respect equal opportunity, so the US has Black General Colin Powell, Black Senators, Black Representative, Black billionaires, and the first Black President Barrack Obama. In Europe, Australia, the Black politicians elected in Parliament House and Senate, even the Catholics have Black priests, Black Cardinals.

President Barrack Obama is the culprit and perpetrator of the global disorder, he is also the global warmaker but awarded the Nobel Peace Prize in 2009. During 8 years in power, President Barrack Obama dug up the ashes of civil war, he developed the hatred by the racial war between the Black and White. Initially, he used the racial shield to gag the Republican candidates into the presidential campaigns and debates in 2008 and 2012. On the other hand, President Barrack Obama destroyed the harmony in the US society and developed the Black people discriminates against the White people to spread worldwide. The Black people in Africa have treated badly to the White people like Zimbabwe and South Africa, the Black people killed and confiscated the White farmers. Therefore, the left media and Barrack Obama always concealed, instead, they have dug up the White's hatred in Western countries.

President Barrack Obama, Democrats, domestic thugs, and foreign enemies have exploited the personal conflict between the White and Black people to excite the Black people protest with riots. The White police officers have become the targets of racism when a Black person died in custody or struggle with police officers as the circumstance of a serious felony George Floyd. Indeed, there were many cases of death in custody and the struggles that occurred between the police officers and the suspects.

The Black Lives Matter appeared under President Barrack Obama's rule. President Barrack Obama promoted and supported Black Lives Matter and this movement becomes the **BLACK SUPREMACY**. There is not only in the US, but the Black Supremacy globalized. It covered by Black Lives Matter and racial weapons to make trouble in society. The death of black man George Floyd has politicalized, Democrats, the left parties incite the Black people to rally with riots, loots, killing the police officers, abuse the people and vandalized the statues, monuments as the Culture Revolution of Mao Tse Tung applied from 1966 to 1976 in China's mainland. The Black Guard of Black Lives Matter replaced the Red Guard of Mao, the uprising of Black Lives Matter responds to the conspiracies of Democrats, China's Communist Party, former President Barrack Obama, and presidential candidate Joe Biden. The first week of Black Lives Matter protested after the death of George Floyd, they burned down and looted the businesses in the 20 largest metropolitan areas, the damages were more than $US 400 million. There is only Minnesota, after George Floyd's" *Black Lives Matter "*, the damages estimate over $US 500 million.

The first Muslim and communist US President Barrack Obama created dire consequences in the US and the world. Certainly, Barrack Obama is a professional communist, nevertheless, his top adviser was Valerie June Jarrett is a hardcore communist, so both experienced in the communist tactics and communist's technical struggle.

In communist countries like Soviet-Union, China, Vietnam, Cambodia *(Khmer Rouge)*, North Korea, and others. The communist party creates hatred for each other in the people. **The class struggle** is the first stage after the communist party robbed the government. The poor people denounce publicly under the sponsor of the communist regime empowering the low-educated components and illiterate peasants labeled proletarians or revolutionists. The so-called revolution means bloodshed in a communist country. The wealthy families and intellectuals became the victims of Proletarian Lives Matter. The revolutionists have the right to kill, rob, confiscate the assets, enslave the family members of the counter-revolutionary enemy. The class struggle also applies flexibly in the domestic purge campaigns and the power challenge occurs between the rivals in the communist party.

President Barrack Obama and his top adviser Valerie Jarrett could not apply the class struggle in the US and Western countries. Instead, **the racial struggle replaced the class struggle,** it currently creates mayhem in society. The innocent Black people become the victims of Barrack Obama who brainwashed the Black people throughout 8 years in the US, the ill-concerned Black people have been intoxicated by Obama, Democrats, and the left media has propagated the hatred. So the Black Lives Matter prides itself as the Black Supremacists, behind Black Lives Matter are Democrats, possible billionaire George Soros, and China's Communist Party.

The protests with riots went too far, the free speech and democracy turn nasty, the Black Supremacists pressure the brand Colonial beer in Australia to change the name, it is racist. Possible, Black Lives Matter can tell the English dictionary to remove the word" **Colonial**" because of the racist. The Black Lives Matter wants to remove all White statues including Jesus, the statues of US presidential heroes at Mount Rushmore while the White statues being torn down around the Western countries, but the statue of Black President Barrack Obama alongside his youngest daughter Sasha was unveiled in South Dakota, the statue located on the corner of Fourth and St. Joseph Street.

After the greatest funeral of a serious felony George Floyd, the Black Supremacy develops in the high tide of the Black revolution in the Western. They complain about the racism in the entertainment industry, the Simpsons will no longer have a White actor's voice of a non-white character. The Missourian newspaper issued an apology for the racist cartoon. Somewhere, the apology's pandemic has spread in sport, media, government

The left media promotes Black Supremacy by the propaganda, so the Black Lives Matter act as the superpower in the country, they ignore the government and police, even the Coronavirus pandemic waived. Unfortunately, after the protests, the second wave of COVID-19 re-outbreak in Victoria (*Melbourne)*, conducts the state locked down while all states and territories in Australia eased the restriction.

Western countries respect free speech and demonstration, therefore, the Black Lives Matter and Antifa have gone too far with the riots, so the government must apply the law to restore order and social safety. All lives matter, not only the Black Lives Matter, certainly, the Black Lives Matter can not rally in China, Vietnam, North Korea, and other communist countries. Even the protest of Chinese people's lives matter, Tibet lives matter, Falun Gong lives matter can not rally in the world's largest communist paradise. There is not only Black Lives Matter, but let's live together in a harmonious society./.

68. NO ISLAMOPHOBIA BUT THE CULTURE LOSS FEARS

The tolerance and generous heart of the Western people are the radical policy of multiple cultures. If the Western has not opened the heart, the United Nations would face the difficulty to raise the fund for the humanitarian program, actually, the other ethnic couldn't arrive and live peacefully.

Almost, the Western people have no racist, but there are some cases, moreover, the law strictly punishes whoever shows racial discrimination and violence against other people. Nevertheless, the racist doesn't apply to the patriot, the concerned people protest against the illegal migrant for border protection and preventing the terrorist infiltrate under the human rights label. However, the innocent component, the hypocritical element, the left parties, and the domestic thugs label the racist, right-wing, or supremacist to the concerned citizen. The false accusation propagated by the left media and the innocent politicians (*the left parties, actually the Greens Party*), have misled the public. **The major Western people oppose the human rights violation, they have no opposed Islam as the false accusation, but they fight against the Sharia Law, actually, the Sharia Law's activists have tried to bring the inhumane culture to intoxicate the Western's society, moreover, the Sharia Law conflicts the UN's Universal Declaration of Human Rights.**

The multiple cultures contribute to the different nuances of ethnic groups and economic development. Therefore, the negative aspects of multiple cultures warn when every ethnic

340

group wants to dominate and impose their culture, actually their religion into the adopted countries harming multiple cultures. The arrogance and selfishness cause **the untold civil war** to silently occur in society. It causes the multiple cultures to fail, the country doesn't unify instead, instead, it divided a hundred tiny nations. Nevertheless, the national budget spends more on security, police when the ethnic groups conflict with each other by the rallies. Nevertheless, the extremists could create the bloodshed and society faces more the problem.

Muslim is the hardline religion, the faith is different, moreover, their culture conflicts with the other religions and social valuation. Muslim's dress being controversial, actually, the Burqa becomes the problem of security and the lawmaker's argument. The strict worship obligates at least 5 times a day that could raise the problem into the working places, certainly, the factories, companies are not the mosques. Nevertheless, sometimes Muslims gathered at the public place to pray, it causes traffic congestion, the public places are not the mosques. Muslims are allergic to pork, they have tried to force the Western to ban the pork at school and somewhere else. Moreover, some bigot Muslims slammed whoever eats the bacon at their front, it insults Muslims. Moreover, the Western people fear the extremists hide in the Muslim communities and mosques, when the bloodshed occurred, the people could know the culprits, it is too late. The arrogant clerics, the bigot preachers plus the extreme leaders launch the hateful propaganda to society, it causes terrorism. The cultural hardline and the arrogant leaders of Muslim that creates the misunderstanding into the adopted countries that cause social complication and social conflict.

Despite, Muslims are a minority in the Western, but they demand a lot of changes in adopted society. The Allah-certified food being controversial, even the small number of Muslims in the Australian army, but they require the Allah certified ratio. The Muslim parents inserted the culture into the students, **they pressure the school to remove the Cross and Father Christmas, the Muslims complain about the labels that insult Muslim while the other religions respect religious freedom. In 2019, Victoria state (*Australia*), a Child Care Center in South-East of Melbourne canceled the Christmas event is due to cultural sensitivities.**

There is just a small Muslim population complicates the society, certainly, their hard-line culture couldn't integrate the society. Therefore, the most left media in Western is keen to promote the Muslim culture and the leaders, it is clever advertising. The people doubt the left media companies and journalists should receive the privileges of the Muslim countries or corruption as in the Vietnam war, the left media should be financed by the communist undercover activists and the left media released the fake news, fabricated stories, and concealed the cruelty of Vietcong.

The most dangerous problem is **the government shield tactic** that Muslims have activated into the adopted country's government system. In the US, a Muslim Barrack Obama succeeded the government shield's tactic, he ruled the US in 8 years and now, this country shattered, actually, President Barrack Obama deserved the facilities and created the Muslim infiltrated the government in federal, states and local. Despite the era of President Barrack Obama is gone, but the numerous Muslims in the US government at multiple levels overwhelmed that alert the US people. After the midterm election in 2018, the Muslim politicians added more two women, the fresh term Muslim Representative Rashida Tlaib used coarse language to President Donald Trump and Ilhan Omar destroyed the Congressional rule in 181, the hat bans removed, she wore the headscarf in the House of Representatives. Nevertheless, the Muslim politicians swore in with Koran's bible, the US Constitution ruined.

In the United Kingdom, the first London Muslim Mayor Sadiq Khan often raises the big voices as the national leader, he becomes the most controversial in the public by his ugly behavior. Moreover, the numerous Muslim politicians in the United Kingdom's Labor Party cornered Great Britain, actually the concerned British fear the cultural loss. On the other hand, the UK Labor Party helped the internal conqueror is Sadiq Khan who controls London, the heart of the United Kingdom.

Australia faces the same situation, the Muslim politicians in the Labor Party swore in with Koran's bible, the Constitution destroyed. The inhumane rules of Sharia Law derived from the Quran bible, so the Western Constitution to be eradicated. Labor Representative Anne Aly is calling for a blasphemy law to protect the Muslim, therefore, she ignores to call the blasphemy law to protect the other religions, actually, the Muslim hurt the Catholic and Christian, they always claim removal of the Cross, Father Christmas, and forcing the school bans the pork in the canteen or the fairs. The Vatican being threatened after Pope Francis signed a pact to merge Catholics and Islam that calls the One World Religion.

The left parties are selfish, they favor the ballot and the

343

seats in the parliament than the country, the social valuation. The left parties are the wonderful places for Muslims developing the government shield's tactic, so Democrats in the US, Labor Party in Australia, United Kingdom, the socialist party in France...the Muslim politicians seem Allah certified congress despite the Muslim member is small, but they influence the other members, actually the left party.

The Western people have no Islamophobia, but the people fear the Muslims have changed society, politics and wiping out the original cultures ever. The phenomenon occurred in Western like the United Kingdom, Australia, and somewhere else, the Muslim's resident changed the electorates, so the elections rigged by the donkey Muslim voters, they elect the representatives, mayors on religious faith, so the adopted countries lose the democracy in its Constitution./.

69. THE SHARIA LAW IS THE INHUMANE CULTURE ON THE PLANET

Whatever, any discrimination form has harmed the society, human history spent the terrible eras of the abnormal theories that caused the human disaster:

–**The racism** developed in Germany by dictator Adolf Hitler, the Third Reich killed more than 6,000,000 Jewish, the massacre has never forgotten.

-**Mind discrimination** has become the most dangerous discrimination's form on the planet. The mastermind is Karl Marx, a dishonest academic, his crazy theory transformed to reality by the genocide Lenin who succeeded the so-called October Revolution 1917 in Russia. Communism killed more than 100,000,000 people and the other a billion people lost freedom. In the communist country, whoever speaks differently from the communist party would be killed or faced the long term into the prison camp, mostly the forced labor camp. Mind discrimination also influences worldwide, even democratic countries and Western. The left media performs the mind discrimination, so the left journalists, left columnists, and the left media companies often attack whoever tells the truth as President Donald Trump in the US.

-**Gender discrimination** represents Sharia Law, it is an obsolete culture still remains and develops into Muslim countries and also spreading into the Western. The world condemns racism, communism, gender discrimination. Actually, the UN's Universal Declaration of Human Rights promotes fair treatment and respect for the people, so Sharia law opposes human valuation. Its reason noted Saudi Arabia failed to impose the Sharia Law at the United Nations, despite Saudi Arabia has the Muslim countries in Middle-East and Africa backed but the major countries opposed.

The Sharia Law derives from the Quran bible, so every Allah adherent is an activist of Sharia Law. The Sharia Law and faith practice into society and insert into religion, so gender discrimination socialized and legalized into the Muslim countries. Nevertheless, the Muslim migrant has brought the inhumane culture into the adopted countries and they have attempted to legalize it. However, the Sharia Law badly treats the female as Quran bible 4.34:" *Men have authority over women because Allah has made the one superior to the other and because they spend their wealth to maintain them. Good women are obedient. They guard their unseen parts because Allah has guarded them. As for those from whom you fear disobedience, admonish them and send them to beds apart and beat them. ".* The Quran bible applies to society, a child bride is a form of serious violation of human rights. The world condemns child pornography, but the child bride accepted somewhere else as Germany Federal Supreme Court rejected Anti-Child Marriage law. Almost, the legal system and the court in the Western applied heavy punishment to the child pornographers, but German Federal Supreme Court ignored and the Justices accepted the Child bride. Nevertheless, the Sharia Law deserves the death sentence to whoever breaches the law, the punishment carries out the barbarous methods as the stone-throwing, beaten to death, hanging...

The world, actually the Western countries respect human rights, equal treatment between the social components including gender, certainly, the Sharia Law unfits the social valuation. Therefore, the left parties are such as Democrats in the US, Labor Party in the United Kingdom, Australian Labor Party, Socialist Party in France, and the other left parties are keen to get the ballot, so they recruited the Muslim politicians in the crowded Muslim's resident of electoral units. The Muslim politicians activate the Sharia Law into the House of Representatives and Senate, it conducts the Constitution ruined when the Muslim politicians swear in by the Quaran bible. It is a contradiction because of the Sharia Law derived from the Quran bible. It means the Western country accepted the human rights violation while the country opposes it.

In Western countries, the people, society, and government have not accepted racism, Communism, and gender discrimination. Therefore, the left parties support and protect Sharia Law's followers. The blasphemy law's bill introducing into the Western parliament to protect the inhumane law's followers while almost the other religions have never required the blasphemy law to protect the Catholic, Christian, Buddhism, Hindu, and others. Moreover, when the concerned citizen's rally to oppose the Sharia Law's followers are the asylum seekers or the illegal migrants invade the country under the label of human rights but the Sharia Law's followers are the left parties support for the futuristic voters. Unfortunately, the domestic thugs (left parties, the innocent people) labeled the patriot and the concerned people are racists. Indeed, the people who fight for human rights, gender equalizes, social safety, to the protection of the country are not racists, nor right-wing, neither far-right. The left media stand alongside the left parties and the Sharia Law's followers into the propaganda. The people support the UN's Universal Declaration of Human Rights by fighting against the inhumane law of Sharia to be condemned and criticized. What is going on in the Western country?

The concerned politicians raise the danger of Sharia Law but the hypocritical politicians of the left parties attack and criticize racism. The Muslim migrant always respects the Quran bible and activates the Sharia law. The Western government opposes human rights violations, gender discrimination. Therefore, they favor and support the followers of Sharia Law. The incident of Brunei has issued the cruel punishment on the LGBT outrage the world, including the left parties and the left media. However, inside the left parties already have the Sharia Law's followers, they are the politicians who always want the Sharia law legislation as same-sex marriage.

The people don't know the stable stance of the left parties. How could the people trust ALP, UK Labor Party, Democrats, and Greens? The police must fight against the crime, but the police can not fight against the crime but also standing with the felons. The Western countries have not opposed the Muslim, but the left parties plus the Muslim bigot, the aggressive clerics labeled Islamophobia, certainly, the people oppose the inhumane law of Sharia, it discriminates the gender, actually, the Sharia Law advocates the bad treatment to the Muslim female./.

70. THE TINY MUSLIM NATIONS SILENTLY GREW UP IN THE WESTERN

The silent invasion of Muslims has thriven into the Western countries that become the real threat of the adopted countries and the social valuation. The negligent immigration policy and the ill-religious freedom's concern of the innocent Western people plus the hypocritical components bringing the bight to kill the countries and destroy the society. The Muslim changes Western society, deeply affects the government, courtesy. The people have never heard the terms are the insult Catholic Christian..or religious blasphemy. But Muslim labels to the non-Muslim people, some adherent condemn whoever eats the bacon at their front, it is the insult Muslim, some Western countries applied the blasphemy law.

Nowadays, there are many unofficial tiny Muslim nations presented and have grown into the soil of Western. The crowded Muslim population in a region influences, the original electorates are no longer reflect the voice of people. The Muslim resident affects the politics, actually, the ballot lover's politicians follow the demand of Muslims to carry out the policies if they want to elect or retain the seats. Nevertheless, the left parties in the Western are the wonderful places for Muslim politicians recruited and influenced the Muslim cultures as the Sharia law, the Allah certified food. The **Government shield's tactic** has become the essential method to expand the tiny nations into the Western countries. The Muslim representatives in parliament drive the nation in the wrong direction, mostly the Muslim representatives serve for their religion than the electorates and the adopted country's interest. The government shield's tactic has applied to multiple government's levels, the Muslim politicians have joined the federal, state, and local governments. They have exploited democracy and the authority to develop the tiny Muslim nations. Actually, the Muslim politicians are keen to deserve the priority and privileges for the Allah adherent, so the Mosques flourished despite the local resident strongly oppose and protest. Moreover, the Muslim worship army has become a problem when they gathered on the streets, the traffic-congested. The hard-line culture of Muslims being controversial on Burqa, Allah certified food, the Sharia law, all are allergy with the society into the adopted countries. While the other religions respect the Muslim's culture, but they want to impose their way on everyone, **there is no pork, but Allah**.

The tiny Muslim nation represented in Victoria state,

Labor Party's Premier one belt-on road Daniel Andrews who puts the national interest and national security for the ballot of ethnic, so the Sudanese in Melbourne snub the anti-terrorist law of federal government while **Premier Daniel Andrews flagged on October 2015, he officially announced to accept the violent extremism is part of contemporary Australia**. Melbourne considers the commercial center of Australia, therefore the heart of business unofficially became the Muslim's tiny nation running by the Sudanese under the silent endorsement of Labor's state government, actually, the gangs currently threaten the Victorian's resident and the business including the tourist.

In the US, Democrats favor the faction and the party's interest, they recruited the Muslim representatives in the House, after the midterm election, two female Muslim politicians join the new force in the Congress. On the first day of new faces in Congress, the Palestinian representative of Michigan is Rashida Harbi Tlaib exposed the aggressive attitude by the coarse language to the US President Donald Trump, she terrorizes the US president with the lawmaker's weapon. The Muslim politicians in Democrats influenced the new budget, the wall deleted but the foreign aid increase, mostly, the Muslim countries as Palestine, Syria, Pakistan will get the aid from the US taxpayers while the wall's fund hampered the border's protection abandons.

In Minnesota, Ms. Ihan Omar became the Representative of Democrats, she exited the Amazon's Muslim workers strike to demand the time for its religious worship at least 5 times a day. The Muslim cornered the working place in the Western country, **there is the job, not Allah.** Democrats strongly endorse the Muslims in the US, actually, Minnesota state crowded the Somali, they established the" tiny nation's cabinet" names Confederation of Somali Community. Nevertheless, the local government in this state promoted the Muslim police, the Somali police officer Mohamed Noor shot dead the Australian woman Justin Damond, despite the murder incident is clear, the motive comes from racist of Black against the White, but the Muslim community pressures the state government, so the justice has delayed while the public and the victim's family are waiting for the verdict.

The heart of Great Britain is London became the tiny nation of an unofficial president is the first Muslim Mayer Sadiq Khan, he behaves as the national leader in the United Kingdom. The situation worsens in Europe, the crowded Muslim resident became the tiny nations boomed in the land of the wealthy continent. The Muslim politicians of the left parties, the Muslim representatives are going to Allah certified the parliament, so the phenomenon of the Muslim politicians sworn in with Koran's bible, the traditional Constitution of Western lost when the democracy turned the trash. Nevertheless, Allah certified the Justice, the courts accepted Sharia law that alarms the legal system being driven to the Muslim law.

Belgium clearly appeared a Muslim tiny nation, Belgium's Islam Party activates transforming Belgium into the Muslim State in 2030, they call" Islamist democracy". The negligent immigration's policy, actually, when the left party rules Belgium, the Muslim migrant throve and now, the consequence to be paid. **The French magazine Causeur believes the next twenty years, the European capital Brussels will be the Muslim land**. The growth of the Muslim party in Belgium alerts the Western countries while the Muslim exploits the so-called Islamicphobia to protect their invasion. In Australia, the Australian Muslim Party founded, they aim to contest the federal and states in the elections. Certainly, the Australian Muslim Party should have some seats in the Muslim's crowded resident, they have the power in parliament, actually, the Australian Muslim Party has the allies are Labor Party and Greens Party, the reference ballot could have Muslim gains the seats and Labor, Greens have more votes.

The socialism Pope Francis is generous, he is keen to integrate with Muslims, but they want to remove the Cross and Father Christmas. In the United Kingdom, the well-known preacher Anjem Choudary called the Buckingham Palace renames Buckingham Masjid, the Arabic World for the mosque, and the Mall that approaches the Palace would become Masjid Road.

The left media often stand alongside the Muslim, almost the left media certified Hallah, so the newspapers, online, radio, and Television deserve the Muslim leaders to appear, they speak as the national leaders. Actually, the Muslim leaders promote Sharia Law and trying to demote it after the terror occurred.

The local people stand up to protect the country and society while the silent enemy gently has invaded under the religious shield and the religious freedom's weapon. However, the left parties including the Muslim communities label the concerned citizen is racist or far-right…the patriots protect the country they are not racist or far-right. The people must remove the title of the enemy and the hypocritical components colluded with the enemy to demote the patriotic spirit. The Western people and government wake up before too late.

The Muslim tiny nations develop, the hard-line culture of Allah adherent causes the non-Muslim resident moving out the region, so the Muslim tiny nations expand. Nevertheless, the Muslim politicians in federal, state and local governments always deserve the priority for them, a day, the Western countries will be the Muslim, it is possible while the threat appeared clearly./.

71. THE FREE RELIGION OR THE RELIGION FREE?

The common sense, all religions mutually respect and everyone has a free choice on the belief, the UN, and the democratic country observes the different religion's practice in the equality treatment. According to the free religion, the most democratic states confirmed by law, the nation has no allowance the religious discrimination by any form. Moreover, the United States Commission on International Religious Concern listed the nations as China, Vietnam, Arab Saudi... in the Countries of Particular Concern (CPC).

However, in most Islamic states, there is no God but Allah, the saying presents into the heart of every Muslim. Mostly the countries currently rule under the Muslim's influence likely Iran, Turkey, Indonesia, Malaysia, Arab Saudi, Sudan, Yemen....almost have no recognition of the other religions present in their country. It causes the church to burn down, the Catholic and Christian's followers killed, despite the government condemn the violence against the religion, but it is just the mouthful speech likely the government's courtesy. Therefore inside the ruling government of the Muslim country, the high profile officials have no intention to crush down the hostile behavior of their Halal fellow to the other religions.

The tourist or even its people just say:" I don't like Muslim, neither Allah", they would be met in deep trouble, the Muslim government labels the religious insult, it is the serious crime, and the legal system deserves the heavy punishment for whose break the law. There were the foreign tourists, mostly came from the western country, who were charged in the Islamic country when they made the mistake the law, moreover the using alcohol or eating pork, those could be restricted. But in the western country, everyone could say:" I don't interest Catholic, Christian...neither I don't like Jesus" they couldn't be charged, they have free speech and free religious concern.

The western country strictly bans religious discrimination, according to the law, any religion freely practices worship. As the routine, normally the worship could happen in the religious firms, sometimes if they want to celebrate a gala, they must apply for the government permission, because it relates to the public and government arranges the security protection. Therefore, in the western states are such as Europe, likely in French, sometimes the Muslim flocked the streets with multiple thousands blocked the traffic during their worship's time, it is an outrage because the Muslim break the law and illegally occupy the public places, but the government did nothing. Probably they extremely respect the Muslim, because, behind the Muslim residents, there are the oil tycoons in the Middle East, the key provides the energy for the western country. The Muslims exploit the free religion by using the worship to invade public places, if the government ignores, a day, they will transform smoothly the adopted country to a Muslim state, the invasion without armed force or bloodshed. The Muslim phenomena in Europe and somewhere else raise the alerts to the world.

Most western countries are generous and kind, but the Muslim exploits and gently occupy public places with the worship's reason, sometimes they organize the rallies with the slogan, dress (Burqa) and wearing the mask shown off at the public places. Therefore the western country government respects the religion, including the Muslim.

In Australia, despite the Muslim student is the minority, but some universities deserved the special restroom for the Muslim student because they could pray everywhere and a toilet is a private place, but the special toilet built by the taxpayer paid. Nevertheless, some Muslim parents went too far, they requested the school removal the Cross and Father Christmas because those are not convenient for their children, if the school wants the student to study from there, they must remove those. Some schools gave up the pork sausages or the pork meat in the festival because a minor Muslim student couldn't eat. However, in a democratic country, the government respects the majority, not especially deserves for a minority or a religion, likely the election, the winner to be met the major ballet voted. But some countries did, it is the victory of the Muslim ethnic in the adopted country.

In Australia, the minor Muslim agitates the companies and government (mostly the left politicians and Greens) apply the Allah food certified, if not they boycott. Even though in the Australian Royal Army, despite the Muslim armed force personnel's is the small number, but they propose the ration Allah certified. The Allah food certified being controversial in Australia, therefore a minor party is Greens (the viral party as someone concern) and some Labor party's politicians should agree while the major population strongly oppose. The Allah food certified raises the problem in the society and divided the country, it steals money from the taxpayer when the companies accept the Allah certified in the brand, obviously, the Muslim community makes a profit from the companies paid as the illegal tax and the companies claims the tax deduction, they add more cost in the product and the consumer has to pay more for the Allah certified. There is also a story in the Down Under, in Queensland, Mr. Raymond Akhtar Ali who bashed his newborn baby to death in 1998, but during the serving period in the prison, he complained the food didn't meet his religion, he ate the vegetarian meals in 3 months, he sued the government and the magistrate decided to compensate $AUD 3,000, the money comes from the taxpayer. It is outrage but happened in Australia.

The Muslim asylum seeker's wave shattered Europe and alert the US, Australia, Canada…Actually, in Europe, the threat has presented the terror's scenes in French, Germany, Belgium, Spain…The Muslims in Europe raises the tension between Germany, Dutch, and Turkey, a Muslim country when the Turkey prime minister Recep Tayyip Erdogan and the ministers want to appear in Germany, Dutch, Turkey's leaders excite the Muslims rally against those governments. It is an outrage, not a form of foreign relationship or international diplomacy. The Turkey government unofficially declare the war on Dutch and Germany, they had a Muslim force with millions of people, the domestic thug. It is the lesson for the nation has the Muslim resident. However, the Turkey government scares China's communist regime, the Muslims in Sinkiang Uighur have been oppressing, why didn't Turkey have no reaction?

The reaction of the western people proved with the nationalist movement in Dutch, French, US, Australia...the rallies oppose against the Muslim and asylum seeker currently occur. Sometimes two sides clash, the police have to keep the public security, but the government spends more money on police and intelligence agencies.

The multiple cultures failed, it doesn't unify the country, indeed divided into hundred tiny nations. Badly the Muslims are keen to impose their religion on the adopted countries. In Australia, the government grants the fund for the ethnic, including the school, but they use the taxpayer for the own culture, actually, the Muslim has the concern their religion is orthodox of God, they should encourage the hatred and the extremist exploits the religion for the terrorism. Likely in the Vietnam War, the Vietcong used the countryside as the base, the most guerrilla came from the peasant with the terror war, and the communist cadres propagated the low or uneducated peasant. Nowadays the extremists hide behind the Muslims and the mosque, Muslim schools should be the dens of the hatred propaganda, mostly the fellows keep quiet while they seeing the terror conspiracy. The government funding to the multiple cultural ethnicities to be overhauled or scrap, the taxpayer wastes.

Not all Muslims are terrorists, but every Muslim could be a terrorist because the religion raises different concerns with the others. Moreover, the living style of Burqa wearing being controversial, it raises the security problem when the Burqa wearer hides the face, some Muslim women refused to take off the Burqa when police request.

Sharia law is not suitable the nowadays society, the sex discrimination has no allowance in western countries and also the UN. In Australia, a senior Muslim leader, president of the Australian Federation of Islamic Councils, Dr. Kysar Trad said using violence against women is a "last resort" for men. (News.com.au on February 23, 20170).

The Muslims in the western country bring alien cultures to the adopted country, the child bride is a human rights violation, the female genital mutilation (FGM) raises controversy, as the predict 15 million teens between 15 and 19 years old add by 2030 will be victimized. But in the world, there are at least 200 million girls and women who were cut the genitals.

Certainly, the Muslim could have the free religious practice in the free speech country, but they have not consented to the free religion in the Muslim country, which is unfair. The differently religious concern that causes the social conflict, the rallies support and oppose currently occur, sometimes causes the violence, it is the domestic war.

Mostly the Muslims and their supports as the Greens (in

Australia), Labor (left), and Democrat (in the US)...label the reaction against the extremist behind the Muslims are racist. The patriot fight for the country, national security, the border's protection...have been titled as the racist, so the most Muslim rallies appear the banner" Racist" as the weapon to defend the Muslim and the government should protect them despite the major population recognize the real face of the domestic thug.

The people respect the free religion, therefore the Muslims exploit it, they have no respect for the other religions in their native nation and also snub in the adopted country. Most people in the western country are not racist, so the different ethnicities live peacefully, actually, the western people have a lenient heart and warmly received and welcome the refugee, while the wealthy state as Arab Saudi waives the Muslim fellows.

However, the generous heart of the western people limited, nowadays they know the title HUMAN RIGHTS turns HUMAN WRONG when the people smuggling, thug, criminal...exploit the loopholes of the immigration law for penetration. Moreover, the Terrorist War wakes up the western people and the patriotic movement arouses in the US, Europe, Australia... the tolerance has no room while the thug attacks in the homeland. The country's protection is not racist, whatever the right or left-wing stance in the western country let's put the national interest first. Remember when the country lost, the citizen couldn't protect the property and the life. There is only the treasonous person who waives the border protection, but the martyr has not given up the fighting for the country./.

72. THE EXTREMIST HARMS THE ALLAH'S FAITH

The most religion loves peace, humanity, tolerance, lenient heart. As common sense, the Muslim behaves likely most religion, certainly the human life to be respected and its bible doesn't encourage the killing or harming anyone. On the other hand, religion helps society, the government reduces crime, but the criminal, gang, felon are the social danger and everyone needs to stay away.

Allah to be believed the God of Abrahamic religions or the God in Islam. The name of Allah is the religious symbol of the Muslim, but what is Allah look like? Therefore all the Muslims absolutely believe" there is no God, but Allah".

Allah expects the God of Islam, the people of different religions respect the Muslim's faith and the Muslim must respect the others, it is fair and equal treatment of each other. Religion is the free choice, there is someone who promotes their religion is only the orthodox, and snub the other religion, moreover, the bigots consider the other religions are evil and they self-confirm as God's representative and destroy the other evil religions. The wrong message comes from the extremists and the bigots, they propagate the hatred to the other religions in the mosque, community and the terrorist mind has been starting, it is the prime stage of terrorism.

When the Muslims migrated to the western country, the society has different religions as Catholic, Christian, Buddhist, including Muslim. Therefore the extremists and the bigots want to transform the adopted country converts to Islam, but the terrorism's method couldn't convince the people, instead of the love, generous treatment is the true belief. However, the extremist's concern using terror to spread religion, it is terribly wrong. Nevertheless, the Muslim bigots want to impose their religious pattern into the adopted society, but the Sharia law or the Islamic law is just the Islamic tradition, it reflects the Quran and the Hadith (written by the Muslim Prophet Muhammed and Muhaddiths collected) have appeared into the Muslim community overseas. However the Sharia law is not suitable in the western country, female discrimination is a serious form of human rights violation, actually, the child bride is a form of a sexual slave. The world respects religion but Sharia law couldn't accept it.

The extremist exploits the religion and uses the name of Allah for terrorism, nowadays the world knows the terrorist threatens everywhere and anytime, all come from the Muslim. The extremist harms the Allah, they insult the religion and Allah by the killing, terror... Moreover, where Allah's citizens present, the people watch out and fear the happening could occur.

The extremists and bigots created the misunderstanding to the world, certainly, the religious Muslim is innocent but the extremists hide behind the Muslim that causes the fear, they create the hatred of the world to the Muslim. Whatever, after the terror with the bloodshed, the victim of the terrorist blames" there no God but killing" not" there is no God but Allah".

Not all Muslims are terrorists, therefore, every Muslim could be a terrorist because the extremists hide in the religion, they could be the clerics, Muslim community leader in the western country or the teachers in the Islamic school, the terrorist growth that comes from the religious firms. Likely in the Vietnam War, not of all peasants were terrorists Vietcong, but every peasant could be a guerrilla, so South Vietnam's security agencies worked very hard. The rural region in Vietnam was the base of the Vietcong's terrorist, the Vietcong cadres propagated the hostility and recruited the guerrilla.

The western country being faced the domestic thugs, they penetrated under the migrant policy and the innocent concern of the government, mostly the ruling government is the left party plus the Greens (the viral party in the democratic state). Europe shattered and shocked by the terror that occurred in Spain, Belgium, French, Germany, UK (the attack on March 23, 2017)…the migrant or the asylum seeker covered under the refugee's label, the HUMAN RIGHTS turn HUMAN WRONG. The UN just encourages the refugee, but they don't distinguish between the refugee and asylum seekers, likely the python and tiger snake are reptiles but the tiger snake could kill anyone with venom. In Muslim countries as Indonesia, Pakistan, Iraq, Turkey, Yemen, Syria, Libya….most of the population are Muslim, but the people couldn't recognize who is the terrorist or not? So the western country, including the security agencies, anti-terrorist, the terrorist's recognition is very difficult, but they could know well after the terror occurred, it is too late likely after a horse ran away, the owner thinks making the fence.

The innocent people in the western country wake up, the domestic thugs could uprising or raise the terror right in their homeland. The US woke up after 8 years of the first Muslim president Barack Obama, they voted for President Donald Trump who recognizes the most threat to the country is the citizen of Allah who could turn from the religion's worship to terrorist. However, the US has many judges in 50 states, but there are only two judges from small states as Seattle (James Robart) and Hawaii (Derrick Watson) use the so-called court order to block the presidential travel ban's order. The district judges like the frog but the left media puffed and bubble like the dinosaurs. It is a farce of the legal public servants, therefore they power themselves as the superpower above the president. While the president prevents the thugs penetrate, the Democrat, Liberal, and two liberal judges try to open the door for the unknown guest to come.

The Muslim and Allah to be respected, the Muslim considers the peace, love, so its religion has about 1.7 billion adherents. But the extremists and the bigots have driven the Muslims in the wrong direction. Allah is God, not killing, unfortunately, the extremist exploits the name of Allah for terror. A Muslim extremist is like Mr. Ziyed B who attempted to grab a gun of female police at Orly airport (French), he shouted:" I am here to die for Allah-There will be deaths"…Allah has never command anyone to die for Allah, but the terrorist uses Allah for killing. Mostly the terrorist act, shout Allah as the faith, but the faith of terror, they harm Allah and religion. The right Muslim adherents have to eliminate the extremist and live in peace, it is Allah's will" there is no God but Allah" not" there is no God but terror". Most Muslims love peace, respect human life, so terrorism has no place for Allah's adherents. The right Muslims have to protect Allah from being harmed by terrorism./.

73. THE NEGATIVE ASPECTS OF AUSTRALIA ECONOMY

On square kilometers, the sixth-largest country on the planet *(Russia, Canada, China, the United States of America, and Brazil*). Therefore, Australia's population just is 25 million, with rich national sources, and huge farmland plus a good education system, Australia is among the favorite universities that attract China's communist students. Unfortunately, the Lucky Country turns misfortune nation while the sovereignty is threatening by China's Communist Party with the company of innocent component and corrupt politicians plus the naïve businesses that have conducted the country into China's vassal. Nevertheless, communism silently infiltrated society and education to kill patriotism. Moreover, the left parties like the **Australian Labour Party, the Greens Party** contributed to the national disaster with the demagogic policies are the hoax climate change causes the nation to divide, the same-sex-marriage legislation cost the taxpayers $AU 122 million by the postal survey to carry out by the Labor's undercover activist *Malcolm Turnbull who climbed higher and dived deeper in Liberal Party,* so Prime Minister Malcolm Turnbull did the Labor's policy and the asylum seekers labeled the human rights but it turned human wrong, the taxpayers also wasted tens of billion dollars for the unknown people, moreover, the terrorists, criminals, and espionage agents have exploited the refugees to infiltrate. Australian society is complicated by the negative multiple cultures cause multiple trouble, the country divided into a hundred tiny nations of ethnicity, so the patriotism faded, indeed the patriotism is the key to develop the country, the samples of Taiwan, Singapore,

South Korea, Japan proved the failure of Australia that conducts the economic development lagged behind those Asian nations above.

The innocent and corrupt politicians that caused Australia to lose anything, the bribery's tactic of China succeeded to buy the politicians and the political parties with donations, so China can get a good policy with the Labor and Liberal Party, China's Communist Party succeeded to deploy the trade trap, debt trap, and government trap, particularly, the bribery tactic created an opportunity for China to control Australia after 28 years of establishing relations. The domestic traitors placed the country for sale plus the negligent immigration policy to shatter the nation and social mayhem. The major economic aspects were lost, China took control and corner the economy, the financial system, and colonizing the country. Moreover, China's espionage agent infiltrated the government including the parliament from the federal, state, and local councils. The concerned people warn about Liberal Representative Gladys Liu who is pro-Beijing, China's communist Pierre Yang becomes the member of Legislative Council in Western Australia of Labor's Premier Mark McGowan and its state government granted the contract of $A 136 million for Huawei to operate 4G in the train's system, the national security risks. The trade with democratic countries based on mutual development and fair trade, instead, China has exploited the trade for the global hegemonic ambition, moreover, China has never respected the law, instead of the bush law and wild rules have applied and bullied the counterparts

1-The land and natural sources: China's communist regime owned at least 9,300,000 hectares including coal mines, farmland, and other economic facilities. The strategist port in Darwin leased 99 years with $AU 506 million under the rule of Prime Minister Malcolm Turnbull and Treasurer Scott Morrison. The airport at Merriden in Western Australia leased 100 years with one dollar. Despite the Australian government established the Foreign Investment Review Board (FIRB) but it is useless. China's state-owned company bought water in Murray-Darling, Beijing controls 732 gigalitres (*1.89% of the water in the market*). Chinese wealthy persons inundated the home buyers in Australia, mostly, the communist members and families occupied the luxurious properties at the good locations in the capital cities including Canberra, instead, the Australian citizens moved out.

2-The industry: Australia has not much industry, the farmland, and mines are the backbone of the economy. Nevertheless, the companies and factories owned by Australian investors have suffered a high wage, union, superannuation, insurance, and tax. So they moved to China or the cheap laborer's countries in Asia. Certainly, China attracted profit-lover investors, so Australian products were ruined from the household appliances, clothes, shoes, even toilet papers made in China. When the Coronavirus pandemic outbreak, the people rushed to buy toilet papers, the consequence paid. The made in Australia and buy Australia is just a relief, indeed, the major supermarkets ordered China made to sell at cheap prices.

3-The businesses and investors are keen to make a profit than the national interest, they have forced the Australian people to buy the poison, contaminated, and short life products imported from China. The Australian consumers have suffered the shoddy products including clothes, footwear, but they couldn't do anything because the supermarkets ignored and snubbed the customers. They killed the native economy and helped China to take control of Australia.

China's Communist Party has manipulated the economy of Australia since its country fell into the traps. The Australian people live in their homeland, but Chinese businesses manage the economy, and China's Communist Party commands. It means, Australian loses independence and sovereignty, the naïve traitors have become the actual henchmen of China, so former Prime Minister Bob Hawke (*he died in 2019*), Paul Keating Kevin Rudd, Malcolm Turnbull, and the Australian Labor Party have stood alongside with China, despite they condemn the dictatorial regime and human rights violation, the hypocrisy of the high profiles is a farce, it is like police fighting against the gang but collaborates with Mafia.

The war to fight against China's global economic terror debunked the global hegemonic ambition of the den of thieves, the hub of counterfeit, and the center of a cheat. Nowadays, China becomes the land of pandemics after the biological weapon is launched worldwide. Australia is among two hundred nations of Coronavirus, but the economy and financial system being cornered by China, so the rogue regime terrorizes to cut the imports after the Australian government proposed the independent inquiry of Coronaviruses. China's communist regime and its ambassador treated Australia like a province, the arrogant intimidation proved Australians being trapped. How can Australia escape the traps of China? Initially, politicians must do something to get back the sovereignty.

However, the Australian people doubt Prime Minister Scott Morrison, he confirmed Malcolm Turnbull is my leader in the leadership spill, so Scott Morrison is the vestige of Malcolm Turnbull after the coup of the concerned member Peter Dutton. Indeed, the people favor Peter Dutton, but the Caucus helped Scott Morrison taking the leadership and became the Prime Minister as Joe Biden robbed the presidency of President Donald Trump in the rigged election in 2020. Australian security is threatened by China while the government neglects or falling into the bribery trap of China. Recently, the Coalition government of Prime Minister Scott Morrison hands over the top secrets of defense to China's Communist Party while the People's Liberation Navy currently threatens the region. It means a hundred million dollars to fight the cyber spy wastes because the Coalition government provides the defense secrets to China. Moreover, the F-35 Lightning II has arrived at the Australian Defence Force, certainly, China does need the technology of F-35 and other secrets. The Australian people and patriots alert about China, so if the Coalition still respects the patriotism, the concerned party can do something:

-The Australian government can revoke the land, waters, port, airport, and national assets sold to China that bases on the Foreign Investment Review Board (FIRB). The Australian lawmakers can make the national security law to protect the national interest and national security.

-To repatriate the companies back homeland, the people need the job: from many decades ago, the negligent investment law plus the profit love businesses, investors moved the companies to China. The Australian government can cut the tax for companies to operate in the homeland and increase the tax to operate offshore, and the products of Australia made in China, Vietnam must pay more tax. The solution can help the Australian factories keep the job and selling the products to the people.

-The Australian government may scrap the free trade agreement with China and choosing democratic counterparts like India, Japan, South Korea, Taiwan, Indonesia, Malaysia, Singapore, and others. China's Communist Party has exploited the trade for global hegemonic ambition, not economic collaboration. The Australian government made big mistakes after 28 years dealt with China. Nevertheless, the Reserve Bank of Australia can cancel the currency swap agreement with the People's Bank of China in 2012 *(Labor government)* with $AU 40 billion or 200 billion Yuan, because China's financial system is on the brink of collapse, nevertheless, China's currency can be kicked out from the Wall Street anytime because the rogue state has cheated the US and the world.

-Limit the union power and scrap the tax-deductible on union fees, it is the stolen money from the national budget. Nevertheless, the union fees cause the corruption of union bosses and the stolen taxpayers help the Australian Labor Party in the elections.

-Creating industries like the car factory *(Holden shut down which is an economic disaster)*. The Australian government encourages factories to produce consumer products as household appliances. The defense industry doesn't contribute to the national product, nevertheless, the Australian economy is keen to collect the taxes from its people, the fuel tax, GST, car, and many taxes that burden the people. Taxes are not a good form of economic development. If the Australian government makes the budget from the companies, factories contribute, not squeeze from the people's pocket. The company's tax cut helps the employers getting more workers when people get a job, they spend, and the economy regulates, the consumption enhances. Certainly, the workers reduce taxes, it is the enable solution to help Australia's development and reducing the pressure of China.

Patriotism education focuses on futuristic development, the patriotic investment is the key to make the country's growth as Japan, Israel, Taiwan, and South Korea. The Australian may keep out the union and politics from the education system. The young generations have ruined and intoxicated by communism, so the young people neglected the country, and become the pupil of Karl Marx after graduated from the university./.

Notes: Writer Hoa Minh Truong, author of 5 books published in the US, graduated from the Political Warfare Academy at Dalat (Vietnam) in 1973. The graduate thesis" *The Economic Development of the Poor Countries*" with 100 pages. The tutor was Professor Trần Long (*Dalat University in Vietnam*). The graduate grade 25 among 165 cadets./.

74. THE DILEMMA OF CHINA BUSINESSES OVERSEAS

Almost, the communist concerns the wealthy and intellectual components are the main enemies of the so-call working class, it is an essential theory of Karl Marx, a dishonest man, and jobless avenges society by writing evil books to teach the social dregs how to kill and rob the people that labeled the revolution. The pupils of Karl Marx killed the people without pity, instead, the felons pride the crimes opposing humanity.

When a communist party robbed the government, the wealthy families and intellectuals killed or sent to the forced labor camp, instead, the illiterates plus the low educated cadres to be promoted as the peak of society. It becomes a strategic disaster in a communist country when the talented component eliminated from the economy, education

The social purge, the obscurantism, and impoverishment policy pulling the communist regime lagging the invention, the national talents framed into the Red Noble class. Commonly, people who live in a communist country must struggle daily to pay the cost of living, their children couldn't afford the discrimination's policy in the education's system with the rule" *the family history wins over the talent*" and in government's working places apply the rule called" *the Red is than professionals*". **The communist families occupied the national economy, and other privileges, their children sent to Western for study, and the tycoons like Chinese businesses, investors overseas are the government's assets or linking with the Political Bureau.**

The global biological warfare terror launched by China's Communist Party in early December 2019 hits back hardly the regime and also affecting worldwide. Initially, China's industry in the mainland disabled, certainly, China's communist tycoons suffered the big losses ever, moreover,

China's tycoon also spread the investment overseas, the targets are Western countries. The assets of China's communist government can not retrieve from the Western countries and elsewhere.

The global stock market plunged by Coronavirus, so China's tycoons couldn't escape the potential losses while the investors in the Western just deal with the losses in their countries, except the investors and companies collaborated with China, they worry and nervous when China's economy crippled. China's tycoons face big losses from the mainland to overseas, they are dealing with the dilemma when China's economy is on the brink of collapse.

Every nation on the planet is the victim of the **Chinese Virus**, whatever, China's communist regime can not escape the full responsibility of the death toll, infected population, and global economic damages. There are many countries that are going to file a lawsuit against China, the massive compensation estimates a hundred trillion US dollars, China appalls the bankruptcy that causes China attacking the countries require the investigation of the original Coronavirus, certainly, a criminal fears the investigation of Police. China's Ambassador to Australia is Jingye Cheng who acts like a kid, he intimidates to stop the import and tourists.

The legal actions can apply to the International Court or the local courts, so China's companies and investors can lose the assets after the court order to confiscate the assets of China owned overseas. Its reason flinches Chinese businesses and investors linking the communist government like the assets of Huawei, ZTE, Landbridge Group, the Greenland Holdings, China Telecom Corp, China's retail companies have operated a long time in Western's soil and others. Nevertheless, Western companies have major Chinese shareholders who should face the problem if the court order seeking compensation, and China's companies, shareholders should be targeted to pay. The Western companies have Chinese shareholders (*Chinese tycoons*) who will face the crisis if the major shareholders become the compensation. During the Chinese Virus attacking worldwide, the Western companies deeply involved with China's communist tycoons rushing to sell off the shareholders, which causes the stock market faltering and Western investors can buy with the low prices. Chinese Virus kicks out and eradicates China's communist tycoons from the stock market.

After more than a half-century, China's Communist Party exploited the free market to make a profit and cornered the global economy, nowadays, offshore China's businesses, and investors facing the dilemma from the mainland to overseas. Particularly, the **China-phobia** caused by the Chinese Virus becomes the psychological economy, so China's tycoon will confront the problem while doing the businesses and investing overseas. The world abominates the Chinese Virus and China's tycoons, certainly, China's businesses will not easily operate as before.

The Australian government refused to bail $AU 1.4 billion to save Virgin Australia, China has 19.85% shares in its airline company, before, China wanted to take over, but now, China flinches by the pressure of compensation. Now, Virgin Australia owed $AU 6.8 billion, there are more than 10 groups attract to buy, including transport billionaire Lindsay Fox. The fate of Virgin Blue is adrift, Perth (*Western Australia*), and Adelaide (*South Australia*) airport seized the planes of Virgin Blue is due to the debt.

The Wollogorang and Wentworth stations straddle the Northern Territory and Queensland spreading to the Gulf of Carpentaria sold by Chinese magnate Xingfa Ma's TBG Agri Holden for $Au 53 million, the Australian's McMillian Pastoral Company takes over (*the assets include 700,000 hectares, 30,000 heads of cattle*). Xingfa Ma's TBG Holden bought it with the price was $AU 47 million in 2015, despite Chinese tycoon get $AU 6 million, but the selling off occurs during the Coronavirus pandemic, Australian currency loses the valuation.

Offshore China's companies panic about the compensation caused by the Chinese Virus, moreover, the Australian government clashes with China about the inquiry of Coronavirus, which arouses Australian patriotism. The major Australian people recognize China's communist regime as a very dangerous enemy, moreover, the Coronavirus pandemic appeared the real faces of tycoons Andrew Forrest, Kerry Stokes, they eat the democratic bread but adore red evil communist China ./.

75. KARL MARX, A DISHONEST AND THE MOST KILLING'S MASTERMIND IN THE HUMAN'S HISTORY.

In the world, everyone knows Osama Bin Laden is the mastermind of Al Qaeda, the dangerous terrorist organization, a condemned culprit who attacked the US' soil on September 11, 2001, and continuing to threaten the world, despite he was killed but the affiliate is still operating the terror.

Therefore, the most killing mastermind Karl Marx has been ignoring for more than a hundred years, despite his theory causes the death of more than 100,000,000 people and more than billion people lost the freedom. Unfortunately, Karl Marx's genocide theory could attract innocent people, actually the western country, they have received the evil theory as the best of social modern. The people who are living in the democratic country but are still dreaming the other one, but they don't know what is it look like? Certainly, they have never seen, lived in a communist country, therefore they endorse it. Karl Marx's believers are like the drivers without a map but they just know a vague destination is a communist paradise. From the modern of the communist regime have appeared on the planet, the tyranny governments around the world have tricked the people about the dream world, but they don't know when will it come? Instead, the promise that cheats the people, some communist leaders predicted the communist paradise will come, but have to wait couple hundred years, even mastermind Karl Marx who didn't know yet.

Karl Marx's theory is like a beautiful cloth covers the trash bin, so the innocent people mistake when just read the theory but they have never known it is the theory that deserves for the dishonest and the human disaster.

Karl Marx was born in Trier, German on May 5, 1881, and died on March 14, 1883. He conflicted the stance with homeland's government and fled to French then joined the secret league, but the birth land of revolution 1789 was not suitable for his thought, so later on the resettled the life in

England until he deceased. His thought is socialism, but it is just a painting that covers the cowardice personality and the unreasonable anger poured into the society after the life ruined by the incumbent governments in Europe, actually his homeland.

An honest deals with the difficulty in the living condition, they accept the situation and tries to work hard, and the life would be improved or getting better. But the dishonest behaves differently, someone breaks the law as fraud, robbery, thief, drug traffic….nevertheless, the high dishonest level as Karl Marx wrote the books, exactly the evil books guide the dishonest how to kill and robbery in the large sphere. Karl Marx's theory instructs the malefactor how to do, actually setting the communist party, a super gang legally operates ever in the earth.

In the crime's history, the criminal always has to avoid the police, government, but the communist super gangs around the world occupy the government also have the representatives of the United Nation and have a diplomatic relationship with the democratic country. The UN, actually the international court bows out the human rights violation. Moreover some super gangs of communist elected the members the UN Human Rights firm, some term they were elected as the chairperson. Karl Marx's theory to be used for the genocide's protection, the killing, robbing, and enslave the people, all cover under the title of revolution. Comparing with Al Qaeda or ISIS, the communist party is fiendish more than any terrorist organization and Mafia. On the other hand, Karl Marx's theory transforms the dishonest to honest by the tricky dialect, so the genocides honored the national heroes are such as Mao Tse Tung who killed 65,000,000 people, Ho

Chi Minh killed 1,700,000 people…but when the democratic leaders from the US, Europe…visit China, they pay the adoration at Mao's portrait, it is a farce.

Karl Marx's theory defends the dishonest whose cover the serious crime that opposes against the humanity by using the tricky words as revolution, socialism, class struggle, and justice. But he couldn't hide the fallen person that strongly attacks to the wealthy people, he angered the rich, but couldn't help the poor how to improve the life, instead of guiding the bobber, killing. The key of Karl Marx is the avenging to the wealthy people by the evil books or the communist bible.

Do you accept a person being faced the hardship and living in the poverty, but you are generous to help food, accommodation, finance…the recipient has no the grateful attitude, indeed who wants to kill and rob you, it is the Karl Marx's character. During living in London, Friedrich Engels, a wealthy family totally supported income for Karl Marx and their family, but he wrote the books Capitalism, he condemned the wealthy people and instructed how to kill, castigate the asset and imprisoned the capitalist. The malicious teaching of Karl Marx has become the world's disaster after his evil bible transformed into reality, obviously in Russia, Lenin applied and succeeded in the so-called October 1917 Revolution. The communist epidemic spread worldwide to most continents.

In the Second World War, the German dictator Adopt Hitler applied the racist policy, his Third Reich killed 6,000,000 Jew, it's a genocide crime to be condemned ever. Therefore Karl Marx is the mastermind of mind discrimination. The merciless mind discrimination has no based on gender, skin, but everyone has a different view with the communist, they are the enemy and to be purged. Karl Marx's evil bible created the biggest crime in human history. Why the world did condemn Hitler but waived Karl Marx?

Despite Karl Marx came from a religious family, but his stance was atheism, the religion to be rejected by his thoughts. Nevertheless, Marx influenced from Georg Wilhelm Friedrich Hegel's and Ludwig Andreas Von Feuerbach. Karl Marx used both German philosophers for the dialect, actually the Historical Materialism of Marx based on them.

Karl Marx's subjective point of view about the history that testified wrongly. He predicted the so-called revolution comes from the distance between poverty and wealthy classes in society. The gap recedes and the poor class adds more people after the wealthy class purged the others. When the proletariat becomes the major population, the revolution has to have and the working class takes over the country and they form the government. The so-called proletariat government repeated the dictatorial regime likely the dynasty in the medieval, the communist regime is barbarous more than any dynasty's era.

The revolution has never happened in French, England after Karl Marx published the pamphlet the Communist Manifesto in 1948 by Engels. Moreover, despite Karl Marx appealed as the beneficiary for the working class but his funeral at Hyde Park just had 8 people, mostly his family and a close friend Friedrich Angels. In Karl Marx's era, he failed to convince the people to join the revolution, but later on, the dishonest as Lenin, Mao Tse Tung, Ho Chi Minh, Kim IL Sung, Fidel Castro...cheated the people, they raised the barbarous and inhumane revolution, the massively dire massacre occurred in the communist countries around the world. The main force did the revolution was the most working-class as Karl Marx's concern, but in the appliance, the low educated or uneducated peasant helped Karl Marx's pupils seized the power and became the communist emperors.

The communist uses the red flag, the bloodshed is the key policy of the cruelly social reform of Karl Marx. The massive massacre doesn't frame into the wealthy class, but the proletariat peasant was targeted too, Lenin and Ho Chi Minh quoted:" the proletariat peasant daily approaches toward the landlord". In the landlord revolution at North Vietnam after 1954, after used the proletariat peasant as the main force for the massive killing, Ho Chi Minh ordered killing and imprisoned the peasants who applied the extreme policy, despite Ho Chi Minh ordered them, but it also relieved the people's anger and avoided the uprising.

Nowadays, Karl Marx's theory has never happened in Europe, the working class has no uprising by the violence when the national economy being declined as Greece's circumstance. Instead, the government collapsed and the other replaced by the election.

The union in the democratic country couldn't occupy the government and carry out the revolution, indeed the union protects the worker on safety, wage, working conditions. However, those targets take care of the government law, so the Union being lost the member because some union bosses exploit the strike for the political purpose of the left-wing party. In Australia, the union is the backbone of the Labor party, the members of the senate and representative filled up by the former union boss.

However, in the western country, the innocent people who don't know the real face of communist, either the cheating of Karl Marx's theory that came from a disappointed man, he poured the angry to the society, so Karl Marx's theory is like the crazy revenge and it is suitable for the dishonest. Karl Marx's books could be stored in the library as a historic evil document, but the leftists still apply to society despite the most population reject the inhumane communist.

Karl Marx's followers in the western country, actually in the US as Jane Fonda, John Kerry, Joe Biden, Bill Clinton, Hillary Clinton, Walter Cronkite…who have never met the re-education camp, lived in the communist country, so they blinded supported the Vietcong in Vietnam War, likely a mechanic does the job of a medical doctor, the patients engage the danger or risk the life by the unqualified doctors. South Vietnam is the victim of Karl Marx's pupils in the western state.

Karl Marx's evil theory is the human disaster ever on the planet, but the blinded followers who have not seen the coffin, not cry yet. They receive the evil theory with the wrong concern, they also apply the communist communication into the democratic country. The left media destroyed the mainstream's credit and affecting a long time damage control.

In the passage of time, the most anti-communist people, particularly the academics, scholars found the negatives in Karl Marx's Books are such as Capitalism, Historical Materialism, and the material dialect. Therefore the personality is the source of the thoughts. The disappointedly fallen life excited Karl Marx tipped the extreme anger into the society, his books come from the revenge and jealous the wealthy people. If Karl Marx was rich as Angels, the evil bible couldn't have. The personality is the fundament for the thinking, so the anti-communist people missed out on the main target, they just research in the books, it is the shadow, but Karl Marx's personality originates his theory.

The Karl Marx followers in the western country have no expert communists, but they blinded apply so the society being crisis and controversial. The debate with the inexperienced communist is like talking the knee. On the other hand, the leftist distances the reality, they deny trust and desert justice. Karl Marx's theory has no way to exist, it is like the dead body revives the zombie.

The Karl Marx and communist lovers, if they recognize the communist is the best, why didn't they migrate to the paradise in China, Vietnam, Laos, Cuba, North Korea to find wonderful places for a living? The democratic country always deserves free choice, if not, they must know Karl Marx's social pattern has no exist and became a human disaster and please do not try to support the evil theory and the tyrannical regimes killed more than 100,000,000 people in the fake revolution.

The concerned people don't do anything that they don't know. Therefore the Karl Marx's lovers don't have the communist experiment, but they follow. Moreover, the leftists in the western country lost the mind, blinded the eyes while seeing the current human rights abuse in the communist regimes, they also knew the genocides occurred in the communist country. The leftists in the western country try to convert the wrong to right, but they apply in the wrong place, because the democratic level of the people boycott Karl Marx's followers, even though they hide under the progressive element. Do not listen to communist and leftist talk, let's watch what they did.

Nowadays Karl Marx's theory is making history, the dead body has never revived. The birthplace of the Global Communist in Russia collapsed and followed the advanced Eastern Europe Bloc threw the evil theory into the bin, but in the democratic countries as US, Europe, someone still believes in the deadly theory, they isolate themselves the society and become the domestic thugs in the homeland./.

76. CHINA OWNS NOTHING IN THE INTERNATIONAL WATERS

China's economic management is different from the western country and democratic nation. Mainland China is ruled by the dictatorial regime, according to the inhumane regime character, the most national interest, and the asset being controlled by the communist party, the communist government congregates monetary fund from 1,35 billion people, Beijing has got the free and huge loan, they could buy anything with the high prices, but China aims to the long term strategy to control the world by the migrant, economy and even though using the military as recently, they have done at the Southern and Northern Pacific

Indeed China owns nothing the international water, actually, the disputed waters being controversial among the neighboring nations has not decided yet by the UN with the maritime international law. In the reality, China has no ownership of the disputed waters with neighbor nations, likely your house has a common fence, yard, but named of a neighbor, so when the legal process, you will be lost the case.

After took over the mainland, China's communist regime has exploited the largest population in the world as the strength for the modern strategic invasion. They have launched psychological warfare around the world, the main target is the Western country, the Chinese academics and scholars live in China or overseas, they convinced the innocent intellectuals in the democratic country, they titled the disputed waters with the name CHINA SEA, now Han's ambition appears the conspiracy of the red empire and also the traditional invasion, the aggressive behavior in the region could be alerted, the world, actually media has to return the reality, the replacement title China Sea needed to correct the China status, proposal THE SOUTHERN PACIFIC or EASTERN PACIFIC and INDOCHINA PACIFIC (in the disputed waters between China and Japan).

The China growth helped by the US since President Richard Nixon took the first visit in 1972 and president Jimmy Carter fortified the relationship between the two countries, continuing Bill Clinton, Barack Obama helped China escaped the low tide of revolution, and step by step, Beijing exploited the western currencies, mostly the US dollars, technology and also the free market. However China has never considered the Western countries as friends, but enemies, now the high tide of revolution coming up, China becomes the second-largest economy and turn the back, nowadays the Beijing becomes the real threat to the world.

Moreover, the most wealthy companies or business

owners of democratic countries do love profit, so they could sell the asset to China at a high price. Since China joined the WTO, there are many nations sold the mine, business to China, therefore the China product wouldn't be trusted, those have been facing so much problem as contamination, poison, poor hygiene process, not long-lasting.... The democratic states as Latin American have to be extremely careful when trading with China, actually selling the natural resources, company and others, moreover the China food products could harm people's health and the country will spend more money on the health issue. China gives one dollar, but they will get back 100, the Chinese will migrate then expand the population, it is the new strategy of Han's invasion today.

China's aggressive behavior in the region raises grave concern to the neighboring nations, despite the negotiation that has been applied, but Beijing is malice, the speaking and doing are different. As an experience of communism, do not trust anything the communists talk about, let's watch what they did. The threat of China's invasion is noted and the Philippines government won the case at the international court. The artificial islands built in the international waters is disqualified by the court, China illegally occupied the maritime road could not be acceptable, recently Mr. Rex Tillerson, US secretary of state represents the US government and also reflects the common interest of the countries in Asia, he required China to stop building the artificial islands (the sand provided by Vietnam government, a close vassal of Beijing in the area) and also asked China not to occupy the international waters.

Despite China has no ownership in the disputed waters, but they aim to occupy the region that has the rich oil and gas resources, nevertheless, the region is the most important maritime road, the worth of goods transport estimates a trillion US dollars./.

77. CHINA COULD CLAIM THE OWNERSHIP EVERYWHERE

China's communist regime is keen to apply the bush law and the wild rules as the Ape lives in the jungle with the trees, mountains, hills, bushes, and anything are the places the herd of Ape. Despite, the jungles, including the national parks, those belong to a nation, but all kinds of animals can live in nature, certainly, the animals own nothing. Nevertheless, the animal is not a human being, they live and act that based on the instinct, not the human mind.

China communist is not Chinese people in the mainland, including Hong Kong people, Taiwanese, and the offshore residents (*except the pro-Beijing components*). Instead, China communists accepted the descendant of Ape as great master Karl Marx labeled in Historical Materialism. Chinese people respect righteousness, justice, and honesty while the Ape super communist gang ruling in Beijing has applied the animal law as an animal herd. Therefore, the international community is not the jungle, the nations respect each other, actually the international law.

China communist exposes the global hegemonic rapaciousness, the Ape super gang could claim the ownership everywhere by themselves, although China communist has no owned the waters in the region, it called the China Sea. But China communists should hire innocent academics, the left media *(or the evil media)* have misled the world, they suppose the China Sea belongs to China. The wrong title fortifies China illegally occupied the disputed waters and built the artificial islands threatening the neighbor countries and aiming to control the most important maritime entering Asia, annual goods transport estimates $USD 5 trillion. The world needs the correct the title of China Sea, it can call the **Indochina Pacific.** The Ape super herd re-mapped the maritime's region, China's Communist Party calls the **Nine-Dash Line**, it labeled " *the Great Wall of Sand*". The regional countries strongly react against China. Japan accuses China has attempted to occupy the Senkaku islands, the tension has raised between the two countries. Recently, China's communist regime exposes the aggressive attitude with India at the border and China also provokes Indonesia, the Philippines, Malaysia. Moreover, China intervenes in Hong Kong by the security law's approval or bush law of henchman Carrie Lam, China ignores the agreement with the deadline that confirms Hong Kong people can live independently to 2047.

The Ape dynasty in China has conspired to control the world, the first Ape Emperor Mao Tse Tung said" *we must control the world*". The famous Chinese communist General, Defense Minister of Ape Emperor Deng Xiaoping was strategist Chi Haotian expected the first Chinese people discovered the Americas, it was Chinese Admiral Zheng He who sailed to this new continent in 1492, the same time as Christopher Columbus. General Chi Haotian hinted the United States of America must return half land to China. In 2005, General Chi Haotian spoke at the Chinese Communist Party's convention, he proposed China using the army to defeat and colonize the United States. This invasion was planned in 1992 that concerned:" *Russia would get Alaska and parts of Canada. China would get the lower 48 states, with other countries invited in for LOOTING RIGHTS".(* *Nowadays, Antifa and Black Lives Matter apply the looting rights in the U*S). General Chi Haotian advised China to use biological warfare to defeat the US and nowadays, Ape Emperor Xi Jinping launches Coronavirus to attack the world.

The global hegemony carries out the project of one belt and one road, China arrayed the trade trap, debt trap, and government trap to control the road crossing multiple nations. So One Belt and one road's brace are controlled by China. On the other hand, one belt and one road linking the continents as Mongolian invaded Asia, Europe in the 13th century. When one belt and one road completed, China's communist regime will expand the military stations setting along with the strategic road, China will argue the security reason to patrol the road as Chinese police officers joined the patrol with Italian Police in Italy. In 2018, the Australia Labor Premier Daniel Andrews illegally signed an agreement of one belt and one road with China, now Victoria's state locked down 310,000 residents to deal with the Coronavirus outbreak the second wave while all states and territory eased the restriction.

Despite China traced behind the US the technology and space discovery, but Beijing claims ownership on the moon, the Ape super gang based on the fairy tales of Chinese people, the fairy tales depict Emperor Yau who came to Kunlun Mountain and met the Queen Mother of Jasper Sea then she gave him the herb of immortality. Therefore, his wife was

Tschang O who used, and she flew to the moon, she became the Lady of the Moon. The other fairy tales describe the Emperor of the Tang dynasty who used the bamboo ladder to climb to heaven and he reached the moon. It is so funny as a kid's dreams but China communist uses the fairy tales to claim the ownership on the moon.

The failure of the Lunar Rover Jade Rabbit becomes the disaster of China communist competes for the space race with the US and Western, India succeeded in the mission to Mars while China didn't.

However, China communists owned the excrement of Chinese people living in the mainland while the Western staying away from the excrement field and has no excrement race with Beijing, so China could claim the excrement's ownership without challenge. Vietnam has launched the excrement race with China since Ho Chi Minh's era. The economy is led by socialism maximally develops the human in agricultural products. Certainly, China is a pioneer to use the excrement on the planet, so Chinese people fear the products come from the farmland and they favor the US although Xi Jinping imposed the retaliatory tariffs. China could claim the ownership of fake products and stolen technology, but the Western oppose the thieves. China communist is the first country owned the formula of medicine that used the unborn baby's carcass cooked with the herbs for virile male. The US and Western have not challenged China in the medical field.

China can claim ownership in Hell and the central earth, the US has never wanted to come to those places. Therefore, North Korea is the first state to land successfully the sun,

China can learn and launch a spaceship landing the sun without cremation.

However, China's communist regime has never confirmed the Coronavirus comes from Wuhan's Biosafety Level 4 Laboratory despite the enormous evidence proved China is the owner of the Chinese virus. Therefore, everyone knows Coronavirus is the biological warfare of China./.

78. THE GLOBAL BIOLOGICAL WARFARE TERROR OF CHINA

Since the evil and dishonest man Karl Marx created the Ape, the human mind replaced by the animal brain, and social humanity has faced the longest disaster. Initially, the first Ape super herd appeared in Russia, the herd leader Lenin succeeded the Ape Revolution in October 1917. The Ape super herds appeared in China with King Ape Mao Tse Tung who led his Ape herd to occupy the mainland. The Ape super herd led by Ape king Hồ Chí Minh who killed more than 1,700,000 Vietnamese people. The Ape herd Khmer Rouge massacred 2 million Cambodian people from 1975 to 1979. The Ape Super herds killed more than 100 million people and the major Ape super herd still conspires to control the world and impose animal rules into human society. Nowadays, the Ape super herd in China is the most dangerous killer on the planet.

China's Communist Party doesn't represent Chinese people, indeed, the Ape super herd robbed the authentic government of Chinese people from 1949. The people can recognize the wrong and right, the good and bad, evil and

God. Therefore, China's Communist Party has exposed the animal instinct, they have enjoyed killing, oppressing, and enslave the people, the genocide labeled the moral revolution. Unfortunately, the Ape herd has ruled the mainland for more than 70 years, it is the shame when the intellectuals, academics, scholars have served the animals.

Chinese history has destroyed, the social valuation wiped out by the Ape super herd labeled themselves Maoist. Moreover, Chinese people obey the orders of the Ape Super herd to adore its Ape's herd leader Mao Tse Tung as the angel, despite Mao Tse Tung killed more than 65 million Chinese people. From 1949, Chinese people in the mainland have behaved as the French proverb" *le Mounton de Panurge"*, they have accepted the animal rule applies to the human society in the mainland. The society in China has overturned, it is so sad for Chinese people.

The Ape super herd barbecued a million lives of the People's Liberation Army in the Korean War, the Ape super herd killed tens of thousands of Chinese people in Tiananmen Square in 1989. Nevertheless, the Ape Super herd conspired to use the biological weapon to destroy the people on the planet. Indeed, 22 tyrannical Ape including Ape leader Xi Jinping couldn't make the biological weapon, but Chinese academics did, they obeyed the orders of Ape to steal the technology and made biological warfare to destroy the people on the planet.

The Ape super herd in China has conspired the global hegemonic ambition for a long time. From more than two decades ago, the Ape General Chi Haotian advocated using the biological weapon to carry out the global hegemonic ambition. Nevertheless, the animal herd in Beijing wants to control the people on the planet and impose an animal rule on human society. The Ape super herd cheated the innocent politicians and profit lover's businesses in the Western, even some academics of Harvard and Yale University in the US work for China's Ape super herd.

The Ape super herd has carried out **the global economic terror** from many decades ago. Therefore, President Donald Trump cracked down on animal ambition. From the Ape Super herd cheated the world and bluffed the innocent politicians in Western, China's Ape super herd has applied the strategies:

1-In the mainland: the brainwash plus terror tamed Chinese people, the impoverishment's people, the obscurantism blind Chinese people.

2-The outside China: the Ape super herd cheated the world, doing malicious business, intimidating and apply the bush law into the countries fell into the trade trap, debt trap, the government trap. Moreover, China's Ape super herd set the plan of one belt and one road-building the" **monkey trails**" with 63 nations including 18 countries in Europe fell into the monetary trap of China's Ape super herd. Italy and Europe received a dire consequence when the governments deeply collaborate with China's Ape herd.

The global economic terror that failed by the tariffs of President Donald Trump. The Ape super herd conspired to launch **a global biological warfare offense worldwide**. Unfortunately, the Ape's character called socialism causes the biological accident in Wuhan from December 1st, 2019, but Ape's bosses concealed it. Moreover, the World Health

Organization stands with the Ape super herd, Dr. W.H.O director-General Tedros Adhanom Ghebreyus distorted the career and skewed the function of the international medical organization to delay the Coronavirus outbreak. Dr. W.H.O director-General Tedros Adhanom Ghebreyus helped the Ape super herd deceive the world, so the Coronavirus outbreak spread from Wuhan throughout China and the world. W.H.O director-General Tedros Adhanom Ghebreyus acts as a medical clown of China's Ape super herd. He is an accomplice with China's Ape super herd into the global biological warfare terror. After the Covid-19 outbreak, the world can not trust W.H.O, Doctor Tedros Adhanom Ghebreyus becomes a DOGTOR who transforms W.H.O to be the medical propaganda machine of China's Ape super herd.

China's Ape super herd launches **the global biological warfare terror**, their deadly biological weapon shattered the mainland, Europe and threatening the other continents. The world is complicated by China's Ape super herd with the dyed black hair's head Congress. The Ape super herd in China still conspires to control the international human society by the bush law or the animal rules. The world and Chinese people unite to fight against the Ape super herd if not, the world will destroy. It is the shame when the left media has propagated for the Ape super herd from the Cold War. The animal's character based on instinct, but the people have a human's mind. China's Ape super herd doesn't care about human life, so China's Communist Party launches global biological warfare to attack the world. The death toll, the infected population, the world's economy faces the crisis, China's Ape super herd is the culprit. The global disaster can stop when China's Ape herd to be expelled in the mainland and the democratic government replaces the Ape government. There is only Chinese people can help the world to eliminate the most disaster on the planet including Chinese people in the mainland./.

79. THE LIFE OF CHINESE PEOPLE HAVE BEEN ENDANGERED

Throughout the thousand historic years, Chinese people have been ruled by dynastic governments. Nowadays, Chinese people still live in the worst monarchic era although the world changed, it is the misfortune of the world's largest population country while Taiwanese, Hong Kong people afford democracy, freedom, and the living standard promoted, the free speech respects. Mostly, Chinese people have lived in dictatorial governments, those are the dynasties:

-Xia Dynasty (2100 B.C. to 1766 B.C.)

-Shang Dynasty (1766 B.C. to 1047 B.C.)

-Zhou Dynasty (1047 B.C. – 256 B.C.)

-Qin Dynasty (221 B.C. – 206 B.C.)

-Han Dynasty (206 B.C. – 220 A.D.)

-Jin Dynasty (265 – 420)

-Sixteen Kingdoms or Dynasties (304 – 409)

-Southern and Northern Dynasties (420 – 589)

-Sui Dynasty (581 -618)

-Tang Dynasty (618 – 907)

-Five Dynasties and Ten Kingdoms (907 – 960)

-Liao Dynasty (916 – 1125)

-Song Dynasty (960 – 1279)

-Yuan Dynasty (1279 – 1368)

-Ming Dynasty (1368 – 1644)

-Qing Dynasty (1644 – 1911)

However, from 1912 to 1949, it was the first time, Chinese people lived on a democratic government. Unfortunately, the Ape herd was led by Ape King Mao Tse Tung deceived Chinese illiterate, low-educated, and innocent components, eventually, the **Ape Revolution** succeeded in 1949. The demagogic propaganda helped the Ape herd took over the mainland in 1949. The Ape robbed the Chinese's authentic government and established the APE DYNASTY. It is the worst dynasty in Chinese history. The Ape dynasty has dominated China by the bush law and wild rules, certainly, China's Communist Party is not Chinese people, instead, the animal without a tail (*Karl Marx labeled and the communists pride the original Ape)* is heartless, barbarous, the animal acts on instinct, not the human mind.

The Ape dynasty promoted the **APE SUPREMACY**, Chinese people must obey the orders of the Ape regime. In the US, the first Muslim and communist President Barrack Obama is the comrade of the Ape herd in China. When Barrack Obama ruled the White House for 8 years, he promoted the **BLACK SUPREMACY** by using the label of the racial shield, he created the actual tool **Black Lives Matter** and globalized. The innocent components in Western have been brainwashed by a **comrade of Ape is Barrack**

Obama like China's mainland, so they knelt to pay the respect of a serious felon George Floyd who is promoted and polished as the idol likely the Ape King Mao Ste Tung canonized in China. Former President Barrack Obama succeeded the obscurantism applying the Western, so House Speaker Nancy Pelosi led her Democratic members to kneel 8 minutes at Congress praying George Floyd, former President Jimmy Carter, presidential candidate Joe Biden and many high profiles of Democrats comply with Black Lives Matter and also Black Supremacy to adore the felony icon. The Black Supremacy spread worldwide, the footballers in the United Kingdom, Australia knelt to pay the respect of George Floyd and support Black Lives Matter.

There was just Ape King Mao Tse tung who killed more than 65 million Chinese people from 1949 to 1976, Ape King Deng Xiaoping massacred tens of thousand Chinese people at Tiananmen Square in 1989. Moreover, the Ape dynasty killed the people in Tibet, Sinkiang Uigur, Falun Gong. The Ape kings were Jiang Zemin, and Hu Jintao continued to apply the animal rules to Chinese people. Nowadays, the incumbent Ape King Xi Jinping launches biological warfare to kill Chinese people and the world. However, the Ape dynasty always denies the culprit of Coronavirus, despite the enormous evidence proved Coronavirus comes from Wuhan's Biosafety Level 4 Laboratory. The massive compensation estimates a hundred trillion US dollars that appalls the Ape dynasty. Nevertheless, China's Communist Party often issued false reports about the death toll and infected cases, and the left media in Western concealed the happenings in China, instead, the death toll and infection in the US, Europe highlighted. Therefore, the world knew the massive deaths and infected population in the mainland must high. Particularly, Wuhan's residents are the victims of the Chinese virus, China's communist government couldn't explain more than 21,000,000 mobile phone users vanished without a track. Commonly, the communists always lie and conceal, but when the monetary loss, they speak out.

Recently, on June 13, 2020, the Ape dynasty alerts the new cases of Coronavirus appeared in Beijing, within 24 hours, there are 57 cases, and China's communist regime locked down 11 residential communities near the Xinfadi market. The world and Chinese people in the mainland fear the Ape dynasty conspires to reduce the population and kill the massive jobless by using Coronavirus.

The high unemployment rate causes the collapse of the dynasties in the days of yore, so the Ape dynasty appalls the old lesson should repeat anytime. China suffered jobless in the trade war, the export sector employed about 120 million workers. The Coronavirus worsens, despite China and the left media concealed while the high unemployment rate in the US, Europe, Australia, Canada, and the world are high. China's economy disabled, the domestic companies, businesses, and industry crippled plus more than 20,000 foreign companies moved out and relocated to India, Indonesia, and other countries except Vietnam is China's vassal. Certainly, the massive jobless in China is inevitable, in the mainland, the job loss predicts from 400 to 500 million and the situation aggravates when the world community isolates and sanctions China by a deadly pandemic. After more than 70 years, the Ape dynasty succeeded the impoverishment with 2/3 population live in poverty, daily income is $US 2 to $US 5, but the communist regime has no income to support the Chinese people.

The new wave of Coronavirus appeared in Beijing, the life of Chinese people have been endangered because the Ape dynasty should use Coronavirus to kill the opponents, the jobless to keep the regime remains. The Coronavirus also helps the Ape dynasty to stray the worst living condition in the mainland, and Chinese people must fight the pandemic, so they forget the ruthless regime. Once again, the life of Chinese people has been threatened, the Ape dynasty could do anything to keep the regime. China's Communist Party should release the Coronavirus to the crowded population as Beijing, Shanghai, Fujian, Guangdong, and other provinces. Possibly, the Ape dynasty has not forgotten to use the virus to kill the people in Sinkiang Uigur, Tibet, Manchuria, and other ethnicities. Chinese people can not ignore Coronavirus that is the biological warfare of Ape herd applying in the mainland. Chinese people must act, the Ape dynasty can kill the massive population to remain the regime./.

80. CONFUCIANISM CONFUSES THE SOCIETY AND VIOLATES THE HUMAN RIGHTS

Foreword: There is someone in the Western country who doesn't understand or has not much knowledge and experience about Confucius and Communists. In Australia, the former prime minister's Bob Hawke, Paul Keating, and Kevin Rudd are keen to advise the Australian government standing alongside China, despite their era was gone. The people don't think Australia's former prime ministers have not understood China, therefore they should impose the personal stance or individual interest above the national interest. This article sends a strong message to everyone as the extreme alarm China's hegemonic strategy. Recently, the Foreign Affairs Department of Australia government has released the White Paper that is aware of the unstable situation in Asia and confirmed ally with the US.

Hoa Minh Truong.

(author of 5 books)

Confucianism is the most tendency has influenced Chinese society and government for multiple thousand years. Nevertheless, Confucianism has attached China's history from the monarchy to the communist regime. Its thoughts have affected deeply into Chinese society, actually, Confucianism conducts the Chinese people on living ways, moral concern, education, and politics.

Almost all Chinese people expect Confucius as the timeless greatest master and pride the outstanding theory, mostly the Chinese people concern the Confucianism is the golden frame, the precious stone's rule of society, and instructing the moral. Nevertheless, the Confucian thoughts became the religion Ruism and Confucius also recognized as the greatest philosopher. Confucius appeared in Chinese history from 551 to 479 BC, he spread the ideology and also recruited the pupils. Therefore,. in the days of yore, Confucianism helped the most dynasties ruled the country by its moral rein that conducted the people absolutely obeyed the order of emperor and regime, although the king was fiendish and lustful. The Confucianism teaching forced the people to adore the emperor as God's representative or the son of God, supreme power in the country. The emperors self-proclaimed the right to kill anyone, some vague conviction was as snubbing the emperor that would face the death sentence. Nowadays, the communist regime is the same rule, in China or any communist country, the people forced to obey the communist party and absolutely adore the leaders like Mao Tse Tung, Lenin, Stalin, Hồ Chí Minh, Fidel Castro, Kim Il Sung, Kim Jong Il, Kim Jong Un…whatever, the leaders are still alive or dead, the people in the Red dynasty have to adore as the communist leaders, so any criticism banned strictly, whoever dares to criticize or have the dislike behavior to the leaders, they would be killed or long-term in prison.

However, Confucianism complicates the people, actually, Chinese people have been treated unfairly from the Ruism born. The social relationship between the government and people classified the priorities:

1-King is the supreme power, Chinese monarchy only expected the head of the dynasty was male, so the emperor authorized to the throne is a prince, not a princess. Therefore, there were some females controlled the dynasties, but it was rare, the female could not mandate ruling the dynasty, mostly the powerful women had to hide behind teen emperors or a weak king. Nowadays, the communist regime is the same rule, the most top jobs are Secretary-General, Prime Minister and chairperson are the males. Communists and Confucius are the same treatment, it is gender discrimination.

2-Teacher is second priority in the old days in China, actually, Confucius respects as the greatest teacher. Nevertheless, in the old days, the most teacher was male. Moreover, the student was male and female didn't allow to go to school and didn't permit to attend the examination. The dynasty recruited the male officials in the central dynasty and local government.

3-Father (not mother despite mother works hard, take care the family and children)

The relationship levels between the king and family members are also unfair and always deserve the priority of the male as the king and father:

1-The people must put the king above the country, even the emperor was cruel and lavish the national assets. In China's history, the brutal suzerains and benighted king killed the people but the local people must follow blindly, whoever was treason if disobeyed the king's decree, even king ordered the death sentence, they had to accept as the loyalty. Nowadays, the China Communist Party is the group of the king, although the inhumane regime killed more than 65,000,000 people under Mao Tse Tung's rule, so Chinese people respect the genocide and its red dynasty. It is the extraordinary impact when the leaders of democratic countries, all respect human rights, therefore, when they visit China, some leaders paid respect to Mao Tse Tung's portrait, although Mao is the most genocide in the 20th century. What is going in on? Moreover, the communist regime coerces the people must be loyal to the communist party and the leader.

2-The children absolutely obey the father, it is the filial treatment. Therefore the mother places behind and served as a slave in the family.

3-Husband always dominates over the wife. It is a form of gender discrimination in the family as Muslims treats unfairly females and the man could have many wives.

Confucius morality encourages the cannibal to prove the loyalties and filial children. In the Chinese tales, a story about a daughter-in-law who used her arm meat to feed the mother-in-law, a loyal member cuts his body to feed the disgraced prince being run. Nowadays, Chinese people in the mainland use unborn babies cooked with herbs for virile drugs. Before, the only child policy killed millions of unborn girls. Confucianism has been endorsed by the monarchy, so throughout multiple thousand years of history, almost the dynasties used Confucianism to rule the country and also applied the invasion to the other states in the region as the Yun Yu book of Confucius endorses the hegemony. The Han's ethnic succeeded the hegemonic strategy, the orthodox king is a son of God, the good emperor has been encouraged, endorsed, and authorized to invade the other countries. Confucianism temporarily suspended under the communist regime, because Confucius is Theism. From 1949, Mao Tse Tung considered the religions were the enemy of atheism, actually, the Culture Revolution was a hard time for the Chinese culture, the Buddhist temple, historic relics to be targeted, so the Confucious temple suffered the same fate. The essential Confucianism taught Five Virtues, the moral conduct navigates the Chinese people in the social treatment that Confucianism encouraged the respectable people, it is the genuine gentleman's concern:

1-Ren: it is humanity. Unfortunately, in Chinese history, the good emperors of the dynasty invaded many countries in the region and the conquerors applied cruel policy to the occupied land. Vietnam is a hard evidential circumstance of the" Ren", in thousand years was governed by Chinese sovereign with the barbarous treatment that left the historic scars forever in the Vietnamese people with the saying echoes to nowadays" Chinese administration forced the Vietnamese went to the jungle for finding the ivory, the Rhino horn and went to the shore collected the pearl". North Korea has tested the" Ren" with the actual hands are Kim Il Sung, Kim Jong Il and now Kim Jong Un, they ignored more than 2,000,000 North Korean who died by the famine for the hegemonic strategy of China with the nuclear program. The massacre at Tiananmen Square in 1989 isn't the Ren?

2-Yi is honesty and uprightness: but China has the most stolen record on the technology from the Western, the China-made is the quality dishonest. China's communist regime sent the espionage agent and network worldwide, the cyber-spy has threatened the security of the counterparts. Certainly, the steal is not honest.

3-Shu taught reciprocity and altruism to each other as the golden rule of Confucianism" what you don't want yourself, don't do to others". Therefore China re-mapped the disputed waters and brazen attitude in the region, the descendant of Confucius built the illegally artificial islands and militarized them. The illegal islands become piratical stations in the Southern Pacific, it is a form of the old days in China, when the dynasty being weak, the dishonest set up the mountain stations to collect the gold and robbery the pedestrian.

4-Zhi is knowledge, but China stole the technological knowledge and the intellectual property of the Western

5-Li is the correct behavior: the poor quality, poisoned, contaminated, and short life product made in China those are the correct behavior?

Nowadays, China's communist regime couldn't use Karl

Marx's theory or Maoist to apply to the society, moreover, the economic pattern diverted the capitalist" free market is led by socialism". The world's democratic trend erodes the dictatorial regime on the economy. China communists must apply the lizard changes skin's tactic for survival. The Communist theory has been rotten, so China communist party recycles Confucianism for keeping the regime's existence because most Chinese adore the timeless greatest teacher Confucius. Nowadays, the Confucious temples and schools revive in the mainland.

Confucianism is obsolete that conflicts the humanity and opposes the Universal Declaration of Human Rights of the United Nation. However, China spread the Confucious Institute into Western countries. The multiple cultures don't conflict with humanity, but Confucianism was. Nevertheless, the offshore Confucious Institutes are the den of psychological warfare and the spy. The Western countries alert the Confucious Institutes established in their soil. Once again, China's communist regime cheats the world, they lie the Confucius Institute is a non-profit public educational organization but its affiliated with the Ministry of Education of the People's Republic of China. Confucius hides under the culture and teaching language in the Western countries from 2004 and nowadays there are 300 Confucius Institutes presented in 90 nations, actually in the US has 70 Confucius Institutes. China plans the Confucius Institutes will approach 1,000 by 2020.

China communist regime shows off the ludicrous attitude with the so-called Confucius Peace Prize that proposed by a business person Liu Zhiqing, the Confucius Peace Prize insults the Nobel Peace Prize, so the garbage disgraced prize has boycotted the winners since the first recipient was Mr. Lien Chan, a politician, formerly Taiwan's vice president and an essential member of the Chinese Nationalist Party (Kuomintang). He wanted to return the island nation to the mainland, but he did not come to get the award. Next, in 2011, a winner was Vladimir Putin, but he didn't come, also. In 2012, former Secretary-General Mr. Kofi Annan was awarded Yuan Longping, but Mr. Annan didn't come to Beijing to receive the funny prize. In 2013, the prize winner was Yi Cheng, and in 2014, a former dictator of Cuba, Fidel Castro, won the prize. In the future, how will a clown in Beijing award the Confucius Peace Prize? In the future, Kim Jong Un will be a Confucius Peace Prize Winner because he carries out the hegemony of China in the region. Nevertheless, there are some brilliant candidates for Confucius Peace Prize as Robert Mugabe, Raul Castro. Confucianism is the early communist on the planet, but Confucius is Theism and Karl Marx is Atheism. On the other hand, Communism and Confucianism are the same practice, so China's communist regime favors Confucius with the demagogy, cheats the Western and exploiting the Confucianism as the religion for keeping the inhume regime./.

81. DONALD TRUMP FALLS IN LOVE THE PATRIOTISM

Under 8 years the US ruler by the first communist and Muslim President Barack Obama, plus the leftist Vice-President Joe Biden who has always served China's interest, so the United States of America shattered, the superpower disabled after an actual pupil of Karl Marx climbed higher and dived deeper into the White House. It is like a virus Meningococcus infiltrates the human brain, the patient would be killed, paralyzed, or amputated.

The consequence made by Barrack Obama has left the long-time damages of the US society and the world. Particularly, the US people lived in the" *terrible communist paradise*" of Barrack Obama who applied the impoverishment policy to the US people. It is the **SATAN** era of a man who raised the mouthpiece's slogan" *yes we can change*". Nevertheless, Mr. Barrack Obama is the global thug and the global war-maker, therefore, the Nobel Peace Prize Committee awarded Obama in 2009, which humiliates the most valuable prize on the planet. President Barrack Obama made America the worst ever. There were just in 8 years, President Barrack Obama, Vice President Joe Biden, Secretary of State Hillary Clinton, John Kerry created the dire consequences that shattered the US and remain in the long term after the global thug left the office.

1-The domestic: the society divided by the hoax climate change, the same-sex marriage legislation, the **Black Supremacy** promoted with the **Black Lives Matter** that turns **Black lies Matter** and the riot, loot assimilates the **BLACK- LOOTS- MURDER** (BLM). President Barrack Obama and the left media brainwashed the people by misleading the public, concealed the truth, it causes social disorder.

The high unemployment rate, the national debt was up to $US 20 trillion, the illegal migrants wasted a hundred billion dollars a year, the drug syndicates, criminals, terrorists, and espionage agents freely infiltrated the US to cover under the Human Rights but turn Human Wrong.

2-Foreign: the allies distrusted the US after the policies of Barrack Obama pushed the allies to become hostile. China nearly controlled the US, so Xi Jinping considered President Barrack Obama as an executive. In the last visit on September 4, 2016, the US president must access a staircase without the red carpet. If Hillary elected in 2016, China will control the world in 2025. President Barrack Obama neglected Taiwan, Israel, India, and others, so the US lost the world's credit.

President Barrack Obama cheated the US people with the slogan" *yes we can change*" in the election 2008. Therefore, he created an opportunity for Islamic State founded by withdrawing the US troop from Iraq. Formally President Barrack Obama called to fight against the terror, indeed, he provided the finance, weapons, and training for Islamic State. The taxpayers wasted, the life of US servants and soldiers risked, the death of Ambassador Chris Steven and 3 officers in Benghazi was among the" *great achievements*" of President Barrack Obama and Secretary of State Hillary Clinton. Moreover, the deaths of the Navy Seal team killed Al Qaeda leader Osama Bin Laden, the people and families suspect President Barrack Obama destroyed the witnesses. On the other hand, former President Barrack Obama, Vice President Joe Biden, and other high profiles Democrats are treason, despite the justice have not indicted yet, but the US people recognized the traitors.

During two-term, President Barrack Obama placed the US for sale, he flagged comrade China built and militarized the artificial islands at Indochina Pacific *(not the China Sea because China has no ownership in the disputed waters).* President Barrack Obama prepared China to control the important maritime road, to enter Asia, annually goods transport estimates $US 5 trillion. China also sieges the US in Asia and Islamic State bars the US in Middle-East, it is the deep conspiracy of Barrack Obama to destroy the US and paving the way for China to dominate the planet.

The appearance of **patriot Donald Trump** saves the US and the world. Certainly, the essential tactics of China to be cracked down, it causes Democrats and China always conspire to remove the US patriotic President Donald Trump from the office by the malicious tactics. On the other hand, Democrats represent China to impeach President Donald Trump through dirty campaigns like legal terrorist Robert Mueller and the Special Counsel to spend $US 34 million on the taxpayers. Nevertheless, the left media always snoops for every move of President Donald Trump, family members, and the White House's administration. Almost, Democratic politicians deserved the most time to impeach President Donald Trump, the US taxpayers paid for the thugs and traitors. The border wall was a crucial battle, the dirty method of porn star stormy Daniels and her illiterate law is lawyer Michael Avenatti. Continuing the tax returns have abused the US president including the coward Justices of the Supreme Court avoided the violation of the Constitution consents" *the incumbent president can not show the tax returns"* but the ill-concerned Supreme Justices passed the responsibility to a local court in Manhattan, it is like an ant to remove an elephant. On September 28, 2020, before the first debate, the prominent fake news New York Times recycled the tax returns of President Donald Trump in the election of 2016 to defame and help Sleepy Joe Biden. However, the obsolete tactic doesn't affect the US people who decided to elect the patriotic President Donald Trump in the second term. President Donald Trump wins people's hearts. Nevertheless, the first debate biased, the moderator Chris Wallace was treated unfairly by President Donald Trump in the first debate. Therefore, President Donald Trump beat Joe Biden and Chris Wallace. The US people are the arbiter, not the left media and a moderator. The Fox News host Chris Wallace distorts the career, he places the moderator for hire, so President Donald Trump said:" *I guess I'm debating you, not him, but that's OK. I'm not surprised*". The unfair treatment of Chris Wallace creates public anger, the conservative Dana Loesch wrote on Twitter:" *Never allow Chris Wallace to moderate another debate again. This was an absolute shit show. The viewer wasn't even a secondary concern*". Even the leftist Mikel Jollett reacted on Twitter:" *Dear Chris Wallace: You are a national embarrassment*". Despite some left media companies released the false polls after the first debate, therefore, President Donald Trump got 86,86% and Joe Biden got 13,15%. The people's power win over the malicious methods, the cunning tactics including the leftist moderator Chris Wallace.

The patriotic heart of a man who makes America great again, the enemies fear, the allies trust, the domestic thugs appalls the White House's swamp-draining out, the felons, traitors will be found. President Donald Trump and family members serve the country without salary. Particularly, **President Donald Trump sacrifices a wealthy life for the country**. Moreover, President Donald Trump can afford the luxurious living conditions of a billionaire, but he denies the wealthy life. The patriotic motive urges Donald Trump to use the time to serve the country. Instead, **Democrats sacrifice the country for their wealthy life**.

President Donald Trump won over the malicious tactics of Democrats and also defeated China's communist regime in the trade war to save the world to escape the red empire conspiring to control the world. China launches a viral war to attack the US and the world. Despite the left media, Democrats have tried to exploit the Coronavirus to destroy President Donald Trump, but, the biological warfare of China's Communist Party hits back the culprit, and an actual henchman Joe Biden will lose the presidential election in 2020. Moreover, communism uprising in the US and spread to Europe, Australia, Canada debunked. The Black Lives Matter and Antifa lose the people's sympathy after the protests with riots, loots, burned down the businesses, killed police officers, abuse the people. On the other hand, former President Barrack Obama, Democrats, and China failed to revive the Black Culture Revolution in the Western. President Donald Trump proves the potential commander in chief, he cracked down on the global hegemonic ambition of China, the economy of the world's largest communist country disabled, financial system is on brink of collapse. The world community arouses and lining up to fight against China./.

NOTES: The motive to write this article:

"The writer is a Vietnamese refugee who fled Vietnam to find the freedom in 1982 after 6 years imprisoned in the hell of so-called re-education, never returned to Vietnam, now the writer lives in Australia, not a voter in the US election on

November 3, 2020, but the writer recognizes the patriotic heart of President Donald Trump who sacrifices the wealthy life to serve the country while Joe Biden and Democrats sacrifice the country for the wealth life. Certainly, the concerned people know the wrong and right, therefore the left media doesn't. Nevertheless, the ill-responsible components in the US have tried to protect the treasonous party to attack President Donald Trump by the dirty tactics including fake news, fabricated stories. Even the Vietnamese community, some Vietnamese refugees are living in the US, but they have used fake news to propaganda as Vietcong in Vietnam. The prominent organization is the Vietnam Reform Party's vestige of former Admiral Hoang Co Minh, his young brother Hoang Co Dinh commands this fake anti-communist party by using the radio (Chân Trời Mới, Tiếng Nước Tôi) and media to create the mayhem in the Vietnamese community overseas, misleading the public in the Vietnamese community. Moreover, most Vietnamese media in the US is pro-Vietcong like Người Việt, Việt Báo, Cali toady (San Jose). SBTN despite they always claim the political refugee, the victims of the Vietcong have never welcomed the fake refugees who eat the democratic bread but adore the evil communist. "/.

82. TERRORIST OBAMA STORMED THE WHITE HOUSE IN 8 YEARS

When a terrorist storms a building like Café Lindt in Sydney, Australia on December 15-16, 2014, terrorist Man Monis held 10 customers and 8 employees, the terror incident awoke Australia, actually, the terrorist wanted to talk with Prime Minister Tony Abbott. After 16 hours standoff, eventually, Police killed gunman Man Haron Monis and freed the hostages. Therefore, two hostages were Tori Johnson and Katrina Dawson killed and a police officer injured. If the terror incident occurs at a government building, actually an important office of government, the damages are much more than Café Lindt. In a war or any conflict, the headquarters is the main target of the enemy. China's communist regime has conspired to infiltrate into the Australian parliament and using the super-espionage agents covered under Australian politicians to drive Down Under into a colony (*or vassal*) of China. When the enemy penetrated the headquarters as a human body being risked when the deadly virus like Meningitis infiltrated the brain, the patient life endangered. President Barrack Obama *climbed higher and dived deeper* into the most important office of the US government, so the potential damages are inevitable and perpetuating in the long term.

President Barrack Obama is the first communist and Muslim became the commander in chief of the US Army from 2008 to 2016, President Barrack Obama exploited the democracy of the US for the terror's mission carried out at the high-level. He legally infiltrated the White House by the election and stormed the United States of America. Actually, the Democratic Party (*hidden communist party in the US*) has propagated the demagogic policies, and the donkey voters of Democratic fan plus the innocent American wrongly elected a terrorist into the White House in two terms. On the other hand, President Barrack Obama is the most dangerous terrorist, he deceived the US public by the slogan" *yes we can",* indeed, the high-level terrorist Barrack Obama changed the US society from peace to war, he eradicated the social valuation and also applied the communism to brainwash the US people in 8 years.

President Barrack Obama also was the global thug by activating the **gender war** conflicts between a minor homosexual couple with a major natural couple in the US and the world (*the same-sex-marriage legislation spread in 29 nations*), it becomes the global gender war. The **racial war** dug up the Black and White in the US, actually, the *Black Lives Matter movement* appeared under Obama's rule in the US. The racial war spread to Africa, the White farmers in Zimbabwe, South Africa are the victims. Nevertheless, President **Barrack Obama acted as the terrorist at the high-level**, he used the US taxpayers for the global terror's mission. Formally, President Barrack Obama often raised the mouthful declaration to fight the terrorist, indeed, Obama also flagged the terrorism to attack the US and the world. Obama's double-Cross war game cost the US taxpayers $USD 10 trillion.

After getting the office in 2008, President Barrack Obama silently carried out the will of Al Qaeda leader Osama Bin Laden by withdrawing the US troop from Iraq, it created an opportunity for Islamic State founded. President Barrack Obama secretly provided the finance, weapon, and training for ISIS, he pushed the life of US soldiers at risk in Middle-East. Moreover, The US people suspect President Barrack Obama and Secretary of State Hillary Clinton were the perpetrators of four deaths in Benghazi in 2012 including Ambassador Chris Stevens. The US people doubt the deaths of the US servants that destroyed the key witness of a terrorist link.

The bloody lesson of Vietnamese people happened in the Vietnam War, President Nguyễn Văn Thiệu was commander in chief, he was a former district commander of the Viet Minh Front (*mostly, Viet Minh Front controlled by Ho Chi Minh and the communist party*), so Vietnamese people suspect the role of President Nguyễn Văn Thiệu like the super double agent who held the highest position in South Vietnam's government. Moreover, he destroyed a million soldiers of the South Vietnam Army (ARVN) in March 1975 to help North Vietnam Communist troops easily took over South Vietnam in 55 days. Therefore, before launching Ho Chi Minh's campaign with 20 divisions, North Vietnam's Four Stars General Văn Tiến Dũng predicted the campaign would take at least 2 years but the victory wouldn't know yet. Luckily, the US has a solid fundament, so the terrorist Barrack Obama couldn't exploit the commander in Chief's authority to destroy the United States of America. If the US is like Vietnam, the Americans will exile as Vietnamese people after the betrayal of President Nguyễn Văn Thiệu disbanded the army.

However, the US commander in chief Barrack Obama destroyed the US army by multiple methods. He put the life of US soldiers endangered in Middle-East while Obama supporting Islamic State. President Barrack Obama permitted homosexuality, transgender in the US army. The high-level terrorist Barrack Obama shattered the US from A to Z, he also flagged" *comrade"* China illegally built and militarized the artificial islands into the disputed waters. On the other hand, President Barrack Obama created an opportunity for Islamic State and China to siege the US in Asia and Middle-East while the US shattered and the society divided.

Unfortunately, the high-level terrorist and the global war

maker Barrack Obama awarded Nobel Peace Prize in 2009 although he had no record about the peace. The consequences of terrorist Barrack Obama still remain in the US and the world after he expired the second term on January 20, 2017. Therefore, terrorist Barrack Obama sowed the legal terrorists into the court's system, Justice Department, FBI, CIA, and the US government, so the legal thugs are the Obama judges issued the court's orders to prevent the presidential orders of the travel ban, border protection released by President Donald Trump.

The high-level terrorist Barrack Obama currently attacks President Donald Trump despite he is no longer rules the White House. However, terrorist Barrack Obama still earns the pension plus the privileges and the taxpayers burden his office after retired. The US government may overhaul the pension and former presidential allowances pay for terrorist Barrack Obama, instead, the treasonous and terror crimes are available for a man who stormed the White House in 8 years. Guantanamo Bay is a place to deserve Barrack Obama if the justice found guilty.

The Democratic Party appeared the real face of a hidden communist party in the US. Nevertheless, Democrats have activated as the terror organization, they have terrorized the US president, the national interest, and national security after President Donald Trump getting the office. Terrorism has carried out in multiple forms:

1-The extremists are the Muslim bigot incite the terror in Western including Muslim countries like Indonesia, Pakistan, Afghanistan, Iraq, and others. The prominent terror organization is the Islamic State to be wiped out and recently, their supreme leader Abu Bakr al Baghdadi exploded himself while the US special force raiding his place. Certainly, after President Barrack Obama was no longer to rule the White House, Islamic State lost the support of the weapon, money, and training.

2-The global economic terror of China has faced potential damages in the economic war with the US after many decades, China's communist regime has struck the world by the soft army with the trade tie, free trade agreement, the debt trap, government trap plus the bribery's tactic.

3-The left media's terrorists failed the fake news, fabricated stories, and the false polls mission to mislead the public and terrorize the people's minds, actually, President Donald Trump granted the fake news certificate for the enemy of people, the foe of public and the garbage in mainstream media.

4-The Democratic Party is the terrorist party in the US carrying out by the high-level terror's mission:

-The legal terrorist Robert Mueller and Special Counsel inserted into Justice Department to terrorize President Donald Trump by $USD 34 million of the taxpayers. After 22 months to terrorize President Donald Trump by the most witch hunt in US history. Ultimately, the legal terrorist Robert Mueller failed the terror mission and Special Counsel disbanded.

-After the mid-term of Congressional election in 2018, the Democratic terrorist gang stormed the Congress, the lawmaker terrorist's leader Nancy Pelosi terrorized the wall's fund and she also leads her gang to terrorize President Donald Trump by the unlawful impeachment./.

83. POPE FRANCIS WHO DERAILS THE CATHOLIC FAITH

Pope Francis has exposed a funny and odd attitude since he replaced Pope Benedict XVI to lead the global Catholics. Mostly, the decisions of Pope Francis conflict with the TEN COMMANDMENTS and also opposing the Catholic faith.

Pontiff Francis is generous as a global Catholic leader in the Vatican, therefore, the refugee and asylum seeker's status is quite different from the radical despite the refugee and asylum seeker are the same circumstance when they just came to the other country. Moreover, the asylum seekers hide the reason to leave from its country by the false declaration to an adopted country and United Nations (UNHCR), actually, the asylum seekers often destroyed the personal identifications, so the immigration department and national security agencies have dealt the difficulties to find the background of the unwanted guests, actually, the terrorists infiltrated under the label of HUMAN RIGHTS that turns HUMAN WRONG.

The innocent politicians are like blind pet lovers, so they couldn't distinguish the difference between the tiger snake, Cobra, Taipan, and python, all assimilate the reptiles. The critical mistake has become the long-term damages for national security, actually, the different faith of Muslim conflict adopted countries silently become the civil war exposing to a religious war.

Pope Francis supports the asylum seeker's wave invaded and shattered Europe despite Pope Francis doesn't care about the terrorists hide inside the illegal migrants. Nevertheless, he also clashed with President Donald Trump on the border protection policy since the US presidential campaign launching. Certainly, Pope Francis just has the power and authority over Catholics, plus the church's system. Moreover, he is not a scientist but Pope Francis promotes the hoax climate change while there are more than 30,000 scientists confirmed that climate change is not real. China favors the hoax climate change to curb the Western industry, creating mayhem in Western by the support and oppose the hoax climate change, actually, China has made a profit from selling solar power and equipment.

Pope Francis merged Catholics to Islam, it calls the **One World Religion**. Therefore, Muslims always want to eliminate the Catholic symbols like Father Christmas, Virgin Marie, Jesus, and Cross. Moreover, the Quran bible totally conflicts with the Catholic bible and the UN's Universal Declaration of Human Rights. Actually, Sharia law is the backbone of the Quran's bible. How can Catholics merge with Islam?

The Muslims hate pork, so Allah's adherents who live in Western countries always pressure the government and adopted countries to eliminate the pork in school, and somewhere else. When Catholics merged Islam, it means Catholics to be wiped out the faith, bible, worship, and the faith" *there is no Jesus but Allah*". The generous heart of Pope Francis that causes the heavy security deployed at Rom in the main events of Catholics, the terrorists hide inside the Muslim community could create the bloodshed any time and everywhere in the Western, actually, the Catholic churches are targeting. The massive killing occurred at the Catholic churches in Africa, Middle-East that wakes the Western's government, actually, a series of bombings struck the churches and hotels in Sri Lank still alerts the people.

On December 7, 2019, during visiting Thailand, Pope Francis has compared US President Donald Trump to King Herod who massacred innocent children in the days of yore because King wanted to kill baby Jesus.

The ancient Roman Emperor Herod ordered to kill the innocent babies to eliminate Jesus. However, Pope Francis wrongly compared US President Donald Trump with Emperor Herod, in the record, Pope Francis has no sympathy with the US president. Nevertheless, the border protection policy of President Donald Trump making the US people living safely, keeping out or preventing the drug cartels, the terrorists, and felons from the US's society.

Pope Francis goes too far, he is the king of Catholics but not the US president. So Pope Francis has no qualifications to intervene in the US's security policy and any policies. Moreover, Pope Francis can not prove the massive number of babies killed by President Donald Trump, his slamming is baseless, even overriding the sphere of a pope. Pope Francis said:" *Yet for drugs, there's no wall to keep them out*". Under the rule of the first Muslim and Communist President Barrack Obama, the illegal migrants cost the US taxpayers a hundred billion dollars a year and the US security divided by the conflict between Muslims and the other religions, nevertheless, the terrorists come from the Muslim communities. President Donald Trump must protect the people, so the border protection carrying out by the wall located between the US and Mexico. Actually, President Donald Trump completes the wall built by the previous presidents.

French proverb quotes:" *Il faut tourner sept fois* ***sa langue dans sa bouche avant de parler"*** after Pope Francis compared President Donald Trump and Roman's Emperor Herod that can not convince the people including the Catholic followers. Roman Emperor Herod killed the children to protect his Roman empire while President Donald Trump protects the border and taking care of the national security, protect the society keeping out the threat of terrorists, the drug cartels. Pope Francis compared King Herod as President Donald Trump that conflicts with the basic Catholic teaching from the bible: *" a lie consists in speaking a falsehood with the intention of deceiving".* The Lord denounces lying as the word of the evil" *you are of your father the devil".* The Ten Commandments of nine consent*:" You shall not bear false witness against your neighbor. ".*/.

84. THE RENOVATION (ĐỔI MỚI): THE TRICKY POLICY OF COMMUNIST VIETNAM.

The low tide of revolution downgraded the Global Communist Bloc, previously the signal of Poland's crisis that had predicted the communist movement would be declined. Therefore the Soviet Union was the birthplace of communist, but the inhumane regime collapsed in the 1990s after more than 7 decades of built-in violence with tens of millions of people killed.

Nevertheless, the total of the most advanced communist country in Eastern Europe transited to democracy, the people strongly rejected the most killing theory Karl Marx, a mastermind, it has had ever in human's history. The communist countries leftover are such as China, Vietnam, North Korea, Lao, Cuba have to find a way to escape the elimination. Among, there are China and Vietnam pretend to open the door, however, they have also wanted to remain the cruel regime by appliance an ugly economic pattern:" the free market is led by socialism" it is like a rotten house painted the new coat, but inside has no change.

The so-called" the renovation" (đổi mới) of Vietcong is cheating on the western country, but the Vietcong regime couldn't blind the Vietnamese people. The communist has no comrade, but the interest is the priority. In the Vietnam War, Vietnam communist party ruled the northern government swung the relationship between two great masters Soviet Union and China, in this period Ho Chi Minh had the pro-Russia's stand because he wanted to receive the modern weapon, but he also didn't want to upset China. Therefore inside the Vietnam communist party, the Soviet Union's rival seized the power, so China's rival to be purged; the mysterious deaths currently occurred in the central communist party and the downgrading position for China's wing applied to the whole government. Remarked, the General 4 stars Nguyễn Chí Thanh who was sent to the southern for invasion, but he was killed by a bomb of the South Vietnam air force, therefore the rumor leaked his death to arranged by his comrades of Soviet Union's rival, they sent the secret agents with him and while the South Vietnam airplane bombarding, the agent broke his skull with a pistol K-54 and General Nguyễn Chí Minh died immediately on his commanding shelter at the Tây Ninh's jungle. Hanoi mourned and they also lied about the death of a high-profile communist party, they broadcast General Nguyễn Chí Thanh killed by airplane raids. In the Vietnam communist party, besides the public security guard department (likely the police department), under Ho Chi Minh's rule, there was a secret agency name The central security firm, it just receives the order from Ho Chi Minh and the chief public security guard executes. In the Vietnam communist party, the Central Security firm assassinated the high profiles as Dr. Phạm Ngọc Thạch (a first health minister of the Democratic Republic of Vietnam), Senior Lieutenant General Hoàng Văn Thái, Chu Huy Mân...

After Vietcong claimed the unpredicted victory on April 30, 1975, the leadership conflict between two great masters had been accelerating, but the Vietcong regime was pro-Soviet Union, they challenged with a former master China, so Vietnam had been facing two battlefields: South-West with Khmer Rouge (a hand of China) and north with China. The Highline was the battle that so-called China teaches Vietnam a lesson. The fierce battle in 1979 killed tens of thousand troopers on both sides.

However, after the Soviet Union and the Eastern Europe Communist Bloc collapsed, Vietnam got lost an opportunity for independence, they led the country to be China's vassal and also promulgated the Renovation Policy. From the 1980s Vietnam communist party issued its policy had consented in the general communist convention VI in 1986, but it is a tricky policy.

The renovation policy is like cloth covers the trash bin, they pretend to apply the free market to the fields as the government business (key of the economy), the corporation (mostly the communist family's member of relatives), small business, personal business, and the foreign investment.

In 1994, the embargo lift on the US president Bill Clinton created an opportunity for the Hanoi regime, they received foreign aid, trade, but Vietcong just targets keeping the dictatorial regime, they have no will to develop the country, neither the patriotic heart, instead the communist party's interest is the priority. Hanoi increases the close relationship with the master China and now Vietnam's situation worsens as Tibet, Sinkiang Uighur because both the master country and vassal are the same characters, but Hong Kong is different despite its land returned to China in 1979 but the territory remains the democracy. Hanoi's regime waives the massive migrant of Chinese, also provided the sand for China to build the artificial islands into the international water.

The tricky renovation policy of Vietcong has not changed the country from poverty to wealthy or better, while the next-door state in Cambodia could make the electrical vehicle but Vietnam could make a screw, therefore Vietnam produced hundred thousands of academic, so the Ph.D., Doctor, engineer...have plenty likely the flies. The Hanoi regime propagates and promotes themselves as the peak of humans, but almost is cheat. Let's see a Vietcong doctor names Nguyễn Chánh Khê who is proud of the technical success with the generator runs by water.

The renovation of Hanoi changed the life of the communist members, they became the capitalist and more than 300 high profiles became the millionaires and billionaires of US dollars. While the major population just has enough income for the daily meal, but the children of communist family afford for the overseas study, the communist seed could laundry money, legally immigrate into the democratic countries.

The world could make the mistake while seeing the renovation of the Vietnam communist party. The communist's character has never changed, actually, the economic management between the communist and democratic country are quite different likely the fire and water. However, the trick policy of renovation duped the innocent leaders of the western country./.

85. IN GOD WE TRUST BUT IN POPE WE DOUBT IN CATHOLICS

God and evil have never reconciled as hell and heaven, fire and water, wrong and right, black and white, honest and dishonest, communist and democracy, theism and atheism. The Vatican always adore God, but communist adore Karl Marx, the mastermind of the most massive massacre on the planet with more than 100,000,000 killed and a billion people still lost the freedom into the communist countries are China, Vietnam, North Korea, Laos, and Cuba. The religious faith relies on God, therefore, the communist believes the killing and robbery, actually the hell called communist paradise.

The Catholic and the other religions as Buddhist, Christian have been oppressed in the communist countries, many priests, monks, and pastors are sent to the hell of prison, the living condition worsened as the concentration camp of Hitler. There were many priests killed, nevertheless, the communist is malicious, the inhumane regime brainwashes the religions and gently replaced the priests, monks, pastors by the communist's cadres. The atheist religious leaders could conduct the religions following socialism and the bible mixed with Marxism-Leninists-Maoist-Ho Chi Minh's thoughts. So in the communist regime, the religions to be cornered and the regime transforms the religions to serve a communist party. On the other hand, the communist changes the internal religion but the label still remains. Despite communist considers religion as a dangerous enemy but the Karl Marx's followers often exploit the region to cheat and make a profit.

After Lenin imposed the communist regime in Russia from October 1917, the Catholics spent a hard time in Russia, the Eastern European states, and the other countries. Nowadays, the Catholic in China, Vietnam, Cuba, North Korea, and Laos still face the difficulty, therefore, in the formality, the communist regimes above propagate the religious freedom, but inside the religions, communist-controlled and bluffed the Western, actually, the evil disguised priests with the monks, priests to cheat the people and Vatican for charity, money.

Catholic pride with Pope John Paul II, the follower's respect, therefore, after Pope John Paul II died, Pope Federick 16 but he resigned then Pope Francis replaced. The Catholic has been faced with child sex abuse, the highest priest is Cardinal George Pell has been investigated and appeared at court in Australia.

Pope Francis is considered as the socialist pope in the Vatican, it is like Karl Marx's pupil Barrack Obama became the US president in 8 years. Pope Francis visited Cuba on September 19, 2015, he had a historic meeting and photos with the evil Fidel Castro. Pope Francis also criticized Presidential candidate Donald Trump for the border protection with the wall. Therefore, Pope Francis is not the global political leader in the US or somewhere else, he doesn't authorize to command the US, except the Catholic churches.

On September 23, 2018, Pope Francis has signed a Provisional Agreement to confirm the priests pointed by China communists. The Agreement accepted 7 previous bishops selected by China communists. The communist priests would earn the privileges of the Vatican as the wage and the others, but they serve for China communists, so China communists inserted the cadres into the Catholic priest line. Cardinal Joseph previously called the Catholic to be sold and he refused to join the State Chinese Catholic Patriotic Association, it is a communist Catholic organization in China.

In the communist regimes as Vietnam, the Hanoi regime trains the communist Buddhist monk and priest in Police Academy (or Public Security College). The Regime produced atheist monks, priests as police officers. The atheism monks and priests to be arranged at the Buddhist temples and the Catholic churches. Nevertheless, the Vietcong monks and priests also sent overseas, the Buddhist temples and Catholic churches of the Vietnamese community appeared the Vietcong's police officers or the intelligence agents covered under the religious leaders. Certainly, the Hanoi regime deserved the facilities the visa for the fake monks, fake priests who migrated to the US, Europe, Australia, Canada....instead, the real priests and monks the to be oppressed and probated at the temples and churches in Vietnam. Moreover, Vietnamese communists often sent the monks and priests to the Vietnamese community overseas for propaganda and collection of the money under the form of charity and reparation from the religious firms.

The Western government may eye on the Buddhist monks, the Catholic priests come from Vietnam, China...they are the communist cadres disguised under the religions. Nevertheless, religion is a good place for an espionage agent to activate under the cover of monks and priests. In the Vietnam War, the Ấn Quang Temple at Saigon was the den of Vietcong's undercover activity, so after South Vietnam lost on April 30, 1975, the Vietcong's monks as Venerable Thích Trí Quang, Thích Hộ Giác...Zen Master Thích Nhất Hạnh and many monks appeared the face.

Pope Francis surrenders the Red evil by the agreement, so the Red evil authorizes to select the priests and the Vatican approves. The agreement signed between Pope Francis and China communist will open the way for the communist countries as Vietnam communists to infiltrate the Vatican, now Hanoi arranged many communist priests in the churches. A day, the Vatican will have a communist pope made in China, it is possible. The deal between China communist and Pope Francis raises the grave concern about the global Catholic in the future, despite **in God we trust, but in Pope we doubt./.**

86. PRESIDENT BARACK OBAMA BRAINWASHED THE U.S PEOPLE IN 8 YEARS.

The most communist regime has applied the brainwashing method, it is the essential strategy of the so-called socialism that the communist titles as the dawn of the communist paradise, it is like a drawn cake that cheats the world since Karl Marx devised his social modern, but the paradise comes from the imagination. Brainwashing is the key policy in the tyranny regime, it comes from the research of Ivan Petrovich Pavlov, a Russian scientist, and the first Russian to win the Nobel Prize in Physiology or Medicine in 1904. The Pavlov's study that applied his dog, he could change the habit, it became the brainwashing method of the communist, actually after Lenin succeeded to apply Karl Marx's theory into reality.

The communist is like the super gang, they violate the human rights as the so-called the social reform, indeed the robbing, killing and transform the people into slave are the unchanged strategy, even though they are facing the low tide of the revolution, therefore the high tide of revolution is barbarous.

The consequence of the communist crime has ever haven in the world since the so-called October Revolution 1917 did by Lenin, the global communist killed more than 100,000,000 people and also has enslaved the other billion people from the 20th to 21st century.

The brainwashing method is just the way that replaces the human habit, including the social valuation, all to be turned to the oriental communist. Like the dogs of Pavlov, after spending the disaster or the difficulty, the habit to be changed. The pauperized policy plus the currently spiritual terror with armed force, public security guard force, the secret agent, and the dictatorial governance system from the local to center, that transform the brain of the people to the communist policy. Moreover, the hardline prison system so-called the re-education camp is the brainwashing center of the communist regimes, so in the tyrannical regime, the re-education camp set up everywhere.

The brainwashing method wipes out the old memories, the belief in religions, the social valuation and imposes the new one. The brainwashing drives the people into the wrong acceptations, the right is wrong, so the genocides as Ho Chi Minh who killed 1,700,000 people, Mao Ste Tung killed 65,000,000, Kim Il Sung (late Kim Jong ill, Kim Jong Un), Fidel Castro…are the heroes, the communist force the people believe the evils are national symbols and the humanitarian lovers.

The brainwashing has happened in the communist regime, therefore in the US, a sample of a democratic country, the US people to be brainwashed through 8 years under the rule of a first black and also communist, Muslim in White House, the president Barack Obama who applied successfully this method, but the most US people have not recognized yet because president Barack Obama gently applied the brainwashing method, he is a clever man. The wrongs to be accepted, are the first stage of brainwashing. President Barack Obama applied to the US people on:

-Homosexuality: although same-sex marriage is the minority Obama used the Supreme Court as the tool to force

50 states to obey the court order, the homosexuality being controversial. Certainly, the Supreme Court's judges should be a tool of Obama.

-President Barack Obama is also a commander in chief as the constitution consented, he allowed homosexuality in the army, despite the major armed force personnel's opposition, the most generals reacted but they did nothing to stop.

-President Barack Obama opened the border, the illegal migrant invaded with the criminals, terrorists…Obama used the taxpayer paid for the unwanted guests and the undocumented migrant…the US people knew, but they did nothing because of the president's power.

-President Barack Obama used the taxpayer for weapon and finance's provision the ISIS and he also appealed the US fighting against the ISI with the taxpayer. The congress and people knew but all accepted the wrongdoings and the national security risks.

-The Clinton Foundation is a family business but they exploited the US government for money collection, they play to pay, but the FBI and congress surrendered. The 32,000 emails, the classifies leaked by Hillary…all the wrongdoings waived but the US people quietly accepted while the law punishes the criminal but the high profile of the national fugitives ignored.

-The Sharia law is suitable for the medieval stage, but president Barack Obama flagged the worst social method being existed in the US, he forced the US government to make the toilet for the transgender that cost about $7 billion. He forced 300 million people to accept the injustices and those would be remained a long time in the society and become the habit likely in the communist regimes.

-Mr. Barrack Obama is the first US president to honor Jane Fonda, also called Hanoi Jane. Everyone knew she is a traitor, she behaved as a treasonous person, therefore Obama imposed unfairly on the people, actually the Vietnam veteran, despite the people recognized it is totally wrong but they have to accept the wrong, so Obama succeeded in brainwashing people.

-The US to be pauperized, so under two terms, the US dived into the deep debt ever with $23 trillion. He wanted to bankrupt the US by the destruction of the economy, brought the job to China (his comrade), he, his wife, and his family spent the taxpayer as a billionaire.

Under 8 years, the 44th US president brainwashed the people, he chose the top adviser Madam Valerie Jarred, a hardcore communist's brain, she was subjected by the FBI but Obama protected her. President Obama also had 6 essential advisors, they are Muslims.

President Barack Obama behaved likely as a Secretary-General of the communist party. As the routine, the communist leader puts their name in the national event likely Vietcong replaced Saigon by Ho Chi Minh City, the Soviet Union changed Saint Petersburg by Leningrad. President Obama named the national health scheme Obamacare, but he cares nothing, the taxpayer paid. Barack Obama is a cheating punter who has no money but uses the people's money in the gamble if he wins, he gets all if he lost, and the people paid. It is incredible in the US, people lived under the communist regime, but mostly they didn't know Obama brainwashed all likely in Asia, the people could boil a frog smoothly, and they just put it in a cold water's pot and fired gently underneath, a frog to be cooked without reaction. Despite the 44th US president Barack Obama brainwashed the US people, pauperized the superpower state to bankruptcy, but the left media and the Democrats promoted Obama as the best president, indeed he is the worst president in US history. Likely the Vietnamese joke the Vietcong regime, the communist party cheats the people from its super gang founder on February 3, 1930, the saying spread into the population:

The fallen harvest comes from a natural disaster. The successful harvest creates by the communist talented party.

However, President Barack Obama's record in 8 years, the US history has never promoted that man who destroyed the US and left long term damage control for society, the US being shattered, the racial conflicts are the Obama's consequence./.

87. CHINA IS THE PROFESSIONAL BURGLAR ON PLANET

After joining the free market and WTO, the largest communist country appeared the real face of a rogue state. The world identified China as the den of thieves, the hub of counterfeit and the center of a cheat, the bush law, and the totalitarian regime couldn't accord the international community. The appearance of China in the free market is like a gang officially operates in society. The US and democratic countries developed without China before the sanction lifted.

China's growth comes from dishonest methods. The clever and professional burglar is the giant with the foot of clay also became the current member of the UN's Security Council and has the diplomatic system worldwide. Certainly, the thieves are criminals, there is no school, university, a college that opens the course teaching the burglary career. Therefore, communism and socialism is the place for teaching the burglary.

The communist paradise of Karl Marx, Maoist, Hồ Chi Minh's thoughts, and the others are the paradise of burglary. The pauperization's policy of communism or socialism originates from the social problem, the poor people without the income's support from the government, become the casual burglars. In the communist paradise, the thieves can steal anything including excrement because the human release provides the fertilizer. In Vietnam, **Hồ Chí Minh defines the excrement as a precious asset**, the nation wide's economic development called Uncle Ho's Fish Pond helped the family solve the toilet and also feeding a kind of fish called" **Cá Vồ**" does love the human excrement. The Fish Vồ processes the Ba-Sa fillet and export to the Western to make money, it is the pattern" *the free market is led by socialism"* has applied in China and Vietnam. The lizard changes color's skin tactic has deceived the innocent politicians in Western and the naïve national leaders.

The paradise of burglary in communist countries as Vietnam, the people always watch out the thieves, the saying:" *socialism means the toilet mus fence"* that reflects the outstanding of communism and Hồ Chí Minh's thoughts. The Western and democratic countries concern the human excrement is the wasted materials, actually, the hygiene's concern. Therefore, the communist countries have used excrement into economic development. In Vietnam, Hanoi's suburb has the excrement market at Cổ Nhuế's village (*someone created the fake excrement for sale and the local government arrested*). In a communist country like Vietnam, even the excrement can make the fake, so the communist paradise couldn't trust. The Vietcong's supporters like Jane Fonda (*Hanoi Jane*) concealed the excrement market and the cruelty of North Vietnam's regime in the Vietnam War. The sibling of the communist is the left media, the left journalists, the left reporters could release the fake news, it is the character of Karl Marx's pupils.

The people who live in the communist paradise recognize the agricultural products meet the poor quality, poison, contamination, actually, the hygiene concern, so the agricultural products of Western favor Chinese people in the mainland. It causes China to fail to impose retaliatory tariffs on the US's agricultural products, China's tariffs hit back Chinese people.

The model of socialism in Vietnam exposes the multiple forms of burglary are dog thieves, cat thieves, log thieves, soil thieves, and other burglaries. The professional thieves and casual burglars snoop everywhere in the communist paradise, so the foreign tourists must be careful while visiting Vietnam, China. The legal burglars are communists, actually, the high-ranking cadres stole the people's sweat, they become the millionaires and billionaires. The stolen money deposits at Western banks and purchased the asset at the capitalist countries.

China is the great master of the Vietcong's regime, so China is a professional burglary at a high level. China has arrayed the global burglary system that carries out into multiple forms and malicious methods. The stolen technology is a vital tactic, China also stole the trademark of the Western brands. The foreign factories in China are the victims of the stolen trademark plus the technology. Therefore, they couldn't take legal action because China has never respected the law, but the bush law can apply to the legal argument. China makes a profit from the loss of Western and the money comes from the burglary using the money for the global hegemonic strategy.

The den of thieves illegally built and militarized the artificial islands in disputed waters, the sand provided by Vietnam, an actual vassal of China. The debt trap is a high level of invasion or the clever burglary of the lands of counterparts. The growth of China is like Nazis in the Second World War, the global hegemonic ambition of the giant burglar has never stopped, China has stolen the fish in disputed waters and also stole the soil of Philippine territories. The cargo ships of China stole the soil of Davao Del Notre Province of the Philippines, the position located at the West Philippine sea or the Spratly islands, the government alert the soil burglary. The Philippines won the International Court, the artificial islands of China are illegal, therefore, Beijing ignores international law including the neighboring countries by the brazen and aggressive attitude. The world watches out the global burglar and the cunning conqueror using the soft army to colonize the counterparts by the trade ties, free trade agreement./.

88. BEHIND THE SHODDY TECHNOLOGY OF CHINA

While Taiwan and Hong Kong people pride the economic development, the living condition promotes, the key comes from democracy. Therefore, the so-called People's Republic of China became a professional burglar, on the other hand, China's Communist Party transformed the mainland to be the den of thieves, the hub of counterfeit, the center of a cheat, and now, the lair of pandemics. However, Ape's dynasty has no shame, instead, they please about the outcome of stolen technology that makes the rogue regime strengthens and also helps China's communist regime carrying out the global hegemonic ambition. China's growth comes from deception and stolen technology.

The record marks about Socialism or Communism completely failed to build a communist paradise. In China, despite it renamed Maoist in the mainland after Ape herd robbed the authentic government of Chinese people in 1949. Therefore, the socialism ethos is rotten itself by the cheating revolution, mostly, the social purge plus the dishonest character of Karl Marx's pupils impoverished the people, so the wealthy component and intellectuals eliminated from the society, instead of the low educated and illiterate peasants manage the country. The bush law and socialism framed the invention, the communist regime succeeded obscurantism to keep the totalitarian government, but the invention limited and the national talent ruined by socialism.

The global hegemonic ambition urges China's Communist Party must apply the stolen technology while the technology lagged behind the US and Europe. After many decades carried out the burglary mission, China became a professional burglar. China stole the Intellectual Property then using to make the products and selling back to the invention countries with the cheap prices, China made a profit from the Western loss

The technological thieves have applied the stolen tactics into multiple forms including establishing contacts with the dishonest academics who handed over the technology to China from many decades ago. China's Communist Party has developed the stolen mission, the main places are Western countries, particularly, the US is a wonderful place. China succeeded in the burglary job, it reflects a quote of Sun Szu:" *create something from nothing*". China acquired technologies like the US and Western, so the professional thieves pride themselves on the stolen technologies and challenging the US, Western. The arms race, the space race, and the military provocation to wake the world, nowadays, China becomes the global enemy after Xi Jinping launched biological warfare to the world community. China couldn't escape the culprit of Coronavirus when the enormous evidence founded Chinese virus originated from Wuhan Safety Level 4 Laboratory. The massive compensation obsesses China, therefore, the Ape's dynasty sowed the wind and will reap the whirlwind.

President Donald Trump unmasked the global burglar after granted the death certificate to China's giant telecommunication Huawei. The 5G ban causes the cyber spy threat in the US and its allies. Huawei's product reflects a proverb*:" borrow a big head to cook soup*", the US and its allies banned Huawei that debunked the professional thieves to appear the real face when the foreign companies stop to provide the chips from Taiwan Semiconductor Manufacturing Co, America chipmaker Qualcomm and others. Huawei's head of consumer business unit Richard Yu alerts its company is running out the chips within a month and their own chip Kirin being faced with the problem. Possibly, Huawei will not make the newest smartphone after September 2020, the funeral of Huawei set, and Chinese people face more jobless. The Tik Tok is going to follow Huawei, the telecommunication companies, the propaganda tools, and the cyber spy of China crippled. Despite the military conflict doesn't happen yet but the US and allies discovered the military technology of China is shoddy. Moreover, the chips are very important in military equipment, but China couldn't make it. The mouthful propaganda released about the aircraft carriers, fight Jet J-15, J-20, and newest J-20B stealth but installed the Russian engine. The left media failed to polish China's strength on the economy and army, the negative aspects of China appeared, they couldn't make the chips and invention, instead, the stolen technologies can not expose the quality as originals. The stolen technological products couldn't compare with the originals, so the Jade Rabbit died after touching the Moon while India succeeded in the Mars mission

The US, Europe, Taiwan, South Korea, Japan, Singapore just cut the technological equipment, the giant with the foot of clay will disable, moreover, the US and Western isolate and sanction China, the communist paradise will be the famine paradise and jobless paradise, China's communist regime lose anything after stealing something./.

89. MARK ZUCKERBERG STANDS ALONGSIDE WITH CHINA

When a country is engaging in the war, every citizen must line up to support except the traitors and the enemy's undercover activists, the spy network helps the enemy by multiple tactics, the domestic thugs are dangerous than the enemy. Therefore, in the Vietnam War, the traitors were Jane Fonda, John Kerry, Joe Biden, Bill-Hillary Clinton, and others plus the left media supported Vietcong, the enemy of the US people and democratic countries, but the traitors have not indicted yet. The war fights against terror, including the Islamic State which confirms the border to separate between the terror and the people, whoever supports finance, recruit, propaganda for terror, would face the criminal charge. The Vietnamese people, Vietnam veterans, and victims of Vietcong want the traitors to pay for the crime despite the Vietnam War was over after Vietcong claimed the unpredictable victory on April 30, 1975. The Jewish people, particularly, the Holocaust survivors have never forgotten the crime of the Nazis. In the same circumstance, millions of Vietnamese people including ten thousand families of Hue's massacre in Tết offensive 1968, have never forgotten Vietcong and genocide of Ho Chi Minh who killed 1,700,000 people.

Nowadays, the world is fighting against global economic terror and the global biological war, China's Communist Party repeats Nazi in the Second World War. Despite this, China has never declared war as Hitler did, but Ape Emperor Xi Jinping attacks the world by biological war. The US leads allies and the world to fight against the global enemy, therefore, the domestic thugs in Western-like Democrats in the US and the left parties plus the left media have attempted to hamper the war against the biological warfare's culprit in Beijing. The domestic thugs appeared in the face after the action showing the endorsement's China into multiple forms.

From many years ago, Facebook has exploited the technical communication to delete the articles, comments accusing China and Vietcong of the human rights violation. On the other hand, Facebook is the left technical company founded in America but serves China's communist regime. Despite Facebook and CEO Mark Zuckerberg often released the mouthful stance to support free speech and democracy. Indeed, Facebook silently has applied the business is like the propaganda machine of China, but its company operates in the US. Nevertheless, Facebook is keen to advertise for Democrats and the left parties, so many comments and videos, pictures deleted by the bush rules, it is the censor's rules of the pro-China company in the US. On the other hand, Facebook becomes the technical communication tool of China like the left media companies since the Cold War.

CEO Mark Zuckerberg snubs the US government although his technical communication operates under the license granted by the US government. Nevertheless, Mr. Mark Zuckerberg goes too far, he issued the wild rules as China applies the bush law in the mainland and Hong Kong (*the security law of Carrie Lam*). Possibly, Facebook conflicts with free speech and promotes China's propaganda. Many Facebook users are the victims of Mark Zuckerberg. Recently, Mark Zuckerberg announced the discrimination policy to delete the posts of politicians, the target focuses President Donald Trump. Nevertheless, Facebook has deleted the information about COVID 19 from the US government, it is a serious violation and the US government reacts but Mark Zuckerberg ignores, he prevents the information about Hydroxychloroquine, Mark Zuckerberg is heartless, he wants the people to die by Coronavirus. Democrats and China have tried to use the death toll and infection of Coronavirus to help the rotten candidate Joe Biden in the election 2020, and Mark Zuckerberg does the same.

Mark Zuckerberg often exposes the arrogant attitude as the most powerful man in the US, indeed, Facebook is just a technical communication company like Google, Twitter, and others. The users around the world and the US, Europe condemn Facebook, so its company lost the advertising of more than 160 major companies.

Republican Representative of Florida is Matt Gaetz filed the referral against Mark Zuckerberg who made the false statements to Congress while under oath in two hearings in April 2018 and the documents sent to Attorney General William Barr. Nevertheless, US Attorney General William Barr joined Australia, British to send a letter to Facebook's CEO Mark Zuckerberg urging to abandon the plan of encryption on all Facebook-owned messaging services. The encryption process changing the information or signals into a secret code, so people can not understand or use it without special equipment. **China is the global enemy and three out of the Five Eyes strongly react against Facebook plus CEO Mark Zuckerberg**. Encryption is the malicious technical communication of Mark Zuckerberg who conspires to use technical communication to censor free speech in China. Therefore, in the US, Western, Mark Zuckerberg can not cheat, certainly, the law can tell Mark Zuckerberg if

Facebook violates and exploits the technical devices to censor free speech and serve for China's propaganda.

Recently, the US people surprise when the major den of fake news is The New York Times has deleted hundreds of advertorials carried out by China's propaganda outlet. The incident has started in June 2020 when a group of Republican lawmakers wrote a letter to Nancy Pelosi to end China Daily delivery to the Congressional office. Republican Jim Banks said:" *We require foreign outlets, propaganda outlets, to register as foreign agents in the United States of America, and yet we have them appearing on our chief decision-makers in America, our lawmakers', doorsteps. We have this propaganda newspaper show up on our doorsteps* ".

The prominent media of China is China Daily divulged to the US Justice Department to show China's communist government paid more than $US 4.6 million to the Washington Post (*owner is Jeff Bezos*), and nearly $US 6 million to The Wall Street Journal since November 2016, particularly, in 2018, The New York Times got $US 50,000. So the people and Facebook users don't know Facebook should receive the payment of China, its reason causes Mark Zuckerberg always stands alongside China in the propaganda and attacks the US government, particularly, President Donald Trump is the main target. The henchman of China must learn a spy-proverb:" *when a hunter recognizes the dog can not do the job properly, a hunter must know to eat the dog's meat*". It is the circumstance of The New York Times, Washington Post, The Wall Street Journal. A day, China should release the payment to Facebook if the job can not do as the requirement.

However, The New York Times deleted the advertorials of China's propaganda that should deal with national security while the US and allies being fought the economic war and the global biological warfare's attack from China. Certainly, Facebook has no experience as the New York Times, CEO Mark Zuckerberg ignores the law and national security, he will face the problem when he declares the war with the US government and stands alongside China's communist regime, now it is enemy of the US and the world community. Possibly, The New York Times tries to avoid the treason, but CEO Mark Zuckerberg doesn't recognize or he has deep relations with China./.

90. THE RIGGED ELECTION CHALLENGES PATRIOTISM

The bush Constitution of 1871 is the hidden slavery contract that made by the lenders have become the bosses of America to control the government, Congress, Senate, and Supreme Court including economy, financial system, actually, Federal Reserve (F.E.D) owned the US dollar and printing the paper currency to create the debt, so Federal Reserve is the infinite treasure, certainly, the CEO (*the US president*) of The United of America has no worry about the debt, moreover, the potential CEO exposes the deep debt as Barrack Obama, George W. Bush and now the presidential robber Joe Biden to spend broadly, and the bosses of the Deep State are very happy with the mad, mental health illness CEO Joe Biden.

Since 1871, the Deep State has squeezed the sweat of a hundred million workers to pay the high taxes despite the people have never accepted it and imposing the President, the Representatives, Senators, the governors, and 50 state governments. The US people have lived in a fake democracy to shield the hidden slavery form. The Deep State has never respected the life of people, the national interest, instead the interest is the prime purpose of the filthy rich components. The merciless magnates have ignored the patriotism, but the people wake up after the rigged election in 2020. **The Deep State snubs the patriotism by imposing the bloody old mad imbecile mongrel ape Joe Biden to storm the White House on January 20, 2021.**

The presidential robbery prepared for a long time, therefore, the rash deception of the rigged election created more public outrage, moreover, everyone knew Joe Biden commits treason, corruption, pedophile, and an actual henchman of China's Communist Party. The corruptions publicized the media, actually, the laptop of Hunter Biden proved the blatant evidence. Moreover, Hunter Biden behaved Joe Biden's representative to receive $US 1.5 billion from China to reward the best services of Vice President Joe Biden from 2008 to 2016. The incident proves the 25th Amendment is a farce after the traitor, corruption, and mental health illness Joe Biden sworn in the office on January 20, 2021, while Democrats exploited 25th Amendment to impeach President Donald Trump with the fabricated dossiers written by the former British Intelligence agent Christopher Steele and after the 45th President Donald Trump leaving the White House when the presidency expired, although the second impeachment failed, the people know the 1871 Constitution grants the license to rob and it is the statement to deserve for the dishonest white collar using the radically legal rules to focus the political purposes. The 1871 Constitution drives the American people into the dictatorial regime as the communist regimes in China, Vietnam, North Korea, and others. It is the shame of America.

The presidential robbery humiliates the US Republic, the law, Constitution, the people, and the social valuation. The greatest rigged election in 2020 exposed the rotten and corrupt Congress, Senate and the Supreme Court represented the Deep State to legalize the rigged election and conducted the traitor Joe Biden illegally inaugurated on January 20, 2021, with the disgraced celebration without the people or 80,000,000 voters of Joe Biden, instead 400 thousand flags and 65,000,000 National Guards plus the Police, the FBI, CIA, Secret Service agents, and intelligence agencies plus the private security guards of Joe Biden to tie the security (*Joe Biden doesn't trust everyone, so he hires the private bodyguards, Chinese security guards are the most trust of Joe Biden*). Certainly, the presidential robber Joe Biden with thuggish Chief Justice John Roberts, the evil House Speaker Nancy Pelosi, Satanic Senate leader Chuck Schumer, the Democratic Representatives, Senators and turncoat Republicans like Mike Pence, Mitt Romney, Mitch McConnell, and other RINO currently fear 75,000,000 people, the losing job's victims of Joe Biden and other concerned citizens to expose the patriotism by the action as Russian people stood up to eliminate the communist regime in the Soviet Union in the early 1990s. The extreme fright of the presidential robber Joe Biden who has not lived in the White House in two months as Press Secretary Jen Psaki confirmed. Certainly, Joe Biden is not the 46th US president, instead, the 45th President Donald Trump still remains the presidency despite the first term expired. The extreme fear of Nancy Pelosi and the Donkey super gang expose on the high fence with razor wire and the checkpoints with 5,000 troops remain in Washington D.C despite the inauguration is over. Moreover, Democrats currently alert about the militias and the angry people can transform to outrage to action, the consequences are immeasurable, possibly, the life of the traitors being risky, no one can know what will happen when the patriotism is provoked by the traitors to challenge to people. The destructive executive orders of the mongrel mad ape Joe Biden increased the patriotism and the people's livelihood are threatening. American people choose between freedom, and slavery, it is the strong message sending to Joe Biden, Democrats, and the RINO while the traitors are living and besieged by the people.

Nevertheless, Democrats have developed a slight majority in the Congress, Senate to create the bush law as the second impeachment applied to the 45th President Donald Trump, the protection's rigged election bill should pass the Congress and Senate, so the election in America is like China, Vietnam, Venezuela as Joe Biden confirmed on the campaign with" *the most extensive VOTER FRAUD organization in history*", so the futuristic elections including the presidential election will happen as the presidential election in 2020. It is the vital problem that Republicans alert and review. The bloody lesson of the 45th President Donald Trump has not solved when the Congress, Senate, and the judges including the Supreme Court dismissed and rejected all lawsuits against the rigged election. The world laughs at the democracy of America when the presidential robber Joe Biden inaugurated with traitor Mike Pence certified the 306 fraudulent electoral colleges of Joe Biden and Chief Justice John Roberts presided the illegal president Joe Biden.

Recently, the $US 1.9 trillion relief bill of Joe Biden has passed the Senate although the bill doubts about the spending. Nowadays, American people live in the hiddenz communist regime when the Democrats control Congress, Senate, the White House, and the Supreme Court become the highest legal tool to protect the bush law and the denouncement publicly of Democrats. The US government is not different from China's communist regime when the Congress, Senate, Supreme Court are controlled by the hidden communist party that called Democrats. The demagogic policies and the label of progressive party collapsed after Joe Biden robbed the White House.

The extreme tension that has occurred between the Donkey super gang and American people have never ended, except the conditions below:

-The rigged election solved after the Supreme Court reviewed the files at the swing states plus more than other 30 states, and the presidency of Joe Biden to be disqualified, certainly, the 45th President Donald Trump will return the office, he is the victim of the presidential robbery. Despite the Supreme Court distorted the justice to protect the rigged election, therefore, the virtual jury is 75,000,000 people, so Chief Justice John Roberts and other robbers with the wooden hammer confront the people and challenge the patriotism. On the other hand, the Supreme Court robs the justice of the people as Joe Biden robbed the White House, the Senate and Congress currently rob the lawmaker's function of the bush-lawmakers.

-The people stand up to force Joe Biden ousting from the White House and the traitor will have the virtual inauguration in the prison.

-The US Army responds to the patriotism to arrest Joe Biden and its animal cabinet plus the corrupt politicians involved in the rigged election in 2020 with the interference of China and 65 nations. The EO-13848 can apply to restore the law and Constitution of 1776.

-The Republican states and the Democratic concerned states can secede, it is AMERICAXIT is the only solution to form the **Federation of America**. Certainly, CEO Joe Biden will lose the job, the rotten Congress, Senate, and the Supreme Court will be nullified, and Federal Reserve will lose $US 27.8 trillion of debt and added $US 1.9 trillion of Joe Biden's bill has passed the Senate.

-The civil war should happen after all solution is the deadlock.

Certainly, 330 million people can not suffer the communism applying in America, the traitors will pay the consequences when the people's outrage and the livelihood are threatened by the crazy executive orders of Joe Biden plus the oppression of Democrats./.

91. BIDEN IS THE FIRST US PRESIDENTIAL ROBBER

The US presidential robbery prepared after President Donald Trump getting the office on January 20, 2017, the sudden loss of Hillary Clinton in the White House race in 2016 rushed Democrats finding any way to remove

447

President Donald Trump, so Democrats currently attacked President Donald Trump throughout four years. The perpetrators are former President Barrack Obama, the fallen presidential candidate Hillary Clinton, Nancy Pelosi, Chuck Schumer, and China's Communist Party plus the Deep State attempted to remove the potential commander in chief Donald Trump with the impeachment to apply into multiple methods. Initially, the fabricated dossiers of former British intelligence agent Christopher David Steele handed over to turncoat Republican John McCain, and Democrats develop to impeach President Donald Trump. Therefore, the Special Counsel of legal terrorist Robert Mueller found nothing Russia interfered in the US presidential election in 2016, but the taxpayers wasted $US 34 million for the game of Democrats.

The Deep State, China, and Democrats exploited the presidential election in 2020 to make a coup with the rigged election to carry out into multiple methods. The 25.2 million illegal ballots inserted, the dead people voters, and the Dominion voting system decided the bloody old mad, imbecile, mongrel ape Joe Biden illegally inaugurated on January 20, 2021, without the people, instead, 400 thousand flags and 65,000 National Guards remained the security.

Nowadays, human society currently has been threatened and complicated by the enemies:

1-The communism with the prominent threat is Maoist, the den is China's mainland. Moreover, the left parties in democratic countries are the siblings of China's Communist Party.

2-The dishonest judges and Justices of the Supreme Court are robbers with a wooden hammer. The dishonest lawyers are the robbers with the paper-knife

3-The criminals and gangs threaten society with violence, robbery, killing the people.

4-The left stream media and the left tech communication companies are the thug of people, the foes of the public, and the garbage of mainstream media

5-The fraudsters

The major enemies of the US people are the thuggish Chief Justice John Roberts and former Mike Pence plus Nancy Pelosi. Moreover, Justice Brett Michael Kavanaugh, Amy Vivian Coney Barrett, and Neil McGill Gorsuch were appointed by   President Donald Trump, but they betrayed the country and stabbed in the back of President Donald Trump. On the other hand, Justice Brett Michael Kavanaugh, Amy Vivian Coney Barrett, and Neil McGill Gorsuch joined the line of the robbers with the wooden hammer with the leader is Chief Justice John Roberts. Those Justices above take responsibility for the peril of America when the mad mongrel ape Joe Biden stormed the White House, therefore, after January 20, 2021, America has two presidents:

-The expired president Donald Trump, but he still remains the 45th president when 75,000,000 people mandate Donald Trump to lease the White House in the next four years. Donald Trump is the virtual President with the office in Florida and continues to lead the people

-The presidential robber Joe Biden colluded with Chief Justice John Roberts and Mike Pence to storm the White House. Indeed, Joe Biden is not the 46th US president, on the other hand, Joe Biden is the president of the Deep State, Democrats, China, John Roberts, Mike Pence, the left stream media, the left tech communication companies, and the turncoat Republicans like Mitch McConnell, Mitt Romney, and others. The presidential robber Joe Biden just signed the destructive executive orders and the left stream media propagates to mislead the public, nevertheless, they conceal the serious mental health illness of an old ape Joe Biden. Certainly, the 25 Amendment waived plus the laptop of Hunter Biden sinks and ignores the investigation when the Department of Justice and FBI are the tools of Democrats.

It is the first month of the presidential robber Joe Biden storms the White House, the US people have been suffered the dire consequences:

-Schools closed as China's virus pandemic.

-Keystone Pipeline canceled, it lost ten thousand jobs despite the Keystone workers and Union supported Joe Biden, now they must pay the big mistake.

-Radical immigration bill introduced to accept the felons, drug syndicates, espionage agents

-Iran Deal coming back

-Political rival impeached (*the Democrats and turncoat Republicans attempted the second impeachment, but failed*)

-Mexico City Policy rescinded

-1776 Commission scrapped, China and communism freely propagate and intoxicate in the US education system

-The hoax climate change restores with Paris Agreement.

-The taxpayers wasted to World Health Organization but turned the World Hell Organization in China virus pandemic (*Joe Biden bans to use of the term" China virus"*).

-Deserve the priority for China in trade and other facilities

-Democrats introduce the bill to ban President Donald Trump's burial at Arlington cemetery.

-The Black Lives Matter and Antifa terrorize the people and the presidential robber Joe Biden backs, the US society is threatened.

-Democrats plus the Supreme Court to force the 45th President Donald Trump to show the tax returns despite, Donald Trump still remains the presidency while the rigged election has not solved yet.

The inauguration was over, but 6,000 National Guards remain in Washington D.C. Moreover, the White House, the Supreme Court, and Capitol Hill circled the high fence with the razor wire and the security ties with the checkpoints deploy as the war zone. Lawyer Lin Wood:

"ARMY WILL SYSTEM EVERYTHING!

Calm down, take care of yourselves for the next few weeks, make sure you and your families are safe.

And then you go on and you go up.

Many countries around the world, will take back their land and recreate the "REPUBLIC".

They will all be free.

It's a beautiful time to be alive now. And Donald TRUMP will come back!!

According to the "NEW CONSTITUTION", TRUMP should stay in the WHITE HOUSE with MELANIA for 8 more years, because TRUMP is a man of God!

But he will definitely be President for another 4 years!

So make sure you have everything at home and safe, the next few days and weeks could be busy.

We'll see what happens.

BUT EVERYTHING WILL COME OUT!!!

May GOD bless the whole world."

The 44th President Barrack Obama is the first Muslim and communist-ruled White House from 2008 to 2016, the US people lived in Satan's era. Certainly, Vice President Joe Biden shared the worst time or Satanic period. Unfortunately, the rigged election imposed Joe Biden to occupy the White

House. The political parasite Joe Biden is the professional robber, he robbed the wife of Bill Stevenson, now he robs the presidency with the certification of Mike Pence and inauguration of the thuggish Chief Justice John Roberts.

Indeed, the presidential robber Joe Biden is a pawn of Deep State, an actual henchman of China, including the Vice Presidential Kamala Harris, who is keen on the term" *let's go to bed*" that is the political tactic to help Kamala Harris stepping the succession from Senator to the Vice-Presidential robber. Therefore, in the shadow, former President Barrack Obama is the supreme president, he rules the third term in the White House with the robbers are Joe Biden and Kamala Harris.

The future of Americans is uncertain, even it worsens when the robber Joe Biden and Kamala Harris rule the White House in the next four years. Moreover, Democrats control the Congress, Senate, and the Supreme Court, so the next presidential election in 2024 will face a rigged election and the White House will not change, even President Donald Trump can not overturn the rigged election in 2020 when all the lawsuits are rejected by the Supreme Court. So **AMERICAXIT is the only solution to save America, the Republican states can reform the FEDERATION OF AMERICA**, and the presidential robber Joe Biden or Kamala Harris will be no longer rule the Corporation of the United States of America. The original Constitution of 1776 restores and the debt of $US 27.8 trillion nullified after the Corporation collapsed, Joe Biden must file the bankruptcy, and 50 states have no responsibility for the debt because the federal administration borrowed from the Deep State's lenders. /.

92. THE HUMANITY CONCERN OF APE AND ANINAL

Certainly, the animal has no human mind, neither religion *(atheism)* nor humanity, instead of the instinct to apply for every action. Karl Marx is the greatest master of the communist, every word of Karl Marx highlights as the golden frame, so the communists pride their ancestor comes from Ape, a kind of monkey as Karl Marx concerned. The Ape has no humanity concern, so the communists have enjoyed the genocide as the revolution, therefore, it is the revolutionary Ape. Particularly, China's Ape greatest leader of China's Communist Party is Mao Tse Tung who killed from 49 to 78 million people from 1949 to 1976 *(the victims were Chinese people, the occupied territories like Tibet and Sinkiang Uighur).* In Russia, Joseph Stalin killed about 24 million people from 1958 to 1961. Pol Pot killed 2 million people in Cambodia from 1975 to 1979. Kim Il Sung killed 1.6 million Korean people from 1948 to 1994. Leonid Brezhnev killed about a million people in Afghanistan. Tito killed 570 thousand people in Yugoslavia from 1945 to 1987. Ho Chi Minh killed 1.7 million people in Vietnam from 1930 to 1969. Mostly, the humanitarian disaster from the 19th century comes from the Ape.

When the communist party or the Ape herd occupied the countries in China, Russia, Vietnam, Laos, Cuba, Cambodia, and others, the people have been suffered by the animal rules with cruel methods. The Ape has no human rights concern instead, the merciless actions have become a grave concern about human rights. Unfortunately, the prominent Ape herd in China has exploited the trade ties, the diplomatic relations carrying out the global hegemonic ambition applying to impose the animal rules on the planet. China's Ape herd uses the money to corner the counterparts, even the United Nations has been abused and bullied by China's Ape representative, so China's Ape and Vietcong's Ape issued the different definition from the UN's Universal Declaration of Human rights and Ape herd always violates the human rights in the occupied countries. Moreover, the mongrel Ape in Western-like Democrats in the US and the left parties accompany China's Ape herd into the global hegemonic ambition.

Unfortunately, the Western politicians received the money, privileges, and the boons of China's Ape herd, they sold the mind to animals, so the left parties expose the mongrel Ape or the Ape comrade with China. The mongrel Ape party in America considers America as the jungle, the Democratic Ape herd doesn't respect the people, instead, the animal character applied in the rigged election in 2020 with the interference of China's Ape herd plus the Dominion voting system, and the **bloody mad, imbecile mongrel ape Joe Biden** stormed the White House on January 20, 2021. The US people have been controlled by the Ape herd with the Democratic Congress, Senate, and the Chief Justice Ape John Roberts created and throned Ape Biden as the 46th president of the people. Indeed, the 45th President Donald Trump just expired the presidency while the rigged election has not solved yet, so Ape Joe Biden is not the 46th president as the left stream animal media and the left tech communication animal companies propagate and support Ape's, King Joe Biden.

Everyone condemns the rigged election, but the Ape's regime in China, Vietnam, Cuba, Venezuela, and others have applied to deceive the people with the so-called election to choose the Ape's representatives in the Ape's sole parliament.

It is a farce when the Ape's herd appoints the candidates and the people vote, but the outcome election is decided by the Ape's herd. Unfortunately, the Ape's election method brings to America. In the US, Democrats or America's Ape herd prides the rigged election, so Ape's presidential candidate Joe Biden confirmed in the campaign" *to create the most extensive and exclusive voter fraud organization in the history of American politics"*

After Ape Joe Biden illegally occupied the White House, the US people face the disaster, Ape's king Joe Biden ignores the living condition of Americans with 52 destructive executive orders signed within 20 days, it causes the loss of a million jobs, and abortion threatens many million unborn babies. Moreover, the Ape's herd in America attempted twice impeachment the 45th President Donald Trump, therefore, all failed. After January 20, 2021, Americans have been ruled by the animal regime of the Ape's king Joe Biden with his Ape's cabinet is like the animal farm of George Orwell. Humanity concerns nothing under the rule of Ape, so Joe Biden downplays the natural disaster in Texas, instead, he keens to protect the turtles from being frozen while the people died by the severe weather. Nevertheless, Biden's son is Hunter Biden received $US 1.5 billion from China's Ape herd, so Ape Joe Biden must obey the orders of Ape's emperor Xi Jinping. President Donald Trump condemns the human rights violation in Uighur, therefore, Ape's King Joe Biden praises the genocide in China as the culture.

The US people have been suffered the animal rule when the Ape's herd controls the White House, Congress, Senate plus the Supreme Court. Unfortunately, the US Army protects the Ape's herd in Washington D.C, it is funny of the most powerful army on the planet. The US people need to remove the Ape's herd called Democrats and the bloody mad, imbecile mongrel Ape Joe Biden as soon as possible, if not, Americans will have the same situation as Chinese people have been suffered in the mainland from 1949./.

93. IN GOD WE TRUST BUT THE ATHEIST PLUS LEFTIST ATTACKS GOD

Atheist considers the God is their enemy despite they have never seen God. Nevertheless, God has never harmed anyone, including the atheist, why do they hate God? The hateful God comes from their great master Karl Marx who dared to confirm the people came from the Ape and his blind pupils follow, certainly, Karl Marx didn't qualify nor authorize to tell about the origin of human. Karl Marx could label the origin of a human came from an Ape, so everyone can tell the people derived from the lion, tiger, and any kind of animal. Karl Marx didn't tell where was the Ape come from? Therefore, his crazy theory is baseless and it has become the human disaster on the planet by communism.

Karl Marx hates God without a reason, he concerns" *Religion is the opium of the people*". Since Lenin succeeded the **Ape-Revolution in 1917**, human society has faced disaster, the Ape regimes around the world killed more than 100 million people and enslaved a billion people. The Ape brain covered by the human body has never loved and cared the people, the animal has instinct replaces the mind, so the people must fight to remove the Ape without a tail on the planet.

The communist is Ape, they are the siblings of the left media, left parties, so the people easily recognize the Ape brain disguised the human body, the Ape characters are a lie, cheat, demagogy, ruse, cruelty if they seized the government, the Ape regimes created the bloodshed occurred in China, Vietnam, Russia, North Korea, Laos, Cambodia…

The Ape brain in the Western represents the left media, left parties and whoever hates God… the Ape always exposes the allergy against God. The Ape politicians activate to remove God when they swore in. The rumor spread that the lawmaker terrorist and commander in thug Nancy Pelosi conspires and activates to remove 150-year-old sign" **In God, we trust**" at the House Chamber Entrance. Moreover, Fox News released the news on January 2019:" *A key committee in the* <u>Democrat-controlled</u> *House of Representatives is moving to eliminate the God reference from the oath administered to witnesses testifying before the panel, as part of a new rules package expected to be approved this week, according to a draft obtained exclusively by Fox News.* ". Karl Mark's pupil hates God, certainly evil and Satan always fears the sign of God as the felon appalls and frightens the police.

The atheist attorney is Michael Arthur Newdow born on June 24, 1953, he also is an emergency medicine Physician. He always hates God, he announces the title of God is unconstitutional as a phrase*" under God"* of the pledge of allegiance in public school. In 2009, attorney Michael Arthur Newdow filed the lawsuit to stop God's reference in the second term's inauguration of President George W. Bush, but he lost the case. Moreover, in 1997, attorney Michael Arthur

Newdow has started the atheist religion called" First Atheist Church of True Science".

Recently, attorney Michael Arthur Newdow files the lawsuit at Supreme Court to remove the phrase" *In God, We Trust*" which is the national motto has used on the US currency and coins from the Department of Treasury. Certainly, the US Supreme Court rejected the foolish lawsuit of the Ape attorney. The law school may review the qualification granted by attorney Michael Arthur Newdow who distorts the legal career and opposing religious freedom and conflicts with the US valuation. Besides the honest lawyers, there are the dishonest lawyers who practice the career as the robbers with the paper-knife.

Despite Karl Marx's pupils hate God, therefore, most communist leaders want to be God. Terrorism plus the propaganda canonized the number one genocide in the 20th century *Mao Tse Tung" goes to the pope*". The crime oppose against the humanity of Mao Tse Tung ruled the Ape regime in China from 1949 to 1976, he killed more than 65 million Chinese people. Therefore, the Ape dynasty portrayed and built Mao's statues everywhere on the mainland. China communist has applied the ruse's tactic from many decades, actually, the taxi drivers are the late generations after the bloodshed campaigns were Great Leap Forward, Hundred Flowers, the Culture Revolution, the Landlord Reform, they don't know the massive killing of Chairman Mao and his Ape communist party. The taxi drivers in Beijing and the other cities believe Mao Tse Tung is the benefit angel when they hang the portrait of Mao in the cabs, but the drivers have not Mao's portrait, they often get bad luck. China police deserve the facility for the taxi has Mao's picture. Moreover, the communist artists displayed Mao's paintings in the Western and the left media companies like ABC, SBS and the other left media companies in Australia introduced Mao's painting.

In Vietnam, the Great Ape's leader Ho Chi Minh who killed more than 1,700,000 people, raped a 15-year-old girl named Tuyết Lan in 1929 in Thailand, moreover, Ho Chi Minh was a famous pedophile in Vietnam. Therefore, Vietcong's Ape communist super gang has canonized Ho Chi Minh as the successful Buddha. Almost all the provinces in Vietnam have Ho Chi Minh's temples, actually, Ho Chi Minh portrait and statue displaced at the public places and government offices. The famous temple promoted Buddha Ho Chi Minh is the Đại Nam Quốc Tự at Bình Dương province, this temple owned by Mr. Huỳnh Uy Dũng, nicknamed Dũng Lò Vôi who was former Public Security Guard of Vietcong regime (as SS of Hitler), moreover, Mr. Dũng Lò Vôi also is an adopted son of Prime Minister Võ Văn Kiệt's wife. In the main altar hall of Đại Nam Quốc Tự Temple, Ho Chi Minh's statue placed with Buddha and Hùng King (Vietnamese ancestor).

The Ba Vàng Temple is the historic Buddhist pagoda located at Uông Bí (Quảng Ninh province), Vietcong Ape's regime displayed the Ho Chi Minh's statue as the successful Buddha and they pointed the communist monk to take care plus collect money. Vietcong is malicious as great master China to propagate Mao Tse Tung into Western countries. On January 26, 2009, at Little Saigon, the capital of Vietnamese refugees in California, a young Vietnamese refugee named Brian Doan opened the Arts gallery of VAALA promoted Ho

Chi Minh with the painting has Red flag of the Ape regime.

In Australia, the successful clown ANH DO is a Vietnamese refugee who wrote the book" The Happiest Refugee", but he returned safely to where he escaped finding freedom after South Vietnam invaded by Vietcong's Ape gang in April 30, 1975. Therefore, Anh Do carried out a show in Vietnam and broadcast on Channel Seven's television, he stood at Ho Chi Minh's Mausoleum and said: " Ho Chi Minh is a good guy ". So the left media companies are such as ABC, Channel Seven are keen to promote" The Happiest Refugee" Anh Do on the television screen.

After the great Ape's king of Vietcong super Ape gang is Ho Chi Minh returned to the communist paradise to reunite with Lenin, Stalin, and the other comrades on September 2nd, 1969. Vietcong spent a billion USD dollars to mummify Ho Chi Minh's body and the Ape regime has a current military plus Public Security Guard unit to protect the security and taking care of Ho Chi Minh's body. The special team serves for Ho Chi Minh's embalmed body fables Ho Chi Minh's body is holy, although Ho Chi Minh died, therefore the hairs and nails still grow, so every month they cut the hair and trim the nails.

The atheists in Western have exploited the legal system to attack the social valuation, actually, they hate God. The left lawmaker Nancy Pelosi and Ape attorney Michael Arthur Newdow conspire to remove the phrase" In God We Trust" or any title links with God. A day, when the House of Representatives crowded Sharia law's politicians, the motto" In God We Trust" will replace" In Allah we trust"./.

94. THE APE PROPAGANDA MINGLES WESTERN MEDIA

W hen the oil mixed with water that makes the ugly stuff, the dishonest priests stand with genuine priests, it causes religious damages, the adherents doubt, the religious trust loses. China and Vietnam are the communist regimes, those dictatorial regimes stole the democratic economy's method and mixed with the dictatorial management, it called" *free market is led by socialism"*. The ugly economic pattern bluffed the innocent politicians, but the Western countries received dire consequences after China deployed the trade trap, debt trap, and government trap around the world.

The mainstream media has lost credibility when the left media mingled and driving communication to propaganda as China has applied in the mainland since 1949. It is very hard to believe the educated component in the Western media line has a long record to endorse communism since the Cold War and nowadays, the left media continues to propagate for China's communist regime. **The left media + Ape media = rubbish tip**, so the left media companies become the center of a cheat, the hub of fake news, and the den of propaganda as China, Vietnam, North Korea to brainwash the people. Unfortunately, the left media companies and their journalists apply the phony propaganda in the wrong place, the democratic countries respect free speech.

Karl Marx promoted Communism, so leftists, socialists, the left media, left academics, and the left parties they are the siblings. Nevertheless, **Karl Marx granted the Ape Certificate** to his pupils, and the Marxism followers pride original Ape, certainly, the Ape is not a human being, the human mind replaced the instinct. The action or behavior of Karl Marx's descendants is not different from the animal, the Ape has never given up the animal character, certainly, Ape has never loved the people. Since Lenin succeeded in the Ape Revolution in October 1917, the Ape regimes around the world killed more than 100 million people and enslaved a billion people. Particularly, the Ape regime in China killed 65 million Chinese people by the first Ape Emperor Mao Tse Tung, and on June 4, 1989, the Ape Emperor Deng Xiaoping massacred tens of thousand people at Tiananmen Square. Nowadays, the incumbent Ape Emperor Xi Jinping conspires to control the world with global hegemonic ambition. In early December 2019, Ape Emperor Xi Jinping attacks the world by biological warfare.

The left media or the Ape media in Western exposes the animal character that conflicts with the human being. The people recognize the wrong and right, good and bad, god and evil…but the Ape media assimilates those are the same. The Ape media represents the character by the formula is **3 F=3 Frauds=False poll+Fake news+Fabricated story**.

The animal tamers exploit the instinct to train the lion, tiger, elephant, and the other by giving the food after the animal did as the order. The dog trainer does the same, and they could tell a dog does something then a trainer rewards the dog's favorite food. The left media is the same circumstance, if they are human beings, they deny the wrongdoings and strongly react against whoever harms the society, the social valuation. The left media knew that Communism opposes humanity, violates human rights, the communist regimes are barbarous, and genocide. However, the left media currently released fake news and chimed the propaganda of China while the world knows China communist is the world's rogue regime.

The war fights against the global economic terror launching by President Donald Trump it is like the warfighting against terror has begun after the event of September 11, 2001, by President George W.Bush. Therefore, the Ape media should have finance from China, so the left media conceal the potential damages of China, instead, they propagate the damages in the US and Western. Moreover, the Ape media often praises the dire weapon of China despite the people knew the weapon of the People's Liberation Army mimed the Western and stolen the technology, copied the uniform, but the fighting doubts. The Ape media lies about China's military strength, they applaud the aircraft carriers, Jet-20 but criticized the US jet fighter F-35, therefore, Japan, Australia, Israel, and the allies bought F-35, even some countries want to buy F-35 but the US doesn't reply or deny. The Ape media's journalists are not aircraft engineers but they dare to tell the fields that they don't know as a farmer telling about the cancer treatment instead, a specialist of medical doctor authorizes to tell that deadly illness and treatment.

The Ape propaganda has mingled into the mainstream to harm the communication, the Ape media has never respected the truth and human concern. Instead of the animal instinct responds to an animal trainer that could control the animal by the food rewarded. The Ape media ignores the truth, therefore, whoever including China communist pays and they have good services, so the Western mainstream media has distorted the communication to propaganda as the communist regime.

The mainstream media needs to eliminate Ape propaganda that has infiltrated communication since the Cold War. The media disaster causes the loss of people's trust, it conducts the public abandoned the left media companies like CNN, The New York Times, The Washington Post, and the other fake news companies have destroyed the free speech. The left media companies cut a thousand employees while the US reduced the unemployment rate to 3.6% it hits the lowest record since 1969 before the Coronavirus outbreak, China is the culprit of biological warfare. Social media and impartial sources replaced fake news.

The Ape media destroyed the mainstream at least a half-century, the mainstream media in Western must take a long time to recover the people's trust that comes from the thug in media. Once again, the left media conceals the massive death toll and infected population in China when the Chinese Virus outbreak in Wuhan in December 2019 and spread worldwide. The left media snubs the public, no one trusts the reports based on China's officials about the Coronavirus. Nevertheless, the leftists hide into the communication companies like Facebook, Twitter, and others using the technology to gag free speech, they apply the censorship in Western countries. Its reason, President Donald Trump issues the executive order that relates to section 230 of the Communication Decency Act which added to law 1966 after Twitter breached free speech:" *No provider or user of an interactive computer service shall be treated as the publisher or speaker of any information provided by another information content provider ".*

After the Second World War, the left media has overridden the authority of media. Instead, the media workers are arrogant, they promoted themselves as the kingmakers and the left media companies operate the communication like the superpower to control the country. Nowadays, the golden time is gone, the world changes, the era of high technology and social media to defeat the dishonest media's companies and media workers. Certainly, the leftists failed to use the technology to censor free speech, and competitive media strips the exclusive right of the left media companies. The communication companies are the business, they must comply with the law and respect the public, possibly, the government can apply the law and Constitution to punish whoever breaches the law and damaging free speech. The left media companies and the communication companies could not sit above the law and ignore free speech, the US government can issue the law to punish the violation, the heavy fines and retrieval license can apply. Moreover, other countries like Australia, Europe can file a lawsuit against the communication companies if they breach the law and the contract./.

95. CHINA HAS PAID FOR THE LEFT MEDIA FOR HIRE

The people including the media line knew China's communist regime is genocide, the first Ape king Mao Tse Tung killed more than 65 million Chinese people from 1949 to 1976. Continuing, Ape king Deng Xiaoping massacred tens of thousand Chinese people at Tiananmen Square in 1989, and nowadays, Ape King Xi Jinping attacks the world by biological warfare. China's Communist Party killed more than a hundred million people without pity.

Everyone knew the serious crimes oppose the humanity of China's Communist Party, therefore, the left media in Western has propagated for China and its Global Communist Bloc since the Cold War. Particularly, in the Vietnam War, the major left media companies like CNN, NBC, CBS, MSNBC, The New York Times, The Washington Post...BBC, The Guardian in the United Kingdom, Australia with ABC (*funding by the government*), Seven Channel, Nine Channel, and others supported Vietcong terror inciting the innocent people to protest with violence by misleading the information, plus fabricated stories and concealment about the cruelty of Vietcong. Nevertheless, after the Vietnam War ended on April 30, 1975, the left media in Western ignored 800,000 soldiers and public servants of South Vietnam imprisoned in the concentration camps, the worst treatment that killed 165,000 political prisoners. The left media in Western has no mind, they have practiced the communication's career like the instinct's animal, the human character disappeared, instead, the conscience replaced by profit and privileges to grant by the enemies.

In the Cold War, the Global Communist Bloc led by China and Soviet-Union, certainly, couldn't apply the propaganda and brainwashing into Western countries, actually, the US. China, Soviet-Union, Vietcong, and others couldn't use their journalists, reporters, and columnists to propagate as they carried out in communist states. So, the local media workers and native media companies have become the actual tools and henchman into the propaganda plus intoxicate the Western people.

China's Communist Party has not spent much money to

establish the propaganda machine in the Western, but Beijing could pay for the left media companies and evil journalists, Satanic reporters, dishonest T.V hosts and China already has acquired communism's propaganda into the lands of the capitalist. The money could buy profit lovers as media companies and dishonest media workers, therefore, the outcome is greater than money. Since the Cold War, innocent people, particularly, the young generations have been brainwashed and intoxicated by the enemy of people, the foe of the public, and the garbage of the mainstream.

After Soviet-Union and Eastern Europe, Communist Bloc collapsed in the early 1990s, China's Communist Party gathered the communist vestiges Vietnam, North Korea, Laos, Cuba into the new battle. The Cold War transformed into COOL WAR, the economic battle highlighted to array the trade trap, debt trap, and government trap into the world. China and Vietcong have applied the ugly economic pattern" *the free market is led by socialism*", it is the lizard changing the skin's color tactic to cheat the innocent politicians in Western. The left media has supported China into the global hegemonic strategy after China has hired dishonest media workers and paid the den of left media companies. Almost, the major media companies have become the propaganda machine of China in Western including the US. The fake news, fabricated stories exchanged the profit and privileges granted from China. The left media companies and media workers are the traitors, they were born, grew, and have lived in the Western (*democratic countries*) but they have served evil China's Communist Party.

Nowadays, people distrust the left media and doubt the

media line. The fake news killed the people's trust. China's Communist Party destroyed the mainstream media by using the money to hire the left media companies and journalists to mislead the public with fake news, so the mainstream media in Western assimilated as the media's machine in the mainland. The money ruined free speech and the left media has driven the media into socialism. China's Communist Party has used the money to buy Western media and also kill the people's trust in free speech. Moreover, the left parties are siblings with China, so Democrats in the US have collaborated with China into the fake news. The people know money can control and command the Western media, possible, the payment occurs in secret, therefore, the corruption couldn't hide, the den of fake news is CNN has the journalists Sean Callebs, Anand Naidoo, Karina Huber, William Evania, Asieh Namdar, Jim Spellman, they have served for China's Communist Party in propaganda and released the fake news, fabricated stories. Certainly, China's Communist Party rewarded the henchman.

Evil media worker Sean Callebs was a reporter of CNN in Afghanistan in 2011. Therefore, in the US presidential election 216, evil journalist Sean Callebs created fake news about Russia intervened in the election to support the legal terrorist Robert Mueller and his tool is Special Counsel into the impeachment's conspiracy. Moreover, this journalist praised China for climate change's response, but everyone knows China is the most dioxide releasing on the planet.

Satanic journalist Anand Naidoo propagates the death toll and infection of Coronavirus in the US but concealed China. Moreover, Anand Naidoo incited the people to protest after the death of a felony George Floyd, conducts the riots, loots with the Black Lives Matter, Antifa.

Karina Huber always exploits the media to applaud China's Communist Party and misleading the public about the tariffs of President Donald Trump to fight against China's global economic terror.

William Evania who attempts to release the fake news about China expands the operation in the US, indeed, from President Donald Trump getting the office, China's espionage network, students shrank. Journalists Asieh Namdar and Jim Spellman, both often have attacked President Donald Trump into the national interest and national security. The prominent fake news in CNN is evil reporter Jim Acosta who exploits the career as a burglar, he often snoops the patriotic President Donald Trump for every move and releasing the fake news

There are just a few evil journalists and Satanic Reporters of CNN, it is just an iceberg floating on the surface. Possible, the dens of fake news like The New York Times, The Washington Post, NBC, ABC, MSNBC, CBS, and others have become the media for hire, certainly, China's Communist Party is keen to pay for the hungry money's media workers, Beijing does need to use the Western media to intoxicate and brainwash its people. The Western lawmakers need to reform the media law to limit the fake news, false polls *(the numerous survey must have at least 1% of the population)*, and fabricated stories. The fake news's activist is a form of fraud, therefore, the fake news creates an immeasurable consequence, it affects the public and country, the social disorder while a fraudster just cheats a person../.

96. APE EMPEROR XI JINPING PLAYS THE RISKY GAME

Biological warfare is the heartless plan of China's Communist Party that has conspired from two decades ago. Possibly, the inhumane offense by a biological weapon proposed by General Chi Haotian, China's famous strategist and defense minister of Deng Xiaoping. China's communist regime has never denied any crime opposing humanity, the genocide in the mainland from 1949 with a hundred million Chinese people killed and 1.4 billion people enslaved. The communist doesn't care about the life of people but the Marxism-Leninist-Maoist-Ho Chi Minh's thoughts prioritize. Leon Trotsky, the hardcore communist said: *"the end may justify the means as long as there is something that justifies the end"*. Eventually, his close comrade Stalin applied his theory and killed Trotsky on August 12, 1940, while he fled in Mexico. The leftists and left media, the profit lover's businesses, and the innocent academics ignored the bloody circumstance of Trotsky. The essential method of communists is throwing the lemon skin after the juice emptied.

The world knew China's communist regime is ruthless, but the left media and left parties blindly support it since the Cold War. The global hegemonic ambition urges China to rush the arms race, the space race. Therefore, finance and technology are the keys to carry out the dream, China solves the problem by stolen technology and exploiting the free market to make a profit.

The global economic terror has applied malicious methods, those are trade trap, debt trap, government trap.

Since China joined the free market after the historic visit of President Richard Nixon in 1972, China made a profit from the Western loss. The actual henchmen of China were President Bill Clinton, Barrack Obama led the US into China's orbit. If Hillary Clinton elected in 2016, China will control the world in 2025. Unfortunately, the cunning conspiracy defeated by the US people to elect patriotic President Donald Trump who cracked down on China and Democrats' plans.

The global economic terror of China failed by Intercontinental Ballistic Tariff Missile of commander in chief Donald Trump. Eventually, China's Communist Party launches the global biological warfare terror, it is a form of the THIRD WORLD WAR unofficially declared by China's communist regime, the commander in viruses Xi Jinping who plays the risky game with the biological war attacks the world. The death toll, infected population, and global economic recession caused by China. Nowadays, **the world recognizes China's Communist Party is the most enemy of humanity including Chinese people in the mainland**. The world's most wanted criminals are 22 tyrants in Political Bureau is led by Ape king Xi Jinping, the culprits of biological terror appeared on the faces. Ape Emperor Xi Jinping and its central communist party are the genocide, the global hegemonic ambition of Xi Jinping should lead the end of China's Communist Party after more than 70 years ruled in the mainland by bloodshed and bluffing the world by global economic terror:

- China's Communist Party wants to solve the excessive population by the virus: the heartless plan of China's communist regime to reduce the population has no surprise. The historic genocide proved in the mainland, after robbing the authentic government of Chinese people in 1949, Mao Tse Tung and his communist party massacred more than 65 million people to carry out the communism or Maoist by the bloodshed campaigns. China's Communist Party killed the intellectuals, academics, and wealthy families to stabilize the regime and reduced the opponents. Nowadays, the old lesson applies, China's Communist Party aims to killed hundreds of millions of people to keep the regime. Nevertheless, the massive jobless occurred in the mainland after China lost the trade war with the US that risks the regime. Certainly, China's Communist Party fears the old lesson of dynasties collapsed from many thousand years of Chinese history when the massive jobless and economy paralyzed.

- China's Communist Party stops the democratic movement in Hong Kong by Coronavirus.

- China strays the massive jobless by pandemic, a hundred million people locked down that stop the people stand up.

- Using the deadly virus to take down the US, Europe, and the democratic countries. The medical supplies made in China sending under the so-called humanitarian aid, but the countries pay. Therefore, China provided false test kits and inserting a virus in the face masks (*). Indonesia is the victim of China's biological warfare offense, on March 25, 2020, China sent the medical supplies to Indonesia because the hospitals were short of medical equipment. The Indonesian government got the medical supplies from China, including 125,000 COVID-19 test kits. Therefore, on April 7, 2020, and 24 doctors died from Coronavirus. New York's Governor Cuomo is an unofficial executive of China, he hid the ventilators and encourages the New York residents to use the personal protective equipment made in China, so the death toll and infected cases rise. On the other hand, **New York Governor Cuomo supports China's biological warfare attack in the US, a murder he did.** In Western Australia, billionaire Andrew Forrest ordered $AU 160 million in medical supplies made in China, his donation raises the safety concern of the medical workers in state hospitals. Chinese embassy to Australia slams the outlet media defames China's companies about the medical supplies (*Magnate Andrew Forrest who has done a long time business with China*).

The global biological warfare of China attacks on the full scale, initially, China used the life of Chinese people in Wuhan plus Hubei province to spread the Coronavirus and using the people of countries that fell into the trade trap, debt trap like Italy to carry out the biological spread when the virus transmits from human to human.

When a house is on fire, the mouse appears, the Coronavirus is the biological weapon of China, the Chinese Virus spread worldwide and the Western can find the domestic thugs appear, the hidden enemies launch the full-scale battle with China. The spy network of China appeared, the left parties, the wealthy components have done the business with China, the left media can not hide the face.

The risky biological warfare game of Ape king Xi Jinping hits back China's communist regime from the mainland to abroad. China's communist regime must pay the price, Chinese people in the mainland are the victims of the genocide carrying out by the pandemic, the undercover activists, spy network in Western uprooted. China's Communist Party lose all after more than half of the century built and sowed the red seeds worldwide. After the Coronavirus, China's communist regime isolated, Chinese people's abhorrence. The new world order without China will develop. Certainly, the Ape super herd will be eliminated, Chinese people decide the national fate.

Ape Emperor Xi Jinping plays a risky game that purposely kills the hundreds of millions of people in the mainland to reduce the people standing up and also destroying the US and the world's economy as one *stone kills two birds*. The hypocritical morality of China can not cheat the world as a stratagem of Sun Tzu:" *hide a knife behind a smile*". The fake gentleman Xi Jinping is a fake hero name Yue Buqun of Hong Kong's author Jin Yong. China sends false medical supplies and masks contain the virus to kill more people and on April 6, 2020, Ape Emperor Xi Jinping called President Donald Trump seeking the collaboration to fight against Coronavirus, indeed, Xi Jinping is the commander in Coronavirus. It is the malicious tactic calls talking during the fighting of communists.

However, the Ape Emperor Xi Jinping commits suicide

after the world recognized Coronavirus as the biological weapon of China and the Chinese Virus has never removed. **The ruthless regime doesn't care about the people, but the money is death vulnerability.** Certainly, the world stays away from China and the global China-phobia kills China products. Moreover, the US and victim countries are eligible to file the lawsuit against China, the compensation estimates a hundred trillion of US dollar, which is enough to make China bankrupt. The biological weapon hits back China's communist regime as a says" *the sword made by China to stab Chinese*". The political party in democratic countries woo the people by the policies, but China's Communist Party keeps the regime by genocide./.

Notes (*)

British PM Boris Johnson is said to have decided to pull out of the 5G contract with Chinese firm Huawei.

It has been reported that the British PM came to the decision after he was furious about a recent shipment of test kits bound for the UK were found to be contaminated with coronavirus.

Furthermore, Boris Johnson too is said to have gone into self-quarantine after being tested positive for Coronavirus. The test kits were assembled in Luxembourg by food safety and laboratory testing services firm Eurofins. The infected elements are "probes and primers," the long, thin swabs that medical personnel use to collect samples from the nasal and oral cavities.

Eurofins has said that the infected elements were

supplied by China.

British politicians across party lines are angry that China did not inform the world about the true spread of Corona in time and also for not taking the crucial consignment of test kits seriously as they have come infected with Coronavirus. Many have started to question if the Chinese government deliberately hid the information about the contamination as many other countries have alleged.

The contamination of the test kits will further delay the testing of British citizens which has everyone in the country concerned.

China has also been indulging in massive PR exercise the world over in a bid to stop anyone from blaming them for the Coronavirus.

First the, Chinese government tried to blame the US soldiers and later pinned the blame on Italy itself.

People and governments the world over are waking up to the evil machinations of the Chinese government to take control of the world using dubious means.

Chinese companies have been trying to influence decisions in many African countries and Australia too.

In India too, many organisations have warned the government to be extremely wary of the Chinese and their products. In January, Swadeshi Jagran Manch (SJM), requested the central government to ban participation of Chinese companies in 5G trials in view of national security and privacy issues.

The SJM had said that there is 'ample evidence that lead to suspicion of Chinese companies indulging in the ex-filtrating sensitive information from, devices and equipment thatit exports', Huawei must be stopped from the 5G trials.

https://www.organiser.org/Encyc/2020/4/6/Britain-pulls-out-of-5G-contract-with-Huawei.html./.

EPILOGUE

Writing a letter, story, a book requires some conditions and skills, actually, a non-English speaking like me, writing deals with difficulties. I have invested in learning English for nearly a half-century, I would like to share my expert writing, I believe everyone can write. Therefore, writing a foreign language as English must take some categories:

1-The mechanism language: the materials are words, grammar, and other basic writing

2-The writing style to recognize the ethos of an author. It is like an architect draws a style of the house.

3-The writing tactic is like a battle, every author can have the tactic.

4-The spiritual language reflects the writing skills, in the same story but someone excites the readers, instead, the boring story describes by an author.

5-The soul of language combines the skills and the ethos of an author

I spent nearly a haft century learning and practice, now I have five published books and editor of the daily news online thedawnmedia.com. I think my writing experiences can help everyone to write.

Hoa Minh Truong.